THE COLLECTION PROGRAM IN SCHOOLS

Library and Information Science Text Series

THE COLLECTION PROGRAM IN SCHOOLS

Concepts, Practices, and Information Sources

♦ **Third Edition** ♦

Phyllis J. Van Orden

and

Kay Bishop

With the assistance of

Patricia Pawelak-Kort

2001
LIBRARIES UNLIMITED
A Division of Greenwood Publishing Group, Inc.
Englewood, Colorado

Libraries Unlimited
A Division of Greenwood Publishing Group, Inc.
P.O. Box 6633
Englewood, CO 80155-6633
1-800-237-6124
www.lu.com

Library of Congress Cataloging-in-Publication Data

Van Orden, Phyllis.
   The collection program in schools : concepts, practices, and information sources /
Phyllis J. Van Orden and Kay Bishop ; with the assistance of Patricia Pawelak-Kort.--
3rd ed.
    p. cm. -- (Library and information science text series)
   Includes bibliographical references and index.
   ISBN 1-56308-980-7 (cloth) 1-56308-804-5 (paper)
   1. School libraries--Collection development--United States. I. Bishop, Kay, 1942- II.
Pawelak-Kort, Patricia. III. Title. IV. Series.

Z675.S3 V334 2001
025.2'1878--dc21

2001038297

Contents

Part I
The Setting

Part II
Selection of Materials

Part III
Administrative Concerns

List of Figures and Tables

Figures

Tables

Authors' Comments

For me, writing this book involved solitary reflection as well as engaging in dialogues about the ideas expressed. So this work is dedicated to those who will explore and refine those ideas and to all my colleagues who participated in the dialogues.

A comparison of the first version (1982) and this one reveals the obvious: the expansion and impact of technological development. At the same time, a steady thread has been the ongoing commitment to intellectual freedom and the rights of students to access, evaluate, and use information. May that commitment continue in the future.

Phyllis J. Van Orden

It has been my privilege to work with Phyllis Van Orden in the preparation of this book. I think her knowledge in the area of collection development for school library media centers is unsurpassed; thus, I learned much from this experience and was able to contribute to the information presented.

I would also like to express my thanks to the following graduate assistants from the University of Kentucky and the University of South Florida, who provided clerical and online searching assistance for portions of the book: Sara Garrison, Liz Engel, Roseanne Sasso, Gina DuBois, and LaVerne Jenkins.

Kay Bishop

Introduction

Collection development can be an exciting challenge that demands special knowledge, skills, and positive attitudes. Although the general principles and techniques of collection development are applicable to most library settings, the unique characteristics of each media program produce new and changing demands that require flexibility and creativity. To help media specialists face these challenges, this work

describes the environment within which the collection exists;

presents principles, techniques, and common practices of collection development;

raises issues that affect all collections but that must be resolved in accordance with the goals and needs of a particular collection;

identifies sources of help, including documents, Websites, agencies, and associations; and

suggests approaches to handling a wide range of situations and demands on the collection.

This introductory text provides an overview of the processes and procedures associated with developing, maintaining, and evaluating a collection at the building level. The processes and procedures practiced in school library media centers are discussed in relation to educational theory and principles of collection development.

The book reflects the opinion that the collection is a key element of the media program, providing the means for meeting the information and instructional needs of the school. To serve these needs, media specialists must consider the collection a physical entity composed not only of its internal resources but also of the informational and instructional resources available through community resources, human resources, resource-sharing plans, and telecommunications.

An underlying assumption is that collection program activities interact in a cyclical pattern. The principles of collection development, selection, resource sharing, acquisition, and maintenance are addressed in policy statements. Other important policy statements should address students' rights, intellectual freedom, fair use, and acceptable use issues.

This book is divided into three parts. Part I examines the media collection in relation to its educational setting and discusses general principles of collection development. This part of the book establishes the environmental framework that is the collection's external tie to educational and informational systems and its internal relationship to the media program. Chapter 1 presents an overview of the external and internal relationships of the media program. Chapter 2 examines six perspectives of the concept of collection on which the process of collection development is based. Chapter 3 identifies the activities involved in building and maintaining a collection. These principles are the framework for the remaining chapters, which provide fuller discussions of each activity. Chapter 4 describes the basis for children's rights to access information, raises issues media specialists will encounter, identifies barriers to access, and identifies the media specialist's responsibilities. Scenarios of situations media specialists face are included to prompt discussion about how to handle such incidents. Chapter 5 describes the external environments that influence the collection and to which it must respond. Chapter 6 describes how policies (collection development, acquisition, selection, evaluation, copyright, and acceptable use) and procedures address these relationships. Chapter 7 outlines steps for developing a selection policy and requests for reconsideration of materials statements. It identifies associations, agencies, and Websites that offer assistance.

Part II moves from the theoretical aspects of Part 1 to the practical considerations of materials selection. Chapter 8 identifies selection tools and suggests ways to involve teachers and students in the selection process. Chapter 9 identifies criteria that apply to all formats. Chapter10 describes the characteristics of each format as well as its advantages, disadvantages, selection criteria, implications for collection development, and copyright considerations. Sources of information about each format are listed. New formats added in this edition include e-books, DVDs, and Websites. The remaining chapters of this section identify criteria and sources of information about materials to meet specific needs. Chapter 11 examines the educational environment and ways that educational perspectives and models of teaching create demands on the collection. Chapter 12 identifies needs for materials to address concerns of individuals and groups (staff members; reference services; multicultural; poor, reluctant, and ESL readers; and people with disabilities).

Part III describes the operations involved in developing and managing a collection. Chapter 13 describes traditional acquisition activities and identifies resources to use in this process. Chapter 14 addresses fiscal and access issues, including licensing, alternative funding, the Internet, Websites, online catalogs, virtual libraries, and resource sharing. Chapter 15 describes maintenance policies and procedures, emergency planning, security, inventory, and re-evaluation of materials. Chapter 16 describes techniques for evaluating collections using collection-centered measures, use-centered measures, and simulated use studies. The chapter identifies selected standards, guidelines, and resources to guide media specialists through the evaluation process. Chapter 17 discusses the issues and procedures involved in creating, shifting, and closing collections.

Lists of recommended readings and electronic resources point readers to in-depth coverage of many of the processes and techniques the book describes. For example, students' rights and intellectual freedom are cornerstones of the media program and are worthy of far greater coverage than this book can provide. The recommended readings and electronic sources in Chapters 4 and 7 provide in-depth treatment of these topics.

While recognizing the importance of bibliographic control, this work does not address the issues and operations involved in that process, nor does it address the circulation and housing of materials. An evaluative assessment of computer programs for managing collections is beyond the scope of this work.

This book addresses people who are preparing to work or are presently working in school library media centers. Even though the examples are from public school library media programs, the principles, practices, techniques, and materials discussed also apply to parochial and independent schools.

Many standard works cover various aspects of the school library media program. This work is not intended to duplicate those efforts. They are referenced in the text or lists of resources for various chapters and are listed in Appendix B.

Appendix A identifies agencies and associations that provide information and services to media specialists. A brief annotation describes those services. Information about how to contact them by mail, telephone, fax, electronic mail, and Websites is listed. Appendix B is an annotated bibliography of resources identified in the text or in recommended readings and electronic sources listed at the end of chapters. Appendix C reprints statements about intellectual freedom.

NEW FEATURES

The text was revised to reflect the philosophy and goals articulated in the American Association of School Librarians and the Association for Educational Communications and Technology's publication *Information Power: Building Partnerships for Learning* (1998).

The chapter on policies and procedures has been expanded into two chapters to accommodate attention to policies relating to copyright issues (fair use) and Internet use (acceptable use). Developing technologies, such as e-books, DVDs, and Websites are included in the chapter about finding, selecting, and evaluating formats. E-books, Websites, and virtual libraries are addressed in terms of their effect on access to information, resource sharing, and handling of acquisition matters.

With the increasing demands on the collection, the expanding array of resources, and technological developments, additional attention is given to alternative funding and grantsmanship.

A new source of information is the listings of electronic resources at the end of appropriate chapters. Some include sample policies, offer guidance in use of the Internet, help in the evaluation of Websites, or provide links to further resources. The addresses provided were accessed during November 2000. With the constantly changing status of Website addresses, our goal was to provide sufficient information to help you locate the Website.

Part I

The Setting

Where is that green book I used for my report last year? Where can I find a picture of Saturn? This video says Pluto is 1,150 miles in diameter, and the electronic encyclopedia says 1,430 miles. Which is correct?

Does this symbol mean I can get this magazine through interlibrary loan from the university library? How can I copy this map? Why won't the computer accept what I entered?

Do you have a story that will make me cry? Don't we have any new horse stories? I've read all of these. Do you have the Star Wars series?

Why don't we have any good recordings? Are the computers available after school? Is there a time limit then? How much does a printout cost? Questions such as these bombard the media specialist as students seek information.

Teachers' voices enter the fray to make requests. *I need a video on potential and kinetic energy for my science class. Do you remember which poem I used for Martin Luther King's birthday last year? Will you show Ned how to make a computerized chart for his report? One of my friends said his Spanish class used electronic mail to correspond with a class in Brazil. Can we set up a similar experience for my class?*

How do I find Web pages dealing with the global economy? Can you arrange a teleconference lecture for my social studies classes? Will the local college's satellite courses be available?

What can I do to get Meaghan to read something besides dog stories? Sean and Heidi need help in videotaping this report. I have five new Albanian students. Do we have any materials they can use?

How can a collection satisfy all of these requests? A responsive collection results from the planning and care of dedicated media specialists. They are the people who think about the purpose of the collection and ways to meet the diverse needs of the users. An effective collection does not simply appear and endure unaltered; it must evolve, responding to changing demands. The following chapters describe the setting of the collection with the media program and suggest ways collections can meet the continuing challenges of their users.

1

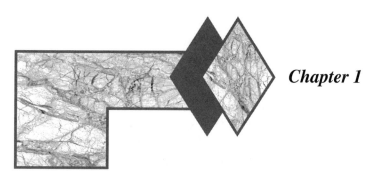

The Media Program
and Its Environment

A MEDIA PROGRAM SCENARIO

An opening-day scene: You arrive in late August for the teacher preparation days before students arrive for the new school year. As the new school library media specialist[1] at Maple City Elementary School, you are eager to learn about its curriculum, access to resources, faculty, and students and to prepare the media program for the coming year. As you familiarize yourself with the collection, teachers arrive in the media center.

First to arrive is Valerie, a fifth-grade teacher who has obviously been planning for classes. She wants to arrange a series of meetings with you to discuss the resources and information literacy skills instruction she needs for her first two units in science and social studies. Valerie alternates these subjects over a period of weeks so the students can concentrate on one at a time. The unit on light will cover the first four weeks and will be followed by four weeks on colonial America. To stimulate her pupils' curiosity, Valerie plans to have a discovery corner in her classroom. The children will be able to handle and compare lenses, prisms, and other sources of basic information before the formal instruction begins. After presenting general information to the class, Valerie will organize students with common interests into working groups.

Valerie researched the characteristics of her students. Their reading levels range from the second to the seventh grade. Valerie recognizes that not all children are motivated to read, so she wants to display not only books but also videos, study prints, realia, and software programs. As you talk with Valerie, you realize she knows her students' needs and abilities and tries to provide a wide range of experiences for them using various media and teaching strategies.

Keyona, a kindergarten teacher, looks for study prints about the school environment to help the children feel at home in their new surroundings. She is interested in having some stories to read aloud when children become overly excited. Keyona also asks for your assistance in locating cassette audiotapes and instructions for simple folk dances and musical activities.

Jessica, an experienced fourth-grade teacher, arrives with Kevin, a new teacher. Kevin's academic background and preparation were for secondary education. He is assigned to teach a fifth-grade class. Jessica tries to alleviate some of Kevin's anxieties and seeks your advice about materials that appeal to fifth graders. In her own class, Jessica likes to start the year by observing each child's interests. You watch her gather a variety of items: books on the care of pets, biographies of sports figures, a rock-specimen display, a kit for making puppets, maps of the moon, play scripts, craft magazines, recordings of homemade musical instruments, and some science-fiction titles. She also asks about software and scheduling computer time. Jessica explains to Kevin that she places the materials around the classroom to attract children into groups with common interests.

Across town at Kennedy High School, your colleague Michael faces similar challenges. He meets Willie, who teaches five sections of American history. Although each of Willie's classes uses the same outline, he gives more independent assignments to the class for college-bound students. For the honors class Willie wants Michael to instruct students in how to prepare a pathfinder before they begin their online searches for their independent research papers. Students in three other sections will supplement the textbook by writing short biographical sketches. These students will need Michael's help in locating videos, books, biographical reference materials, and homepages on the Web. The remaining class is made up of students who read below grade level. For this group Willie needs visual and manipulative materials that will help him cover the prescribed content.

Next to arrive is Heather, chairperson of the English department. She wants to arrange a series of meetings with Michael to discuss the resources available and the information literacy skills her students will need for the first two units. She asks Michael to join her in teaching her research class on search strategies that students can use with the electronic databases. Heather plans to start the unit by showing a videodisc to help the students remember the techniques of note taking. She mentions that last year several English teachers wanted to use the videodiscs on the same day and expresses concern about scheduling to meet everyone's needs. Dinora, another English teacher, joins the conversation in hearty agreement about the demand for the videodiscs.

Both Dinora and Heather want ideas for encouraging expository writing. They ask whether Michael can recommend magazine covers, posters, or art prints that could serve as incentives for writing.

Carlos, another English teacher, joins the conversation. He needs ideas for motivating students' interest in poetry. Does the media center have any recordings of popular music? Perhaps students could listen to them, read the lyrics, and discover poetry. He asks whether Michael knows any composers or lyricists who would perform for the class and describe how they work. He also wonders about local poetry workshops at the public library or bookstores and the availability of funding from the state council for the arts to bring poets into the classroom. Would Michael be interested in cosponsoring a student publication?

Dieter, from the mathematics department, wants to know whether the computer software he requested last spring has arrived. He asks Michael when his students can come to the media center to use the programs. Will aides be available to help students?

Rodrigo, an assistant principal, is planning a talk to a community group. His topics include teenage pregnancy, substance abuse, the increase in teenage suicide, and alienated youth. The group members want to know how they can help with these problems. Rodrigo asks Michael to help him gather materials for the presentation. Can visuals be made to display the facts?

These incidents, occurring in the first hour of opening day, represent only a few typical staff requests. They illustrate the day-to-day challenges media specialists encounter. They also show that the media program is not limited to activities within the media center itself. The media program (its administration, services, staff, facilities, and collection) is an integral facet of the entire school program and must be responsive to the needs of individuals, groups, and programs.

ENVIRONMENT OF THE MEDIA PROGRAM

The media program should be based on well-defined policies and procedures to make its resources, facilities, services, and personnel an integral part of the school's program. Before these policies and procedures can be established, one must have a clear understanding of the needs and demographics of the school and community, which can be achieved by conducting a school and community analysis. A school analysis might include information such as the number of students enrolled in the school, courses taught, students' ethnic backgrounds and socioeconomic status, and special school programs, such as literature-based reading or electronic reading programs. Helpful demographic data relating to a community include factors such as the population, major employers, and setting (urban, suburban, or rural).

The media program is an integral part of the school in which it functions, and thus the school's media program should reflect the school's philosophy and goals. School and media program goals are frequently affected by a school district program and are governed by policies established at the district or system level. Additionally, state-generated guidelines and policies will affect the individual school media program. The school program may be part of regional activities: For example, a regional center may provide electronic bulletin boards or other services. Guidelines and standards produced by professional organizations at the national level also influence the goals of a media program. Finally, with the emerging technologies, the school media program is linked to and affected by the global community.

LEARNER AND MEDIA PROGRAM

In the 1998 guidelines for school library media programs, *Information Power: Building Partnerships for Learning,* the learner is the main focus. The goals of today's media programs center on literacy standards for authentic student learning. A creative, energetic media program sustains these standards (American Association for School Librarians and Association for Educational Communications and Technology 1998).

The 1998 guidelines retain the mission introduced in *Information Power: Guidelines for School Library Media Programs,* which were adopted a decade earlier: "The mission of the library media program is to insure that students and staff are effective users of ideas and information" (American Association of School Librarians and Association for Educational Communications and Technology 1988, 1).

ROLE OF THE COLLECTION

The media center collection plays an important role in ensuring that the media program is integrated with the overall school program and that it provides access to information within and outside the school. Most media specialists would agree that to meet the school's media needs effectively, the media program must

be an essential part of the total school program;

respond to the curricular needs and interests of teachers, administrators, and other staff members;

respond to the multicultural diversity of the student population, to the developmental level and learning styles of students, and to the needs of students with disabilities;

provide guidance in the use of and access to a full range of resources—print, non-print, and electronic—with appropriate equipment;

cooperate with other institutions to provide the widest possible access to information, which may involve interlibrary loan, coordinated collection development, and other forms of resource sharing;

exemplify the total media concept, providing access to varied materials, necessary equipment, trained personnel, and resources housed inside and outside the media center; and

have a staff that adequately plans and carries out the selection, maintenance, and evaluation of resources.

The media specialist is the person responsible for ensuring that these conditions exist and these functions take place.

Although answers to students' questions were traditionally found in the collection housed in the school media center, the answers today may or may not be found within the items on the shelves of the media center. The collection goes beyond the walls of the immediate media center and contains many sources that can be accessed through online services. Thus, the media center is connected electronically to a far-reaching world of sources and information.

ROLE OF THE MEDIA SPECIALIST

The new *Information Power* (American Association of School Librarians and Association for Educational Communications and Technology 1998) identifies the following key roles of the media specialist as they relate to the total learning program: teacher, instructional partner, information specialist, and program administrator. Three basic ideas or strategies—collaboration, leadership, and use of technology—are identified as the unifying themes for guiding the effective media specialist.

The responsible media specialist supports the philosophy, goals, and objectives of the school within which the media program functions. This person collaborates with teachers and administrators in the planning process to ensure that the media program is an integral part of the school program, manages the media program's operations, selects materials and other resources (including electronic formats), and instructs students and teachers. The media specialist who understands the value of the media program acts as its chief advocate by planning informational, instructional, consultative, and production services; evaluating the services and collection; and promoting the media program through public-relations activities.

All members of the school faculty share responsibility for the media program. A media specialist cannot run an effective, integrated program alone. The media specialist's leadership and human-relations skills are called upon to involve others in the program. The media specialist needs to collaborate with teachers in curricular planning; in turn, teachers need to collaborate with the media specialist in planning and evaluating the media program.

The media specialist may find it difficult to involve administrators, teachers, and students in planning, implementing, and evaluating the media program. However, collection-related activities (with print, non-print, and electronic resources) provide a range of opportunities for a media specialist to involve everyone.

First, the media specialist should identify the characteristics of the users and the demands of the curriculum. What are the needs and interests of the students and teachers? Second, the media specialist should take steps to involve administrators, teachers, and students in the development of policies. How can policies reflect their needs and interests? Third, the media specialist should make an effort to invite others to participate in the selection of materials and online resources for the collection. How can the media specialist involve students, teachers, and administrators in the process? Fourth, the media specialist facilitates inter-agency borrowing and lending of materials. Are students and teachers aware of resources available through other agencies? Are they familiar with the use of online databases or other forms of electronically delivered information? Do they understand the procedures for obtaining information located outside the collection? Fifth, the media specialist alone cannot judge the effectiveness of a collection. Does the collection meet the students' and teachers' needs? Do the policies support the needs of the school? How can the media specialist involve teachers, students, and administrators in the evaluation of the collection, the materials, and the policies?

The media specialist makes many decisions about the collection: what to add, what to access through resource sharing, and what to remove. Others can help with these decisions. The media specialist must have an overview of the total program, take responsibility for the decisions, and manage a responsive collection while involving others in the planning and evaluation process. In a discussion of collection program activities, later chapters address examples of techniques for involving others.

CONCLUSIONS

Although the media program traditionally centered on a collection that was internal to the facility, that collection has now expanded beyond the walls of the media center. Authentic student learning is the focus of the media center program. As a teacher, instructional partner, information specialist, and program administrator, the media specialist now provides the leadership to build a community of learners, working collaboratively with teachers, administrators, and students. Both the media specialist and the collection play important roles in the media program in that the media specialist serves as the interface connecting students to the collection (both within and beyond the walls of the media center) and ultimately to the answers to students' questions.

NOTES

1. The term "school library media specialist" is the currently accepted title for this position. In this work it is shortened to "media specialist." In like fashion, the term "media program" is used in place of "school library media program."

REFERENCES

American Association of School Librarians and Association of Educational Communications and Technology. 1988. *Information Power: Guidelines for School Library Media Programs*. Chicago: American Library Association; Washington, D.C.: Association for Educational Communications and Technology.

———. 1998. *Information Power: Building Partnerships for Learning*. Chicago: American Library Association.

ADDITIONAL READINGS

American Association of School Librarians and Association of Education Communications and Technology. 1998. *Information Power: Building Partnerships for Learning*. Chicago: American Library Association.

Part One lists nine student learning standards that indicate what an information-literate student should know and be able to do. Several indicators of proficiency are included. Part Two deals with three integral components of an effective media program: collaboration, leadership, and the use of technology. The four roles of the professional media specialist—teacher, instructional partner, information specialist, and program administrator—are also discussed, with specific principles and goals indicated.

Loertscher, David V., and Blanche Woolls. 1999. *Information Literacy: A Review of the Research*. San Jose, CA: Hi Willow Research and Publishing.

Covers reviews of research on topics relating to information literacy. Includes applications of the research studies.

ELECTRONIC RESOURCES

American Library Association. 1999. "Information Power: Because Student Achievement Is the Bottom Line." [http://www.ala.org/aasl/ip_implementation.html]. (Accessed November 6, 2000).

Includes links that deal with *Information Power: Building Partnerships for Learning* and its implementation.

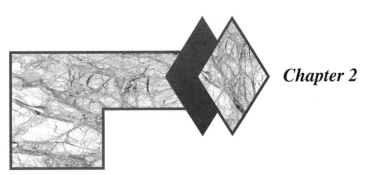

Chapter 2

The Collection

Traditionally, the term *collection* described the resources (mainly print items) housed in a single room of a school. This room, called the library at that time, contained some books, a few magazines, and perhaps a newspaper rack. A student or teacher searching for information went to this library—a collection confined to the printed matter within its walls. If Andrew, a fifth-grade student, entered this library with a rock, he could look for information about the rock in the encyclopedias and books about geology. If he could not find a picture of his rock, he probably would leave the library disappointed, unable to find out what kind of rock he had found.

In today's media center, Andrew can compare his rock with those housed in the realia collection or illustrated in an electronic encyclopedia. If he wants to learn about the formation and geological history of an area, he can use an interactive video or correspond via electronic mail with a student in a county where similar rocks are found. If he wants to know more, the media specialist can help him locate sources outside the school. Andrew can use interlibrary loan to obtain materials from other libraries, or the media specialist can arrange a loan of natural history museum materials.

Andrew's older sister Erika also can use electronic tools to explore any number of research topics. She can use a modem to communicate with university researchers on a distant site or request a fax of a document from a government agency. Today, walls do not limit searches for information.

Today's wider access to information calls for a definition of the term *collection* that reaches beyond four walls to almost the entire world and indeed at times to space. How one defines *collection* influences how one makes information sources available and accessible. Defining a collection as merely the holdings of an individual facility is no longer a viable option. An analysis of several overlapping perspectives of the collection reveals a comprehensive definition. A collection is a physical entity;

includes materials in print and in visual, auditory, tactile, and electronic formats with appropriate forms of delivery;

serves school goals and programs;

meets the developmental, cultural, and learning needs of all students;

provides both physical and intellectual access to information resources of all types;

provides access to human and materials resources in the local and global community;

accesses information and materials from other libraries and information systems through interlibrary loan, resource sharing, and electronic resources; and

is only one element of the media program.

The ways in which these perspectives overlap indicate their multifaceted external and internal relationships (see Figure 2.1).

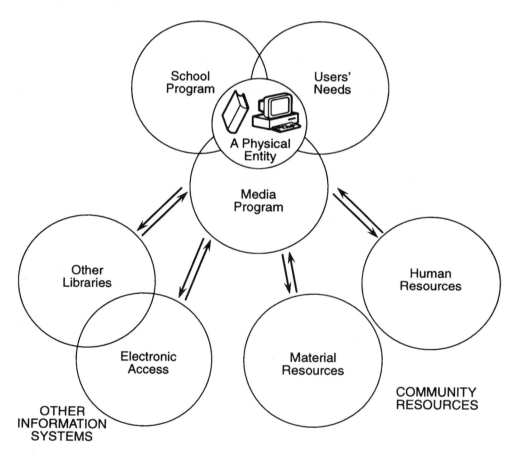

Figure 2.1. Overlapping perspective of the collection.

ACCESSIBILITY AND AVAILABILITY

Accessibility and *availability* are key concepts in the definition of *collection*. When information can be researched, it is accessible. When the item is actually at hand, it is available. Today Andrew, the budding geologist, may go to the media center's online catalog to find a wide range of resources. He knows that the items he needs are in the collection, and he finds them; at this point, the information is available. If, on the other hand, he learns he can go to the local natural history museum to obtain the information, the information is accessible. When Andrew goes to the museum, he finds the information available there. He also can access information through an interlibrary request or through visiting a Website.

The interval between accessibility and availability can be crucial for those students with a limited attention span. It is also critical for the classroom teacher whose students need information now—not after they move on to a new subject. The media specialist's definition of collection and the resulting practices affect both accessibility and availability. Today the media center program offers services to help users locate, obtain, and use resources external to the collection. Online catalogs representing the holdings of numerous media centers, fax machines, and online databases all decrease the time between an expressed need and having the information available for the user.

The Americans with Disabilities Act requires all institutions serving the public to provide access to everyone. Students with cognitive and perceptual disabilities will find toys, audio, video, and multimedia materials more useful than traditional formats. Deaf students may need captioned materials. Blind students can obtain resources through the National Library Service for the Blind and Physically Handicapped. Chapter 12 discusses ways the collection can meet the needs of students with disabilities.

Accessibility goes beyond physical access. Media specialists, as teachers and information providers, also are responsible for providing intellectual access. Helping students locate, access, select, and evaluate information is an important element in information skills instruction. With the access to information on the Internet, it is even more critical to help students learn how to evaluate the information they find.

PHYSICAL ENTITY

The collection is a physical entity; the individual items collectively create a whole. The value of a single item must be viewed in relation to other items in the collection as shown in Figure 2.2. When deciding whether to add or withdraw a specific item, the item should be evaluated both as an entity and in relation to the collection:

◆ Is the same information already in the collection, but in a different format?

◆ If so, will this format make the information accessible to more people?

◆ Is the same or a similar item quickly accessible through a resource sharing network or the Internet?

◆ Does this item uniquely fill a particular need?

Questions like these help identify the relationship of one item to another in the collection.

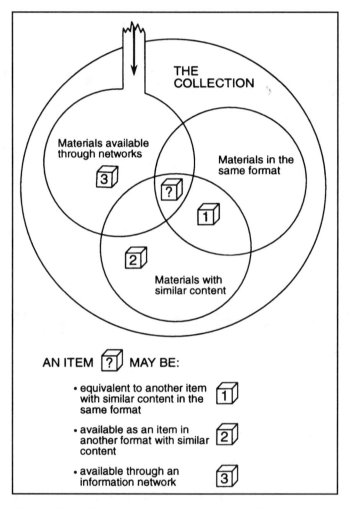

Figure 2.2. Relationship of an item to the collection as a whole.

Schools that intershelve subject-related materials in various formats physically show how the individual items relate. If inadequate physical space or other limitations do not allow this integration, the user must rely on the catalog to reveal all potential information sources.

Centralized bibliographic control informs people of the locations of materials, whether in the media center or elsewhere on the school's campus. This approach to identifying the collection is particularly important in schools with team teaching, where resources are housed in the area of highest use. Centralized bibliographic control also provides access to materials in departmental libraries housed throughout a campus. Centralized bibliographic control is not limited to materials; human resources (for example, teachers' notes about field trips) can be made available through entries in the bibliographic record. All materials should be treated as information resources for the entire school and should be accessible to all potential users.

With access to information through resource sharing and electronic means, media centers are definitely moving away from a philosophy of ownership to one of accessibility. The immediate physical collection provides only a starting point for students as they begin to search for information. Through online catalogs they can learn about information resources in other schools, public libraries, community college libraries, and other sites. In the large sense of accessibility, anything—including interlibrary loan items and information found on the Internet—that users can obtain through the media center constitutes the collection. In the broadest sense of availability, everything that users can find using tools in the media center makes up the collection. In this context, the collection as a physical entity provides a starting point for coordinated collection development practices and resource sharing with other media centers, libraries, and institutions.

MATERIALS

A wide range of learning experiences can be offered through a collection that includes materials in various formats. To support these materials, the collection must provide appropriate equipment. Formats commonly found in collections include printed materials (books, periodicals, newspapers, pamphlets, and microforms); visual materials (filmstrips, slides, transparencies, graphic materials, and videos); tactile formats (games, models, sculpture, and specimens); and electronic formats (computer software, CD-ROMs, and online). Collections also may include postcards; live animals; materials that support creative activity, including carpentry tools, easels, paints, printing presses, and puppets; Braille materials; clothing patterns; and calculators. The list is virtually endless, for people gather information in a variety of ways and from many sources.

Considering the collection as materials in various formats acknowledges that students with different learning styles comprehend information in different ways. Competent readers may find print materials most useful; individuals with aural or visual literacy skills may find audiovisual materials more appealing. Computer-literate students may prefer software, electronic encyclopedias, and information on CD-ROMs. Learning activities involving several individuals may call for games. Programmed texts or software may be the most effective format for practicing skills.

The term *integrated* describes a collection that includes materials in a variety of formats selected to meet the information-seeking habits of its users. This variety can accommodate the range of teaching patterns, learning styles, and uses of small-group, large-group, and individualized instruction.

The media specialist must be familiar with each format's characteristics, advantages, disadvantages, compatibility with other formats, equipment needs, and copyright regulations. In evaluating formats, one considers their technical and physical characteristics, content, potential use, and relationship to other items in the collection.

PURPOSES

The collection has purposes. First, it serves school goals and programs. Second, it should meet the developmental, personal, and learning needs of all students. Although these purposes often overlap, each has specific implications for collection activities.

If the collection is to fulfill its purposes, one must evaluate the materials in terms of the school's goals and purposes and the users' needs and interests. High-demand materials should be readily available. Rarely requested materials or ones not anticipated could be obtained through interlibrary loan, networking arrangements, or other avenues of resource sharing.

School Goals and Program Needs

If the media program is to be an integral part of the school, the media specialist must learn about the school's programs and goals. To do this, the media specialist becomes familiar with the school's philosophy; programs (curricular and noncurricular); people (administrators, teachers, students, staff, and parents); and facility. Each of these elements has implications for planning, building, and evaluating the collection.

Media specialists and teachers must study and discuss curriculum plans and teaching strategies. Does the school have programs for gifted students, speech therapy, remedial reading, deaf students, students with a visual impairment, or career guidance? Does it offer short-term projects, such as an Earth Day program, women's history month, Black history month, or public-relations projects? Does the school sponsor a student council, safety patrol, Spanish club, drama club, after-school programs, and so on? What resources do these programs need?

One can analyze the implications of goals and programs for the collection by asking these questions:

♦ Does the collection need to house formats suitable for large groups and small groups?

♦ Is individualized study stressed?

♦ Is there an emphasis on subject- or skill-oriented information?

♦ What range of subjects and learning styles occurs in the school? Do advanced-placement and remedial classes exist?

Informational, Instructional, and Personal Needs

A collection comprises communication media designed to meet the users' informational, instructional, and personal needs. Materials may be designed to instruct, inform, or appeal to the interests of individual users.

People use the collection for many reasons. Administrators require materials for in-service programs, publicity, speeches, and communicating with parents about educational issues. Teachers need professional information, including up-to-date ideas about accepted learning theories and effective teaching practices as well as current scholarship in their subject area. Non-teaching personnel and caregivers use the professional collection to aid them in their work with students.

The student population exhibits a wide range of needs, abilities, and interests. Students' ages, gender, interests, experiences, personalities, learning styles, and physical characteristics affect their use of materials. The media specialist needs to know the abilities and interests of each student. Some students develop high levels of proficiency in computing, reading, listening, or viewing skills. Others may be weak in one or more of these areas, contrasted with sophisticated users of all types of media. Students from homes with access to the latest technology will be more familiar with its uses than will some of their teachers.

Within a single class, students' abilities in all skills may vary by many levels. For example, a sixth-grade class may include children who read from the second-grade through the eighth-grade level. In a middle school, reading levels may range from second-grade through college level.

Many other differences exist as well. People with physical disabilities may require special materials and equipment. Recent immigrants may need the help of translators. Some students may be employed on a full-time basis, others on a part-time basis. Students may live alone, be responsible for younger members of their families, or even be parents. Any of these factors may affect which formats students find easiest or most convenient to use.

PHYSICAL AND INTELLECTUAL ACCESS

Two types of barriers can limit access to information: physical barriers and a lack of policies and practices that demonstrate a commitment to intellectual freedom. Examples of potential physical barriers are height of shelving, width of aisles, and lack of necessary equipment for using materials. A small child or short person may not be able to reach an item on a shelf. A person in a wheelchair or on crutches may not be able to move between the shelving. A partially sighted person may not be able to view a document without being able to enlarge the image.

A principle for information access and delivery is that "the library media program is founded on a commitment to the right of intellectual freedom" (American Association for School Librarians and the Association for Educational Communications and Technology 1998, 91).

This commitment is not new. It is part of the profession's history. The position is equally significant today as we help students become critical thinkers and competent problem solvers who can contribute in a democracy. Chapter 4 presents relevant issues and offers readers an opportunity to explore their own thinking and to formulate their position on these topics.

COMMUNITY RESOURCES

Another perspective of the collection is as a gateway providing access to the community's human and material resources. Museums, businesses, industries, and local government agencies often encourage field trips or provide personnel to visit schools. For example, a natural food store's distribution of cookies made from kelp provides an effective learning experience about the resources of the sea.

In some cases the media center staff visit the business to create a field trip on video. A media center staff member might videotape a local newspaper's operations to prepare a class for a visit by an editor. The range and potential use of available resources is limited only by a media specialist's imagination and priorities.

People are valuable information sources. They can provide career information, present travelogues, relate local history, or demonstrate hobbies and crafts. Many government officials, business people, and other members of the community make themselves available for student interviews. The school's occupational specialist can help identify such people.

Teleconferences and electronic mail are transforming the school's community and expanding its borders to the world and outer space. The Internet offers myriad opportunities for students to expand their queries beyond geographical boundaries.

Integrating community resources expands the collection. Access can be provided through listings in the online catalog, in information packets distributed to teachers, and on the library or school's own Website. Such listings identify the institution or agency, name a contact person, describe the resources and services available, identify the intended audience, and note the areas of curricular interest.

RELATIONSHIPS AND INFLUENCES

Building Level

Finally, the collection can be viewed as an element in the school's media program. From this perspective, the collection is a tool that supports the roles and activities of the media specialist. The media specialist's roles can be characterized as direct or indirect. They operate in a cyclical pattern as shown in Figure 2.3. The direct roles involve interaction with patrons. The media specialist's *direct* roles include professional services as teacher, instructional partner, and information specialist for students, teachers, staff, parents, and community members. The role of helping students evaluate the information they find is increasingly important as students face the multiple and varied information sources available through the Internet. The media specialist's *indirect* roles provide the means for carrying out the direct roles. In these roles the media specialist serves as program administrator, including developer and evaluator of the collection.

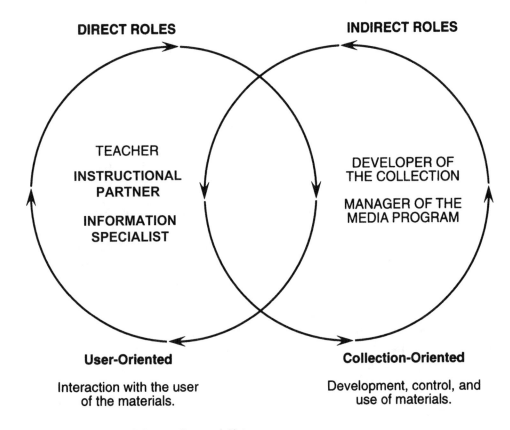

Figure 2.3. Roles of the media specialist.

The direct and indirect roles are interdependent. Acting as a teacher, instructional partner, and information specialist, the media specialist gains knowledge that is then used in making decisions about the collection.

As teachers, media specialists help students develop skills in accessing, evaluating, and using information from multiple sources. They work with teachers and administrators to help them develop skills in information literacy, including the uses of information technology.

As instructional partners, media specialists join teachers in linking student information needs, curriculum content, learning outcomes, and a wide range of information resources. Media specialists work with individual teachers to design and assess learning tasks for the student and to integrate this with the information and communication abilities required in subject matter standards.

As information specialists, media specialists acquire and evaluate information resources, while working collaboratively with teachers, administrators, and students to make them aware of information issues. As information specialists, media specialists demonstrate mastery of sophisticated electronic resources and maintain a focus on the quality and ethical uses of information resources.

As program administrators, media specialists are responsible for the management of staff, budgets, equipment, facilities, and evaluation of the program. They must interpret and communicate all this to school personnel and the public. In carrying out these responsibilities, media specialists work to ensure that programs meet goals directly related to the collection. These include providing

intellectual access to information and

physical access to information through selecting and organizing the local collection and acquiring information and materials from outside sources.

In any particular setting, the collection must support the media specialist's roles as teacher, instructional partner, information specialist, and advocate for the effective use of information and information technology.

Yet another perspective of the collection emphasizes resource sharing—providing access to materials owned by other institutions. Media programs share resources by participating in networks and coordinated collection development plans. In one school district with four high schools, each school has a unique area of collecting responsibility. The school with a strong music department collects in that area and has the district's only copy of Grove's *Dictionary of Music*. The second high school collects social studies materials; the third, science materials; and the fourth, humanities materials. All four high schools have basic collections in all other areas but rely on the other schools for a more in-depth array of resources. In multi-type library networks, schools may do major collecting in career education materials, professional materials, ethnic materials, and high-interest/low-vocabulary materials. Statewide online catalogs, such as Florida's *Sunlink,* provide ready access to the holdings of other collections.

District Level

Many building-level media programs (those designed to meet the needs of a single school) are units of a school district media program. The district's goals and objectives apply to the building-level media program, and the district-level media program personnel and resources provide a wide range of services to the building-level program. The district may provide centralized purchasing and processing of materials. The online catalog or wide-area networks (WANs) may include bibliographic and location information about items owned by the district and housed in the media centers throughout the system.

Collections housed in the district media center often include items that supplement materials owned by individual schools. The district collections may include materials that are expensive or heavily used at limited intervals, museum items with curricular value, and backup equipment. They also may include video libraries, professional collections, and materials examination collections. District-level collections are available to all school personnel within the district.

State Level

In the United States, education is the responsibility of each state. Each has its own philosophy, goals, and objectives for its educational programs. These responsibilities are assigned to the state education agency. Their staff may serve as consultants and information disseminators. Their products and services may include printed publications, sponsorship of listservs or other electronic services, statewide online catalogs for the holdings of all the schools in the state, and the maintenance of examination centers. For media specialists working without the benefit of a district-level media program, the state media consultant is a key contact. In addition to consultants, state educational agencies may offer recommendations and standards for the media program and collection, as well as other useful works for media specialists.

Other state agencies are information resources. They provide information about all aspects of the state, sponsor Websites, identify speakers to talk to students about environmental or economic concerns, or offer materials such as video programs. They may provide lists of resources available from the state.

Regional Level

The media program and the media specialist have formal and informal relationships with groups and agencies within the county and regions of the state or nation. County-level professional associations provide programs and contacts useful to the media specialist. Some states have regional examination centers where the media specialist can personally evaluate materials and attend in-service programs.

Regional accrediting associations issue standards for schools. When a school seeks accreditation, the school's media specialists are involved in self-studies prepared for visits by association representatives. (See Appendix A for a list of regional accrediting associations.)

National Level

The school and the media program are elements within the education and information systems of our society. Society's concerns can influence the building-level media program. A few examples illustrate this relationship.

Society's concern about people with physical disabilities spawned several pieces of legislation that affect school and media programs. In 1990 the Americans with Disabilities Act (ADA) mandated that public services and facilities be accessible to people with disabilities. The media specialist should assess whether the media center fulfills that mandate.

Another piece of legislation that directly affects the operation of the media center is the Copyright Act of 1976. Designed to balance the interests of authors and artists with the user's ability to access information, the law guides media specialists in carrying out their responsibilities.

Both the school and the media program have national affiliations that provide guidance and information. Two professional associations directly involved with media programs are the American Association of School Librarians (AASL) (a division of the American Library Association) and the Association for Educational Communications and Technology (AECT). Their joint efforts led to the publication of *Information Power: Building Partnerships for Learning* (1998). Each association offers other sources of information and assistance. This book cites various documents and services offered by these and other professional associations.

Global Level

With the increasing availability of access to the Internet, our opportunity to tap into resources on a global basis is growing. Teachers and students can "surf" the World Wide Web (WWW) to sites throughout the world. Through listservs (discussion lists), such as LM_NET, media specialists can share ideas with their counterparts throughout the world (LM_NET appears to be mainly in English-speaking countries).[1]

CONCLUSIONS

The media specialist's perception of the collection affects how the media program functions with the school program. Thinking of the collection as limited to the materials contained within one area of the school limits the resources available to students and teachers. Extending the definition to include resources available throughout the building and from the global community greatly increases access to materials. Ensuring physical access to information and having a commitment to intellectual freedom are important aspects of carrying out one's professional responsibilities.

A knowledgeable media specialist can ensure that the collection is an integral part of the school's program, meeting the needs of the program and its users. Policies and procedures should be designed to facilitate this integration.

NOTES

1. To join LM_NET, send an e-mail message to LISTSERV@LISTSERV.SRY.EDU. In the first line of the message, type SUBSCRIBE LM_NET Firstname Lastname.

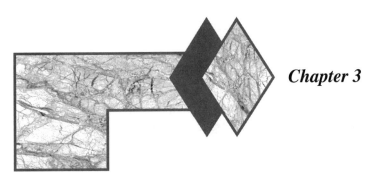

Chapter 3

The Collection Program

The term *collection program* denotes the processes necessary to develop and maintain a collection. The media specialist carries out the program by

becoming knowledgeable about an existing collection or creating one;

becoming familiar with the community (that is, the external environment);

assessing the needs of the school's curriculum and other programs as well as the needs of the users;

establishing collection development policies and procedures (the overall plan);

creating the basis for selection (including policies and procedures to guide selection decisions);

identifying criteria for evaluating materials;

planning for and implementing the selection process: identifying and obtaining tools, arranging for personal examination of materials, and involving others in the decision making;

participating in resource sharing through networking and coordinated collection development;

establishing acquisition policies and procedures (that is, guides to obtaining materials);

setting up the maintenance program; and

evaluating the collection.

These activities draw on the information presented in the previous chapters and establish the framework for the remaining chapters of this book. The purpose of this chapter is to present an overview of the relationships among the processes involved, as illustrated in Figure 3.1. While the media specialist is the primary actor in the processes, he or she cannot control all the factors influencing collection activities. The school or district programs, financial concerns, or the facility may impose constraints.

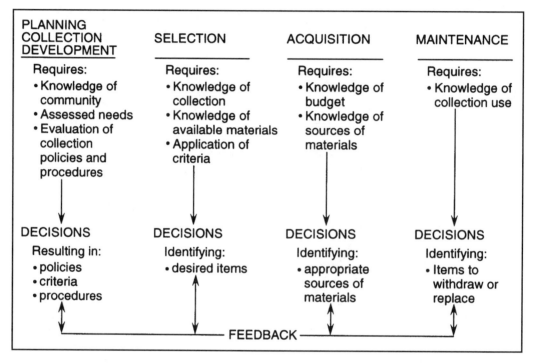

Figure 3.1. Processes of the collection program.

COLLECTION PROGRAM ACTIVITIES

How the media specialist carries out collection activities determines how well the collection achieves the goals of the principles addressed in the perceptions outlined in Chapter 2. Knowledge, skill, and sensitivity are required to systematically plan and carry out collection activities.

Learning About an Existing Collection

If a collection is to serve as a communication and information base, the media specialist must know both the users' needs and the collection's available resources. Browsing is an easy way to learn about a collection. When walking through the collection, do you recognize titles and equipment? Are materials housed in unusual areas? Will students overlook them? Are materials housed in unmarked cabinets or drawers? Are signs clear and accurate? Put yourself in a student's position. Would you find those materials? Will the online catalog help you? Test a few entries.

Are you familiar with all the formats you find? Are encyclopedias available in print, on CD-ROM, online, and/or in videodisc formats? What evidence do you see of access to electronically delivered information? Are connections to the LAN available throughout the school or only in the media center? Are there signs of distance learning delivery systems, such as campus cable systems or satellites?

As you roam through the facility, scan items new to you. Take note of the software manuals. Are there programs with which you are unfamiliar? Make notes about materials that are new to you. Also notice areas that need a sign to make materials easier to find. Equipment should be housed in an area convenient to the materials that require it. Is there a ready reference area? Are these materials duplicated in the circulating collection?

Remember that the collection extends to materials housed outside the media center. The teachers' lounge or department offices may house professional journals or other materials. Check other resources in the school. Is there a staffed career center that assumes responsibility for collecting vocational materials? Are there other departmental collections? The collection development policy should identify these as well. Does the catalog note storage locations throughout the school?

As you gather these first impressions, check the media center's procedure manual for explanations of unusual situations. Ten copies of one videotape may seem unusual, but the manual may state a good reason for having them. As the school year progresses and you become involved with teachers and students, you will soon become quite familiar with the collection.

If you face the task of creating a new collection, guidelines will help you get started. This challenging and exciting opportunity is discussed in Chapter 17.

Knowing the Community

A basic consideration of all collection development activities is the interaction of the media program with the school, other educational or informational institutions and agencies, and the external environment. The community (its geographical, political, economic, cultural, and social characteristics) influences the collection. Changes in school objectives, in access to other collections, or in citizens' attitudes about education affect decisions about the collection.

Today, the global community is a prime resource. Students have computers in their homes and access to them in their public libraries. Teachers electronically communicate with colleagues around the world. Telefacsimile (fax) machines speed the delivery of an article for a student's report.

Assessing Need

To ensure that the collection fulfills the informational and instructional needs of its users, the media specialist must identify those needs. Whom does the collection serve? What are their informational needs? What are the teachers' instructional needs? The media specialist can begin to answer these questions by researching the users' characteristics, the preferred teaching methods, and the preferred size for learning groups. Two local sources of statistical information are the automated circulation systems and the logs for online and CD-ROM searches. Analysis of interlibrary loan requests identifies gaps in the collection. Knowledge of the existing collection, the school, the community, and assessed needs must all be considered in plans and policies that guide the development of the collection.

Developing Collections

The plans and policies for collection development should reflect the short- and long-term goals of the media center. The media specialist must integrate into the policies and plans factors such as audience demand, need, and expectation; the information world; fiscal plans; and the history of the collection. Involvement of teachers and administrators in the development of such documents is an important collaborative effort to ensure understanding of the issues addressed. High-school students can play a role in these efforts. Attention to collection development ensures informed selection decisions, not just an accumulation of materials.

Collection development policies guide acquisition, selection, and evaluation activities. They identify the goals and limitations of the collection, including the use of materials covered by the Copyright Act of 1976. Procedures guide methods of handling collection activities, including censorship challenges.

Chapter 6 addresses the differences between policies—which identify the reason for doing something—and procedures—which identify how to do it.

Selecting

While the collection development policies and procedures address the overall development and management of the entire collection, parallel policies and procedures are needed to guide the selection decisions for each item. Such documents may be part of the overall plan; frequently they are the only documents that exist.

Selection policies articulate the media program's commitment to the right of intellectual freedom and reflect professional ethics, rights of users, and concern for intellectual property. Again, this is a document that benefits from the participation of teachers, administrators, and students in its development. The selection procedures are the specific processes that carry out selection policies.

Identifying Criteria

Criteria, the standards by which one evaluates items, are a major part of the selection policy. One must establish criteria for assessing the item itself and its relation to the collection development policy. Generally accepted criteria include literary quality, currency, accuracy of information, appeal and value to students, application within the curriculum, quality of presentation, and format. One needs to establish criteria for specific formats and for materials that specific types of people use.

Selection Process

Selection is the process of deciding whether an item will be a valuable addition to the collection. During this process one keeps in mind set criteria and makes decisions within established policies. Personal examination and favorable reviews can provide the basis for selection decisions. Sources that provide reviews include selection tools, reviewing journals, and bibliographic essays. These are valuable references to consult during the selection process; they should be readily available.

To plan for the selection process, the media specialist should obtain bibliographic and selection tools. These resources tell whether an item is available for purchase, rent, or loan. Materials should be secured for reviewing or previewing. Plan to involve teachers, administrators, and students in these processes.

Established criteria, policies, and procedures are not the sole factors that influence a media specialist's choices. One's selection skills, values, interests, and even prejudices influence these decisions. To make sound selection decisions, the media specialist sets aside personal biases and makes objective choices. Self-awareness helps the media specialist know when to seek the opinions of others.

Resource Sharing

Networks created by multi-type libraries sharing resources provide access to information materials and services housed outside the school's facility. A school that participates in a network has access to a plethora of resources and services; however, participation carries with it certain responsibilities and perhaps financial obligations. If your school participates in a network, what are your responsibilities? Has your school been assigned the task of collecting specific subjects or formats? In a typical example, one school collects high-interest/low-vocabulary materials while another collects reference works about a specific subject. Schools may have responsibilities for materials presented in different languages. The public library or the historical museum collects local history items while the school collects yearbooks. What materials, services, and financial obligations does the agreement include? Networks offer cooperative purchasing programs, cataloging and processing, computerized databases, delivery systems, production services, examination centers, serials cooperatives, and other forms of resource sharing. If your school does not participate in a state network, inquire about how you can join.

Some facilities serve both the school and the public. Meeting the needs of patrons with ages that range from preschool to senior citizen creates advantages and disadvantages for the collection. A distinct advantage is the media specialist's knowledge of the community, but a disadvantage is conflicting demands on the collection. The media specialist should address questions such as these: How can one resolve such a conflict most efficiently? Should the collection be directed to the curricular and instructional needs of the students or toward the general informational and recreational needs of the public? Do separate budgets exist? Are materials for adults and children housed together? Policies and procedures statements should address these questions.

Acquiring

Acquisition, the process of obtaining materials, is a direct result of the collection development policies and the selection policies and procedures. Acquisition policies determine who will supply materials; acquisition procedures establish the process for obtaining the materials. Acquisition policies establish methods of determining the appropriate source for material, that is, the most efficient and most economical source. Acquisition procedures establish the processes by which the media specialist orders, receives, and pays for the materials. Using the policies and procedures as a guide, the media specialist selects the appropriate source. Purchases of books may be from a *jobber* (a company that handles titles from several publishers), a publisher, or a local bookstore. Purchases of computer software and audiovisual materials may be from vendors who handle materials from several companies or direct from the company. Examples of other sources of materials include renting, leasing, and subscribing through online services or magazine distributors.

Other questions to address include the following: Which is the best format for specific information? For example, should a reference work be bought as a book, as a CD-ROM, or as an online service or obtained through use of the Internet?

Maintaining

Collection maintenance is an important and often neglected function of the collection program. The media specialist must make decisions about replacing, removing, mending, or rebinding and keeping magazines and similar materials. Equipment must be kept in working condition. Is an appropriate number of personal computers available so patrons may use the software in the collection? Are sufficient supplies of consumable items such as projector bulbs and slide mounts available for prompt replacement? How will often-used items be replaced? Must items be completely unusable before they are replaced? If so, will replacements be available when they are needed? Obviously, the media specialist must establish policies and procedures for maintenance activities.

Inventory time provides an excellent opportunity to systematically check the condition of all items, but the collection may not be inventoried frequently enough to spot the gradual deterioration of some items. Planning for the systematic maintenance of all materials is important in keeping the collection usable.

Establishing Plans for Evaluation

Both the collection and the policies and procedures governing its growth demand evaluation and need to address many issues. What factors determine the value of the collection? One can assess the value quantitatively, that is, by the number of items in the collection, and qualitatively, for example, by how well the collection fulfills users' needs. A collection is an evolving entity that must be responsive to its environment; evaluation is the method by which media professionals assess a collection to determine whether it is responding effectively. Ideally, evaluation is a continuous process; however, daily routines often receive higher priority. Evaluation of a collection is also complex. Planning is required to create an evaluation system that is both manageable and comprehensive, one that allows media specialists to respond to changes in the collection or its environment.

Interaction of the Activities

One can view collection development activities as a continuum in which one activity leads to and influences the others (see Figure 3.2.). Activities are not isolated; rather, their interaction is cyclical. Thus a change in one activity affects others.

The collection development policy establishes priorities that directly affect both selection and acquisition activities. When Fermi Middle School adopted a critical thinking approach to teaching science, the goal was to have students learn through observation, experimentation, and individual or group investigation, not through textbooks. The collection development policy was altered to reflect this change. If budgetary constraints prevent the collection from meeting all the demands of the new program and the other informational and instructional needs of the school, one may need to revise the collection policy. The new wording could be as follows: "Priority will be given to the purchase of materials in the most desirable and effective format that supports the concepts and skills presented in the science curriculum."

The media specialist should establish policies that provide guidance with flexibility to anticipate and meet changes. With the rapid developments in technology, the media specialist can expect to add new formats to the collection. The media specialist should incorporate appropriate selection criteria for these in the policy.

Figure 3.2. Interaction of collection activities.

FACTORS THAT GOVERN COLLECTION ACTIVITIES

The media specialist is responsible for the development and implementation of the collection program. However, the media specialist cannot control all the factors that influence collection activities. The media program must operate within policies that the board of education adopts. The program must also meet the goals of the district and the school. The "attendance districts" established by the school board may change yearly and affect the composition of the student body or potential users of the collection. State or federal legislation may dictate requirements about the student population, the curriculum, and other school programs. Shifts in the student population will impose new demands on the collection that the collection program must accommodate. The constantly changing availability of electronic access creates continual shifts in the equipment needed and requires the media specialist to seek updating skills.

District Media Program

A building-level media program that is part of a district media program offers many advantages to the entry-level media specialist. The system's media program coordinator or director is someone to turn to for guidance. The district-level guidelines for media programs and the selection policy that the governing body adopts also aid the media specialist. The district-level media program may offer opportunities for the media specialist to examine new materials and invite teachers to exhibits and demonstrations at district-level media program meetings. District-level media programs offer many services to help establish and maintain the collection program.

Regional centers or intermediate school districts also provide personnel and services, including consultants or technicians, cooperative collections, examination centers, in-service programs, and clearinghouses for information about new technology. Internet sites and distant-learning opportunities are other ways these centers can extend the resources of the building media center.

Although such systems offer many benefits, they may also impose constraints on the school media program. An approved buying list generated by a districtwide committee may limit the range of titles that a media specialist can purchase. If you encounter this situation, learn the procedures for ordering items not on the list. In some systems, you must order titles on specific subjects at specified times. A typical pattern is to order science materials in December, replacements in March, and so on. Although this practice is efficient for the processing operation, it severely constrains the collection program. Fermi Middle School's science curriculum changes would have had a difficult, if not impossible, task of fulfilling curriculum needs under such regulations. Other schools find greater flexibility by acquiring materials via the jobber's electronic system, which enables one to place orders, track them, and ask questions on a regular basis.

Financial Support and Control

The institution's funding policies, including its policies regulating use of outside funding sources, impose constraints on the collection program. Accrediting agencies may also make budget demands. Media specialists operate within the limits set by budget allocations. In addition to the size of the budget, the accounting system can affect collection activities. A traditional line-item budget establishes a flat amount for media program materials. Line-item budgets divided by format impose further restrictions. This type of funding can prevent the collection from responding to school programs and individual users. For example, funds designated for computer software cannot be used for video formats. Collection development is more successful when budgeting allows program objectives and needs to determine priorities.

The school board's or the administrator's position on the use of outside funding affects the collection. Some school districts opt not to use outside funds; others encourage media specialists to seek grants or endowments. These may specify materials to be purchased or may limit the type of use or user for whom materials may be purchased. For example, some funding may be used only for materials for student use.

Across the country, media specialists face challenging questions: What percent of their limited funds should be spent on technology, and what should be spent on traditional formats? Should encyclopedias be bought only on CD-ROMs and no longer purchased in book format? Should online databases replace print indexes? Are CD-ROMs more effective than online databases for teaching students how to conduct searches?

At some point in your career as a media specialist, a school official may inform you that you must spend a large sum of money earmarked for materials for special uses within 7 to 10 days. This situation does not encourage thoughtful planning or selection but is typical of outside funding announcements. Try to stay alert to sources of outside funding to learn what they will fund and when the funding will occur. A file of materials that you are currently considering for purchase is essential in these situations.

Budget control and authorization of purchases are sensitive issues for the media specialist. A salesperson may visit the principal, who controls the budget, and promote a package deal that sounds like a bargain. If the principal buys the package without consulting the media specialist, the principal may learn after the purchase that (1) the collection already contains these materials, (2) the materials do not meet any needs of the collection, or (3) the materials require equipment not available in the school. Establish professional rapport with principals and purchasing agents to avoid such problems.

School Facilities

Limitations of the physical facilities or the physical plant can create constraints on the collection. Adjustable lighting will help accommodate the use of a wide range of formats. The lack of an adequate number of safe electrical outlets limits the use of media. If the media center serves a multistory building, equipment should be available on each level. As information delivery systems change, spatial accommodations and equipment needs change. Usage patterns such as after-school programs or programs for preschoolers may precipitate further changes. As media centers change from predominately print collections to ones with electronic collections, less shelving space is needed, but more workstations are required. Curricular changes with an emphasis on critical-thinking skills require different modes of delivery and a wide range of materials to meet individual learning styles. The flexibility of the facility influences the use of resources.

Many items in the collection (such as picture books, large study prints, art prints, and maps) require specialized storage units. When evaluating materials, consider how and where they will be stored and used. Will sound from equipment interfere with other activities? How many terminals will be needed?

CONCLUSIONS

At the most basic level, media specialists cannot make information accessible unless they are aware of its existence. The importance of knowing the collection increases as you learn about the users and their needs. Users may overlook poetry books, art works, and picture books that deal with mathematical concepts if you or the mathematics teachers consider only the items classified in the 500 section.

To ensure that information is accessible, media specialists must alter policies and procedures to meet changing needs. However, they must consider all the demands on the collection when initiating changes. The Fermi Middle School media center staff faced an awkward and demanding situation when the new science curriculum was implemented. Materials in the collection were inadequate to support both the new curriculum and the needs of individual users. As a result, the school had to limit the circulation of science materials to teachers; this was difficult to explain to the students but necessary to support school priorities. Even the maintenance policy was affected. For two years the priority for mending and repairing went to science-oriented materials. Titles dealing with science were removed from the collection only when the information in them became obsolete.

How did the situation affect requests from teachers for materials on other subjects? The whole language curriculum called for a wide range of materials and multiple copies of individual titles so that several students could read them at the same time. The program required many materials written for the third- through ninth-grade reading levels but failed to satisfy these needs.

Such situations illustrate the danger of overreacting to an immediate problem at the expense of the collection as a whole. Changes in one program activity affect other program activities. Media specialists must find diplomatic solutions to the demands on the collection.

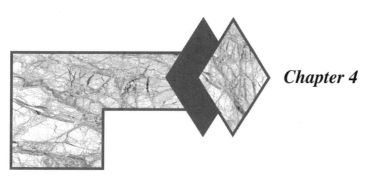

Issues and Responsibilities

Media specialists continually call on decision-making skills while building a collection. Each decision reflects personal perceptions of the characteristics of collections, views about the responsibilities of a selector, and philosophical positions on issues. For example, the materials selected reflect the media specialist's stance on intellectual freedom and students' rights. The media specialist's position on these and other issues consciously or unconsciously influences decisions about the collection. To explore these critical issues, this chapter examines the following questions:

♦ How does the concept of intellectual freedom apply to children and young people?[1]

♦ Should there be limits on students' rights to read, view, and listen? If so, who has the right to impose those limits?

These issues are complex and can arise within a variety of contexts: social, ethical, economic, political, religious, psychological, or in regard to pornography.

To explore his or her own perceptions about the characteristics of the collection and views of selection responsibility, the media specialist should consider the following questions:

♦ What is a balanced collection? Is balance a legitimate goal?

♦ Should all sides of issues be represented in the collection?

♦ Should popular materials have priority over materials with greater literary value?

♦ What barriers to access exist?

♦ What professional responsibilities do media specialists have?

The issues are not new. We constantly scrutinize the opinions of both society and our profession, and in this chapter we present various viewpoints. Media specialists need to reflect on the opinions expressed here and by the writers of the recommended readings listed at the end of the chapter. You, the media specialist, must know yourself. Where do you stand on these issues? At the end of this chapter are scenarios involving intellectual freedom, students' rights, access equality, and copyright. As you study them, bear in mind the very real possibility that you may one day face such situations.

CHILDREN'S RIGHTS

The information you make available and accessible to students reflects the value you place on intellectual freedom and students' rights.

First Amendment Rights

In the United States, the First Amendment serves as the basis of intellectual rights. A child's intellectual rights can be viewed as legal rights as well as ethical rights. The application of the First Amendment to children generally arises in matters dealing with public education, particularly in court cases concerning censorship.

Intellectual freedom is the basis of the First Amendment's three major sections: freedom of religion, freedom of expression, and freedom of association. These three rights have been the topic of controversy and court cases. Although the U.S. Supreme Court has taken a dim view of restrictions based on content, it does allow the government, when it has legitimate reasons, to restrict the time, place, or manner of expression. Schools may limit speech by prohibiting the use of vulgar or obscene language in school activities. In like fashion, the government may limit freedom of association (by which one expresses views alone or in association with others, perhaps by demonstrating against the government). For example, the government may require permits from groups that wish to demonstrate.

Consider the implications of the First Amendment's guarantee of freedom of expression. This section guarantees freedom of speech and of the press. It extends the scope of intellectual freedom to all ideas, not only those of a religious nature. David Moshman reminds us that "these clauses refer most directly to the expression of ideas. It is clear, however, that one cannot *express* ideas unless one *has* ideas, and that one cannot *have* ideas unless one *forms* them. Thus the right to form and hold beliefs is implicit in the right to express them" (Moshman 1986, 4).

Accepting this interpretation of the First Amendment influences the way you view a student's right to speak in an open assembly or to write an article for a high-school newspaper. Moshman's interpretation also provides a basis for teaching critical-thinking skills.

Application to Children

How does the First Amendment apply to children? Moshman describes its relevance in terms of five aspects of constitutional interpretation: text, intent, constitutional theory, precedent, and values. As in other areas of constitutional law, there is no clear-cut answer; the five aspects do not fully support each other.

First, according to Moshman (1986), the text of the First Amendment does not distinguish between children and adults and does not indicate that the amendment applies only to adults. Second, the authors of the amendment intended it to apply to people in general. (One could argue that the authors of the Constitution were referring only to white males. The Fourteenth Amendment includes women and nonwhites but does not mention children.) However, constitutional theory, the third test, finds nothing in the amendment to suggest that the word *people* refers only to those of voting age. Moshman's fourth test of the amendment, precedent, is inconclusive: "Application of the First Amendment to children is at best highly complex and multifaceted and at worst mutually contradictory" (1989, 27). Fifth, in terms of values, he argues that

> to limit intellectual freedom based on limited rationality is to restrict the development of rationality itself. Ethical considerations, then, suggest that children have a vital stake in the First Amendment and that society as a whole has a compelling interest in including them within its scope (Moshman 1989, 28).

Indeed, Moshman goes so far as to say that First Amendment rights are more important to children than to adults:

> When one denies an adult access to diverse ideas, one is restricting available input; when one denies such access to a child, however, one is also restricting development of the ability to coordinate differing views. When one denies an adult free expression, one is denying the opportunity to communicate; when one denies free expression to a child, however, one is also restricting development of the ability to form one's own ideas. In short, in denying First Amendment rights to a child, one is restricting not merely the present exercise of those rights but also the further development of precisely those intellectual competencies that make the First Amendment meaningful. Contrary to the suggestion that children have little at stake, it appears that as future adults they may have more to lose than present adults from governmental restriction of their intellectual freedom (Moshman 1986, 33).

Legal and Moral Implications

Moshman proposes that the First Amendment has both legal and moral implications. The first five principles listed in Figure 4.1 limit government action, reflecting the common view that the First Amendment places restrictions on all levels of government, including public schools, but not on individuals acting in nongovernmental capacities, such as parents or private schools. The sixth principle listed in Figure 4.1 limits the extent to which childhood status may be used to limit application of the first five principles. Moshman's moral principles exceed the language of the Constitution; they restate children's First Amendment rights in language that addresses the child rather than the government.

Intellectual Rights of Children

Legal Rights

Free Expression—Government may not control a child's right to form or express ideas.

Freedom of Nonexpression—Government may not require a child to adopt or express belief in a particular idea.

Inculcation—Government may inculcate ideas only when a legitimate purpose, such as to produce educated citizens, exists.

Freedom of Access—Government may not restrict children's access to ideas and sources of information.

Free Exercise of Religion—Government may not restrict children from acting according to their religious beliefs.

Distinction of Child from Adult—Limiting First Amendment rights must be based on compelling reasons by showing that harm would occur because the children in question are less competent than the typical adult.

Moral Rights

Free Expression II—A child has the right to form, express, and communicate ideas.

Freedom of Nonexpression II—A child has the right to choose not to adopt or express belief in particular ideas.

Inculcation II—Children have the right not to be indoctrinated and to be subject to inculcation only when there is a legitimate reason.

Freedom of Access II—Individuals responsible for children's development have an obligation to provide access to diverse sources of information and to diverse opinions and perspectives.

Free Exercise of Religion II—Children have a right to act according to their religious beliefs unless such actions would be harmful or illegal.

Distinction of Child from Adult II—Restrictions on children's intellectual rights should be based on the individual child's circumstances and intellectual limitations.

Right to Education—Children have the right to the type of environment that will facilitate their intellectual development to the extent of their intellectual limitations.

Figure 4.1. Rights guaranteed by the First Amendment. Based on David Moshman, "Children's Intellectual Rights: A First Amendment Analysis," in *Children's Intellectual Rights,* **ed. David Moshman, New Directions for Child Development series, no. 33 (San Francisco: Jossey-Bass, 1986), 27.**

Court Decisions

How do First Amendment rights apply to children? As one example, Moshman examines these rights in the context of censorship cases involving school libraries. He notes

> that schools must make choices; they cannot use every text or stock every book in the library. Selections should, however, be made in accord with educationally relevant, written criteria aimed at providing as wide a variety of views and ideas as students can handle. Removals should follow carefully designed procedures in which these criteria are carefully applied and claims of harm based on alleged lack of cognitive competence are seriously scrutinized (Moshman 1986, 35).

How have the courts interpreted children's rights? The classic court case for children's First Amendment rights is *Tinker v. Des Moines* (1969). This is the first time the Supreme Court declared a government action unconstitutional because it violated minors' rights to freedom of expression. The Supreme Court said:

> School officials do not possess absolute authority over their students. Students in school as well as out of school are "persons" under our Constitution. They are possessed of fundamental rights which the State must respect, just as they themselves must respect their obligations to the State (*Tinker v. Des Moines* 1969).

According to Moshman, *Tinker v. Des Moines*

> clarified that children have First Amendment rights not simply because government respect for their intellectual freedoms is in the best interests of their parents, their teachers, the educational system, or society as a whole, but more fundamentally, because they are persons under the Constitution (Moshman 1989, 13).

This action creates a balance to maximally protect both liberty and learning. School officials may maintain order but do not possess absolute authority over their students. However, confusion exists in the courts about what this means and how far it extends. Edward B. Jenkinson reminds us that, in the courts' responses to cases involving censorship of school materials,

> human beings preside in the courts, and human beings do not agree on all matters. Thus it is not surprising that the courts have not been uniform in their decisions involving the removal of books and other teaching materials from public school classrooms and libraries. The courts do tend to agree that they prefer not to become involved in debates over educational objectives and practices, leaving such matters to school boards, unless they believe that specific constitutional rights have been violated. But when they do become involved, their decisions are not always predictable (Jenkinson 1986, 31).

Tinker v. Des Moines and other cases ensure children the rights to know and to read. Jenkinson quotes attorney Julia R. Bradley:

> A student's right to read, and thus to have available in a school library a full range of materials which reflect differing literary studies, and differing social, political, and religious views, is a variant of a constitutional doctrine described as the "right to receive information" (Jenkinson 1986, 27).

Figure 4.2 highlights court decisions about intellectual freedom that affect children.

President's Council, District 25 v. Community School Board No. 25 (New York City), 457 F.2d (2nd Cir. 1972), 409 U.S. 998 (1972).
First case to consider whether a school board could remove books from the school library. Judge Mulligan declared the board, as statutorily empowered to operate the school, is the body responsible for selection and can remove books.

Minarcini v. Strongville City School District, 541 F.2d 577 (6th Cir. 1976). Circuit Court Judge Edwards stated:
A library is a storehouse of knowledge. When created for a public school it is an important privilege created by the state for the benefit of students in the school. That privilege is not subject to being withdrawn by succeeding school boards, whose members might desire to "winnow" the library for books the content of which occasioned their displeasure or disapproval.

Right to Read Defense Committee v. School Committee of the City of Chelsea, 454 F. Suppl. 703 (D. Mass. 1978).
Arguing that the complainant could not remove a book, in whole or in part, in accordance with standard library procedures.

Bicknell v. Vergennes Union High School Board, 475 F. Suppl. 615 (D. Vt. 1979), 638 F.2d 438 (2nd Cir. 1980).
After the librarian and students protested the board's removal of *The Wanderer* and *Dog Day Afternoon* from the library, a freeze on new acquisitions, and the board's policy to screen all major acquisitions, the courts ruled that the right of professional personnel under that policy "to freely select" materials for the collection are explicitly limited by the phrase "in accordance with Board policy."

Board of Education, Island Trees Union Free School District No. 26 v. Pico, 457 U.S. 853 (1982).
After a politically conservative organization informed it about objectionable titles, the school board appointed a review committee, which recommended retaining five books, restricting two, and removing two. (The committee made no recommendation for one title.) The board voted to remove all but one title. In a 5-4 vote, the Supreme Court upheld the student's challenge. The Court suggested decisions based on educational suitability would be upheld when a regular system of review with standardized guidelines were in place and condemned politically motivated removals.

Figure 4.2. Court decisions about intellectual freedom.

Keep these cases in mind as you read about the development of policies (Chapter 6) or as you review your school's policies.

Media Specialist: Protector or Advocate?

Librarians tend to take one of two positions in response to the question "What intellectual rights do children have?" One position, the protector, assumes that adults know what is best for children: what will harm them, what information they need, and how their needs should be met. Such protectors create barriers. The other position, the advocate, assumes an open stance, perceiving children as capable of defining both their information needs and their resource needs. The first position strives to protect students from themselves, from others, and from ideas. The second strives to help students identify, evaluate, retrieve, and use information.

SELECTION AND CENSORSHIP

What is the difference between selection and censorship? After all, selection is by nature exclusive. In choosing materials to include in the collection, the media specialist excludes the materials not chosen. And, as we have seen, media specialists' choices are colored by their personal values and commitments to such issues as intellectual freedom. Selection and censorship can be differentiated. Selection is a process of choosing among materials. The choices are relative as one item is compared with others. In choosing materials, the media specialist strives to give each item fair consideration and makes a concerted effort to suppress personal biases. In censorship, an individual or a group attempts to impose certain values on others by limiting the availability of one or more items. By examining definitions of selection and censorship, one can see how censorship creates barriers to intellectual freedom and how selection can promote intellectual freedom.

Henry Reichman describes the differences between selection and censorship:

> In general, selection is carried out by trained professionals, familiar with the wide variety of available choices and guided by a clear graph of the educational purposes to be fulfilled. . . . By contrast, the censor's judgment is that of the individual, and it is most frequently based on criteria that are inherently personal and often intolerant. . . . Where the censor seeks reasons to *exclude* materials, those engaged in the process of selection look for ways to *include* the widest possible variety of . . . library materials. . . . Censorship responds to diversity with suppression; the selection process seeks instead to familiarize students with the breadth of available images and information, while simultaneously erecting essential guideposts for the development of truly independent thought (Reichman 1993, 46).

Table 4.1 contrasts selection and censorship.

Table 4.1.
Characteristics of Censors and Selectors

CENSORS	SELECTORS
Censors look for items to exclude.	Selectors apply criteria as they compare materials and choose to include items.
Censors search for what they want to discard.	Selectors examine materials, looking for that which best presents their educational objectives.
Censors judge a book on the basis of a few passages they dislike.	Selectors judge the book as a whole.
Censors rely on the reviews of other censors to get rid of books.	Selectors rely on reviews published in professional journals.
Censors want the collection to include only books that represent their points of view.	Selectors look for books that represent a variety of points of view.
Censors look outside the book for reasons to reject it, for example, the author's religion or politics.	Selectors judge the book on its own merits.

Based on Edward B. Jenkinson, *The Schoolbook Protest Movement: 40 Questions & Answers* (Bloomington, IN: Phi Delta Kappa Educational Foundation, 1986), 21.

Elements of Censorship

Censorship can be described in terms of who is doing the questioning, which materials they are questioning and what is being questioned, and how the questions are handled. Policies and procedures to guide these situations are described in Chapter 7.

Complaints About Materials

The American Library Association's (ALA) Intellectual Freedom Committee (1996) offers the following definitions for various levels of inquiry and challenge to materials in the collection:

Expression of Concern—An inquiry that has judgmental overtones.

Oral Complaint—An oral challenge to the presence and/or appropriateness of specific material.

Written Complaint—A formal, written complaint filed with the institution (library, school, etc.), challenging the presence and/or appropriateness of specific material.

Public Attack—A publicly disseminated statement challenging the value of the materials presented to the media and/or others outside the institutional organization in order to gain public support for further action.

Censorship—A change in the access status of material, based on the content of the work and made by a governing authority or its representatives, including: exclusion, restriction, removal, or age/grade level changes. (American Library Association 1996, 47–48. Reprinted with permission of the American Library Association.)

Two studies conducted in the 1980s reveal patterns of challenges. Dianne McAfee Hopkins studied U.S. high schools that experienced challenges between 1986 and 1989. She found that of 4,736 schools, 64.1 percent (3,036 schools) reported no challenges and 35.9 percent (1,700 schools) reported one or more challenges (Hopkins 1991, Chapter 8, 1). From September 1982 to August 1984, David Jenkinson studied 6,644 public and private schools at all levels and 73 public libraries located in the Canadian province of Manitoba. He found that approximately 25 percent of all school libraries and 40 percent of all public libraries experienced at least one challenge during that time. One school faced seven challenges (Jenkinson 1986, 8).

Recent reports suggest an increase in the number of challenges. According to the ALA Office for Intellectual Freedom, 5,718 challenges were reported to them between 1990 and 1999. Research suggests that, for each challenge reported, four or five go unreported. Books most frequently challenged during the 1990s included *Scary Stories,* a series by Alvin Schwartz, *Daddy's Roommate* by Michael Willhoite, *I Know Why the Caged Bird Sings* by Maya Angelou, *The Chocolate War* by Robert Cormier, *The Adventures of Huckleberry Finn* by Mark Twain, *Of Mice and Men* by John Steinbeck, *Forever* by Judy Blume, *Bridge to Terabithia* by Katherine Paterson, *Heather Has Two Mommies* by Leslea Newman, and *Catcher in the Rye* by J. D. Salinger (American Library Association Office of Intellectual Freedom 2000c).

Common objections to materials include sexuality, profanity, obscenity, immorality, witchcraft, nudity, occultism, and violence. Less frequently cited reasons include incest, mental illness, and slavery. Censors state family values and the immaturity of students as reasons for their challenges.

The ALA Office for Intellectual Freedom defines intellectual freedom as follows:

> Intellectual freedom is the right of every individual to both seek and receive information from all points of view without restriction. It provides for free access to all expressions of ideas through which any and all sides of a question, cause or movement may be explored (2000b).

If either freedom of expression or freedom of access to ideas is stifled, then intellectual freedom does not exist. Ironically, commitment to intellectual freedom obligates media specialists to safeguard the rights of censors. On the one hand, media specialists recognize the right to unrestricted access to information; on the other hand, media specialists recognize the right to protest.

The reports by Hopkins and Jenkinson indicate the importance of working with teachers, principals, and the local media to encourage their support of intellectual freedom. Local authors can also aid in these efforts.

Who Are Censors?

The list of those who initiate challenges is long. Individuals include parents and other members of students' families, teachers, students, principals and other school administrators, school support staff, community members, library media supervisors, library support staff, and even librarians. Groups include school boards, local government officials, and organized groups who share political or religious beliefs. Reichman reminds us that:

> The word "Censor" often evokes the mental picture of an irrational, belligerent individual. In most instances, however, it is a sincerely concerned parent or citizen interested in the future of education who complains about curricular or library materials. Complainants may not have a broad knowledge of literature or of the principles of intellectual freedom, but their motives in questioning the use of educational materials are seldom unusual. Complainants may honestly believe that certain materials will corrupt children and adolescents, offend the sensitive or unwary reader, or undermine basic values and beliefs (1993, 14–15).

The ALA Office of Intellectual Freedom notes that it is unfair to stereotype the censor, but one generalization can provide insight: "Regardless of specific motives, all would be censors share one belief—that they can recognize 'evil' and that other people must be protected from it" (2000a).

Internet and Censorship

Before the 1990s, the majority of censorship challenges dealt with materials that were housed in the school library. However, with the advent of Internet access in school libraries, one of the main targets of censorship has been the use of the Internet.

The Internet is very different from other resources in the school library in that it is made up of a huge number of resources, many of which provide rich research materials for students. However, the Internet also provides access to numerous sites that a school media specialist would not consider useful or appropriate for students' use in the school library. Initially, the choice was an all-or-nothing proposition for school libraries: Either provide access to the Internet or don't provide it. Because of the possibility of accessing inappropriate sites (particularly those that were sexually graphic), many parents, organized groups, and legislators challenged access to the Internet in media centers (or anywhere in the school).

The Communications Decency Act (CDA), hotly debated in 1998, was an unsuccessful federal legislative attempt to legislate "safe" Internet use. Its original intent was to protect children from inappropriate sites, but its broad wording potentially deprived adults of nonsexual information in areas such as science, health, and art. The American Library Association opposed the CDA because it believed that the act would deny the legitimate free flow of information and would provide parents with a false sense of security because its provisions would have been almost impossible to enforce (Haycock, Chapin, and Bruce 1999).

Commercial companies quickly began to produce filters for the Internet, which, according to the companies, would eliminate objectionable materials. Philosophically this presented a problem for school librarians who saw the use of such filters in public institutions as conflicting with the precepts of intellectual freedom. An additional problem was that the filters did not always work as intended, for they frequently blocked potentially educational sites while permitting access to other "inappropriate" sites. The filter programs had significant limitations. Software programmers, however, are continually improving the filters and have made them much more sophisticated. The filters can now allow administrators to determine categories of materials to block and to allow various levels of access determined by user passwords.

Some school districts and states have legislated the use of filters on individual computers in schools. Other districts and some states have moved to proxy servers (on an external computer) that filter all files before they arrive at individual computers. Some Internet service providers (ISPs) also offer a filtering service for a small fee in addition to their regular Internet service fee (Haycock, Chapin, and Bruce 1999). Regardless of whether a filter on each computer or a proxy server controls Internet access or whether there is open access to the Internet, it is important that a school have a written Internet policy or an acceptable use policy (AUP) that includes parental consent of the use of the Internet. (See Chapter 6 for a discussion of Internet policies.) It is essential that school media specialists be well acquainted with any policies (state, district, or school) that relate to Internet access in their school libraries.

ACCESS TO INFORMATION

Access to information involves both intellectual and physical access. *Intellectual access* addresses students' rights to hear, read, and view information; to receive ideas; to express ideas; and to develop skills to receive, examine, analyze, synthesize, evaluate, and use information. *Physical access* refers to an environment that permits the unimpeded location and retrieval of information. This involves provision of adequate media center staff, access to the media center during and after regular school hours; provision of a broad range of resources to meet students' needs in terms of learning styles and linguistic and cultural diversity; use of interlibrary loan; and access to computerized information networks or databases. The media specialist's commitment to intellectual freedom influences the extent of intellectual access provided. The media specialist's commitment to intellectual access and sensitivity to individual needs influence the extent of physical access provided. Commitment to intellectual and physical access affects the media specialist's response to collection issues.

Professional Responsibilities

As professionals, media specialists' responsibilities for intellectual freedom and access extend to collection activities other than selection. As selectors, media specialists need to be aware of their own biases. As managers of the collection, they need to ensure adequate funds to support the collection. As respecters of the creative contributions of authors, illustrators, and producers, media specialists need to ensure the enforcement of copyright practices. In each of these areas, commitment to intellectual freedom and balance in the collection come into play.

Selection

Knowing one's self is a prerequisite for selection. Media specialists should be aware of their own biases and preferences so that personal prejudices do not inadvertently affect selection decisions. A media specialist with a strong belief in higher education may be tempted to purchase more college-oriented materials than those for vocational courses. A media specialist who advocates online searching as a major teaching tool may be overzealous in budgeting for online services. A media specialist whose hobby is cinema may buy numerous materials about movies and equipment for video production. College-preparatory materials, online databases, books on cinema, and video production equipment are all worthy resources; however, the media specialist's personal interests should not unduly influence selection decisions.

Are you an active conservationist? Will your position on such issues cloud your evaluation of materials presenting different views? If you are an advocate of the feminist movement, will your sensitivity to the treatment of women dominate your evaluation of materials? Will you be equally sensitive to the treatment of racial or ethnic groups?

When you next visit a media center, examine the collection. Can you detect any bias on the selector's part? Does this indicate the need to involve others in selection?

One purpose of the collection is to fulfill the needs of everyone in the school. If you sense that your personal views may be outweighing your professional judgment, seek other people's opinions.

Funding

A media specialist's professional responsibilities include obtaining funding that will support and strengthen a collection. This may mean presenting facts about the collection, noting its condition, anticipating replacement costs, informing those who make the budget decisions of the average costs of materials, deciding how much of the budget should go toward the purchase of online databases, or seeking outside funding through grants.

Copyright

As respecters of creative contributions, media specialists have a responsibility to ensure that copyright laws are honored. These professional responsibilities include educating teachers and students about fair-use guidelines and the copyright laws, placing copyright notices near copy machines and computers, identifying copyrighted materials, and monitoring the use of copyrighted materials. (Chapter 10 describes copyright regulations for various formats, and the "fair-use" guidelines can be found on the Websites listed under "Electronic Resources" at the end of this chapter.)

Intellectual Access and Balance

Intellectual access embraces many issues, most of which center on balance in the collection. Pressing questions regarding balance in the collection are these: Should materials in the collection represent all sides of issues? Should selection be based on demand (popularity), quality (literary merit), or both?

One-Versus-All Views

Some people define a balanced collection as one that contains materials that represent all sides of various issues. Advocates of this position express the belief that young people should learn to gather and evaluate information; they believe these skills are necessary to preserve democracy. Opponents argue that students need to be directed or guided to materials selected by adults to reflect the adults' beliefs and values.

Another debate centers on whether it is possible to objectively present any controversial subject. Would oversimplification and generalization result? Attempting to be objective may put constraints on the writer who is well informed about an issue and cares about the outcome. Authors who attempt to present both sides may become bogged down in phrases such as "some experts believe." Fortunately, many writers achieve objectivity while stimulating curiosity.

A more realistic goal of collection development is to maintain objectivity by including works that present differing views. Some students may not be aware of the wide range of viewpoints that exist about a particular subject. To help the student who stops at the first source of information, media specialists should encourage students to seek a wide range of information.

When examining materials about controversial subjects, consider not only content but also presentation. Excluding relevant facts is only one way to slant information. Word choice and connotations, use of visuals, vocal inflection, or filming techniques may be used to elicit emotional responses. For example, videos about alcohol, driving, and sex may include frightening scenes.

One benefit of a balanced collection containing many diverse viewpoints is that there will be materials on hand to counter criticism of controversial works. For example, one can anticipate questions about contemporary works on creation science, sexuality, birth control, and homosexuality. One response to critics is to refer them to works that present a different perspective on adolescents' problems. To address this situation, some media specialists select some works that reflect traditional, conservative, or various religious views.

Popular Versus Literary Merit

To achieve balance within a collection, media specialists must grapple with the conflict between popular appeal and literary value. At one end of this spectrum is a collection that includes only popular items lacking literary merit. At the other end is a collection that contains classic works of little or no interest or relevance to many young people. Proponents on both sides argue vehemently, generating lively debate in conversations and in print. Some say that appeal is more important than quality; others promote the role of libraries in preserving and providing quality materials.

The issue of demand selection versus literary selection cuts across the boundaries of content, format, reading level, and intellectual freedom. Should the media specialist purchase popular material that contains racial, ethnic, or sexual stereotypes? Should one buy mostly visual materials and software because "no one reads anymore"?

Some people argue that if children do not find items they want in the media center, they leave with a negative attitude about libraries that endures for life. Others argue that a media specialist's professional responsibility is to motivate young people by exposing them to materials that will aid the development of their literary and aesthetic tastes. Some people argue that responding to readers' requests encourages reading. Their position is that children will reach a saturation point with a series and will then turn to media specialists for recommendations. Others argue that limited budgets demand that media specialists encourage readers to explore worthy works that are less advertised.

An ongoing debate centers on the inclusion of series titles from "fiction factories," where hired writers complete a prepared character and plot outline ("formula writing"). The debate, active since the 1920s, when the series in question were Nancy Drew and The Hardy Boys, is a prime example of the demand-versus-quality issue. Similar debates center on the widely advertised Goose Bump series for younger readers and the paperback young adult romance series Sweet Valley High, which are only two of the numerous series on display in mall bookstores. As a media specialist you will need to decide whether to include series books in your collection and how to determine which series titles to include.

The issues concerning series apply to other materials as well. Comics, materials from the popular culture, and materials based on popular television programs are a few examples. Should comics be in the collection? On what basis? Are there differences in value among *Peanuts*, *Mad Magazine*, and *Wonder Woman*? Are these materials more or less valuable than graphic novels or nonfiction presented in comic book form?

Those who say comics have a place in the collection call for clear guidelines for selection. These criteria address the visual art, social values, potential use for language development, and quality of the story.

Barriers to Access

Common barriers to access include inequality of access; fiscal limitations; physical limitations of materials, equipment, and individuals; design of resources, such as interactive retrieval systems; attitudes and practices regarding reference and interlibrary loan services; and censorship.

Inequality of Access

We are increasingly aware of inequality in accessing computer-based information. These inequalities result from factors such as the following:

Girls are less computer literate than boys.

Software is designed to appeal to boys, not girls.

Wealthy school districts continue to own more computers than less wealthy ones.

The gap between rich and poor schools is widening.

Minority students may have less computer experience.

Schools without media specialists may have computers but lack trained personnel who are able to assist students in effective computer use.

Delia Neuman (1990) recommends actions to meet the challenge, including the following:

Look for software that appeals to girls.

Provide adaptive input and output devices (for example, guarded keyboards for students with physical impairment and large-print monitors for students with visual impairment) designed for students with disabilities.

Ensure equitable scheduling.

Explore ways to use new technologies to promote equity.

Fiscal Limitations

Budgetary constraints limit available resources, including personnel. Lack of a replacement policy encourages media specialists to hold onto out-of-date materials. Media specialists who automate circulation and cataloging systems or expand software and online services without outside funding have fewer funds for books and audiovisual materials.

Physical Limitations

Physical barriers to access limit the use of resources and restrict the number of people who can use them. The physical environment of the media center can create limitations: lack of seating and work space, shelving beyond people's reach, lack of electrical outlets for equipment, or an insufficient number of terminals. (Provisions for people with disabilities will be discussed in Chapter 12.) Barriers created by administrative decisions include rigid schedules, limited hours for use, restrictive circulation and interlibrary loan practices, and limited pass systems. Inappropriate or missing catalog subject headings can also inhibit access to resources.

Inadequate Design of Resources

Another aspect of access is the effectiveness of interactive information retrieval systems for children. Frances F. Jacobson calls for an evaluation of exactly how children use these systems; such research reveals whether software is properly designed. Jacobson describes the challenge:

> There are clearly many issues to be explored in evaluating information retrieval systems in youth services. Until recently, designers seem to have assumed that products initially developed for adults also would meet the needs of children and young adults. But unlike paper-based systems, electronic systems are fluid in nature. They can be adapted and modified; they also can be developed specifically for targeted

user groups. Researchers and practitioners have a unique opportunity to influence this process by communicating their concerns to product developers. Certainly, the potential for truly responsive systems is worth the effort (Jacobson, 1991, 112).

Publishers, producers, and vendors can benefit from media specialists' alerting them to areas that need materials or improvements. Regional associations can collect comments and suggestions or sponsor a workshop on this topic at a conference.

SCENARIOS

Think about how you would handle the following situations:

1. A board member removes books from a high-school media center because a citizen said the books were objectionable. Neither the citizen nor the board member has read the books in question.

2. The media center clerk draws diapers on the little naked boy in Maurice Sendak's *In the Night Kitchen.*

3. The principal checks out materials he does not like and fails to return them but offers to pay for them.

4. You realize one of your coworkers is not ordering titles that have been challenged elsewhere.

5. One of your teachers is using a computer in the media center to copy software programs that she then installs on her computer at home.

6. The music teacher is making copies of a piece of choral music that is going to be sung at an upcoming school choral concert.

7. Two teachers are coming into the media center after school hours and are downloading pictures from pornographic Websites.

8. A male student continually belittles a female student who has difficulty understanding how to use the Online Public Access Catalog (OPAC).

9. The site-based council informs you that they want the materials budget to be spent on online databases this year, with no new purchases of print materials.

10. The assistant principal, whose hobby is antiques, has requested 15 books on various types of antiques and antique collecting.

CONCLUSIONS

The definition of *child* is at best vague and still evolving. Society in general, and librarians in particular, are beginning to address the rights of children, but existing barriers must be removed to provide children with intellectual and physical access to information. One final thought from David Moshman: "Childhood status in itself should never be a basis for denial of personhood" (1989, 33) and one from Dr. Seuss: "As Horton the elephant says . . . after all, a person's a person, no matter how small" (1954, unpaged).

Your practices as a selector and the resources you make available to students will reflect your position on intellectual freedom and students' rights. As you ponder these issues and the concepts of balance and objectivity, ask yourself, what is your philosophy of collection development?

NOTE

1. For the purpose of this discussion, the terms "children," "young people," and "students" refer to people under the age of 18.

REFERENCES

American Library Association. Office of Intellectual Freedom. 1996. *Intellectual Freedom Manual,* 5th ed. Chicago: American Library Association.

———. 2000a. The Censor: Motives and Tactics. [http://www.ala.org/alaorg/oif/censormotives.html]. (Accessed November 6, 2000).

———. 2000b. Intellectual Freedom and Censorship Q & A. [http://www.ala.org/alaorg/oif/intellectualfreedomandcensorship.html]. (Accessed November 6, 2000).

———. 2000c. The 100 Most Frequently Challenged Books of 1990–1999. [http://www.ala.org/alaorg/oif/top100bannedbooks.html]. (Accessed November 6, 2000).

Haycock, Ken, Betty Chapin, and David Bruce. 1999. "Information Age Dilemma: Filtering the Internet for Young People." In *Bowker Annual Library and Book Trade Almanac,* 44th ed., 235–65. New Providence, NJ: R. R. Bowker.

Hopkins, Dianne McAfee. 1991. *Factors Influencing the Outcome of Challenges to Materials in Secondary School Libraries: Report of a National Study.* Madison: University of Wisconsin-Madison, School of Library and Information Studies.

Jacobson, Frances F. 1991. Information Retrieval Systems and Youth: A Review of Recent Literature. *Journal of Youth Services in Libraries* 5 (Fall): 109–13.

Jenkinson, David. 1986. Censorship Iceberg: Results of a Survey of Challenges in Public and School Libraries. *Canadian Library Journal* 43 (February): 7–21.

Jenkinson, Edward B. 1986. *The Schoolbook Protest Movement: 40 Questions and Answers.* Bloomington, IN: Phi Delta Kappa Educational Foundation.

Moshman, David. 1986. "Children's Intellectual Rights: A First Amendment Analysis." In *Children's Intellectual Rights,* ed. David Moshman, 27–38. *New Directions for Child Development Series,* no. 33. San Francisco: Jossey-Bass.

———. 1989. *Children, Education, and the First Amendment: A Psychological Analysis.* Lincoln: University of Nebraska Press.

Neuman, Delia. 1990. Beyond the Chip: A Model for Fostering Equity. *School Library Media Quarterly* 18 (Spring): 158–64.

Reichman, Henry. 1993. *Censorship and Selection: Issues and Answers for Schools.* Chicago: American Library Association; Arlington, VA: American Association of School Administrators.

Seuss, Dr. 1954. *Horton Hears a Who.* New York: Random House.

Tinker v. Des Moines Independent Community School District. 1969. 393 U.S. 503.

ADDITIONAL READINGS

Censorship/Intellectual Freedom

Barth, Jennifer. 2000. Censorship. *Teacher-Librarian* (May/June): 63–64.
> Annotates several documents and journal articles related to censorship and intellectual freedom in school libraries.

Censoring Bestsellers: Harry Potter Under Fire. 2000. *Newsletter on Intellectual Freedom* 49 (January): 1, 26.
> Discusses challenges made to ban Harry Potter books in eight states.

Cornette, Linda. 1998a. Intellectual Freedom Is a Concern for All Media Specialists. *Ohio Media Spectrum* 50 (Fall): 13–14.
> Discusses the importance of intellectual freedom and ways to ensure it.

———. 1998b. You Can't Judge a Book by Its Coverup. *Ohio Media Spectrum* 50 (Summer): 10–12.
> Offers practical steps for dealing with material challenges.

Haycock, Ken, Betty Chapin, and David Bruce. 1999. Information Age Dilemma: Filtering the Internet for Young People. In *Bowker Annual Library and Book Trade Almanac*, 44th ed., 235–65. New Providence, NJ: R. R. Bowker.
> Covers filtering software, acceptable use policies, and the challenges involved in providing Internet access in libraries.

Johnson, Doug. 1998. Internet Filters: Censorship by Any Other Name. *Emergency Librarian* 25 (May–June): 11–13.
> Discusses the Communications Decency Act and the use of filters.

Oder, Norman. 1999. Several States Face Filtering. *Library Journal* (March 15): 5, 12.
> Summarizes filtering bills that several states are considering.

Peck, Richard. 1999. A Young Adult Author Speaks Out: The Many Faces of Censorship. *Voice of Youth Advocates* 22 (October): 242–43.
> Discusses some of the problems of censorship of books for teenagers and challenges readers with his comment, "You can fear parents or you can teach their children, but you can't do both."

Peck, Robert S., and Charles Levendosky. 2000. *Libraries, the First Amendment, and Cyberspace: What You Need to Know.* Chicago: American Library Association.
> Includes questions and answers, citations from court cases, and a chapter titled "Children, Schools, and the First Amendment" by a First Amendment scholar who teaches constitutional law.

Schrader, Alvin M. 1999a. Internet Censorship: Issues for Teacher-Librarians. *Teacher-Librarian* (May/June): 8–12.
> Discusses Internet filtering and rating technologies.

———. 1999b. Issues for Teacher-Librarians. *Teacher-Librarian* 26 (May): 5, 8.
> Describes and critiques emerging issues concerning Internet access in schools and school libraries.

Small, Robert C. 2000. Censorship as We Enter 2000, or the Millennium, or Just Next Year: A Personal Look at Where We Are. *Journal of Youth Services in Libraries* 13 (Winter): 19–23.
> Presents the author's views on censors and censorship.

Symons, Ann K. 1999. Celebrating the Freedom to "Read! Learn! Connect! @ the Library." *Journal of Youth Services in Libraries* 12 (Winter): 25–28.
> Relates ALA's role and the role of leaders in defending intellectual freedom. Is a revision of a presentation at the Up the Leadership Ladder Conference.

Symons, Ann K., and Sally Gardner Reed. 1999. *Speaking Out! Voices in Celebration of Intellectual Freedom.* Chicago: American Library Association.
> Based on their favorite intellectual freedom quotations, each contributor provides a brief inspirational essay. Read these for their insight, breadth of perspective, and challenges to your personal and professional positions.

U.S. National Commission on Libraries and Information Science. 1998. *Kids and the Internet: The Promise and the Perils: An NCLIS Hearing in Arlington, Virginia, November 10, 1998.* Washington, D.C.: U.S. Government Printing Office.
> Summarizes the hearing and provides transcripts of the actual hearing and written material submitted to the commission.

Copyright

Gasaway, Laura N. 1998. Copyright, the Internet, and other Legal Issues. *Journal of the American Society for Information Science* 49 (September): 1003–09.

> Addresses copyright, online service provider liability, database protection, obscenity, and privacy. Cites cases.

Logan, Debra Kay. 2000. Imitation on the Web: Flattery, Fair Use, or Felony? *Knowledge Quest* 28 (May/June): 16–18.

> The author shares her experience of finding the bulk of her Website copied by another library professional. Provides directions on what to do when dealing with plagiarism.

Peek, Robin P. 1999. Taming the Internet in Three Acts. *Information Today* 16 (January): 28–29.

> Presents the highlights of three acts that could affect the future of Web publishing: the Digital Millennium Copyright Act, the Internet Tax Freedom Act, and the Child Online Protection Act.

Simpson, Carol. 1999. Managing Copyright in Schools. *Knowledge Quest* 28 (September/October): 18–22.

> Includes information on managing copyright issues dealing with video, audio, computer software and hardware, networks, and the Internet, as well as how copyright relates to students and teachers.

Inequality of Access

Mestre, Lori S. 2000. Improving Computer-Use Success for Students of Diverse Backgrounds. *Knowledge Quest* 28 (May/June): 20–28.

> Discusses needs for special computer instruction for minority students and methods of meeting those needs.

Students' Rights

Arnest, Lauren Krohn. 1998. *Children, Young Adults, and the Law: A Dictionary*. Santa Barbara, CA: ABC-CLIO.

> Is a subject dictionary highlighting issues involving children and their legal status.

Daniel, Philip T. K., and Patrick D. Pauken. 1998. Educators' Authority and Students' First Amendment Rights on the Way to Using the Information Highway: Cyberspace and Schools. *Washington University Journal of Urban and Contemporary Law* 54 (Summer): 109–55.

> Discusses the Communications Decency Act. Cites relevant cases. Discusses acceptable use policies and the right of students to freedom of expression.

Kids Have Rights/Parents Have Responsibilities/Librarians Have Ulcers! 2000. *Newsletter on Intellectual Freedom* 49: 5–7, 29–37.
> Discusses children's rights.

Penn, Matthew. 1999. Your Students' Cyber Rights. *Florida Media Quarterly* 24 (Spring): 12–13.
> Summarizes how the material in Mike Godwin's book, *Cyber Rights* (Random House, 1998), applies to students' rights.

ELECTRONIC SOURCES

Censorship/Intellectual Freedom

American Library Association. 2000a. Filters and Filtering. [http://www.ala.org/alaorg/oif/filtersandfiltering.html]. (Accessed November 6, 2000).
> Contains links to Internet filters and filtering, statements and policies opposing filtering, court decisions against filtering, and numerous other related topics.

———. 2000b. Internet Filtering in Public Libraries, A Memorandum from Jenner and Block. [http://www.ftrf.org/internetfilteringmemo.html]. (Accessed November 6, 2000).
> Includes a long memorandum dealing with an overview of filtering software, liability for installing filtering software, legal principles, First Amendment rights of minors, and potential liability for failure to filter. Cites numerous legal cases and provides scenarios.

———. 2000c. Office for Intellectual Freedom. [http://www.ala.org/alaorg/oif]. (Accessed November 6, 2000).
> Offers numerous links dealing with intellectual freedom, including policies, statements, the freedom to read, the First Amendment, awards, programs, publications, and banned books.

Arizona Department of Library Archives and Public Records. 2000. Intellectual Freedom. [http://www.lib.az.us/cdt/intell.htm]. (Accessed November 6, 2000).
> Provides an overview of intellectual freedom, including dealing with censors, intellectual freedom considerations for selection, handling challenges, Internet use policies, and links.

DiBianco, Phyllis. n.d. Internet Issues. [http://home.computer.net/~dibianco/issues.html]. (Accessed November 6, 2000).
> Provides links dealing with Internet issues on topics such as censorship and the Internet, cyber rights, copyright and fair use, and filtering.

Hopkins, Dianne McAfee. 1998. Toward a Conceptual Path of Support for School Library Media Specialists with Library Challenges. *SLMQ Online*. [http://www.ala.org/aasl/SLMQ/support.html]. (Accessed November 6, 2000).

Reviews research studies that deal with garnering support when dealing with a book challenge in a library.

Intellectual Freedom WWW Resources. 1999. [http://www.lib.utexas.edu/Libs/UGL /Banned/free.html]. (Accessed November 6, 2000).

Links to sites dealing with intellectual freedom including quotes, ACLU position papers, and feminists for free expression.

The Internet School Library Media Center (ISLMC) Intellectual Freedom Page. 2000. [http://falcon.jmu.edu/~ramseyil/free.htm]. (Accessed November 6, 2000).

Includes links to the freedom to read, intellectual freedom, banned books, library policies, the Supreme Court, libraries, filtering software, and court cases. Administered by Inez L. Ramsey at James Madison University.

Kids Hit the I-Way. 1999. [http://spot.Colorado.edu/~jobem/educate.htm]. (Accessed November 6, 2000).

Provides links for topics such as "Develop the Skills" and "Consider the Issues and Develop Policies."

Michigan Electronic Library. 2000. Filtering and the Internet. [http://mel.lib.mi.us/social /SOC-filter.html]. (Accessed November 6, 2000).

Provides links to child safety on the Internet and specific filtering programs.

Shimek, Gary. 1998. A Guide to Internet Resources on Intellectual Freedom. [http://www.msoe .edu/~shimek/if_resources_titlepage.html]. (Accessed November 6, 2000).

Includes quotes dealing with intellectual freedom. Gives links to items such as intellectual freedom and the Internet, constitutional law and the First Amendment, children and the Internet, and filters. Prepared for the Intellectual Freedom Round Table of the Wisconsin Library Association.

Copyright

American Library Association. 2000. Copyright and Intellectual Property. [http://www .ala.org/work/copyright.html]. (Accessed November 6, 2000).

Provides information on copyright, intellectual property, and fair use. Includes links.

Becker, Gary. 2000. Copyright in a Digital Age. *Electronic School.* [http://www.electronic -school.com/2000/06/0600f2.html]. (Accessed November 6, 2000).

Provides information on how to comply with copyright laws and set good examples for students.

Harper, Georgia. 1999. Copyright Issues: Multimedia and Internet Resources. [http://www .utsystem.edu/OGC/IntellectualProperty/mmfruse.htm]. (Accessed November 6, 2000).

Addresses topics dealing with copyright including fair-use guidelines, management of copyright, and multimedia.

Lutzker, Arnold P. 1999. Primer on the Digital Millennium: What the DMC Act and Copyright Term Extension Act Means for the Library. [http://www.arl.org/info/frn/copy/primer.html]. (Accessed November 6, 2000).

    Discusses the DMC Act and its effect on libraries.

Media Technology Services Policies and Procedures: Copyright Implementations Manual. 1998. [http://groton.k12.ct.us/mts/egtoc.htm]. (Accessed November 6, 2000).

    Provides the copyright manual of the Groton schools in Mystic, CT.

Missouri Department of Elementary and Secondary Education. 2000. Copyright and Schools. [http://www.dese.state.mo.us/divinstr/curriculum/copyright/index.htm]. (Accessed November 6, 2000).

    Offers brochures on copyright and schools for superintendents, principals, educators, and students.

O'Mahoney, Benedict. 2000. Copyright Web Site. [http://www.benedict.com]. (Accessed November 6, 2000).

    Covers copyright basics, news, and guidelines. Provides audio and visual examples. Award-winning site.

Stanford University Libraries. n.d. Copyright and Fair Use. [http://fairuse.stanford.edu/library]. (Accessed November 6, 2000).

    Links to sites dealing with copyright, including guidelines and policies.

U.S. Copyright Office. 2000. U.S. Copyright Office. [http://lcweb.loc.gov/copyright/]. (Accessed November 6, 2000).

    Includes copyright basics and copyright publications.

Students' Rights

American Civil Liberties Union. 1997. Students' Rights. [http://www.aclu.org/issues/student/hmes.html] (Accessed November 6, 2000).

    Provides links to sites such as the National Child Rights Alliance, the Children's Defense Fund, and Children Now.

———. 2000. Students. [http://www.aclu.org/students/students.html]. (Accessed November 6, 2000).

    Covers topics for students and teachers such as banned book week, speech on campus, and affirmative action.

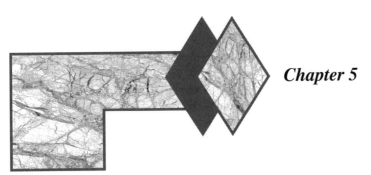

Chapter 5

The Collection's External Environment

The collection is not an isolated entity. It is one component of the media program within a school that is in a district and a state. The school also functions within the local community it serves. Relationships among these components of the environment influence the collection program. For instance, financial support for educational programs may influence and reflect society's attitudes about the quality of education. How a community values information can also be a factor.

To understand the importance of the external environment to the collection program, one must recognize the give-and-take nature of the relationship. A policy is needed to specify who will have access to the collection. The collection will attract a certain number of outside users including other institutions involved in resource sharing. On the other hand, the outside environment has much to offer the school collection. Online databases and electronic networks provide access to myriad external information sources in the community and beyond.

Educational administrators and community officials are often responsible for establishing the directions, limitations, and strategies under which the media specialist will be working. Their goals and attitudes about education and information will support or challenge the media specialist's views and commitment to intellectual freedom. Their actions will influence the financial support and selection policies of the collection program.

If you do not know the decision-makers and their goals or attitudes, you will find it difficult to communicate with them or to offer them useful services. Your daily contacts within the school and the local community present opportunities to discover needs, receive requests, recognize attitudes, and offer services. How well do you know the policy makers at the district and state levels? These people establish policies that affect your environmental structures, budget, programs, and operational activities. Use your initial visit to the district and school to learn about these structures.

LEARNING ABOUT THE COMMUNITY

Beyond the school grounds lie businesses, offices, factories, and residences full of people—the local community—who are interested in the activities of the school program. The term *local community* has two meanings. The first refers to the area that surrounds the physical site occupied by the school, including adjacent institutions, agencies, businesses, and residences. A second interpretation relates to the area where the students live. The latter may be identical to the first setting, or students may be transported to the school from a broader area.

How do you learn about the community? Generally, the seven best sources are the school district, the chamber of commerce, news media, government agencies, service and civic clubs, local census data, and the public library. These sources can provide maps, surveys, brochures, community profiles, lists of local activities, and projections for future population shifts. They can lead you to other information sources, such as planning commissions or historical societies. All of these groups may have Websites that provide information. If the public library surveyed the community's information needs, their findings will be of interest. Is the local public or university library a United States government documents repository? Such libraries will have the United States census data for your community. The summary of characteristics should include the items identified in Figure 5.1.

Demographics

How does this profile help the media specialist with the collection? The demographics can provide useful guidance. You may find a community of young families, who are more likely to support educational programs than a community of fixed-income people. The educational level of the population may be another clue to the willingness of citizens to financially support schools. Active participants in community groups may be more receptive to the importance of the media program.

Remember that neighborhoods in large districts differ drastically. You may find pockets of support—or opposition—in the various neighborhoods.

Census data about racial, ethnic, and language backgrounds indicate types of materials the collection needs. Staff members who serve as translators can be a source of information about students' needs. Other sources include groups organized to serve diverse populations, such as a Hispanic council whose members may be responsible for helping locate tutors to mentor young Hispanics. If children come from Cuban families, you will want to have

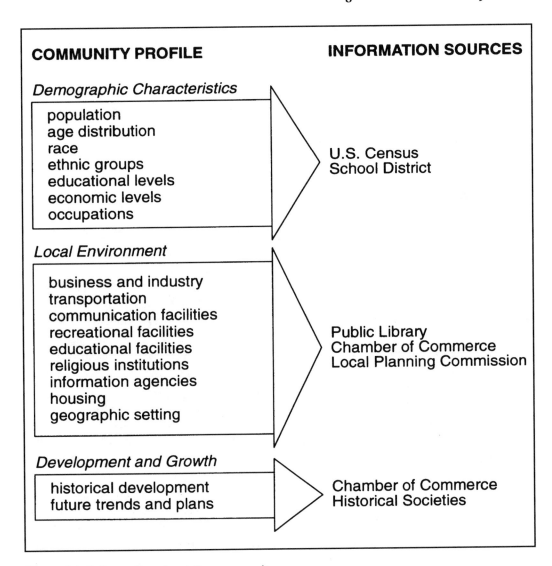

Figure 5.1. Information about the community.

Spanish-language materials. You may also want to incorporate Cuban folklore that parallels literature familiar to American children. In communities with large populations of refugees and immigrants, you will also need materials that help the indigenous young people and teachers understand the new members of their community.

Stability of the population also affects the collection. A community without an influx of young families may face a decline in student population, leading to the closing or consolidating of schools. If you are in a school with low-income workforces, there is likely to be a certain amount of transience. When working with children from such families, you may need to emphasize materials in less-permanent formats. Children of inner-city factory workers or migrant farmworkers may spend only a few weeks in your school. A migrant family's decision to move may happen suddenly. In this situation, it may be better to select mostly paperback books and not fret about the loss of materials.

Schools with a high percentage of students in advanced-placement classes will have demands different from those of schools where students are entering the job force rather than going on to higher education. Advanced-placements students are likely to need materials available through interlibrary loan or on the Internet.

Students' Personal Lives

Even the students' home conditions affect their use of materials. Are there students in your school who support themselves and pay the rent on an apartment? Are there students who hold full-time jobs to maintain cars or trucks, which are their primary concern? The latter group may seek auto-repair or career-guidance materials. How many students are parents raising their own children? How many look after younger siblings? Responsibilities such as these may leave limited time for schooling, even for highly motivated students.

We also need to recognize that some students move among several cultures on any given day. They get up, go to school, go to work, and go home, constantly reacting as each of these cultural environments places different demands upon them. Some students, unable to cope with the regular school setting, may temporarily attend an alternative school. When they are ready to return to regular school, the adults who worked with them can help the school staff understand these students' needs and interests. Other students may be heavily involved in sports, music or other performing arts or have other interests that call for discipline and heavy time commitments. These demands affect the time they have to use the media center.

The effect of students' home environments can be shown through the lives of two elementary school children. Kayla, a third grader, is responsible for seeing that her five-year-old brother and three-year-old sister are fed, clothed, and supervised. A good reader, Kayla likes to read aloud to her younger charges and to the children of another family who share their apartment. Kayla is allowed to take out two books overnight. The media specialist thinks it is unfair to ask Kayla to keep track of books for a longer period. Kayla happily renews her books or takes out new ones each morning. At the same time she receives encouragement and personal attention from the media staff.

In contrast, Stephanie's home has a live-in housekeeper. Stephanie flatly demands materials, then leaves them wherever she pleases as she moves onto other activities. Until Stephanie's mother volunteered to work in the media center, she did not realize how conditioned her children were to having someone wait on them and pick up after them. She also realized that many children lacked the resources available to her own children; Stephanie and her siblings each have their own computer.

In some homes, parent's religious convictions state that children should not watch films or videos. For other reasons some parents do not approve of children using the Internet or spending time reading fiction or poetry. These are only a few of the contrasts one finds in the school's environment.

Community Opportunities and Constraints

The community's layout affects students' mobility and thereby influences demands on the collection. To map students' mobility characteristics, look at your community's transportation patterns. How easily can children get to the public library or other information agencies? You may want to make a simple map of the community, noting where students can find information and how they might get to those places. Limiting factors may include the absence of mass transit, pedestrian walks, or bicycle trails. The children who attend Gaver Elementary School have to cross two major highways to reach the public library. For the students who depend on bicycle transportation, their school's media center was their only sources of materials for instructional or recreational use. The school media center cooperated with the public library in bringing the summer reading program to these students, helping young readers maintain their reading levels over the summer.

The location of the community, its climate, and its recreational patterns also make demands on the collection. You will soon learn whether students are active in 4-H clubs, Scout troops, or other activities. Schools in areas where skiing, snowmobiling, or water surfing are regular activities need appropriate materials in the collection.

Many communities support recreational and educational programs. Young people may regularly participate in functions at museums, zoological gardens, art institutes, and concert halls. These interests result in demands on the collection. If the community planetarium is open to the students, the collection will need stronger astronomy resources than one in a community without such a facility.

COMMUNITY RESOURCES

The school media center's relationship with the community is reciprocal. Just as the media center has much to offer the community, so the community has much to offer the media center in terms of both information and human resources.

Organizations

Each community has a wide range of cooperative organizations and people who provide educational experiences. Typical examples are accountants, airports, cemeteries, city halls, junkyards, mental health workers, nurses, taxicab drivers, tree surgeons, and zoos. A guide to the community resources is a helpful reminder of the vast range of resources within the community. Electronic bulletin boards may list local community activities or announce the meetings of hobby groups.

Students and teachers can gain access to community resources through use of the school's online catalog, which lists holdings of collections throughout the community. The Online Public Access Catalog (OPAC) may include entries for community resources, such as options for field trips. A sample entry for a health food store might be organized as in Figure 5.2.

TITLE:	Green Acres Natural Food Store [organization resource]
SOURCE:	Our town (112 Liveoak Ave., 99999), Phone 555-5555, 9:00 a.m.-4:00 p.m.
SUBJECTS:	Food, Natural. Seafood. Stores, Retail.
CONTRIBUTORS:	Eatright, Mr. Eatright, Ms.
AUDIENCE:	4th-7th grades.
SUMMARY:	Mr. Eatright will visit classes to discuss natural foods. Students can visit the store in groups of 12 for an hour tour that includes sampling foods. The store can supply cookies made from kelp for science units on foods from the sea. Available every day except Saturday and Sunday.

Figure 5.2. Bibliographic record for organization resources. Record provided by John E. Leide, McGill University, Graduate School of Library and Information Studies.

The visit described in Figure 5.2 included a science-related activity about food from the sea. As a reminder of the visit, each participant received a cookie made from kelp. Such entries could also include preferred times and/or dates for field trips; resource people available at the site; time needed to travel to the location; types of experiences; charges; presence of eating facilities and restrooms; rules concerning the use of cameras, tape recorders, and video cameras; and available preparation materials for use before the visit, such as a videotape. Before planning field trips you will want to consult your district's policy about the use of community resources and any restrictions such as a limit on the amount of school time allotted for field trips.

Community Members

Other valuable resources are people within the community. Human resources can also be listed on the OPAC. You may be looking for people with travel experiences, hobbies, collections, talents, or occupations. Other people can serve as role model examples, such as a stay-at-home father or a woman boxer. You can identify people through speakers' bureaus, extension agencies, and directories of local artists, authors, and illustrators.

Like organizations or materials, human resources can be listed in the OPAC. A sample entry might include items similar to those in Figure 5.3. The entry could include the cost, time needed to arrange a program, whether it would be better to interview the resource person in the classroom or at the workplace, and the appropriate audience. The mortician described in Figure 5.3 told tenth graders about the personal characteristics a mortician needs and told eleventh graders about the educational requirements of the profession and the challenges of operating a business.

TITLE:	Mortuary science as a career [human resource]: oral presentation / Jacob Smith.
SOURCE:	Contact the Pleasantville Funeral Home, Phone: 555-5555, 10:00 a.m. — 5:00 p.m.
SUBJECTS:	Undertakers and undertaking — Vocational guidance Addresses and essays. Professions.
CONTRIBUTORS:	Pleasantville Funeral Home.
AUDIENCE:	10th-12th grades.
SUMMARY:	Mr. Smith describes academic requirements, educational costs, admissions procedures, and the advantages and disadvantages of work as a mortician.

Figure 5.3. Bibliographic record for human resources. Record provided by John E. Leide, McGill University, Graduate School of Library and Information Studies.

Libraries and Information Centers

Your most valuable ally may be the public library's children and young-adult specialists. Questions you will want to explore are the following: What services do libraries and other information agencies offer to students? Is there a branch library near your school, or do students use a bookmobile? Do students have access to the Internet at the public library? Can they access the library's online catalogs from their home or from the school? Do school and public libraries offer cooperative programs or services? Can you borrow public library materials for classroom use? If so, for how long? Has the school established a procedure for alerting the public library of forthcoming assignments? Do the two library systems participate in resource sharing plans? Have the two libraries jointly applied for grant funds?

Visit local community college, college, and university libraries. Their collections probably include reference materials, bibliographies, and selection tools too expensive for the school's collection. What resources in special libraries (industry, hospital, government, etc.) are available to students? Their resources can be of particular interest to seniors doing honors papers. One can use networked information services to identify these resources.

Educational Experiences

In addition to the traditional uses of organization and human resources (field trips and guest speakers), information can be found in other ways. Students can gather oral history by interviewing senior members of the community and recording their reminiscences. For example, at Kennedy High School, Willie's American history class visited the Salvation Army's "Golden Agers" group to interview the members about the Great Depression and Prohibition. The students heard about the experiences of "rum runners" who had traveled back and forth between Canada and the United States. The students were enthusiastic about their experiences.

Younger students can also collect oral histories, beginning with questions that interest them, such as "What did you do for fun if you didn't have computer games?" Students in Jessica's fourth-grade class at Maple City Elementary School interviewed their parents and grandparents as part of a state library project to gather history about small communities. Using data sheets prepared by the historical archives section of the state library, the children asked their parents how long they had lived in the community, why they had moved there, and how far this was from their previous home. When possible, children interviewed their grandparents, asking them the same set of questions. Each child kept one copy of the report; the other became part of the archive collection. A similar type of project could be initiated through a local historical society.

These examples represent only a few of the educational experiences available in any given community. As you get to know local community people, ask for their suggestions. People at the school district and state level will undoubtedly have many ideas, but don't overlook the suggestions of your neighbors, students, parents, and everyone else you meet. The school staff should not be overlooked; for example, the school's cafeteria workers may have valuable experiences to share.

THE SCHOOL DISTRICT

A community's attitudes about and expectations of education are inevitably translated into the school district's policies. Awareness of the district's priorities can alert the media specialist to demands that users may place on the collection. If the school board emphasizes basic education, be prepared to relate the collection to that approach; if the district emphasizes computer literacy, be prepared to meet that priority. If a curriculum area is to be reviewed, become involved. Administrators, board members, teachers, or media personnel can make these fundamental decisions, but it is best if a committee representing a combination of representatives makes them.

School Board and Administrators

Attending or listening to school board meetings allows the media specialist to see how the members interact and how they approach the issues. Find out the positions the board members have taken on matters concerning media programs. Keep in mind that many school board policies directly or indirectly affect the media program. If the school board meets on a rotating basis in various schools, offer the media center as a place to meet. Serve them refreshments, whether they meet in the center or not. This can be a drawing card for the board members to visit the media center.

Some states and districts require that advisory committees composed of students, faculty, and community members advise the media specialist on policies, operations, priorities for purchase of materials, and selection. Advisory committees can also do the following:

> strengthen the media program and in turn strengthen the school's overall instructional program;

> promote positive relationships among media personnel, teachers, students, and administrators;

> provide a line of communication between the school and community; and

> assist in maintaining a balanced collection of resources and equipment (North Carolina Department of Public Instruction 1992, A-1).

Advisory committees can also be educated defenders of intellectual freedom. As a media specialist, you will benefit from the contributions of each group, gaining strong support for the media program and identifying people who can help with public-relations efforts.

The district's administrative hierarchy affects communication and decision making. Learn what types of decisions are made at the district and regional levels, along with those made at the individual school level. Is school-based management the pattern? Where do media personnel fit into the organization chart? Where do special projects staff, perhaps those funded by state or federal programs, fit into the organization chart? Are specific personnel assigned to help with the development of grant requests and obtaining of outside funding? Determine how you can participate in the decision-making process.

In a large district with a central media supervisor, the school-level media specialist may have little direct contact with other district personnel; however, in many districts this is not true. Be assertive about establishing good lines of communication. When the central administrative staff visit your building to look into other matters, be sure to meet them. Establishing contact with administrators may be useful; one day you may need to ask the curriculum coordinator for resources that will help teachers.

Teachers' Organizations and Unions

The districtwide teacher organization or union can also serve the media program. Are media specialists represented on the negotiating team? Do they consider media program concerns? Does the contract make provisions for the media staff, collections, or production facilities? Does the contract address intellectual freedom or spell out who should be involved in the selection of materials? Does the contract call for teachers to be involved in the development of policies, such as the one governing selection or use of the Internet? Media specialists should not overlook the mutual concerns they share with teachers about environmental conditions and access to information. Teachers' groups "watchdog" legislation and convey relevant information, including information of importance to the media program, to local districts.

One way you can become involved is to alert the union president to your willingness to serve on committees involving curriculum matters. These volunteer efforts have many benefits. They help you to learn more about curriculum matters and make useful contacts. For example, when a censorship case came up in one school district, a media specialist who was chairperson of the Instructional Development Council was able to use her committee contacts with parents, board members, students, teachers, and the curriculum director to resolve the matter.

District Services

A district's public information office can help you track down information or publicize your program to the community. Their staff will have contacts with people in the local mass media and can guide you to those who can help. Staff can also help to involve the public in the development of policies.

Ask about the district media program. Its history will reveal important clues to the level and consistency of support for media personnel. Decisions at this level also determine the focus of both your services and the collection. In schools with site-based management, the planning and direction, including the hiring, evaluation, and budgetary matters, will be handled at the building level. In other situations, the district media program personnel may handle these activities. Regardless of the situation, it is important to learn about the services that the district-level program offers.

Typical functions of district-level programs include planning, administration, staff development, and services. Planning and administration activities may include designing or remodeling facilities, developing policies, interpreting the media program to the community through public information systems, coordinating federal projects, seeking grants, and all financial matters relating to the media programs. Staff development activities include orientation of new media specialists, consultative services, and in-service opportunities. Services include central ordering and processing, examination centers, producing materials, assisting in developing basic collections, delivery services, and maintenance of media and equipment.

Before you are hired, the media supervisor or district media coordinator may interview you. When talking with them and other district staff members, you will need to raise a number of questions. How is the district media program administered? Is the district coordinator or supervisor part of the central administrative staff? What services does the district media center offer? With what cooperative programs is the district involved? Do coordinated collection development programs exist within or outside the district? Is there a districtwide manual or policy handbook? Are consultant services provided? What roles do the district media personnel play in deciding budgets? Are in-service programs provided for media personnel? What types of support are there for integrating emerging technologies into the building programs? By learning answers to these and other questions, you can identify the magnitude of your responsibilities and identify the services you can expect from the district.

Another group of questions relates to how materials are selected and made accessible to students and teachers. In some states the media program's advisory committee plays a strong role in the selection process. Your state may mandate the creation of such a body. Are selection committees appointed on a district-level basis, rather than at the building level? How does one become a member of the district selection committee? If an "approved list" is used for purchasing, how can you buy items not on the list? Are there delivery services between buildings and the district center? Is the school district involved in networking at the local, regional, or multi-state levels and in a multi-type library situation? What interlibrary loan procedures have been established? The answers to these questions reveal the control you have over selection decisions and the ease with which you can borrow materials from other collections. In examining these relationships, you can learn how much you and the collection can or must depend upon the district organization.

THE REGION AND STATE

At the regional- or intermediate-level media program, one will find functions similar to those described for the district level. Sometimes these services are combined with those for the public libraries in the same region. Consultant services, cooperative programs between schools within one or more districts (or between schools and public libraries), staff development programs, examination collections, production, telecommunication delivery systems, and publications are a few examples of their services.

Another crucial relationship is that between the school and state. School goals and objectives reflect broad guidelines that the state develops. Frequently, legislators encourage or direct goals or standards.

In Texas a committee of school librarians appointed by the Texas Library Association drafted standards for school libraries, which were adopted by the Texas legislature and became effective in July 1997. These standards included a profile of a model school library:

◆ Offers a balance of print, multimedia, and electronic resources based on district adopted, board approved selection policies

◆ Develops and maintains a balanced collection based on curriculum and user needs, proportionate to student populations and special programs

◆ Provides access to state of the art technology

♦ Offers access to resources via world wide networks

♦ Reflects a diverse community ("Texas School Libraries" 1997)

Some state laws address the school library collection. California's educational codes are one example:

> Education Code, Section 18110. County boards of education may adopt lists of books and other library materials for districts not employing a superintendent of schools or a librarian for full time. The lists may be distributed to all school districts in a county for use in the selection of books and other library materials.

> Education Code, Section 18111. The governing board may exclude from schools and school libraries all books, publications, or papers of a sectarian, partisan, or denominational character (California School Library Laws 2000).

Kentucky's *Online II,* the school library media guidelines prepared by the Kentucky Department of Education, discusses resources in its Appendix D:

> The library media center collection is composed of print and nonprint resources that meet the curricular and leisure needs of the students and school community. The collection is weeded annually to eliminate outdates, worn, unattractive and inappropriate material, both print and nonprint. A professional collection for faculty and staff use is provided either in house or in a district resource center (Kentucky Department of Education 1995).

Missouri's *School Library Media Standards Handbook* is particularly thorough, containing all areas of school library media operation, including a long section dealing with resources—both print and non-print, as well as equipment. It also mentions a core collection: "Although no one library media center or school district can meet all the needs of its users, a basic core collection of timely and relevant information resources are [*sic*] essential in every building's library media collection" (Missouri Department of Elementary and Secondary Education 2000).

A few state documents stress the quantity of resources, but today more of the documents coming from state departments of education or state professional organizations emphasize quality. The Massachusetts School Library Association points out the importance of the school library media specialist in relation to the collection:

> The key to providing a quality service is not determined by the quantity of hardware or the number of books that should be in each building. Rather, the key is a skilled and sensitive library media specialist who selects all resources, in whatever format, that support the curriculum

and meet the needs of the individuals who will use them (Massachu-setts School Library Media Association 1996).

Hawaii's Department of Education provides a materials selection policy for all school libraries in Hawaii. They refer to their libraries as "school library instructional technology centers" and stress the use of electronic resources in addition to the print materials, stating that the center should:

> Provide a variety of electronic formats as well as print materials to support student learning needs. These electronic formats include resources found on the Internet and other online networks (Hawaii Department of Education 1994).

Some departments of education are developing technology plans for schools. The plans include the technology that school media centers house. In some cases funds are specified per student; in other situations schools apply through a grant proposal. The funds may be designated for hiring engineers as consultants on wiring, for acquiring equipment and facilities, or for in-service activities. In states with school-based management, media specialists need to be involved in the technology decision making.

Wisconsin developed such a plan with a task force, noting that "Some library media centers are innovative in technology techniques but lack resources to make an impact on classrooms" (Wisconsin Department of Public Instruction 1997). The Wisconsin plan addresses equity, access, and use:

> Equity and access issues are central to any technology plan. Equity refers to the availability of instructional technology to all students regardless of socioeconomic status, culture, religion, gender, age, or race. The state cannot make results of technology perfectly equitable for all students, schools, and districts. The state can, however, lay the groundwork for equity across all districts by providing funding for a common base of technology (Wisconsin Department of Public Instruction 1997).

In several states, departments of education or professional library associations (often in cooperation with one another) have developed information literacy standards for students. These standards, for the most part, are similar to those found in *Information Power: Building Partnerships for Learning*. New Jersey's "Information Literacy Standards for Student Learning and the New Jersey Core Curriculum Contents Standards" (Educational Media Association of New Jersey 1999) and Washington's "Essential Skills for Information Literacy" (Washington Library Media Association 1996) are two such examples. Maryland has a document that is based on student outcomes, listing the library media skills that students should be able to demonstrate in grades kindergarten through eight (Maryland Department of Education 2000).

Indiana, on the other hand, has written standards for its "teachers of library and media." The eleven standards include expected performances, knowledge, and dispositions (Indiana Professional Standards Board 1998).

Some states such as Massachusetts have emphasized cooperation between school and public libraries. Its "Policy on Cooperation Between Public Libraries and School Libraries," which was written by the Massachusetts Board of Library Commissioners, provides support for cooperation between public libraries and school libraries through:

◆ Direct advisory assistance, technical assistance and training for public libraries on effective cooperation at the community level

◆ A program of regional library systems which provide support for resource sharing, shared technology and other cooperative activities, consulting services and training to individual public and school libraries

◆ Grants to public and school libraries for cooperative projects (Massachusetts Board of Library Commissioners 1999)

There have also been many cooperative efforts between public and school libraries in the area of resource sharing. Many states have online databases for sharing materials. Access Pennsylvania is a combined library catalog for participating school, university, and special libraries. Wisconsin has a similar catalog, The Wisconsin Union Catalog (WISCAT). State union catalogs of school libraries are also available; examples are Rhode Island's RILink and Florida's Sunlink.

The school library media state consultant and the state school library media association are two important contact points for up-to-date information about services, programs, legislation, and standards. Your involvement in these activities is an essential part of your professional role.

THE GLOBAL COMMUNITY

With the increasing opportunities for students and teachers to use e-mail and the Internet comes another way to interact with people from other parts of the world. For a listing of epal sites that accept messages from both student accounts and/or staff accounts, see the electronic resources list at the end of this chapter.

CONCLUSIONS

Media specialists can help bring the community to the school. As you explore the resources of any community, you will find individuals and groups who are interested in sharing with students. Contacting members of the community also provides an opportunity to learn about the community itself and how the members of that community view education. Students will benefit from your knowledge of ways to access information from other agencies.

The community, your school district, and the professional associations offer many opportunities for participation. As you engage in these activities, you will learn how the decision-makers impact the collection and how your participation can be most effective.

REFERENCES

California School Library Laws. 2000. [http://www.cde.ca.gov/cilbranch/eltdiv/library/liblaws.html]. (Accessed November 6, 2000).

Educational Media Association of New Jersey. 1999. Information Literacy Standards for Student Learning and the New Jersey Core Curriculum Content Standards. [http://www.emanj.org/s1april99.html]. (Accessed November 6, 2000).

Hawaii Department of Education. 1994. Materials Selection Policy for School Library Instructional Technology Centers. [http://sls.k12.hi.us/selection.html]. (Accessed November 6, 2000).

Indiana Professional Standards Board. 1998. Teachers of Library and Media. [http://www.state.in.us/psb/Standards/lib_media/lib_media.htm]. (Accessed November 6, 2000).

Kentucky Department of Education. 1995. Online II. [http://www.kde.state.ky.us/oet/customer/online2//appendix_d.asp]. (Accessed November 6, 2000).

Maryland Department of Education. Arts and Science Branch. 2000. Library Media Skills-Grades K-8. [http://www.mdk12.org/mspp/mspap/whats%2Dtested/learneroutcomes/library%5Fmedia/k%2D8/clarifications1.html]. (Accessed November 6, 2000).

Massachusetts Board of Library Commissioners. 1999. Policy on Cooperation between Public Libraries and School Libraries. [http://www.mlin.lib.ma.us/mblc/public_advisory/school_public/ps_index.shtml]. (Accessed November 6, 2000).

Massachusetts School Library Media Association. 1996. Standards for School Library Media Centers in the Commonwealth of Massachusetts. [http://www.doe.mass.edu/doedocs/LMstandards/lmstandards.html]. (Accessed November 6, 2000).

Missouri Department of Elementary and Secondary Education. 2000. Library Media Center Information. [http://www.dese.state.mo.us/divinstr/curriculum/lmcindex.htm]. (Accessed November 6, 2000).

North Carolina Department of Public Instruction, Division of Media and Technology Services. 1992. *Learning Connections: Guidelines for Media and Technology Programs* (Raleigh, NC, Department of Public Instruction).

Texas Library Association. 1997. School Library Standards: Resources. [http://www.tea.state.tx.us/technology/libraries/resources.html]. (Accessed November 6, 2000).

Washington Library Media Association. 1996. Essential Skills for Information Literacy. [http://www.wlma.org/Literacy/eslintr.htm]. (Accessed October 10, 2001).

Wisconsin Department of Public Instruction: Instructional Media and Technology. 1997. Wisconsin Educational Technology Plan PK-12. [http://www.dpi.state.wi.us/dpi/dltcl /imt/witekpln.html]. (Accessed November 6, 2000).

ELECTRONIC RESOURCES

CSLA Position Paper: School and Public Libraries. 1996. [http://www.schoolibrary.org /Board/schlpubpp.html]. (Accessed November 25, 2000).
      California School Library Association adopted October 20, 1996. Takes the position that school and public libraries should not be combined but identifies ways in which the two institutions can cooperate and collaborate.

E-Pals Classroom Exchange. 2000. [http://www.epals.com/index.html]. (Accessed November 25, 2000).
      For grades K–12 and teachers. A teacher-based ePAL match site. Has English, French, and Spanish interfaces with translation imbedded. Links to other education project centers. Provides search by country, city and/or school name, grade/age, and/or language.

Guidelines for the Evaluation of Instructional Technology Resources for California Schools. 1999. Stanislaus County (California) Office of Education. [http://clearinghouse.k12 .ca.us]. (Accessed November 6, 2000).
      Identifies standards to meet legal compliance relating to social content of resources.

Intercultural E-Mail Classroom Connections. 2000. [http://www.stolaf.edu/network/iecc]. (Accessed November 25, 2000).
      International, cross-cultural, and intergenerational ePALS listing for adults. "Search All IECC Archives" helps adults match their students with other children by date, language, and country.

Keypals Club. n.d. [http://www.mightymedia.com/keypals]. (Accessed November 25, 2000).
      Designed for students and teachers in grades 1–12. Requires parents' signature on a permission form before students can register. States what information is available and what is not, how school staff monitor information, and what students can exchange. No advertisements. E-mail addresses are not sold. Provides a search form to locate classes based on country, state, grade, class size, or interests.

The Kidlink Network. 2000. [http://www.kidlink.org/english/general/intro.html]. (Accessed November 25, 2000).
      Sponsored by a Norwegian non-profit group. Allows real-time chats. For students up to grade 10 and for teachers. A multilingual and multinational site to connect discussion groups. Takes place in more than 10 languages.

School Libraries on the Web. 2000. [http://www.sldirectory.com/index.html]. (Accessed November 25, 2000).

      Lists of library Web pages maintained by K–12 school libraries in the United States and other countries.

School Library Program Standards: Guidelines and Standards. 1997. Texas State Library and Archives Commission and the State Board of Education. [http://www.tea.state.tx.us] and [http://www.tsl.state.tx.us]. (Accessed November 10, 2000).

      Identifies the state's standards.

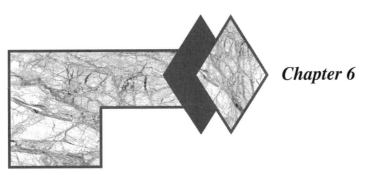

Chapter 6

Policies and Procedures

How can media specialists ensure that a collection reflects the goals of both the media program and the school? A major task that media specialists face is to analyze and articulate the answers to the "why, what, how, and by whom" questions involved in the creation, maintenance, and use of a collection. A number of media center policies address these issues: collection development, selection, acquisition, resource sharing, and evaluation. Individually or collectively they constitute the management tools for long- and short-range planning. Policies address issues such as intellectual freedom, rights of individuals to request reconsideration of materials, fair use of copyrighted materials, and use of the Internet. Such a policy is known as an Acceptable Use Policy (AUP).

By establishing policies and procedures, media specialists

promote collection development principles that reflect institutional goals and user needs;

define the scope and coverage of the collection;

assign selection responsibility;

facilitate quality selection and deselection decisions;

guide evaluation of the collection;

protect intellectual freedom;

acknowledge the rights of individuals to ask for reconsideration of materials;

ensure fair use of copyrighted materials;

ensure student access to materials including those on the Internet; and

create a public relations document to inform the public of the purpose of the collection.

POLICY VERSUS PROCEDURE STATEMENTS

Policy statements and procedure statements guide the activities of the collection program. Policies explain why the collection exists. They state ideal goals in general terms, allowing for flexibility and change. Policies establish the basis for all the collection program activities, identify who will use it, and delineate what will be in the collection, thus defining its scope.

Procedure statements direct the implementation of policies and should be concrete and measurable. By defining the "what, how, and when" questions, they address the tasks or processes for attaining the policy goals. Procedure statements explain how policies will be put into practice and identify the person who is responsible for their implementation. Policies need to be in place before procedure statements are written. Procedures are specific and should be reviewed regularly. Due to the specific nature of procedures, media specialists need to update them on a regular basis. This is an argument for issuing the policy and procedure statements as separate documents. The broad and more general statements found in policies usually require less frequent revision. Labels for policy documents vary from one media center to another. Other titles commonly used are "collection policy," "selection policy," and "materials policy."

As you examine documents, try to determine whether the policies and procedures are clearly distinguished. Questions you can ask yourself include the following: Does the statement

- ◆ address the purpose of the collection? (a policy)

- ◆ identify the types of materials that will be included? (a policy)

- ◆ explain how the collection will be created? (a procedure)

- ◆ state who is responsible for the collection? (a policy)

- ◆ describe the steps for maintaining the collection? (a procedure)

- ◆ explain the basis for adding or withdrawing materials from the collection? (a policy)

- ◆ identify who (students, teachers) will be involved in the selection process? (a policy)

- ◆ describe how teachers, administrators, and students will be involved in the selection process? (a procedure)

- ◆ identify student responsibilities for the use of resources in an ethical and educational manner? (a policy)

VALUE OF WRITTEN STATEMENTS

A written policy statement is more effective than an unwritten one for directing media specialists' activities or for explaining their actions to others. For the reader, the written policy demonstrates that the program is run in a businesslike and professional manner, decisions are not arbitrarily made, and overall planning is taking place.

The written policy statement justifies the presence of specific materials in the collection. This is especially important when someone challenges materials. Without a written policy, challenged materials may be judged by headlines in the local news media, rather than by the professional judgment of educators.

The benefits of a written policy include

justification for inclusions of materials in the collection, for example, defense of selection decisions for materials that may be challenged;

involvement of others in the process, enhancing public relations and understanding of the purpose of the collection;

the community's increased confidence in its schools, based on knowledge of the thorough and reasoned philosophies and procedures underlying the selection of materials; and

promotion of an atmosphere of objectivity in the selection process and the handling of challenges.

POLICY FORMULATION AND ADOPTION PROCESS

Policies must reflect the goals and needs of the individual media program and its institution. To be effective and responsive to these specific goals and needs, policy statements must be created at both the district and building levels. For example, the school district's stance on intellectual freedom, fair use, and acceptable use of the Internet would be developed at the district level; questions dealing with the intensity of collecting specific subjects would be at the building level.

The local group responsible for creating the policy statement must determine which elements to include and how to organize them. The diversity of building-level educational programs and the changing needs of users limits the effectiveness of adopting another school's policy statement. However, it is prudent to examine statements from various sources. This activity can prevent omissions, provide guidance for the outline, and offer suggestions for wording.

All the policies dealing with the collection may be combined in one document, or they can be handled individually. Figure 6.1 illustrates what the table of contents might look like if the policies were combined. Many policy statements found in schools today focus on selection, failing to recognize the importance of the collection development, acquisitions, and evaluation functions. Each topic is important. When presented as individual documents, the collection development policy should present an abstract or summary of them. Combining them into one document does not diminish the importance of the selection policy but emphasizes that selection decisions about individual items should also consider the collection as a whole.

   I.   Introduction

  II.   Collection Development
      A.   General Collection Management and Development Policies
          (gifts, multiple copies)

      B.   Detailed Analysis of Subject Collections

      C.   Conspectus Approach, Narrative Statement, or a Combination

      D.   Detailed Analysis of Special Collections

      E.   Collection Levels

      F.   Language Codes

  III.   Acquisition

  IV.   Selection

   V.   Reconsideration

  VI.   Evaluation

 VII.   Copyright

VIII.   Acceptable Use (Internet)

  IX.   Indexes

Figure 6.1. Table of contents for combined policy statement.

As you consider this responsibility, reflect on the observations of Lillian N. Gerhardt, former editor of *School Library Journal*:

> Writing policy and procedures is not difficult. Identifying support to get them approved is harder. Then ensuring that they are carried out is the hardest part and the loneliest. But, if there were no risks or strains involved, librarianship would not be a profession (Gerhardt 1993, 4).

The policy formulation and adoption process (see Figure 6.2) begins with the governing body as it

1.   Decides to establish and adopt a policy.

2.   Appoints an ad hoc committee composed of representatives of the school community. This body may include parents, students, certified media specialists, administrators, people from other libraries and educational institutions, and community members. If the policy is to cover all instructional materials, including textbooks, then the body should also include subject specialists.

3.   Determines who will use the policy.

4.   Identifies when the statement might be used for evaluating the collection, preparing funding proposals, generating accreditation reports, or guiding cooperative resource-sharing agreements.

5.   Charges the committee with the responsibility of developing the policy and establishes a deadline for the presentation of a draft.

6.   Distributes general guidelines to the committee to facilitate its work.

7.   Studies the draft before discussing it with the committee.

8.   Determines whether and how the policy can be easily updated.

9.   Solicits discussion and suggestions from legal counsel, personnel within the school (such as department heads or curriculum committees), and groups such as parent-teacher associations and the teachers' association.

10. Conducts a closing review of the committee's recommendations and the comments expressed by others who studied the draft.

11. Adopts a formal written statement as the approved policy of the issuing agency.

12. Provides for implementation of the newly adopted policy. This involves disseminating the policy to all staff members involved in the evaluation, selection, and use of materials covered in the policy. A meeting or in-service program should familiarize the staff with the policy so they can respond to inquiries about it. Media personnel and teachers are likely to be the ones who receive requests that materials in the collection or used in classrooms be reconsidered.

13. Disseminates the policy to the community.

14. Plans and conducts school and community activities to make people aware of the importance of the freedom to read, speak, view, listen, evaluate, and learn.

15. Establishes periodic evaluation and revision of the policy. Reviews should be scheduled on a regular basis with intervals of one to three years.

16. Formally adopts changes. Dates of the original adoption and sequential revisions recorded on the document are helpful indicators of the documents' history.

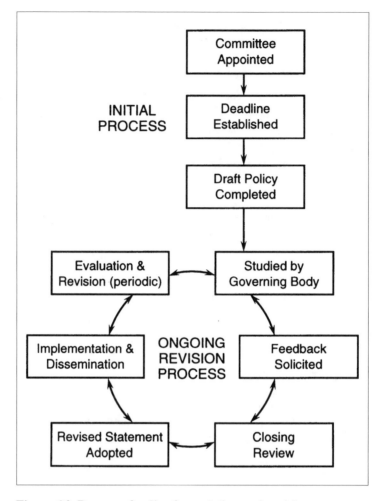

Figure 6.2. Process of policy formulation and revision.

COLLECTION DEVELOPMENT POLICY

The *Guide for Written Collection Policy Statements* defines collection development as "the process of planning, building and maintaining a library's information resources in a cost efficient and user relevant manner" (Anderson 1996, 27–28). The collection development policy

provides a broad overview of users' needs and priorities

reflects the goals of the media program and the school

offers guidance for decisions regarding the procurement of materials on certain subjects and identifies the depth of coverage.

I.   Introduction

The introduction to the statement establishes the authority, foundation, scope, and uses of the document.

A.   *Purpose of the policy statement and audience to whom it is directed.* The policy should identify the governing body of the district as legally responsible and the date the governing body adopts and revises the policy.

B.   *General description of the institution and clientele served.* The introduction can handle this in a sentence or two describing the school, the grades it serves, and other programs. It can refer to other documents that provide this information. Additional statements should address questions such as the following: Can parents use the collection? Can former students use it?

C.   *Mission statement and goals of the collection management and development program.* This section includes the goals of the media program and how the collection will be developed and managed to support the school goals. You should consider the following school library media program goals relating to collections from *Information Power: Building Partnerships for Learning* (American Association of School Librarians and Association for Educational Communications and Technology 1998):

> To provide intellectual access to information through learning activities that are integrated into the curriculum and that help all students achieve information literacy by developing effective cognitive strategies for selecting, retrieving, analyzing, evaluating, synthesizing, creating, and communicating information in all formats and in all content areas of the curriculum (American Association of School Librarians and Association for Educational Communications and Technology 1998, 6).
>
> To provide physical access to information through
>
> a.)   a carefully selected and systematically organized local collection of diverse learning resources that represent a wide range of subjects, levels of difficulty, and formats;
>
> b.)   a systematic procedure for acquiring information and materials from outside the library media center and the school through such mechanisms as electronic networks, interlibrary loan, and cooperative agreements with other information agencies; and instruction in using a range of equipment for accessing local and remote information in any format (American Association of School Librarians and Association for Educational Communications and Technology 1998, 7).
>
> To provide resources and activities that contribute to lifelong learning while accommodating a wide range of differences in teaching and learning styles, methods, interests, and capacities (American Association of School Librarians and Association for Educational Communications and Technology 1998, 7).

To provide resources and activities for learning that represent a diversity of experiences, opinions, and social and cultural perspectives and to support the concept that intellectual freedom and access to information are prerequisite to effective and responsible citizenship in a democracy (American Association of School Librarians and Association for Educational Communications and Technology 1998, 7).

D. *The library's official stance on intellectual freedom, censorship, and copyright issues.* If this statement is in the selection policy, then a reference to its location, rather than repeating the information, is appropriate. This section is usually handled in a sentence or two with reference to documents located in the appendix. Two examples are the "Library Bill of Rights" and the "Access to Resources and Services in the School Library Media Program." See Appendix C.

Note: The following sections E–J should be in the introduction unless they are treated elsewhere in the policy.

E. *Brief overview of the collection.*

1. History of the collection. The history can consist of a sentence or two about when the collection was established. In schools with endowments in memory of someone or with physical areas named after a person, an explanation about that individual would be appropriate.

2. Broad subject areas emphasized or de-emphasized. The definition states the scope of the collection. For example, all instructional materials, including textbooks, or just the materials under the direct control of the media center are part of the collection. This statement describes factors affecting the subject coverage. For example, coverage may be limited to subjects within the curriculum or be more expansive and include subjects useful in extracurricular programs.

3. Collection locations. This information is more apt to be needed in a campus plan or a high school with departmental collections. In an elementary school an example could be a professional collection not housed in the media center.

F. *Organization of the collection management and development program.*

1. Staffing and assigned responsibilities. In situations where there is more than one staff member, specific collection responsibilities should be designated. This could be by subject area, grade level, or format.

2. Liaison with user groups. This statement could describe the role of an advisory committee or state the goal of working with various groups, such as teachers or departments.

G. *Budget structure and allocation policy.* This section addresses questions such as the following:

- ◆ Is the collection the sole source of materials to meet the school's needs?

- ◆ Are instructional and media center materials bought with separate funds?

- ◆ Are funds available from sources outside the regular budget?

- ◆ Is a specified percentage of the budget used only for electronic information?

- ◆ Are funds set aside for replacement of materials and equipment?

H. *Relationship to policies and programs for management of collections, such as preservation, storage, replacement, deselection, and access.* This section addresses issues such as

the scope and purpose of deselection activities;

the criteria for determining which items to replace; and

policies dealing with access to electronic information.

I. *Cooperative collection development agreements.* This section identifies the resource sharing programs, such as networks, interlibrary loan arrangements, and coordinated collection development plans in which the school participates. This section identifies the school's responsibilities in such programs. In a coordinated collection development policy, an example could be that "the district professional collection serves the needs of all teachers within the district; individual schools are assigned specific professional journals to share throughout the system." Chapter 14 presents a fuller discussion of the issues.

J. *Policies related to equipment purchase and technical support for the on-site and remote electronic files and texts.* This section refers to policies about purchasing, leasing, or licensing arrangements for equipment and electronic information.

II.   *General Collection Policies*

This section describes general policies about materials by format, language, use, or situation. These divisions may not be applicable to all media centers. Collecting levels may be assigned on the basis of these divisions.

A. *Types of publications.* This statement identifies which formats are to be collected and which are excluded. For example, only microform materials on a particular subject may be included. Textbooks may be excluded, or single copies of a textbook providing information not covered by other materials will be included. The range of formats is extensive, including the following:

- ◆ books
- ◆ periodicals
- ◆ newspapers

♦ microforms

♦ maps

♦ pamphlets

♦ art works

♦ posters

♦ audio and visual materials

♦ computer software

♦ electronic formats

B.   *Other policies appropriate to the general management of the collection.* Additional statements should address local authors' publications; multiple copies; formats (print, CD-ROM, or online) for reference works; government publications; acquisition procedures affecting collection policies (standing orders, approval plans, blanket orders, gifts, or exchanges); expensive purchases; and replacements.

III.   *Subject Collections*

The conspectus approach involves evaluation and description of the collection, acquisition plans, deselection plans, and established goals. The analysis involves using ranges within the Dewey classification scheme to determine the collection levels (existing collection strengths).

The collection goal for each range is established by designating a collection code. Table 6.1 defines a number of conspectus levels from minimal to comprehensive. Each succeeding higher level includes the types of materials described in the lower level(s). Media specialists using the conspectus approach may use a more extensive version of the levels as established by their coordinating agency. After analyzing and comparing the collection level (existing collection strength) and acquisition commitment (current collecting intensity) then the collection goal (the desired collecting intensity or acquisition commitment), can be established.

All types of libraries, including school library media centers involved in resource sharing, have used the (WLN) Conspectus approach. WLN offers manuals, worksheets, and software and is available to use ranges within Dewey.

Variations on the technique for analyzing collections to establish priorities for ordering can be found in a number of sources. David V. Loertscher designed a collection mapping approach. The Ephrata (Pennsylvania) Area School District uses three levels of analysis. The first level designates areas for de-emphasis, for making a few new selections, and for signaling the possible need to weed. The second is to maintain the current level. The third indicates an area that needs to grow. For further information about these approaches, see listings for David V. Loertscher and for Debra E. Kachel (Ephrata Area School District) in "Additional Readings" at the end of this chapter.

Table 6.1.
Conspectus Levels

Code	Level	Definition/Collection
0	Out of scope	Excludes this subject. The media center will have no materials on this subject.
1	Minimal level	Includes selected current basic titles on this subject. The media center will have a few works on a subject, such as art appreciation, even though the subject is not a part of the curriculum.
2	Basic level	Includes introductory and reference materials, access to appropriate bibliographic databases, and a few key periodicals. This is the common collection goal for many subjects in media center collections.
3	Study or Resource level	Includes basic works in appropriate formats on a subject, representative journals, access to electronic databases, reference works, and basic bibliographies. A high-school honors class may require this level of support.
4	Research level	Includes the major published and source materials required for research. This level could apply to a district professional collection supporting a specific research project.
5	Comprehensive	Is exhaustive in coverage and includes all significant works. A collection of school publications such as programs, yearbooks, and student newspapers could be at this level.

Based on *Guide for Written Collection Policy Statements* (Chicago: American Library Association, 1996, pp. 16–17).

IV.   *Conspectus Approach or Narrative Statement*

Some libraries prefer to present the analysis in a narrative format, whereas others combine the graphic conspectus with a narrative. Narratives should be organized by categories such as subject and each should describe

◆ the purpose or objectives of the program or the needs of the clientele served by that section of the collection.

◆ the scope of coverage and languages collected or excluded.

◆ types of materials (formats) included or excluded and the collecting level codes.

- ◆ who is responsible for selection and resource sharing plans.

- ◆ policies for acquiring access to information for physical or electronic items that the permanent collection will not retain.

V. Special Collections

For media centers with special collections, additional policy statements should cover these materials isolated by form or location. As with the other sections, collection levels should be identified. Examples of such collections include archival, separately housed collections, departmental collections, and endowed collections.

VI. Indexes

An index or indexes should provide references to user groups, specific programs, key words, and concepts. If both the conspectus approach and the narrative statement are used, the index should include cross-references between classified segments and subject descriptors.

ACQUISITION POLICY

The acquisition policy addresses the most efficient and cost-effective process for obtaining or accessing materials. This policy reflects the collection development policy and the selection policy. It establishes the condition under which materials will be obtained through a jobber, a distributor, a vendor, or a local source or by direct order. For example, if one needs a selected item immediately, the policy justifies direct ordering or local purchasing.

The policy might read: "Preferences will be given to jobber services that can supply at least 80 percent of an order within 60 days." The next statement might be, "When materials are needed sooner than a jobber can deliver, the media specialist may purchase appropriate materials from a local source." This exception allows the media specialist to obtain materials quickly under special circumstances. Another policy may address how to obtain other types of materials, such as computer software and electronic journals.

Acquisition policies may address whether the media program will participate in resource sharing through exchange programs, interlibrary loan, and coordinated collection development plans. This section also addresses the following questions: Under what circumstances will the media center use

- ◆ standing orders?

- ◆ approval plans?

- ◆ blanket orders?

♦ exchange programs?

♦ gifts?

Most policies have a statement to the effect that a gift must meet the criteria used in making selection decisions to purchase materials. A proviso that the library will dispose of materials that do not meet such criteria should be shown to people making gifts. Remember that gifts are not entirely free: They have to be processed and stored like all materials.

Ascertain who in your school district is authorized to accept gifts. Some districts require formal acceptance of gifts by the board of education. In other districts individual building personnel, such as the principal or school library media specialist, can accept them.

SELECTION POLICY

The selection policy identifies the criteria for evaluating materials before acquiring them and later in determining which items to deselect. The selection policy also establishes who is responsible for selection decisions and who will participate in that process. Sometimes the selection policy is created as a separate document. In other cases it is with the policies and procedures for dealing with requests to reconsider materials. In some districts both of the aforementioned documents are in a section of the selection policies for all materials in the school. The latter may be titled the "Instructional Materials Selection Policy." See Chapter 7 for a fuller discussion of the selection policy.

REQUESTS FOR RECONSIDERATION OF MATERIALS

This section of the document provides directions for handling complaints and for focusing the complainant's attention on the principles of intellectual freedom, rather than on the material itself. Chapter 7 provides more details.

EVALUATION POLICY

The evaluation policy establishes the basis for evaluating the collection, identifies who will be responsible, and states the frequency of such efforts.

Continuing (or ongoing) evaluation of the collection ensures that it will meet established collection levels. This policy statement specifies

♦ the person who will be responsible.

♦ the scope and purpose of evaluation.

♦ the criteria for deselection of materials.

♦ the disposal policies.

♦ the audience for the report.

♦ the manner of presenting, using, and disseminating the results.

An accompanying procedure manual identifies the frequency or timeline, as time frames are subject to change. Evaluations of the materials should result in the removal (deselection) of deteriorated or obsolete materials. The procedures outline the steps for disposing of materials. The terms *re-evaluation*, *deacquisition*, *weeding*, *discarding*, and *deselection* are sometimes used interchangeably to denote the same process, which Chapter 15 describes.

COPYRIGHT POLICY

The school's copyright policy guides the use of materials by students, teachers, and media center staff. Related procedures (provided in a separate document) specify how to manage the copyright compliance. The policy places the burden of litigation on the person responsible for any illegal actions.

The elements of the policy include the following:

1. *The governing body's intent to comply with the U. S. Copyright Act of 1976* (Title 17, U.S. Code, Sect. 101, et seq.).

2. *The conditions under which copyrighted works may be copied.* Chapter 10, "Criteria by Format," describes guidelines for copyright laws as they affect specific formats.

3. *The location of the procedures.*

4. *A statement identifying the person who is responsible for implementing the policy and keeping records.*

Media centers are required to post copyright warning notices near all copying equipment and to place a copyright warning notice on the first page of copied materials. Media specialists should assume that they are responsible for educating teachers and students about copyright law and for monitoring the use of copyrighted materials. Copyright regulations for the various formats are provided in Chapter 10. Given the legal aspects of these statements, media specialists should seek legal counsel before the school board approves a document.

For further information about copyright laws, see the listings at the end of the chapter. For a comprehensive policy see the Groton (Connecticut) Public Schools manual at the following URL: http://groton.k12.ct.us/mts/egtoc.htm (accessed November 10, 2000). Another example is the Ephrata (Pennsylvania) Area School District policy and administrative procedures in Appendix D of the book by Debra E. Kachel.

ACCEPTABLE USE POLICY

Acceptable use of the Internet policies (AUPs) and procedures are also documents that should be developed by representatives of those whom they will affect. Due to the nature of these documents, legal counsel should review them. Although AUPs are usually developed and adopted at the district level, media specialists should be aware of the elements and issues that such documents address. Figure 6.3 displays an example outline for an acceptable use policy.

Introduction or background.

Role of the Board.

    Educational purpose.

    District responsibilities.

    Parental responsibilities.

    Technical services provided by the district.

    Access issues.

    Student safety.

    District liability.

Student responsibilities or Internet rules.

    Student account agreement.

Employees' responsibilities.

    Employee account agreement.

The Student Related Disciplinary Process.

    Due process.

    Disproportionate punishment.

    Search and seizure.

Plagiarism and copyright.

First Amendment Issues

    Student speech.

    Employee speech.

    Access to information.

    Academic freedom.

Figure 6.3. Outline for an acceptable use policy.

The Minnesota Coalition Against Censorship observes that

> Because the Internet is a fluid environment, the information which will be available to students is constantly changing; therefore, it is impossible to predict with certainty what information students might locate. Just as the purchase, availability, and use of media materials does not indicate endorsement of their contents by school officials, neither does making electronic information available to students imply endorsement of that content (Minnesota Coalition Against Censorship 1994, unpaged).

The Coalition recommends that policies related to the Internet should include language affirming that:

◆ Students have the right to examine a broad range of opinions and ideas in the educational process, including the right to locate, use and exchange information and ideas on the Internet.

◆ Students have the right to examine and use all information formats, including interactive electronic formats.

◆ Students have the right to communicate with other individuals on the Internet without restriction or prior restraint.

◆ School officials must respect a student's right to privacy in using Internet resources and using the Internet as a vehicle for communication.

◆ School officials, school employees, or other agencies responsible for providing Internet access must not make individual, arbitrary, unreviewed decisions about Internet information sources.

◆ School officials must apply the same criterion of educational suitability used for other educational resources to attempts to remove or restrict access to specific databases or other Internet information sources.

◆ If restrictions are placed on student access to Internet resources, it is parents and only parents who may place restrictions on their children, and only their own children. Parents may not tell the school to assume responsibility for imposing restrictions on their children.

◆ Students are responsible for the ethical and educational use of their own Internet accounts.

◆ Students have a responsibility to respect the privacy of other Internet users.

◆ Policies and procedures to handle concerns raised about Internet resources should be similar to those used for other educational resources (Minnesota Coalition Against Censorship 1994, unpaged).

There are many sources of help including templates for agreement forms. Among the electronic resources listed at the end of this chapter, consult the entries under Nancy Willard, Bellingham (Washington) School District Libraries, Groton (Connecticut) Public Schools, and the Virginia Department of Education.

CONCLUSIONS

Written and formally adopted policy and procedure statements guide collection development, aid in selection decisions, assign responsibilities, guide acquisition practices, and ensure compliance with copyright law. These documents also help protect intellectual freedom by establishing policies and procedures for dealing with requests for reconsideration of materials.

The collection development policy provides the broad overview of needs and priorities based on the media program's goals and offers guidance for decisions regarding the procurement of materials.

In practice, elements of the collection program policy may be established at the district level, rather than at the building level. However, the sections pertaining to a specific school's collection, such as the analysis of instructional objectives, the detailed analysis of subject areas and format collection, criteria for selection, and evaluation of the collection must describe the needs of the individual building's collection.

A basic principle is that policies need to "be reviewed at intervals to verify that existing collection goals are being met and that changes in defined goals and user needs are addressed" (Anderson 1996, 5).

REFERENCES

American Association of School Librarians and Association for Educational Communications and Technology. 1998. *Information Power: Building Partnerships for Learning.* Chicago: American Library Association.

Anderson, Joanne S., ed. 1996. *Guide for Written Collection Policy Statements,* 2d ed. Collection Management and Development Guides, No. 7. Chicago: American Library Association.

Gerhardt, Lillian N. 1993. Matters of Policy. *School Library Journal* 39 (January): 4.

Minnesota Coalition Against Censorship. Minnesota Public School Internet Policy. Adopted August 18, 1994.

Wood. Richard J., and Frank Hoffman. 1996. *Library Collection Development Policies: A Reference and Writers' Handbook.* Lanham, MD: Scarecrow Press.

ADDITIONAL READINGS

Bielefield, Arlene, and Lawrence Cheeseman. 1997. *Technology and Copyright Law: A Guidebook for the Library, Research, and Teaching Professions.* New York: Neal-Schuman.

    Useful guide to the impact of copyright laws on the use of technology.

Bruwelheide, Janis H. 1998. *Copyright Primer for Librarians and Educators,* 2d ed. Chicago: American Library Association.

    A practical guide to questions about copyright as it relates to use in media centers.

California Department of Education. 1991. *Suggested Copyright Policy and Guidelines for California's School Districts.* Sacramento, CA: California Department of Education.

    This is a 13-page booklet for $3 available from the California Department of Education, Bureau of Publications, Sales Unit, Box 271, Sacramento, CA 94812-0271.

"Copyright and You" feature. *TechTrends for Leaders in Education and Training.* Association for Educational Communications and Technology.

    This regular feature provides updates on the ever-changing status of copyright law.

Kachel, Debra E. 1997. *Collection Assessment and Management for School Libraries: Preparing for Cooperative Collection Development.* Westport, CT: Greenwood Press.

    Appendix D, "Written Collection Policy Documents," pages 141–93, includes the Ephrata (Pennsylvania) Area School District's policies and copyright, selection, and acceptable use analysis of the collection.

Loertscher, David V., and May Lein Ho. 1986. *Computerized Collection Development for School Library Media Centers.* Fayetteville, AR: Hi Willow Research and Publishing.

    This computerized system allows one to analyze a collection in terms of curricular areas and numbers of students enrolled in courses.

Pennock, Robin. 1997. "Read My Lips: Copyright." *School Library Journal's Best: A Reader for Children's Young Adult & School Librarians,* ed. Lillian N. Gerhardt, comp. Marilyn J. Miller and Thomas W. Downen, 423–24. New York: Neal-Schuman.

    Useful suggestions for media specialists responsible for handling copyright matters.

Smith, Mark. 1999. *Internet Policy Handbook for Libraries.* New York: Neal-Schuman.

    Covers the policy development process, guides the deliberation of the issues to be addressed, and provides examples from existing school library media center policies.

WLN, Box 3888, Lacey, WA 98503-0888. 1-800-DIALWIN.

Manual, worksheets, software for LC or Dewey. Offered at two levels. The smaller one by category level is probably more appropriate for schools.

Wood, Richard J., and Frank Hoffman. 1996. *Library Collection Development Policies: A Reference and Writers' Handbook.* Lanham, MD: Scarecrow Press.

Includes school district policies and samples of elements from other policies.

ELECTRONIC RESOURCES

Bellingham (Washington) Public Schools. 1995. "Bellingham School District Instructional Materials Policy." [http://www.bham.wednet.edu]. (Accessed November 10, 2000).

Includes documents such as "Student Access to Networked Information Resources" and "Parent Permission Letter (Internet and Electronic Mail Permission Form)."

Bellingham (Washington) School District Libraries. 1999. "Library Media Collection Development: Managing Our Libraries for Information Power." [http://www.bham .wednet.edu/library/tablec.htm]. (Accessed November 10, 2000).

Contains policies and procedures related to assessing, acquiring, maximizing access, and maintaining the collections.

Brevard (Florida) Public Schools. n.d. "Acceptable Use Policy—Administrative Procedures." [http://schoolboard.brevard.k12.fl.us/Rules/AcceptUsePol.htm]. (Accessed November 10, 2000).

Provides the authorization for acceptable use policy language.

Groton (Connecticut) Public Schools, Media Technology Services. Rev. 1998. "Copyright Implementation Manual." [http://groton.k12.ct.us/mts/egtoc.htm]. (Accessed November 10, 2000).

Offers a model for other schools.

Missouri State Department of Elementary and Secondary Education. 1997. Revised April 29, 1999. *Standards for Missouri School Library Media Centers.* Jefferson City, MO: Department. [http://www.dese.state.mo.us/divinstr/curriculum/standards/lmcstand .htm]. (Accessed November 10, 2000).

Provides guidelines for sizes of collections, matrix for evaluating collection (particularly materials in Dewey sensitive subjects that are 12 years old), and matrix for collection evaluation/budget. The companion work, *School Library Media Standards Handbook,* is available at the same Website.

Mount, Steve. 2000. "U.S. Constitution Online." [http://www.usconstitution.net]. (Accessed November 10. 2000).

Provides access to the Constitution, Declaration of Independence, Articles of Confederation, and related documents and Websites.

Templeton, Brad. n.d. "10 Big Myths About Copyright Explained." [http://www.templetons
.com/brad/copymyths.html]. (Accessed November 10, 2000).
    Offers practical information, including the fact that after April 1, 1989, every-
thing created privately and originally in the United States is copyrighted and protected regardless of whether a notice is present.

Virginia Department of Education, Division of Technology. n.d. "Acceptable Use Policies: A
Handbook." [http://www.pen.k12.va.us/go/VDOE/Technology/AUP/home.shtml#intro].
(Accessed November 10, 2000).
    Provides links to various policies from a number of school districts.

Washington Office of the Superintendent of Public Instruction. 1996. "Policies and Procedures
Impacting Schools and School Library Media Centers." [http://www.wlma.org/walibs
/poliproc.htm]. (Accessed November 10, 2000).
    Covers selection; fines, damage, and loss replacement; electronic access and
acceptable use; interlibrary loan; confidentiality of library patron records; and intellectual freedom.

Willard, Nancy. 1996. "K–12 Acceptable Use Policies." [http://www.erehwon.com/k12aup].
(Accessed November 10, 2000).
    Includes templates and information designed to help schools develop effec-
tive Internet policies. The materials on the site are protected by copyright, but
schools may download the materials to review them. If schools or districts use the
materials, there is a licensing fee of $50.00 for the set of templates.

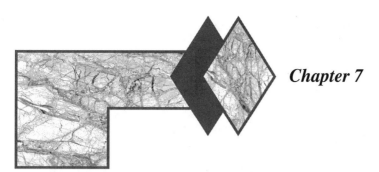

Chapter 7

Selection and Requests for Reconsideration

As a media specialist you will be involved in the creation of updating of a selection policy and the policies and procedures relating to requests for reconsideration of materials. This chapter describes the elements in such policies and offers samples of writing such documents.

FORMULATING SELECTION POLICIES

Policy statements are stronger and more effective when formulated by a group; rarely are they the product of one person. The media specialist's professional responsibility is to ensure that appropriate policies are in place. Involving teachers, administrators, students, and citizens is vital to the process. A major benefit is the participants' advocacy and support of the principles on which the policy is based. This process presents an opportunity to explain the media center's role in the educational process, to emphasize the importance of a commitment to intellectual freedom, to discuss the concept of providing access to information, and to ensure fair use of materials.

If your district does not have a policy, you should alert your administrator and the governing body to the need for one. If a policy exists but has fallen out of use, you should encourage a review of the policy. Ask the director of the district media program to coordinate the formulation of a policy for aspects that are districtwide. If you are the only certified media specialist in a one-school district, you will be responsible for starting the process of creating a working policy. As you work with others, remind them that:

The library media specialist understands that her/his role is not to personally approve of or believe in every item that is in the library media collection, but to recognize the role of applying sound criteria to selection as well as the value of differing viewpoints on subjects of interest (Hopkins 2000).

STATE-REQUIRED STATEMENTS

Many states require school districts to have selection policies. For example, Wisconsin requires each school board to develop written policies and procedures to disallow discrimination against students. Chapter P19 of the Wisconsin Administrative Code specifies that the library media selection and evaluation policies must contain language prohibiting discrimination. Suggested wording to meet this requirement is as follows:

The School District shall not discriminate in the selection and evaluation of instructional and library materials on the basis of *sex, race, national origin, ancestry, creed, pregnancy, marital or parental status, sexual orientation or physical, mental, emotional* or *learning disability* (Folke 1999, 6).

Other states have similar mandates for selection policies and procedures for reconsideration of challenged materials. Contact your state department of education or department of public instruction for information about such mandates.

ELEMENTS OF A SELECTION POLICY

This discussion focuses on the elements of the selection policy when it is issued as a separate document. The procedures for selection are not part of this document.

I. *Statement of Philosophy*

This brief statement presents the school district's values and beliefs. It may refer to the school's mission and goals statement or language from that document, and other relevant documents may be duplicated here. The statement may address how the educational resources help the school achieve its goals.

Other statements in this section may refer to the First Amendment's protection of students' rights to access information to read, listen, view, and evaluate. Another sentence may state the school's or school board's responsibility to provide a wide range of educational resources.

Sample phrases in this section start with "the Board of [school district's name] through its professional staff shall provide," "will provide," or "is committed to facilitating teaching and learning by providing":

◆ materials for students and teachers.

◆ resources of varying levels of difficulty, diversity of appeal, and presentation of different points of view.

◆ materials that will help students develop critical thinking skills and aesthetic appreciation.

Other statements may refer to the needs of a democratic society or a nation with a pluralistic society. An example is found in the Vancouver (British Columbia, Canada) policy that reads:

> The policy of the Board of School Trustees of School District #39 (Vancouver) is to provide a wide range of learning resources at varying levels of difficulty, with diversity of appeal and the presentation of different points of view to meet the needs of students and teachers (Minnesota Coalition Against Censorship 1991, 8).

II. *Selection Objectives*

This section translates the school district's philosophy and goals into collection objectives. The statements show how the collection helps the school meet its goals. Objectives identify the materials that will be in the collection, present a rationale for using a variety of resources in the school, and describe the basis for judging the educational suitability of the materials for use by students and teachers. Examples of main objective statements are:

> To make available to faculty and students a collection of materials that will enrich and support the curriculum and meet the educational needs of the students and faculty served (Office of Intellectual Freedom, American Library Association, 1996, 204).

or

> The primary objective of professional selection shall be to provide the curriculum with a variety of materials. Selection shall represent a variety of attitudes and the points of view of many religious, cultural, ethnic, and social groupings within the community, shall demonstrate artistic value and/or factual authority, and shall be selected as valuable in stimulating intellectual, ethnical, and aesthetic growth in our young people (Dallas Independent School District 1993, 4.3).

A statement identifying the range of materials covered in the policy might read:

> Media center materials are defined as all electronic, print, and non-print resources, excluding textbooks, that students and teachers use for the District's education program.

The combination of materials definition, main objective, board delegation, and sub-objectives are found in the Irving (Texas) Independent School District *Policies and Procedures Manual,* which reads:

> In this policy, "instructional resources" refers to textbooks, library acquisitions, supplemental materials for classroom use, and any other material used for formal or informal teaching and learning purposes. The primary objective of instructional resources is to deliver, support, enrich, and assist in implementing the District's educational program.
>
> The Board generally shall rely on its professional staff to select and acquire instructional resources that:
>
> 1. Enrich and support the curriculum, taking into consideration students' varied interests, abilities, learning styles, and maturity levels.
>
> 2. Stimulate growth in factual knowledge, literary appreciation, aesthetic values, and societal standards.
>
> 3. Present various sides of controversial issues so that students have an opportunity to develop, under guidance, skills in critical analysis and in making informed judgments in their daily lives.
>
> 4. Represent many religious, ethnic, and cultural groups and their contributions to the national heritage and world community (Lankford and Chaney 1993, np).

Another statement of objectives could express the belief that students need ideas beyond those that textbooks present. Other phrases commonly found in objective statements include:

◆ Represent the breadth of the curriculum.

◆ Wide range of the best materials available on appropriate levels of difficulty.

◆ Resources to support various styles of teaching materials that allow students to analyze, synthesize, evaluate, and use information effectively.

◆ Provide resources for students with particular physical disabilities and other special educational needs.

III. Responsibility for Selection

A. *Delegation of responsibility to professional staff.* An important element of the selection policy is stating who is responsible for selection decisions. If the policy applies to all instructional materials, this statement should distinguish between those who are responsible for text materials and those responsible for media program materials.

These statements usually acknowledge that the school board is legally responsible and delegates to media specialists the authority to select. The term *media specialist* may be defined as "professional, certified personnel employed by the district."

B. *Identification of participants in the selection process.* This statement identifies the role and level of involvement of teachers, students, administrators, staff, and community members in the selection process. A statement regarding advisory committees of teachers, students, and community members is appropriate for this section. Some states mandate the role of the advisory committee. Questions to address include the following: Will a committee make selection decisions, will media specialists work independently, or will a combination be used? How is responsibility delegated?

The responsibilities of the board may be described in terms of the operations of the school, policy making, and the determination of the use of monies. The Minnesota Coalition Against Censorship recommends that

> In some school districts, it might be valuable to indicate that the role of the principal is supervising the process, not actually performing the selection (Minnesota Coalition Against Censorship 1991, 17).

IV. Selection Criteria

This section generally consists of two or more parts. The first is a list of general criteria that applies to all materials and relates to the district or school goals stated in section I. A statement that these criteria apply to all materials, including gifts and loans, can eliminate the need to write a separate section about such items.

A. *General Criteria.* Criteria commonly include literary qualities, technical qualities, qualifications of authors or producers, and appropriateness for audience. Chapter 9 identifies general selection criteria that this general section could highlight. Examples of wording used in policies are as follows and indicate that materials should

◆ be relevant to today's world.

◆ represent artistic, historic, and literary qualities.

◆ reflect the problems, aspirations, attitudes, and ideals of society.

◆ contribute to the instructional program's objectives.

◆ be consistent with and support the general educational goals of the state and district.

◆ be appropriate for the age, ability level, learning style, and social and emotional development of the intended user.

◆ be appropriate for the subject area.

◆ meet quality standards in terms of content, format, and presentation.

◆ help students gain an awareness of our pluralistic society.

◆ motivate students to examine their own attitudes; to understand their rights, duties, and responsibilities as citizens; and to make informed judgments in their daily lives.

◆ be selected for their strengths rather than rejected for their weaknesses.

◆ consider the reputation and significance of the author, illustrator, publisher, and producer.

◆ consider the validity, currency, and appropriateness of the content.

◆ consider the contribution the material makes or the breadth of representative viewpoints on controversial issues.

◆ have a high degree of potential user appeal.

◆ reflect value commensurate with cost and/or need.

◆ have integrity.

◆ not represent a personal bias.

B.   *Specific categories criteria.* The second part addresses criteria for specific categories of materials, users, treatment of sensitive issues, and formats. The procedure guidelines may treat these more specific criteria separately because of the changes in topics of concern or changes in the technologies or presentations involved.

V.   *Position on Intellectual Freedom*

In this section the policy addresses the importance of access to information. The wording may indicate that the board endorses specific professional statements, such as the American Library Association's "Library Bill of Rights," or the wording may state that the district supports the concepts or values in one or more named documents. In either case the policy should attach the referenced documents. See Appendix C for reprints of commonly used professional statements. Wording in this section might read as follows:

> The Board of Education of [name of school district] supports the prin-
> ciples of intellectual freedom inherent in the First Amendment of the
> Constitution of the United States as expressed in official statements
> of professional associations. These include [identify statement(s)]
> and form a part of this policy.

VI. *Other Elements*

Two elements found in some policies are (1) statements about potentially contro-versial subjects and (2) the role of reviewing and selection tools in the selection process. There are advantages and disadvantages to such statements. The group formulating the policy will need to weigh those arguments carefully.

Traditionally, selection policies attempted to justify inclusion of potentially contro-versial topics by issuing statements about the variety of approaches sought in the collection on subjects dealing with religious, political, and social viewpoints. That position should be weighed against the position taken by the Minnesota Coalition Against Censorship, who observed:

> By their nature, resources about ideologies, religion, and sex will be considered by some persons to be biased. The identification of areas for special consideration creates a risk that considerations other than educational suitability, appropriateness, and other adopted criteria will be used. We do not recommend special considerations, rather adopted criteria should be applied equally to all resources (Minnesota Coalition Against Censorship 1991, 32).

Some policies identify selection sources to consult for help in locating two or more favorable reviews before an item can be considered for selection. This position is frequently taken based on the assumption that the practice will lead to quality purchases and that the reviews will defend the selections. This practice has several disadvantages that may prove to be restrictive. First, reviewing journals and selection tools often do not review the same titles. Second, a dearth of reviews exists for many formats. Third, a specific list may not be comprehensive or may not identify sources actually used. This creates a problem if none of the cited sources has reviewed a certain item. The problem is exacerbated if the title is pur-chased anyway and later is challenged. The Minnesota Coalition Against Censorship points out other problems:

> This requirement limits the teachers and media specialists and should not be included in policies. While selection aids are useful in helping teachers and media specialists identify titles to be considered for purchase, using reviews as a criterion for selection focuses on the review, rather than the professional judgment of the teachers and media specialists. There are several reasons why a review should not be considered a criterion for selection. Published reviews are neces-sarily general and are written for both school and public librarians. Resources of local or regional interest are not usually reviewed in national selection aids. Reviews do not address educational needs in specific school districts. Whether selection results from a review or actual examination of the resources, professional judgment should be the focus, not lists of acceptable selection aids (Minnesota Coali-tion Against Censorship 1991, 23).

VII.   *Other Situations*

This section addresses other situations relating to selection. Can teachers expect that materials will be procured solely on their recommendation? How much information or justification must teachers submit before an item will be purchased? Will the principal be allowed to make selection decisions without consulting the media specialist? Criteria for equipment should also be established.

SOURCES OF ASSISTANCE

Information is available from a variety of sources including professional colleagues and professional associations. Guides to developing policies are identified at the end of this chapter.

Other organizations offer valuable assistance in handling censorship disputes. These include the American Association of School Administrators, American Association of University Women, American Civil Liberties Union, American Federation of Teachers, Association of American Publishers, Electronic Frontier Foundation, Electronic Privacy Information Center, Free Expression Network, Freedom to Read Foundation, International Reading Association, National Coalition Against Censorship, National Conference of Christians and Jews, National Congress of Parents and Teachers, National Council of Teachers of English, National Education Association, National School Boards Association, and People for the American Way. Appendix A provides their addresses.

REQUESTS FOR RECONSIDERATION OF MATERIALS

This section of the document provides directions for handling complaints and for focusing the complainant's attention on the principles of intellectual freedom rather than on the material itself. A school district may include policies and procedures for dealing with challenged materials in other documents, such as the collection policy, the selection policy, or a separate policy. If issued as a separate document, the collection and selection policies should reference it. However, the elements of the challenged materials policy remain the same, regardless of whether the policy stands alone or is incorporated in the collection policy. Copies of both the selection policy and procedures for handling challenged materials should be available in the circulation area. A copy of both documents should be in the media center's policies and procedures handbook.

Generally speaking, policies and procedures should be separate documents (policies for the public, procedure for internal use), but in this case, a single document for the public's use should combine both policies and procedures. Sharing this information in a forthright manner can alleviate some of the tension that can occur in this situation. To ensure that all queries, whether internal or external, are treated in the same manner, each individual's complaint should be treated according to the school board's adopted procedure.

The Office of Intellectual Freedom of the American Library Association notes that this procedure

> establishes a fair framework for registering complaints, while defending the principles of intellectual freedom, the library user's right to access, and professional responsibility and integrity (Office of Intellectual Freedom, American Library Association 1996, 206).

Hopkins recommends that media specialists:

> Examine your district's materials selection policy carefully. Is the wording inclusive enough to show that challenges initiated by administrators, teachers, and other school personnel are to be included in reconsideration steps outlined in the policy? If not, contact your state library or media association and/or LMC consultants at the Department of Public Instruction/Education. Seek a critique of the current policy as well as sample policies to review (Hopkins 1993, 29).

The Wisconsin Department of Public Instruction offers the following advice:

> When an expression of concern or a complaint occurs, the district should treat the person expressing concern with respect. Everyone has the right to request that a resource be reviewed. Inquiries should not be taken personally; reactions should be pleasant, informative, and initiate the first steps of the reconsideration process (Folke 1999, 11).

Without a collection development policy or even a selection policy as a statement of principles and the basis for selection decisions, a media specialist would very likely feel that the inquiry was indeed personal.

The Office of Intellectual Freedom identifies the following advantages in having a complaint procedure and a prepared questionnaire for the complainant to complete.

> First, knowing that a response is ready and that there is a procedure to be followed, the librarian will be relieved of much of the initial panic which inevitably strikes when confronted by an outspoken and perhaps irate library patron. Also important, the complaint form asks complainants to state their objections in logical, unemotional terms, thereby assisting the librarian in evaluating the merits of the objections. In addition, the form benefits the complainant. When citizens with complaints are asked to follow an established procedure for lodging their objections, they feel assured they are being properly heard and that their objections will be considered (Office of Intellectual Freedom, American Library Association 1996, 209–10).

In summary, the advantages of having the procedures in place are as follows:

Complainants are reassured that their comments will be heard. This recognizes the rights of individuals to express their grievances.

The media specialist knows the procedure is in place and can use it to turn what may be an emotional situation into one in which the complainant's objections are stated in logical terms.

Carefully designed procedures provide a timely and fair review of challenged resources and inform the complainant of what will happen.

I. Statement of Philosophy

To focus attention on intellectual freedom in this policy, rather than on materials or personnel, many libraries endorse and reproduce national statements, such as the "Library Bill of Rights."

II. Handling Complaints

Other items this document may include are statements that establish procedural details.

A. *Who may register a complaint.* In some policies the following people qualify to register a complaint: United States citizen, resident of the community, teacher, student, administrator, member of the board of education, resident of the district, and employee of the district.

B. *Who should be notified when a complaint is received.* Typically this person is the principal, the superintendent, the curriculum coordinator, or some other person responsible for the formal handling of the process.

C. *Whether complaints must be in writing.* Consider the idea of having a person fill out a form such as the one described in the next step. Think about the advantages of having complainants provide the information in their own words and by their own pen. (Be sure they include their signature.)

D. *A form for the complainant to complete* (see Figure 7.1).

E. *Procedures for handling a complaint when the complainant is unwilling to fill out the form.* If this practice is followed, what is the provision for ensuring and verifying the accuracy of the complainant's statement?

F. *A committee to consider the complaint.* This item addresses the following questions: Which groups or authorities should the committee represent? How long will their terms be? How will they handle voting? Under what guidelines will it operate? Is there a specified time period for consideration of any one complaint? Who is responsible for informing the complainant of the processing of the complaint and final action? To whom should the committee report its decision? The New York State guidelines offer this advice:

Request for Reconsideration of Library Resources

Request initiated by: (print name) _____ Date: _____

Address _____

City _____ State _____ Zip Code _____ Telephone Number _____

Are you making the request on your own behalf? _____

Are you making the request on behalf of an organization? If yes, please identify the organization.

_____

1. Resources on which you are commenting:

_____ Book _____ Video _____ Audiovisual Materials

_____ Magazine _____ Newspaper

_____ Electronic information/network (please specify)

_____ Other, please specify.

Title _____

Author _____

Publisher/Producer (if known) _____

2. What brought this resource to your attention? _____

3. Have you examined the entire resource? _____

4. What concerns you about the resource? (Use other side or additional pages if necessary.)

5. Are there resources(s) you suggest to provide additional information and/or other viewpoints on this topic?

Signature of Requestor: _____

Date requested received: _____ By whom: _____

Identification of person or body that authorized the procedure and form.

Figure 7.1. Sample complaint form.

It is recommended that the report be submitted to the Board of Education directly rather than to establish a hierarchy of appeal from principal to superintendent to the Board of Education. The longer the issue remains in question, the more potential exists for creating additional tensions (University of the State of New York, State Education Department, Bureau of School Libraries n.d., 8).

G.   *How challenged materials are to be handled during this process.* Do they remain in use or are they removed? An argument for keeping materials available is that, if they are removed, intellectual freedom is being challenged, not specific materials.

H.   *Whether any item can be reconsidered more than once within a specified time period.*

I.   *Whether an explanation of the final action should be reported in writing to the complainant.*

J.   *Procedures for appealing the committee's decision.*

Both the complaint form and the process for handling complaints should be designed to encourage constructive dialogue. The review committee should be a standing one consisting of members who are informed about the policies and procedures and who are prepared to handle their responsibilities. This facilitates the process, supports the idea that this is an established routine, and avoids the tensions that can occur if such situations are treated as unusual incidents. There is no other area in which interpersonal skills, commitment to intellectual freedom, and sound knowledge affect a situation with such far-reaching implications.

Once adopted, the policy should be distributed to interested people and to those whom it will affect (teachers, administrators, and students). A condensed version might be distributed on a wider basis.

CONCLUSIONS

If your school district has adopted a selection policy, you will need to be familiar with it. Do the district policies reflect the goals of your school or the needs of collection? Is your principal aware of the policy and its implications? When was the last time the governing body studied the policy? Do additional guidelines need to be developed? If no policy exists, you have a professional responsibility to initiate the creation of one.

The involvement of diverse participants in the development of policies is important to ensure students' rights to read, speak, view, listen, evaluate, and learn. An adopted procedure for receiving and handling complaints recognizes the rights of people to challenge school practices. The media specialist has a professional responsibility to ensure that policies are developed and reviewed. The governing body has a responsibility to develop policies and ensure their implementation. Models and policies from other school districts can be examined, but each school district needs to develop policies tailored to its situation. Education associations and agencies provide other examples, offer guidelines for their development, and provide support when complaints are registered. The media specialist has a professional responsibility to ensure that policies are developed and reviewed. The governing body has a responsibility to develop policies and ensure their implementation. Models and policies from other school districts can be examined, but each school district needs to develop policies tailored to its situation.

REFERENCES

American Library Association. Office for Intellectual Freedom. 1996. *Intellectual Freedom Manual*, 5th ed. Chicago: American Library Association.

Association of American School Librarians and Association for Educational Communications and Technology. 1998. *Information Power: Building Partnerships for Learning*. Chicago: American Library Association.

Dallas Independent School District. Media Services Department. 1993. *Library Media Center Handbook*. Dallas: Dallas Independent School District, 1993.

Folke, Carolyn Winters. Wisconsin Department of Public Instruction. 1999. *Dealing with Selection and Censorship: A Handbook for Wisconsin Schools and Libraries*. No. 0046. Madison, WI: Wisconsin Department of Public Instruction. Available for $21.00 from Publication Sales, Wisconsin Department of Public Instruction, Box 7841, Madison, WI 53707-7841 or e-mail pubsales@dpi.state.wi.us. Customer Service at 1-800-243-8782. Also available at http://www.dpi.state.wi.us; see Publications Catalog, Subject Area Contents, Libraries.

Hopkins, Dianne McAfee. 1993. Put It in Writing: What You Should Know About Challenges to Materials. *School Library Journal* 39, no. 1 (January): 26–30. Reprinted in *School Library Journal's Best: A Reader for Children's, Young Adult and School Librarians,* ed. Lillian N. Gerhardt and comp. Marilyn L. Miller and Thomas W. Downen. 1997. New York: Neal-Schuman.

———. 2000. E-mail message to author, February 7.

Lankford, Mary D., and Deborah Chaney. 1993. Policies and Procedures Manual. Irving, TX: Irving Independent School District.

Minnesota Coalition Against Censorship. 1991. *Selection Policies and Reevaluation Procedures: A Workbook*. Minneapolis: Minnesota Educational Media Organization.

University of the State of New York. n.d. Statement Education Department, Bureau of School Libraries. *Selection Guidelines: School Library Resources, Textbooks, Instructional Material*. Albany, NY: Bureau.

ADDITIONAL READINGS

Association for Library Service to Children. 2000. "Intellectual Freedom for Children: The Censor is Coming." Chicago: American Library Association.

> Provides addresses, telephone numbers, and Websites for associations with speakers. Describes policies for materials selection, confidentiality, use of the Internet, and complaints procedures. Includes policy by the Council of the American Library Association and reprints of articles on related topics.

Newsletter on Intellectual Freedom. Chicago: Intellectual Freedom Committee of the American Library Association, 1952– . ISSN 0028-9485.

> Reports events relating to intellectual freedom and censorship.

ELECTRONIC RESOURCES

Buckingham, Betty Jo, ed. 1995. Selection of Instructional Materials: A Model Policy and Rules. Des Moines: State of Iowa, Department of Education. Available: [http://www.iema-ia.org/IEMA116.html]. (Accessed November 10, 2000).

> Provides a comprehensive model for schools.

Electronic Frontier Foundation. 2000. [http://www.eff.org]. (Accessed November 24, 2000).

> Endeavors to protect rights and promote freedom in electronic resources. Updates home page as appropriate news stories appear.

Electronic Privacy Information Center (EPIC). 2000. [http://www.epic.org]. (Accessed November 24, 2000).

> A public interest research center located in Washington, D.C. Focuses on civil liberties issues. Provides a newsletter, online news summaries, a bookstore, and guides to other sources. Guide for the 2000-01 National High School Debate topic, "Resolved: That the United States federal government should significantly increase protection of privacy in one or more of the following areas: employment, medical records, consumer information, search and seizures" included. Provides extensive range of resources.

Free Expression Network (FEN). 2000. Free Expression Network Clearinghouse. [http://www.freeexpression.org/info/about.html]. (Accessed November 24, 2000).

> An alliance of organizations, including the American Library Association, dedicated to protecting the right of free expression. Provides online source of information about this topic. Includes articles that can be downloaded free of charge.

National Coalition Against Censorship (NCAC). 2000. [http://ncac.org]. (Accessed November 24, 2000).

> Reports on recent attempts at censorship and NCAC's responses.

National Council of Teachers of English (NCTE). 2000 [http://www.ncte.org/censorship]. (Accessed November 24, 2000).

        Includes information about how NCTE will help. Provides the text of "Students' Right to Read" and "Guidelines for Dealing with Censorship of Nonprint Materials."

Office of Intellectual Freedom (OIF) of the American Library Association. 2000. [http://www.ala.org/alaorg/oif]. (Accessed November 24, 2000).

        Links to documents such as "Library Bill of Rights" and interpretations of that document.

People for the American Way (PFAW). 2000 [http://www.pfaw.org]. (Accessed November 24, 2000).

        Describes the range of interest and programs offered by PFAW to encourage citizens to participate in a democracy.

Part II

Selection of Materials

Selection sounds like a simple task, but the decisions have broad implications for the quality of education that schools offer. The needs of individual persons or programs often conflict with others. For example, at Edison Middle School, in one of the eighth-grade social studies classes, Letitia wants her students to collect data, analyze them, and draw conclusions. She wants materials that collectively present different opinions about topics. In her other eighth-grade social studies class, students need structured information with constant reinforcement. For these students, open-ended presentations are confusing. The two classes need the same content presented in different ways. Without sufficient materials of both types, the desired learning experience is unattainable.

Wide-ranging needs coupled with limited resources result in conflict. The collection policy identifies the collection's priorities and offers selection guidelines. The media specialist has an item in hand and needs to make a decision. Who will have access and under what circumstances? How will they use it? Does it duplicate materials already in the collection? Media specialists must weigh factors like these when making selection decisions.

Thus, the media specialist must be aware of the teaching methods used, the school program goals, the unique features of the various formats, and the needs and interests of students so that funds are not allocated to items that are "shelf sitters." If the media specialist does not apply selection criteria, items of limited value may be selected. It is disheartening to purchase an item and then to learn about a better one.

The burden of selection is not the media specialist's alone; teachers, administrators, and students can all participate in the decision-making process. However, the media specialist, as the one person who knows the collection and the needs of the school, is ultimately responsible for making wise selection decisions.

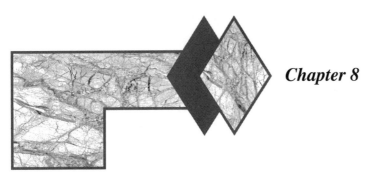

Chapter 8

Selection Procedures

In choosing materials, a media specialist plans and carries out certain activities that culminate in selection decisions. These activities include identifying and assessing evaluative information about materials; arranging for examination of materials through preview sessions, exhibits, and visits to examination centers; and providing ways to involve others in the process. These steps lead to the direct acquisition of materials or obtaining materials and information through resource sharing and electronic means. For bibliographic information and descriptions of the resources this chapter cites, see Appendix B.

OVERVIEW OF THE SELECTION PROCESS

Selection is the process of deciding what materials to add to the collection. Media specialists can identify potential materials through many sources. For example, administrators, teachers, and students request specific items or types of materials. Items in the collection wear out, are lost, or need replacing. The media specialist learns about new materials by reading reviews; seeing publishers', producers', and vendors' announcements; and previewing materials. Materials may be donated to the collection.

Media specialists should attentively record suggestions and requests to purchase materials. The media specialist should record as much bibliographic and purchasing information about the item as one can obtain at this stage, including the identifying source or the person who requested the item. The next step is to determine whether the item is already in the collection or on order. Some media specialists enter the information in the online catalog so users will be aware that the item is being considered or on order.

Once an item is fully identified, the media specialist must decide to include or exclude it from the collection. The media specialist bases this selection decision on several considerations, including collection policy; budget; selection criteria regarding content, format, and use; and immediacy of need. After the specialist has decided to purchase the item, the status of the record for the item is changed from "consideration" to the "order" file. The actions following this step compose the acquisition process.

SOURCES OF INFORMATION ABOUT MATERIALS

The opening-day scene in Chapter 1 reveals many requests for materials. Are there recommended videodiscs that present general information about light for Valerie's class? Where do you find music activity recordings for Keyona's kindergarten children? Which play scripts, science fiction titles, and biographies of sports figures are appropriate for Jessica's fourth-grade class? Is there a videotape that Rodrigo can use for his talk to the community group? Is there a computer software program about note taking? Which posters or art prints will stimulate students to write? Does the collection include visual and manipulative materials for Willie's American history class? Will any of the popular music recordings be useful for Carlos's poetry unit?

To fulfill these requests, the media specialist must investigate the following:

specific formats: art prints, posters, study prints, books, computer software, realia, recordings, videodiscs, and videotapes

user groups (audiences): kindergarten children, fourth graders, fifth graders, college-bound students, students who are reading below grade level, and adult members of a community group

subjects: American history, English, information literacy skills, light, teenage pregnancies, substance abuse, and teenage suicide

literary forms and genres: biographies, nonfiction, plays, science fiction, and poetry

This analysis indicates the broad coverage needed in sources of information about materials.

Bibliographic Tools

Bibliographic tools are a basic source of information about the availability of materials and their cost and whether they are recommended. Two types of bibliographies are useful. Trade bibliographies, such as *Books in Print* (R. R. Bowker 1948–) and *Canadian Books in Print* (University of Toronto Press 1975–), provide information about the existence of materials but do not evaluate them. Selection tools, such as *Senior High School Library Catalog* (H. W. Wilson 1997) and *Elementary School Library Collection* (Brodart, annual), evaluate materials and may include purchasing information.

When considering a bibliography for use or purchase, read the introduction and examine several entries. This will answer the following questions about the work:

◆ Purpose of the bibliography: Does it meet your need?

◆ Directions for use: Are they clear? Does the work give sample entries with explanations?

◆ Format: Is the bibliography available in print, CD-ROM, or other formats?

◆ Extent of coverage: Does it include information about a variety of formats? Does it provide information for many items, or is coverage limited? Does it include materials for a wide range of audiences, preschool through adult? What periods of publication and production does the work include?

◆ Method for collecting the information and designated responsibility: Who wrote the entries? What are the writers' qualifications? Are reviews signed?

◆ Criteria for inclusion: On what basis are items included? Are the criteria stated? Is the selection policy provided?

◆ Form and content of entry: Does the work present information clearly? Does it use symbols and abbreviations? Symbols may indicate levels of recommendation, reviewing sources, interest level, readability, and type of media. What ordering and bibliographic information does the work give? Are the annotations descriptive, evaluative, or both? Are all items recommended equally? Are items recommended for specific situations, uses, or audiences? Are there comparisons with other titles or formats? Does the work include only materials that have received favorable reviews in other tools?

◆ Organization of entries: Are the indexes necessary to locate an item? Do cross-references direct the user to related items? Do indexes provide access by author, title, series titles, audience, reading level, and subject? Does the index include analytical entries? For example, the selection tools by H. W. Wilson Company include analytical entries for individual folktales in anthologies, biographical sketches (not limited to collective biographies), subjects, and short stories in collections. This information is helpful in locating these materials for students and teachers.

◆ Date of publication: Does the work provide the compiler's closing date? How often is the bibliography revised or cumulated? Does it provide supplements? What time lag exists between compiling the information and the publication or issuing of the bibliography?

◆ Special features: Does the bibliography include directories for sources of materials? Does the work include appendices? If yes, about what?

◆ Cost: Does the tool provide sufficient information for a variety of users to merit the expenditure for it?

Selection Tools

Selection tools are bibliographies that include an evaluative or critical annotation for each item, providing

recommendations;

bibliographic information for each item;

purchasing information;

access to entries by author, title, subject, format, and even audience approaches to aid in locating recommended materials; and

analytical indexes, appendixes, or other specific features useful in helping students and teachers locate portions of works that may be in the school's collection.

For example, analytical entries in the H. W. Wilson series (*Children's Catalog, Middle and Junior High School Library Catalog*, and *Senior High School Library Catalog)* are useful for students, teachers, and media specialists in locating materials about specific subjects and people.

Where should one house these tools? Are they shelved in the media center office, or are they publicized and housed for maximum accessibility to all users? How can media specialists encourage students and teachers to use them? You should consider the multiple uses of these resources when justifying their cost and when deciding where to shelve them.

Selection tools exist in a variety of formats: books, reviewing periodicals, and bibliographic essays.

Books

Commonly used general selection tools that appear in book format are the H. W. Wilson series (*Children's Catalog, Middle and Junior High School Library Catalog*, and *Senior High School Library Catalog*). In 1994 the *Elementary School Library Collection* became available in both print and CD-ROM formats.

The lead time required to produce these books creates a time gap between the publication of the last item reviewed and the publication date of the bibliography. As a result, books are not as current as reviewing journals. A careful reading of the introduction can provide clues about whether a new title was not recommended or was not received in time for review in that edition of the bibliography.

Book format selection tools provide a means of checking recommendations for titles that have been available for 12 months or more. These selection tools are especially useful for determining whether titles listed in the teacher's edition of textbooks are recommended. Other book-formatted selection tools list recommended materials for specific subjects, audiences, or formats. (For examples, see Chapter 12 and Appendix B.)

Elizabeth Ann Poe, Barbara G. Samuels, and Betty Carter observe that

> book lists are all too often seen as complications of subjective rec-
> ommendations, when in fact they are the product of rigorous selec-
> tion policies. To eliminate this perception, selectors must share their
> processes and policies with their audiences (Poe, Samuels, and Carter
> 1993, 67).

Reviewing Journals

Reviewing journals evaluate currently published and produced materials. There is a wide range of these journals, each with unique and valuable features. Commercial firms, professional associations, education agencies, and other publishers produce reviewing journals; generally they are written for a specific audience, such as media personnel or classroom teachers. The coverage of materials that journals review may be limited by the following issues:

Format: print materials, audiovisual materials, computer software, text, and instructional materials.

Potential users: children in grades K–6, junior high school students, preschoolers through adults, and young adults.

Subjects: all materials that may be in a media collection or materials on a specific subject.

Particular perspective, such as *Multicultural Review: Dedicated to a Better Understanding of Ethnic, Racial and Religious Diversity* (1992–).

Reviews may be written by journal staff members or by professionals in the field. Signed reviews can provide clues to the reviewer's position or background that may be of value. Reviewing journals may also include articles, directories, or columns of interest to media personnel.

The selection policy printed annually in *School Library Journal* helps potential purchasers understand the basis for judgments in the reviews. Clearly explained symbols, such as those used in the *Bulletin of the Center for Children's Books* quickly clue the user to the recommendation.

Problems media specialists face in using the reviewing journals include lag time between publication and review; lack of access to reviewing journals for specific subjects; and limited coverage of audiovisual, computer software, and electronic resources.

There are legitimate reasons why journals may not review a specific title. One journal will not review a work unless it can be reviewed within a specific time after its publication. The reader of that journal cannot be sure whether an item was received after the reviewing deadline, was outside the journal's scope, or failed to meet other criteria. Each journal's policies and procedures may cause time gaps among various journals' reviews of a work. For example, testing material in the field is an advantage but adds time to the process.

The value of the assessments can vary in quality or in applicability to a specific collection. Note the reviewer's position and geographic location to decide whether his or her situation is similar to yours. The journal *Appraisal* offers a unique feature. Both a librarian and a subject specialist review items. Comparing reviews can offer more insightful information about an item than can be obtained from a single reviewer.

Trying to locate two or more reviews of a current title can be frustrating. Often the problem is caused by the limited number of items reviewed and by the lag time between reviews. Table 8.1 shows the number of reviews of books published annually by the major reviewing journals.

Table 8.1.
Number of Items Reviewed by Major Reviewing Publications

	Books			
	Juvenile		Young Adult	
Journals	**1997**	**1998**	**1997**	**1998**
Booklist	2,429	2,277	832	879
Bulletin of the Center for Children's Books	800	853		
Horn Book Guide	3,312	3,659		
Horn Book Magazine	275	259	78	67
Publishers Weekly	1,800	2,076		
School Library Journal	1,653	1,637	1,353	1,410

Locating reviews for audiovisual materials, computer software, electronic materials, and online databases is a challenge. These materials are reviewed less extensively than books. No one journal reviews all the formats found in media center collections. Table 8.2 displays a sampling of journals that review more than one format.

Cumulated indexes in the journals can be helpful in the search for reviews, but a more comprehensive approach to review indexing can be found in tools such as *Book Review Index, Book Review Digest,* or *Media Review Digest. Book Review Index* is available online (DIALOG file 137). *Book Review Digest* is available as a CD-ROM. The cost of such tools may require that all media centers in the district share them.

Table 8.2.
Reviewing Journals' Coverage by Format

Title	Book	CD-ROM	Computer Software	Online	Recordings	Video
Book Report	X	X				X
Booklist	X	X			X	X
Choice	X		X			X
Kliatt	X					
Library Journal	X	X		X	X	X
Library Talk	X	X	X			X
School Library Journal	X	X			X	X
Teacher Librarian	X				X	
VOYA	X				X	X

Bibliographic Essays

Bibliographic essays that describe and recommend materials about a subject, a theme, a specific use, or an audience can be found in journals such as *School Library Journal* and *Book Links.* These essays can be very helpful, but they demand careful analysis. Readers do not know whether the writer simply overlooked an omitted item or whether the writer deliberately omitted it. Usually, bibliographic essays focus on a specific component of an item and do not provide an overall assessment of the material.

Relying on Reviewing Media

Media specialists use reviewing media on a regular basis. If no selection committee exists, the entire burden of selection rests with the media specialist. To examine every item published or produced within a given year would be an impossible task.

What do media specialists look for in reviews? Janie Schomberg writes,

> I need and expect a lot from reviews. First, book reviews should be descriptive, objective statements about plot, characters, theme, and illustrations. Second, I expect book reviews to have an evaluative statement including comparison of the title being reviewed to similar titles and literature in general. Third, the potential appeal, curricular use, and possible controversial aspects of the title need to be addressed to fully inform me as a potential selector (Schomberg 1993, 41).

Remember that reviews reflect the writer's opinion based on her or his knowledge of materials and students. A variety of sources provide reviews. In addition to the ones noted earlier in this chapter, reviews can be found on Websites of individuals, professional groups, and commercial organizations such as Amazon.com. As with other review sources, try to determine the authority and background of the reviewer. Try also to determine whether there are guidelines for the reviewers and whether selection standards are used.

Whether your evaluation involves personal examination of items or relies on reviews, some materials will, for one reason or another, remain unused or prove to be inappropriate. Consider these situations as learning experiences. Schomberg observes, "There seems to be no way to avoid the occasional 'lemon.'… Selection of materials based upon reviews cannot be expected to be successful 100% of the time" (1993, 42).

You should base your decision whether to use reviews, involve others in personal examination of materials, or use a combination of methods on a number of factors. You must weigh the expense of time and money for selection tools, for subscribing to reviewing journals, and for arranging previews against the opportunity to help teachers and students become knowledgeable about materials and their potential use.

Evaluate reviews regardless of their format in reviewing journals or selection tools or on electronic listings by examining the following provisions:

Bibliographic information

Purchasing information

Cataloging information

Content, description, and evaluation of

> Literary characteristics: plot, character, theme, setting, point of view, and style.
>
> Usability: authority, appropriateness, scope, accuracy, arrangement, and organization.
>
> Visual characteristics: shape, line, edge, color, proportion, detail, composition, and medium style.

Comparison: author, illustrator, and other works.

Sociological: controversial or popular.

Other considerations: total artistic, book design, use, and audience.

In an analysis of reviews of Notable Children's Books between 1994 and 1996 by six standard reviewing journals, Bishop and Van Orden found that all six provided information needed for ordering the books, noting, "The content of the reviews varied greatly from one journal to another, depending on the category being analyzed" (1998, 178).

School Library Journal provided the most comprehensive bibliographic and ordering information. *Booklist* provided the most cataloging information. *Bulletin of the Center for Children's Books* offered the greatest coverage of descriptive and evaluative comments about literary and usability elements. *Bulletin of the Center for Children's Books* provided the greatest number of descriptive comparisons, while *Booklist* offered the greatest number of evaluative comparisons. Media specialists looking for specific features of reviews can consult the recommendations in Table 8.3.

Table 8.3.
Attributes of Reviewing Journals

Categories	Journal(s)
Bibliographic and Ordering Information	SLJ
Cataloging information	Bklt
Literary elements, description	BCCB
Literary elements, evaluation	BCCB
Usability elements, description	BCCB
Usability elements, evaluation	BCCB
Comparisons, description	BCCB
Comparisons, evaluation	Bklt
Potential use: description	Bklt
Potential use: evaluation	BCCB, SLJ
Potential audience: description	BCCB
Potential audience: evaluation	SLJ, BCCB
Total artistic effect: description	BCCB
Total artistic effect: evaluation	Kirkus
Book design: description	Horn Book Magazine
Book design: evaluation	Horn Book Magazine

Other Sources of Information

Information about materials can also be obtained from publishers, producers, distributors, vendors, and wholesalers. The information may be in catalogs or flyers or on the Internet; it is not evaluative.

PERSONAL EXAMINATION

There are many ways to obtain materials for personal examination. The most practical ways include visits by sales representatives, formal previewing arrangements, viewing Internet sites, visiting examination centers, and attending conferences.

Previewing

Previewing is one of the most efficient ways to examine materials personally prior to purchases. This is the practice of borrowing materials from an examination center, a producer, distributor, or jobber for a specific time for the purpose of evaluation.

Materials commonly evaluated through preview arrangements include video formats, laser discs, and software. Previewing is an effective way to involve students and teachers in the selection process. Review groups of teachers, administrators, and students may be organized by subject area or grade level. In his review of research, Daniel Callison observes that one of the arguments for involving students is that

> teachers and students tend to agree on software they do not like, but disagree on software they favor; students tend to favor simulation formatted programs, while teachers tend to favor tutorials that match established lesson plans (1990, 61).

If a committee is evaluating materials on a specific subject, make arrangements with several companies so the committee can examine their materials at the same time. When arranging previewing sessions, however, consider the committee's needs and limitations. Viewing too many versions of the same subject or same format can be fatiguing. Planning can prevent such situations.

An advantage of having the media specialist make the preview arrangements is the avoidance of several teachers requesting the same item for preview within a given school year. Media specialists should establish a previewing plan with the school administrator. This should ensure that the media specialist serves as a clearinghouse, asking all groups participating in previewing to provide evaluations of the materials and arranging for other evaluation sessions.

Previewing is not a free way to supplement the collection, nor should several teachers within one building request the same item for examination at different times. The media specialist is responsible for returning previewing materials in good condition within the specified time. Check the policy of the company from whom you are considering purchases.

Requesting materials you are seriously considering for purchase and planning for their systematic evaluation is an excellent way to make informed selection decisions.

Exhibits

Both teachers and media specialists appreciate the opportunity to examine materials firsthand. Some school districts arrange for exhibits of new materials in a central location during the pre-opening school activities. These exhibits allow media specialists and teachers to compare a wide range of materials, including software, on the same subject. If your school district sponsors such exhibits, invite teachers to examine the materials with you. In this way you can learn how teachers would use the materials, and they can learn about similar materials in the collection. As you watch demonstrations of newer materials and equipment, you can identify which teachers are interested in learning more about them. Exhibits at conferences also provide an opportunity to join teachers in examining materials.

Examination Centers

Another way to personally evaluate materials is to visit an examination center. These centers may serve district, intermediate, regional, or state levels. They may be housed in the district media center, at a university, or in a state agency. Some centers house materials ranging from curricular and instructional materials to trade books, software, CD-ROMs, and interactive video. Other centers or clearinghouses focus on materials for specific users or specific formats. Examination centers, such as the Children's Book Council, provide newsletters and other information.[1]

INVOLVING OTHERS IN SELECTION

The idea that teachers, students, and administrators should participate in making selection decisions is not new, but its practice is not as common as one would expect. Common ways to involve others in the process include:

> routing bibliographies and reviewing journals to teachers and administrators;

> attending faculty, departmental, or grade-level meetings to learn about curriculum changes and to discuss future purchases;

> conducting interest inventories with students; and

> involving teachers, administrators, and students in the selection decision-making process.

Advisory committees are another way to involve others. Teachers, community members, and students may be members of the advisory committee. The committee can play a variety of roles. In some districts, the advisory committee's responsibilities are limited to policy issues and to establishing priorities for acquisition. In other districts, the advisory committee may be involved in the selection process or in making decisions about which materials to remove or replace.

Teachers

Plan to acquaint teachers with the collection. Explain to them or involve them in developing the criteria you wish to use in the selection process and have reviews available for reference. During these sessions you will find yourself providing in-service education on how to evaluate materials. As you work with the group, you are helping people think critically. In addition, you are developing more active users of the media center, users who will support media center budget requests.

With proper preparation, teachers can contribute a great deal to the selection process; however, you must anticipate some problems. Any group made up of people with diverse views will experience conflict.

When you ask teachers or department chairpersons to make suggestions or to participate on selection committees, some may respond that they do not have time or do not view the center as having teaching materials in their areas of specialization. They may actually be expressing feelings of inadequacy about their knowledge of materials. Others may say that selection is your responsibility, not theirs. On the other hand, when you approach them for their expertise, either as subject specialists or as effective users of materials, many teachers will be glad to participate.

The best way to gain cooperation is to sincerely seek others' opinions, act on them, and inform these people of the results. Remember that teachers are busy and may lose interest if you do not accept their recommendations. If you are unable to buy a specific item they recommended, explain why. Be prepared to suggest a similar item. When the requested item arrives, notify the person who recommended the material and explain where it will be housed.

As you work with selection committees, record the reasons for decisions. Forms listing criteria with names of the evaluators and their ratings can simplify record keeping. Holding this information on file can prevent duplication of effort; it is easy to forget which items have been evaluated. The record also provides accountability when a decision is challenged. Ideally, one form should cover all types of materials (see Figure 8.1). In practice, however, it may be easier to develop separate forms for different formats.

Media specialists have found various ways to involve teachers. At Edison Middle School, Letitia, a social studies teacher, suggested establishing an endowment to create funding for unbudgeted or unexpected purchases. After the contract was drawn, Letitia invited the other teachers to be charter members. Later, Junko, the media specialist, invited community members and classes to contribute to the endowment fund. As the practice continued, people thought of the fund as an appropriate place to contribute memorial funds or other gifts.

MATERIALS EVALUATION FORM

Title _____ Author/Producer _____

Edition _____ Series Title _____

Publisher/Distributor _____ Place _____ Date_____

Format: _____

Appropriate Users (circle): P K 1 2 3 4 5 6 7 8 9 10 11 12 Adult

Curriculum Uses Include:

Information Uses Include:

Personal Uses Include:

CRITERIA	RATING				WHY? Comments
	Poor	Fair	Good	Superior	
Authoritativeness					
Accuracy or Credibility					
Organization					
Appropriateness of Content					
Aesthetic Quality					
Technical Quality					
Overall Rating					

Recommendation: ☐ Add 1 copy ☐ Add ___copies ☐ Do not recommend
☐ Uncertain Why?_____

Evaluator(s):_____

Evaluation test group:_____

Date: _____

Figure 8.1. Sample evaluation form.

When the interest from the endowment reached $1,500, a committee was appointed to identify appropriate categories for purchases. Because the collection was weak in software, several programs of interest to various departments were exhibited. Then Junko invited department chairpersons and faculty to attend a demonstration of the software. The group made their selections and prioritized them. When the materials arrived, the participating individuals were notified. Because not all the funds were used for these purchases, Junko took three of the department chairpersons to the district media center for a demonstration of additional computer programs.

Sarah, the media specialist at Bubbling Brook High School, uses a variety of techniques to involve faculty members in selection decisions. She consistently informs people of the arrival of the materials they recommended. In this case, a portion of the budget is reserved to buy materials that new teachers recommend. Sarah tries to purchase the items within a week so that new teachers know their suggestions are taken seriously. This practice gives her an opportunity to meet each new teacher and to share information about the collection.

Sarah encourages all of the teachers and administrators to make suggestions about materials they see at conferences or learn about through in-service programs. When new materials arrive, she displays them in the teacher's lounge or in the departmental areas. She uses a sign to ask teachers to indicate which materials they like or whether other materials should be obtained. When special funding becomes available for purchases, Sarah notifies teachers, giving them a deadline for submitting their suggestions.

She distributes photocopies of reviews to teachers and staff members who she thinks might be interested in specific items. She attaches a note asking, "Do you think this would be a valuable addition to the collection?"

Teachers and administrators also are encouraged to mark reviews and advertisements of materials they spot in their professional journals. Every year at the first faculty meeting, teachers are encouraged to look for materials that should be added to the collection. Teachers are reminded that ideas may come from in-service programs, course work, professional meetings, and professional reading. When the media staff know that teachers will be attending professional meetings, they ask the teachers to look for specific types of materials. As the teachers suggest them, media staff record which teacher suggested which item. Teachers are notified whether the item is purchased, when it arrives, and where it is displayed or stored.

In Sarah's school, students have independent projects and write research papers. She asks teachers which papers received good grades in order to identify papers in which the content met the teachers' expectations. This assessment gives a clue to the quality of the citations. Then Sarah checks the students' bibliographies to identify items that students found in other libraries. Those items are then considered for purchase.

Sarah encourages community members to participate in school activities. When exhibits, book fairs, or demonstrations take place, Sarah encourages the faculty, students, and community to attend. The response by parents has been favorable and has led to donations.

Suzanne, another media specialist, serves Rolling Hills High, a very large high school with buildings on a campus plan. She carries a clipboard so she can readily make notes as she talks with teachers. Suzanne also notifies teachers what action she has taken on their requests.

Students

Students can participate in some of the selection activities that primarily involve teachers, but there are many ways to involve students. When a sales representative brought Spanish materials to Sarah's media center, she took the representative to an area where Spanish-speaking students were working and asked them whether the school should buy the materials. They identified items they thought were particularly useful as well as some they thought were poorly presented or of limited use or appeal.

In Sarah's high school, tenth- to twelfth-grade students are required to take English. With the cooperation of the English teachers, Sarah visits each English class near the end of the year. She starts the session by asking, "In what subject areas did you have difficulty finding materials?" Sarah presents the budget, showing sources of funds and how they are spent. She points out how the students who pay taxes contribute to these funding sources. She also takes a printout of missing materials and shares the estimates of replacement costs.

Two issues frequently arise during these sessions. The first is the reading level of materials. Poor and reluctant readers complain about the difficult materials and about those they consider too technical. More able students complain about the simple materials that do not cover subjects in sufficient detail. The second issue relates to format. Students who are computer literate and competent searchers want greater access to online sources. Visually oriented students prefer materials on interactive videodiscs. The discussion often leads to problem solving, and Sarah tries to follow up within a day on specific suggestions for improvements so that students know they were heard.

At the close of the discussion, Sarah distributes three-by-five-inch cards on which students are asked to answer three questions anonymously. First, "What are your criticisms of the media center, its services, and its staff?" Second, "How do you suggest improving those weaknesses?" Third, "What does the collection need, and what do you as a student want?" She reminds the students that materials can include periodicals, recordings, newspapers, books, videos, software, online services, and CD-ROMs. If they do not know specific titles, they can suggest subject areas.

Sarah's budgeting strategy (she holds a reserve of $500 for items students request) allowed her to follow up on another student's suggestion. Joshua had an avid interest in collecting baseball cards but found few sources of information about the subject in the media center. Sarah spotted a useful title in a local bookstore and bought it. After it was processed, she prepared the book for circulation and took it to Joshua's English class, where she announced she had it ready for him. Such efforts on Sarah's part let students know that their suggestions are important. Joshua's classmates felt free to make other requests. Such practices may seem impractical, but the idea of seeking suggestions and following up on them can be applied in a variety of ways.

At Niles High School, Douglas, the media specialist, sets aside $350 for the purchase of popular compact discs. A student committee evaluates the suggestions from the student body and then recommends specific items for purchase. When the recordings arrive, announcements on the school's daily televised morning program inform students that the items are available.

In other schools students give brief reviews or announcements about new materials over the public address system, through the daily television broadcast, on the school's electronic bulletin board, or in the student newspaper.

If someone in your community reviews materials for the local newspaper or for professional journals, they may welcome students' reactions to the materials. The district media center may have titles that students may review. Through these experiences students learn how to evaluate materials and may find titles they want to suggest for the collection.

Even children in the first and second grade can begin to learn about the selection process. When groups of young children come to the media center to select materials for their classrooms, ask them the following questions: Do all your classmates share your interests? What other topics do they enjoy? Are there children who like more pictures in their books? Are there times when you want something to read quickly? Are there children in your class who prefer facts to stories? Didn't Natasha get a new puppy? Do you think she would like this videotape about taking care of a puppy? These questions help children begin to think about the materials they use.

Students involved in the selection process can help alert others to materials and opportunities in the media center. A classmate's recommendation often carries more weight, certainly more appeal, than the same recommendation from an adult. These examples highlight a few ways to involve students in the selection process and point out the advantages, insights, and excitement that media specialists can generate so easily.

CONCLUSIONS

The selection process calls for professional knowledge and judgment about materials and the sources that review them. The media specialist must be a knowledgeable consumer of the review sources, selection tools, reviewing journals, and bibliographic essays.

Careful planning, initiative, and interpersonal skills help to effectively involve others in the selection process. Collective evaluation of materials through personal examination and group discussion can increase the knowledgeable use of the media center's collection.

NOTE

1.   The Children's Book Council, Inc., is located at 568 Broadway, Suite 404, New York, NY 10012; 212-966-1990. [http://www.cbcbooks.org]. (Accessed November 10, 2000). Publishes *CBC Features* and other informational packets about children's books. Provides an examination center and information about new titles for children.

REFERENCES

Bishop, Kay, and Phyllis Van Orden. 1998. Reviewing Children's Books: A Content Analysis. *Library Quarterly* 68, no. 2 (April): 145–82.

Books in Print. New York: R. R. Bowker, 1948– .

Callison, Daniel. 1990. A Review of the Research Related to School Library Media Collections: Part I. *School Library Media Quarterly* 19, no. 1 (Fall): 57–62.

Canadian Books in Print. Toronto: University of Toronto Press, 1975– .

Multicultural Review: Dedicated to a Better Understanding of Ethnic, Racial and Religious Diversity. Westport, CT: Greenwood, 1992– .

Poe, Elizabeth Ann, Barbara G. Samuels, and Betty Carter. 1993. Twenty-five Years of Research in Young Adult Literature: Past Perspectives and Future Directions. *Journal of Youth Services in Libraries* 7, no. 1 (Fall): 65–73.

Schomberg, Janie. 1993. Tools of the Trade: School Library Media Specialists, Reviews, and Collection Development. In *Evaluating Children's Books: A Critical Look: Aesthetic, Social, and Political Aspects of Analyzing and Using Children's Books*, ed. Betsy Hearne and Roger Sutton. Champaign-Urbana: University of Illinois, Graduate School of Library and Information Science.

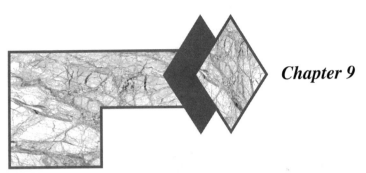

Chapter 9

General Selection Criteria

Selection is a complex decision-making process, not a simple, gut-level "I like this" response. Responsible collection development requires that broad considerations govern the evaluation and choice of a single item. The media specialist is responsible for the collection as an entity and for the individual items. You must base your choice on your evaluation of the item in question and its relationship to the collection. You should also formulate your justification for the choice of an item from an assessment of its contribution to the fulfillment of the policies and goals of the collection program.

Selection decisions require the evaluator to judge materials within the framework of given criteria. However, many selection decisions are subjective. Criteria must be established to guide decisions and lend consistency to this activity. These criteria can help one evaluate the content, physical form, or potential value of materials to users or programs. In the final decision to select an item for the collection, the media specialist must consider all the criteria. This chapter describes general criteria that one may apply to all types of materials, criteria related to intellectual content and its presentation, physical form, and equipment. Later chapters discuss criteria for specific formats; specific subjects; and for instructional, informational, and personal needs.

INTELLECTUAL CONTENT AND ITS PRESENTATION

When making selection decisions, the basic criterion is quality. Two fundamental questions must be considered. Is the format appropriate for the content? Does the presentation effectively address the users' needs? When evaluating an item's presentation, consider these questions: What is the idea (intellectual content)? How is it presented? Does the medium provide the most suitable treatment for the idea? Analysis of these questions provides the framework for this chapter. The criteria we provide are guides, not absolutes. The collection, the users, resource-sharing plans, and outside resources influence the applicability of each criterion to specific items.

How can one evaluate the idea, or intellectual content, of a work? Criteria include (1) authority, (2) appropriateness of content to users, (3) scope, (4) accuracy, (5) treatment, (6) arrangement and organization, (7) literary quality, (8) materials available on the subject, (9) durability of the information, (10) reputation of the author, artist, or producer, (11) special features, and (12) value to the collection.

Authority

The basis for the criterion of authority addresses the qualifications and abilities of the people who created the work. You can judge authority by considering the qualifications of the author or director, the quality and acceptance of other works by the same person, and the dependability of the publisher or producer. Does this work meet the standards expected from this person or organization?

Appropriateness of Content to Users

Appropriateness of content focuses on the content in relation to its intended use and audience. The concept must be appropriate to the users' developmental level. In other words, is the presentation geared to the maturity and interest level of the intended users? Whether the content is factual or imaginative, it should not be presented in a condescending manner, nor should it supersede the users' capacity to understand. An item should be appropriate for the students who will use it and not for some arbitrary standard established by adults.

Scope

Scope refers to the overall purpose and depth of coverage of the content. Examine the introduction, teacher's guide, or documentation for an item to learn the intended purpose and coverage. Evaluate whether the stated purpose meets a need of the collection and, if so, whether the material fulfills its purpose. When the content of the item you are considering duplicates content in the collection, consider whether that item presents content from a unique perspective. If it does, it may be a valuable addition that broadens the scope of the collection.

Accuracy

Information presented in materials should be accurate. Opinions should be distinguished from facts and, as much as possible, impartially presented. Accuracy is often linked to timeliness, or how recently an item was published or produced, especially in technological subjects where changes occur rapidly. Check with a subject area specialist, if necessary, to be sure the information is timely. Remember, however, that a recent publication date does not necessarily show that material is current or accurate.

Treatment

The treatment or presentation style can affect an item's potential value. It must be appropriate for the subject and use. In the best items, the presentation catches and holds the users' attention, draws on a typical experience, and stimulates further learning or creativity.

◆ Are signs (pictures, visuals) and symbols (words, abstractions) necessary to the content and helpful to the user?

◆ Are graphics, color, and sound integral to the presentation?

◆ Are the presentations free of bias and stereotyping?

◆ Do materials reflect our multicultural society?

◆ Is the information accessible to those who have physical limitations?

◆ Does the user control the rate and sequence of the content presentation?

◆ With electronic information, can the user easily enter, use, and exit the program? Are on-screen instructions user friendly? Do prompts and help screens provide clear directions? Is there an introductory or practice program?

The treatment of an item must be appropriate to the situation in which it will be used. Some materials require an adult to guide the student's use of material; other materials require use of a teacher's guide to present the information fully. Treatment may present very practical limitations. For example, is the length appropriate to class periods as generally scheduled, or are schedules flexible? The use of a 60-minute video may be problematic if the longest possible viewing period is 55 minutes.

Arrangement and Organization

Presentation of the material in terms of sequences and development of ideas influences comprehension. Content should develop logically, flowing from one section to another and emphasizing important elements. Does the arrangement of information facilitate its use? A chronologically arranged work may present difficulties for users searching for specific information if there is no subject index or keyword access. A summary or review of major points will help users understand the organization of the work, find needed information, and enhance effectiveness.

Literary Merit

The artistic effect literature serves is another area of evaluation. What theme or idea is the author trying to present? The theme should unfold in a coherent manner and be relevant to the child's real or imaginary world. Organization of plot, setting, characterization, and style should be consistent.

♦ Is the user's interest captured early?

♦ Does the plot develop logically?

♦ Does the story have a beginning, a middle, and an end?

♦ Are changes and developments plausible but not predictable?

♦ Does the description of the time and place evoke a clear and credible setting?

♦ Are the characters' actions convincing?

♦ Is the style or genre appropriate to the theme?

♦ Do the words and syntax create a mood or help to convey ideas?

♦ Is the point of view appropriate?

♦ What is the overall effect of the work?

One component should not stand out from the others, except for emphasis, creating a unity of literary elements.

Materials Available on the Subject

In selecting materials to fill a need for a particular subject, program, or user, availability may outweigh other criteria. This occurs frequently with current events, such as the election of a new president. Biographical information may be needed immediately, and there are few, if any, materials available for younger students. By the end of a president's first four-year term, there is a wide range of titles and formats from which to select, but requests tend to wane.

Durability of Information

The lasting value of information often relates to the scarcity of materials. The idea or subject may be stable or may change rapidly (such as political boundaries, fashions, or automobiles). Thus the subject presented and the information about it may change. An automobile assembly line today may be similar to one 10 years ago, but the materials, processes, and grouping of operations have changed. For rapidly changing subjects, less expensive formats may be preferable to more expensive formats, so replacements can be obtained more economically. As an example, for countries where political boundaries are rapidly changing, one may want to use news clippings until the situation stabilizes and materials that meet other criteria are available.

Reputation of Author, Artist, or Producer

Particular creators (authors, artists, or producers) and specific titles enjoy widespread reputations as essential to the education of students. For example, the classics are a staple of many collections. Does a work you are evaluating exemplify the contributions of its creator? If a particular work falls into this category, buy it and make plans to introduce it to students. This is an area in which a paperback collection might be appropriate.

Instructional Design

Materials designed for clearly defined instructional objectives should meet the expectations of the learner or teacher.

◆ Does the material encourage problem solving and creativity?

◆ Does it promote the understanding of ideas?

◆ Will users have the necessary capabilities (reading ability, vocabulary level, and computational skills) to learn from the material?

◆ Will the presentation arouse and motivate interest?

◆ Is evidence of field tests provided?

◆ Does the presentation simulate interaction?

◆ With electronic materials, do menus and icons always allow direct access to specific parts of the program?

◆ Is the screen well designed?

◆ Are instructions clear?

◆ Is there an effective use of color, text, sound, and graphics?

◆ Is clearly presented documentation provided?

◆ Are there suitable instructional support materials, such as hotlines, newsletters, and guides?

Special Features

Information or features that are peripheral to the main content of a work may be of value to the collection. Distinctive characteristics, such as maps, charts, graphs, other illustrations, and glossaries, can serve as reference materials. A record album may contain biographical information about the composer or performer; the teacher's guide may offer suggestions for follow-up activities or contain a bibliography of related materials. Does the information have an accurate and complete index? These special features can be a decisive factor in selection decisions that are less than clear-cut.

Value to the Collection

After evaluating the specific qualities of the item, the media specialist needs to consider it in relation to the collection.

◆ Does the item meet the needs of the school program or the users?

◆ Can it serve more than one purpose?

◆ Who are the likely users?

◆ How often would they use the item?

◆ Could an individual or a teacher in an instructional situation use the item for informational or recreational purposes?

◆ Is the item readily available through interlibrary loan?

Other Considerations

Series

The media specialist must judge each item within a series independently in terms of its value and known needs. Several authors may write books in a series, but not all the authors may be equally skilled. If one author writes the entire series, is that person equally knowledgeable about all the subjects presented in the series? Even an author of fiction may be unable to sustain the readers' interest throughout a series. Can the works function independently of each other, or is sequential use required?

Sponsored Materials

Particular organizations may produce and distribute materials often referred to as "free and inexpensive." They range from brochures, books, computer programs (*freeware* or *shareware*), games, maps, multimedia kits, posters, videocassettes, videotapes, television broadcasts, and real objects. You may need to return more costly items, such as videotapes, to the supplier after their use. The materials may provide more up-to-date and in-depth information than you will find in other materials. With expendable items, students can use them and incorporate them into their own presentations.

Sponsors include local, state, national, and international groups, such as government agencies, community groups, private businesses, and trade and professional associations. For example, you can obtain posters from foreign countries from airline and cruise ship companies. Embassies can provide information about their country. World Wide Web sites can help you locate photographs and other educational materials. The U.S. Government Printing Office and the National Audiovisual Center identifies materials available on a wide range of subjects.

When evaluating these materials in addition to applying general selection criteria and format-related criteria, one needs to assess whether the information presents a one-sided or biased view of the topic. Another consideration is the amount of advertising. Does it dominate the presentation?

Cost

The price of an item and the expense involved in obtaining it often strongly influences the selection decision. Is the item within the budget specifications? Is a less expensive but satisfactory substitute available?

If the material requires new equipment, peripherals, and supplies, you much consider the price of these. Are there periodic enhancements? Can your budget provide for these? Can the new equipment be used with other materials in the collection? The item should receive enough use to justify its cost.

PHYSICAL FORM

Although content is one basis on which to evaluate an item, you must also evaluate the packaging of the information, or its physical form. The quality of the content can be weakened if it is not presented through the appropriate medium. How does one decide which medium presents the content most effectively? This may appear to be a simple question; it is not. One of the primary criteria you must evaluate is the compatibility of content and format. In speaking of Michelangelo's *David,* Lillian B. Wehmeyer suggests that

> had a reader never seen the sculpture (or its model or photo), a purely
> verbal description, without visuals, would not likely enable him to
> envision more than a vague image. Just as the David must be seen, so

must Beethoven's Ninth Symphony be heard, corduroy be touched, lilacs be smelled, or wonton be tasted before a learner can begin to understand them (1978, 150).

Technical Quality

The media specialist must judge the physical characteristics of the item independently and collectively.

♦ Are illustrations and photographs clear and eye catching?

♦ Is there a reason for soft-focus effects?

♦ Is the balance of illustrations to text appropriate to the content and prospective user?

♦ Do colors express the theme or message?

♦ Are line, shape, and texture used effectively?

♦ Does the use of sound, visual materials, and narrative help focus attention?

♦ Is there a balance of music, narration, and dialogue?

♦ Are sound elements synchronized?

♦ Is the speech clear and effectively paced? Is the sound clearly audible?

♦ Are film techniques, such as clasps, animation, or flashbacks, used to focus attention or reveal information?

♦ Are the mobility of subjects, expressiveness of presenters, multiple camera work, resolution, and clarity used effectively?

♦ Is the result a smooth presentation with appropriate pacing, rhythm, length of sequences, and special effects?

♦ Does the item allow searching using Boolean logic, keywords, subjects, or truncation?

♦ Does the documentation or manual clearly explain how to use the software?

The appearance of the type can be expressive and provide clarity. Typeface used in projected images, such as transparencies, should project clearly and appeal to various audiences.

Aesthetic Quality

Both the external design and the presentation of the content need to be aesthetically pleasing: Separate aspects integrate to form an aesthetic whole. Is the item attractively packaged? Book jackets and album covers should appeal to the potential user. Does the design avoid colors that are difficult for people with colorblindness to distinguish?

Safety and Health Considerations

Safety and health features are particularly important when selecting tactile materials, but you should consider these issues for all materials. Is the item constructed of nonflammable materials? Can one clean the item? Realia present a challenge in terms of cleanliness. What can you do with a piece of salt from the Great Salt Lake that probably will be licked by 905 of the 1,000 students in the school?

Materials with movable parts pose problems, possibly with loss of integral parts. Models and kits may have parts that can cut fingers or be swallowed. Architectural models may collapse. Live animals can create health and safety problems.

Other Considerations

Will an individual or a group use the material? The media specialist must consider the potential number of simultaneous users in selection decisions. For groups, using a videotape based on a book might be preferable to using the actual book. The variety of uses for the material should also be considered. For motivation, games and live specimens invite participation. Videotapes can bring distant places to the user more dramatically than a map can. If creativity is to be encouraged, a programmed text may offer limited options. For example, programmed software can introduce a student to the basic principles of computer programming but may limit the creativity of a more technologically oriented student.

The media specialist should consider users' personal preferences, when they can be discerned.

◆ Will the viewer who first saw a telecast find a print version of the content equally acceptable?

◆ Will the person who first read a book appreciate the videotaped version?

◆ Does electronic access motivate students more than a manual search?

Translating a work from one medium to another can affect the treatment of the subject and the impact of the message. Verbal language differs from visual language. This difference can result in two seemingly unrelated works, ostensibly drawn from the same content.

Ease of use, storage, and maintenance are also important selection criteria.

♦ Can an individual or a group use the item with equal ease?

♦ Will workstations permit use of electronic media by several people simultaneously?

♦ Does the material require special storage?

♦ Is the item durable?

♦ Can it be easily replaced or repaired?

♦ Does the item include more than one part, such as a kit, that may include both print and non-print materials?

♦ Must all the items be used together?

♦ If a single item or part is lost, can the remaining parts be used?

♦ Can missing items, such as game parts, be replaced locally?

♦ Can they be purchased separately?

These practical criteria can be just as important as aesthetic considerations.

EQUIPMENT

Some materials require specific equipment for their use. In other cases one must provide certain conditions such as darkened rooms or rearview projection to use the materials effectively. One of the first considerations in evaluating an equipment purchase is whether the equipment will be used enough, in the short and long term, to justify its purchase and possible alterations to schedules or the physical environment.

♦ If the item is not purchased, will there be a negative impact on the program?

♦ Will teachers be unable to use desired materials?

♦ If the equipment is suitable for use only by a single teacher and class working in only one subject area, is there sufficient justification for purchase?

♦ What alternative approaches might work? For some items, short-term rental may be the best option.

Ease of Use

Complex equipment discourages use. In any case, the media specialist must provide proper conditions and facilities. Projection areas should have permanently mounted screens and adjustable light controls. Are rear screen units needed? These areas will need multiple outlets where the equipment will be set up. Will trained personnel need to operate the equipment? What is the teacher's responsibility? Are trained students or aides available?

Examine the equipment, keeping in mind the potential users.

- ◆ What level of manual dexterity must one have to operate the equipment?
- ◆ How many steps must one follow to run the equipment?
- ◆ Does the equipment have many controls?
- ◆ How operator-proof is the equipment?
- ◆ Does the equipment operate efficiently with minimum delay?
- ◆ Can one remove parts easily and possibly misplace or lose them?
- ◆ How much time does one need to teach students and faculty to use the equipment?
- ◆ Does each piece of equipment come with visual instructions?
- ◆ Are the directions complete, clear, and easy to follow?
- ◆ Are automatic operations dependable?
- ◆ Is there an option for manual or remote control?
- ◆ Are shut-off or cooling-down features automatic? Is the configuration for peripherals, networks, and teacher options, such as sound and record keeping, easy to use and well documented?

Physical properties of the equipment can deter use.

- ◆ Is the equipment constructed of strong materials? Durability is a key criterion.
- ◆ Have established safety specifications been met?
- ◆ Does the size, weight, or design of the equipment require that you use and store it in one location?
- ◆ Can one move the equipment to a cart?
- ◆ If equipment is used in a two-story building, is it too heavy or bulky to carry up the stairs? Circulating equipment should be lightweight and compact.

If the equipment will go out of the building, one must have weatherproof carrying cases. Are there straps or handles that aid in moving the equipment? The straps and handles should be strong enough to withstand the weight of the item carried any distance.

Performance, Compatibility, and Versatility

Equipment should operate efficiently and consistently at a high level of performance. Poor-quality projection or sound reproduction can negate the technical quality of materials so carefully sought during selection. What is the quality of mechanical construction? The noise or light from the equipment should not interfere with its use. Is the equipment subject to overheating?

Equipment needs to be compatible with other equipment and materials in the collection. Can one use the item under consideration with existing equipment and computer systems? Is special hardware or software needed? Is its use limited to materials produced by the manufacturer? Can the CD-ROM drive read other optical disc formats? Can the DVD drive read CD-ROM formats?

Equipment that one can use in a variety of ways may be desirable. Can an individual or a group use the equipment? Can one use it with more than one medium? If one needs to use attachments or adapters to achieve versatility, how easily can one use the peripherals? Will users need special training?

Safety

Safety features demand consideration, especially when young children will use equipment. The media specialist should choose equipment that has no rough or protruding edges. Is the equipment balanced so that it will not topple easily? Users should not come into contact with potentially dangerous components, such as a fan or heated element. Electrical connections should be suitably covered and grounded. If the equipment generates heat or fumes, adequate ventilation is necessary. The item should carry the Underwriters Laboratory (UL) or Canadian Standards Association (CSA) seal.

Maintenance and Service

The equipment should be built to withstand hard use, but plan for regular maintenance and service. What conditions do the warranties or guarantees cover? Can one handle minor repairs or parts replacement quickly and easily? Does the distributor or manufacturer offer in-service training on operating or repairing the equipment? The district or school may have a staff person assigned to do repairs. Some distributors and manufacturers provide on-the-spot repairs, whereas others require that the purchasers send the item to a factory. Does the manufacturer, vendor, or repair center provide replacement or rental while they are servicing the equipment?

Reliability of Dealer, Vendor, Publisher, and Manufacturer

The reputation of the distributor, manufacturer, publisher, and vendor is important.

◆ Does the manufacturer have a reputation for honoring warranties?

◆ Is delivery prompt?

◆ Does the manufacturer handle requests for assistance efficiently?

◆ Does the dealer have outlets near the school?

◆ Does the manufacturer provide support service through e-mail, telephone hot-lines, toll-free numbers, backups, preview opportunities, updates, refunds, and replacements?

◆ Is the support assistance readily available?

◆ Are the service hours convenient?

◆ Does the publisher or manufacturer provide demonstrations or in-service programs for teachers?

◆ Are they willing to negotiate licensing agreements?

Cost

The media specialist should weigh quality over cost but also consider budget constraints.

◆ Does a competitor offer a similar, less expensive item?

◆ Does the lower price represent lesser quality in terms of performance standards, warranties, or service?

◆ Are trade-ins allowed?

◆ Should one lease or buy the equipment?

◆ Is a dedicated machine necessary?

◆ Can the facilities support the equipment?

◆ Will the equipment under review require replacement parts that are different from items already in the collection or additional in-service training to operate it?

◆ Will teachers and students need time to learn to use the equipment?

◆ How much maintenance and cleaning will staff need to do?

◆ Will special technical training be necessary for minor adjustments?

Source of Information

Specifications for equipment can be found in the annual *Directory of Video, Multi-media, and Audio-Visual Products* (Fairfax, VA; International Communications Industries Association, Overland Park, KS: Daniels Pub. Group, 1996–).

CONCLUSIONS

Selection is a subjective activity for which the media specialist is responsible and therefore accountable. To fulfill this responsibility, the media specialist must ensure that the collection, as an entity, fulfills its purposes of meeting both the school's goals and instructional, informational, and user needs. To this end the media specialist must judge the value of individual items to the collection. Although selection decisions may be subjective, the media specialist must be able to justify the choice of any item.

A basic criterion for evaluating material is the impact of its intellectual content. What additional information or new dimensions in presentation will that item add to the collection? Will it appeal to users?

Another criterion is the appropriateness of the medium to the message. Does the form in which the message is delivered promote or hinder the purposes and use of the content?

These are the two basic criteria for judging all potential purchases. The media specialist must also consider additional criteria specific to various formats, uses, and needs.

REFERENCES

Wehmeyer, Lillian B. 1978. Media and Learning: Present and Future, Part I: Present. *Catholic Library World* 50: 150–52.

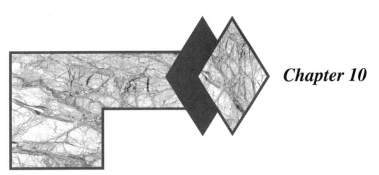

Chapter 10

Criteria by Format

People acquire knowledge through their senses: seeing, hearing, touching, tasting, and smelling. Various formats appeal to these different learning patterns. This chapter focuses on the characteristics of the different formats and how media specialists should consider them in selection decisions. All of the physical forms in which we find messages presented have unique qualities that suggest criteria for us to consider in the selection process. The formats are arranged in alphabetical order. Each description includes physical characteristics, advantages, disadvantages, selection criteria, implications for collection development, copyright considerations, and sources of information such as bibliographic tools and sources of reviews for that particular format.

For addresses of private and public organizations mentioned in the text, see Appendix A. For bibliographic information and fuller descriptions of the resources cited in this chapter, see Appendix B.

Although this chapter concentrates on format criteria, the decision to select an item involves a total evaluation of all of its various components as well as its value to the collection. Who will use the item and for what purpose? Does it fulfill a unique need? Selection decisions must take into account the physical item, its content, potential use, and appeal.

Art Prints *See* Graphics

Audiocassettes *See* Audiorecordings

Audiorecordings

Audiorecording formats commonly found in schools include audiocassettes, microcassettes, compact discs, and mini-compact discs. Each format requires appropriate equipment.

Advantages

1. Recordings are portable and easy to use.

2. A wide range of content is available.

3. Equipment is fairly easy to use and relatively inexpensive.

4. Music and sound effects can create moods or draw attention to specific information.

5. Use can be easily scheduled.

6. Information is locked into a fixed sequence. Specific sections can be easily located through use of bands on discs or counters on tapes.

7. Most students are familiar with the equipment and find it appealing.

8. Compact discs retain superb sounds for hundreds of hours.

Disadvantages

1. Listening for an extended period of time tends to induce boredom.

2. Different types of equipment are needed to accommodate the variety of tape speeds and track arrangements.

3. Use with large groups requires amplifiers.

4. Compact discs and cassettes are theft prone.

5. Cassette cases break easily. Have a supply of empty cases on hand.

Selection Criteria

1. Does narration begin with attention-getting words to capture the listener's interest? Are keywords or key statements emphasized to help the listener? Are the sentences short and simple?

2. Is the sound free of distortion?

3. Are the length and quality of the performance appropriate to the intended audience?

4. Do labels give enough information to distinguish one item from another? Do labels give playback information?

5. Are tapes and discs compatible with available equipment?

6. Is equipment easy to use and portable?

7. Does the equipment ensure accurate, high-quality reproduction?

8. If the recording is based on a book, is the recording true to the original?

9. Does the recording engage the listener's attention?

10. Are the accompanying materials, such as a teacher's guide, appropriate and useful?

Implications for Collection Development

The items should provide for individual and group use of music, documentaries, narrative presentations, and drillmasters. Storage for discs should be easily accessible and prevent warping. Compact discs are less likely to be damaged in circulation than cassettes.

Copyright Considerations

Reproducing musical recordings or converting them to another format requires written permission.

Sources of Information

Recordings are evaluated in *Elementary School Library Collection* and reviewed in *Kliatt: Reviews of Selected Books, Educational Software and Audiobooks,* and in *School Library Journal.* They are listed in *Schwann Opus, Schwann Spectrum, Words on Cassette,* and *Bowker's Directory of Audiocassettes for Children. Books in Print Plus* includes children's titles from Bowker publications (*Ulrich's International Periodicals Directory, Words on Cassette,* and *Bowker's Complete Video Directory*).

Books

Hardback and paperback books share similar characteristics but can fulfill different needs. Variations in size and typeface can affect potential use; layout, graphics, and photographs can enrich a text.

E-books introduce other considerations when purchasing. First, the term "e-book" describes various models. Walt Crawford advises that one should ask people what they mean when they use the term as some are more appropriate than others for media center collections. According to Crawford, the "open e-book" is an XML (eXtensible Markup Language)-based model that can be read on desktop computers, notebook computers, palmtops, and other handheld devices. Crawford warns that the "XML-based model may turn out to be less attractive than Adobe's PDF format, even if it is a standard" (2000, 56). "Instabooks" are digital copies of books and texts in the public domain, available free to download, print, or circulate. He foresees that "E-vanity and self-publishing" books will face the same problems as their traditional formats, the difficulty in being publicized or reviewed. "Extended books," according to Crawford, are those that have diskette or CD-ROM features that make them more than transcriptions; these should be called "electronic media" because they complement and extend print publishing.

Advantages

1. Books are usually designed for individual users.

2. The user can set the pace and stop in the process to recheck information or reread a section.

3. The table of contents and index can provide ready access to information.

4. Books are portable.

5. Books present a wide range of subjects and genres.

6. Books do not require equipment.

7. They are relatively inexpensive.

Disadvantages

1. Use of colored artwork or photography, although adding to appeal or clarity of text, increases the cost.

2. Movement is difficult to illustrate on the printed page.

3. Large-group viewing of the same material is impractical, except with "big books" (oversized paperback books).

4. Contact with books is a personal, internal experience; interaction and feed-back for the learner are difficult to achieve except in programmed texts.

5. Users must have the appropriate reading- and comprehension-level skills.

Selection Criteria

1. Are the shape and weight of the book appropriate for the intended audience?

2. How opaque is the paper? Print that shows through the page may be confusing to a young or disadvantaged reader.

3. Is the typeface suitable for the intended audience?

4. Is the spacing between words and between lines adequate for the young or reluc-tant reader?

5. Is the book jacket attractive? Does it reflect the content of the book?

6. Are the illustrations placed within the text where readers can use them easily, or are they bound together in an inconvenient location? Are they appropriate for the potential user?

7. Is the medium used for illustrations (for example, pen-and-ink drawings, block prints, or oil paints) appropriate to the setting and mood of the story?

8. Do the page layouts and color add appeal and clarity to the book?

9. When a readability formula, such as Fry or Spache, is applied, is the text appropriate for the intended audience?

10. Is the content accurate and current?

For a fuller discussion of selection criteria, see *Selecting Books for the Elementary School Library Media Center: A Complete Guide* by Phyllis Van Orden (Neal-Schuman, 2000).

Additional Criteria for Hardbacks

1. Are the bindings durable and covers attractive and easy to clean? Are reinforced bindings available for titles that very young children will use or titles that will circulate frequently?

2. Will the hardcover books lie flat when open?

Selection of E-books

When evaluating e-books, media specialists should apply traditional criteria and also consider both the licensing arrangement and the equipment necessary for using them. The latter is discussed more fully in Chapter 14.

Implications for Collection Development

Even though selections should cover a wide range of subjects and genres, one should also consider the reading and maturity levels of students. Order additional copies of popular books; paperbacks are an inexpensive way to meet these demands. A paperback book may appeal to some users more than the same title in hardback would. Policies should address questions such as what foreign languages to include and whether there is a need for large-print books.

As with other developing technology, a basic question is whether the media center will circulate the materials and provide any equipment needed to use the material. For discussion of other aspects of "e-books," see Chapters 13 and 14.

Copyright Considerations

Copyright law defines print materials as books, periodicals, pamphlets, newspapers, and similar items. A teacher may make a single copy of a chapter in a book, a short story, short essay, short poem, chart, graph, diagram, cartoon, or picture to use in teaching. For multiple copies the limit is 250 words for poetry and 2,500 words for articles, stories, essays, and picture books, with further limitations on each. A copyright warning notice should appear on each copy of a work. Creation of anthologies, compilations, and collective words are prohibited.

Sources of Information

Reviews can be found in *The ALAN Review, Appraisal: Science Books for Young People, Book Report, Bookbird, Booklist, Bulletin of the Center for Children's Books, Horn Book Magazine, Kirkus Reviews, Kliatt: Reviews of Selected Books, Educational Software and Audiobooks, Library Journal, Library Talk, Publishers Weekly, School Library Journal, Teacher Librarian,* and *VOYA*. Some of these journals are available in electronic format (see Appendix B for this information). To locate reviews, one can use the indexes in the individual journals or *Book Review Digest, Book Review Index,* and *Children's Book Review Index.*

Selection tools include *Children's Catalog, Fiction Catalog, Middle and Junior High School Catalog, Senior High School Catalog,* and *Elementary School Library Collection.*

Information about the availability and cost of books can be found in the following Bowker publications. In book format are *American Book Publishing Record, Books in Print, Subject Guide to Books in Print, Children's Books in Print, Subject Guide to Children's Books in Print, Publishers Trade List Annual,* and *Paperbound Books in Print.*

Cartoons *See* Graphics

Cassette Tapes *See* Audiorecordings

CDs *See* Audiorecordings

CD-ROMs

Compact disc read-only memory (CD-ROM) can provide access to very large quantities of digitally encoded information at relatively low cost. Graphics, sound, software, and other non-text items can mix with text. This format is used for encyclopedias, reference sources, databases, multimedia products, interactive books, games, music, Online Public Access Catalogs (OPACs), computer software, clip art, and graphics.

Advantages

1. A single CD-ROM can store the equivalent of 1,000 books.

2. A single disc can hold more than 650 megabytes of text, graphics, and sound.

3. The user can use the menu to see the interrelationships of people, places, and events as they relate to the entry.

4. With a good index, information retrieval is flexible.

5. Use of CD-ROMs helps students learn search strategies before going online, thus saving online charges.

6. The quality of images is high, and they do not fade as photographic images do. The images take less storage space than if they were individual slides or photographs.

7. CD-ROM discs are small, lightweight, and portable.

8. CD-ROM discs are durable, resistant to fingerprints, and the laser-beam reader does not come into direct contact with the disc.

9. Text downloaded from the CD-ROM is ready for word processing or other manipulation.

10. This format is very appealing to students.

Disadvantages

1. A CD-ROM player is required.

2. To read the screen requires turning on the computer and CD-ROM player. At times this involves a certain sequence of turning on various pieces of equipment.

3. Different CD-ROM discs require different retrieval software.

4. Access is slower than on hard drives.

5. Capacity is limited compared to online databases.

6. Information cannot be updated or changed in any way.

7. Use of a single CD-ROM is limited to one student or a small group, creating scheduling and teacher planning difficulties. Networking their use can alleviate these problems.

Selection Criteria

Criteria for CD-ROM and software are similar (see the discussion in the "Computer Software" section). Additional questions to consider are the following:

1. How frequently is the CD-ROM updated?

2. Does the cost of the subscription include the update?

3. Is there an annual fee?

4. Are on-screen tutorials provided? Are they simple and easy to understand?

5. Will a bundled package of applications rather than individual ones serve your purposes?

6. Is the menu system easy to use?

7. How fast is access to the information?

8. What is the quality of the video and audio production?

9. What is the technical quality of the underlying program, the manual, and the support personnel?

10. Does the CD-ROM contain a large amount of high-quality information?

11. Is there a significant number of hours of information and learning?

12. Are the advertisement and promotional materials accurate about the number of minutes or hours of full-motion video, high-fidelity audio, number of photographic images, and amount of text?

13. Is the CD-ROM truly interactive in the sense that users can explore options? Mambretti compares books and CD-ROMs by observing that "If a book is a 'page-turner,' that's good;...If a CD-ROM is a 'page-turner,' that's not good; it means the CD-ROM is boring" (Mambretti 1998, 40).

Implications for Collection Development

Plan procedures to establish (1) time limits for individual student use of a CD-ROM workstation, (2) number of printouts allowed, (3) fee if applicable, (4) security for discs, and (5) whether to have a dedicated machine for each disc. Plans should also include how to obtain copyright permission of the CD-ROM title copyright holder and to obtain appropriate licenses. These plans must be flexible and are best designed in conjunction with teachers. Administrators may be involved in setting a fee schedule.

When you find recommended titles you want to consider, find out whether you can obtain a copy of the CD-ROM for a trial period on your equipment. During the trial also evaluate the technical support found in the documentation, user manuals, and telephone help lines. If you cannot obtain the entire work for a trial, you might buy a single copy of one of the selections, install and evaluate it before purchasing the entire work.

Free demos can supply you with a look at content but may be technically different from the product. Use of previews (often with slide shows making a marketing pitch) can give you a sense of possible interest to your users.

Copyright Considerations

Unlike books, audiorecordings, maps, and so on, the physical medium (CD-ROM) is purchased, but the content is licensed for use. For multiple users or multiple copies of the disc at multiple workstations, you will need to obtain a site or network license to avoid the limitation of one user or location.

Sources of Information

For a full discussion of CD-ROMs and their management, see *CD-ROM Technology: A Manual for Librarians and Educators* by Catherine Mambretti.

School Library Journal and *Teacher Librarian* carry reviews of CD-ROMs, as does *Elementary School Library Collection.*

Charts *See* Graphics

Compact Discs *See* Audiorecordings

Computer Software

Computer software is available through educational institutes and consortia, commercial vendors, software companies, and textbook publishers. Shareware—courseware available at no cost—is available from the educational agency or other body that produced it.

Advantages

1. Software can be used for creative problem solving, drill and practice, testing, recreation, and guidance.

2. Individual and self-paced interactions are special instructional features of these systems. Programs can provide the reinforcement and stimulation needed by students who have learning disabilities.

3. Programs with branching allow the student with correct answers to move into more difficult questions, while allowing those who need to review and repeat responses the opportunity to do so.

4. These systems allow rapid information retrieval.

5. They provide instant calculations in programs where concept building is more important than mathematical manipulation.

6. Use of computers can be a highly motivating experience for gifted and average learners and learners with disabilities, thus bringing diverse groups to the media center.

7. Desktop publishing allows students to design and enhance their presentations.

8. Teachers can use record-keeping programs to monitor students' progress.

Disadvantages

1. Teachers who are not trained to use computers may be reluctant to use them in teaching.

2. Incompatibility of software and equipment can limit use.

3. Ignorance of special features of computers and poor programming can lead to improper use of the medium to teach material that could be taught more effectively using programmed instruction or other techniques. An extreme example of this is a program that is, in essence, an electronic page-turner.

4. There are more software programs designed to appeal to boys than to girls.

5. Students and teachers may have unreasonably high expectations of how quickly learning will happen.

6. The program may not accept creative or original student responses.

7. A high level of use can limit the amount of interaction of the student with teachers and other students.

8. A technical aide may be necessary to meet demands for assistance and instruction.

Selection Criteria

1. Are the software and equipment compatible?

2. Is the content more appropriate for presentation on a computer than on other instructional media?

3. Is the program designed to run on the user's computer? The computer's brand, model, memory size, operating system, storage format, display technology (monitor and graphics system), and accessories (mouse, game paddles, etc.) must be compatible.

4. Is the computer's disk operating system compatible with the software program?

5. Does the user control the rate and sequences of the content presentation (unless timing is an integral part of the program)?

6. Can the user enter, use, and exit the program with relative ease and independence?

7. Are the responses or feedback to answers (both correct and incorrect) appropriate?

8. Will the software design lead students to correct answers or remedial instruction when they need assistance?

9. Are on-screen instructions clear and easy to understand?

10. Are the student guides and worksheets, the teacher guide, and the technical information adequate and comprehensive?

11. Is the documentation clear and carefully indexed?

12. Does the program require the learner to be familiar with special terms or symbols related to computers?

Implications for Collection Development

What will the scope of the software collection be? Which strategies will it enable: tutorial, drill and practice, simulation, entertainment, or problem solving? Will you seek out teachers' opinions in deciding priorities among these strategies? Will the software circulate? Will it circulate to both teachers and students or only to teachers?

Copyright Considerations

One archival or backup copy of each program is permitted. To do this, you can use a "locksmith" copy to bypass the copy-prevention code on the original. For use at more than one computer (such as on a LAN [local area network] or WAN [wide-area network]), obtain a site license granting that coverage.

Sources of Information

Reviews and recommendations are given in *Elementary School Library Collection, Kliatt: Reviews of Selected Books, Educational Software and Audiobooks,* and *Technology & Learning.*

Availability information can be found in *Software Encyclopedia* and *Swift's Directory of Educational Software for the IBM PC.*

Diagrams *See* Graphics

Dioramas *See* Models

DVDs (Digital Versatile Disc)

DVD, formerly referred to as Digital Video Interactive, is a compact optical-disc format for digital storage and playback of full-motion video. DVD can hold cinemalike video, audio, and computer data. Although a DVD disc is identical in thickness and diameter to a standard compact disc, its storage capacity is seven times greater.

Advantages

1. DVD can deliver near-studio-quality video and better-than-CD-quality audio.

2. Instant search and stopping for a title, chapter, music track, and time code are possible.

3. The compact size is easy to store, and portable players are available.

4. The discs are durable. Wear does not occur from playing, only from physical damage.

5. Since 1993 all television sets sold in the United States have Closed Caption (CC) decoders. This permits the activation of on-screen text captions used by viewers with hearing impairment. These captions are located at the bottom of the screen below the person who is speaking and include descriptions of sounds and words.

Disadvantages

1. Careless production can create visible artifacts (anything that was not originally present in the picture), such as banding, blurriness, blockiness, fuzzy dots, and missing details.

2. The television set must be properly adjusted to handle the clarity of DVD.

3. Production of content materials (video programming, computer software, etc.) lags behind the development of the technology.

4. Poorly compressed audio or video may be fuzzy, harsh, or vague.

5. The production of materials has centered on those for the home-entertainment center, rather than those designed for educational and instructional purposes.

Selection Criteria

Criteria applied to video, audio, and computer software should be applied to materials on DVDs. As with other developing technology, additional questions are the following:

1. Is the standard used to judge the content of the same quality as for other materials in the collection?

2. Are the discs and the players compatible?

Implications for Collection Development

You will want to monitor the production of materials, which currently centers on presentations for the home-entertainment center, such as movies, rather than materials designed for educational or instructional purposes. Development and availability of DVD should also be monitored for its anticipated replacement of audio CDs, videotapes, laserdiscs, and CD-ROMs. When you add DVD drives to your systems, look for those that are designed to play CD-ROM titles.

Copyright Considerations

A number of copy-protection schemes are used with DVDs. One is the SCMS ("serial" copy generation-management system), which is designed to prevent copying. The copy generation-management system (CGMS) is embedded in the outgoing video signal, and one must use equipment that recognizes the CGMS. The U.S. Digital Millennium Copyright Act (DMCA), in which "don't copy" flags are incorporated by the producers, became law in October 1998.

Sources of Information

A comprehensive and updated source of information is Taylor's "DVD Frequently Asked Questions (and Answers)" (2000). As of this writing, reviews are most commonly found on the Internet. Taylor suggests doing searches such as "DVD review sites" at Yahoo. He provides links to a number of reviewing sites.

Games

A game is a simplified model of a real-life situation. It provides students an opportunity to participate in a variety of roles and events. Players must operate within the rules covering the sequence and structure of their actions as well as meet a time limit. Some games require using a computer or other equipment. Games available for use with computers tend to be designed for specific hardware and cannot be used with incompatible equipment from other manufacturers.

Advantages

1. Participants become involved in solving problems.

2. Games simulate a realistic environment, encouraging greater participation than other media.

3. Participation usually generates a high degree of interest.

4. Students receive immediate feedback.

5. Some games contribute to effective learning by motivating and supporting learning and attitudinal changes.

Disadvantages

1. Games can be time consuming, lasting up to several days. The intense involvement in a problem-solving situation is often incompatible with school schedules.

2. The limited number of players can create problems if others want to participate.

3. Games can distort social situations and create stereotypes when details are omitted or the creator has a bias.

4. Some teachers may not be aware of the learning value of games, and their input in selection decisions is highly desirable.

Selection Criteria

1. Is the packaging designed to store and quickly identify missing parts? Can lost pieces be replaced locally?

2. Are the items durable?

3. Are the directions clear?

4. Are the content, reading level, time requirements, and required dexterity appropriate for the intended audience?

5. Does the game require a computer? Will it run on the media center's equipment?

6. Is the game too costly or elaborate for its intended use?

Implications for Collection Development

The media specialist should consider commercially produced and locally developed games for inclusion in the collection. They serve many uses: educational purposes, practice of manipulative skills, opportunities for interacting with others, and relaxation.

Sources of Information

Booklist occasionally reviews games, as does *Elementary School Library Collection.*

Graphic Materials

Graphics are nonmoving, opaque, visual materials that provide information through verbal images, such as tables, and visual images, such as drawings. These materials include posters, graphs, charts, tables, diagrams, cartoons, art prints, study prints, drawings, and photographs.

Posters relate a single specific message or idea and should be selected for their clarity of design and attractiveness.

Graphs illustrate the relationship of numerical data. There are four major types of graphs. *Line graphs* present data on a simple continuous line in relation to a horizontal and vertical grid. *Bar graphs* show relationships through use of proportional bars. *Circle* or *pie graphs* display relationships as percentages of a whole. In *pictographs* or *picture graphs,* symbols present information.

Charts include tables and diagrams to present classified or analyzed data. Tables list or tabulate data, usually in numerical form. Diagrams show relationships among components, such as in a process or device.

Cartoons are stylized drawings, often in series, that tell a story or quickly make a point. Someone may need to explain the symbols in political and satirical cartoons to students.

Pictures include flat prints, art prints (reproductions of art works), and study prints. Study prints may have drawings or photographs on one or both sides, with accompanying text or a guidebook.

Advantages

1. Graphic materials are inexpensive and widely available.

2. Physical detail can be illustrated with X rays, electronic microscope photographs, and enlarged drawings.

3. Carefully selected pictures can help to prevent or correct students' misconceptions.

4. Graphic materials are easy to use, and some are easy to produce.

Disadvantages

1. Sizes and distances are often distorted.

2. Lack of color or poor quality may limit proper interpretation.

3. Students need to develop visual literacy in order to use these materials effectively.

4. The size of the material must be large enough for all members of a group to see the same detail.

5. Motion cannot be simulated, only suggested.

6. If an opaque projector is used, the room must be completely darkened.

7. Today's students are technologically aware enough to prefer presentations of more recently developed technologies.

Selection Criteria

1. Is the information presented in a precise manner?

2. Are less important elements de-emphasized or omitted?

3. Is the presentation unified? Are the basic artistic principles of balance and harmony observed?

4. Is the lettering clear and legible?

5. Is the size large enough for the intended audience?

6. Does an art print give an accurate reproduction of the original work's color and detail?

7. Are the framing and mounting durable?

8. Is a sufficient number of individual pictures used in a series to show a sequence of information?

Implications for Collection Development

If you anticipate a need to display the text on the reverse of a story print, consider ordering two copies of the print. The teacher's guide to the series may also duplicate the text on the reverse of a study print.

Circulating graphics, especially for home use, should be laminated, mounted, or protected in some way. Special storage units may be needed so students can examine the materials without damaging them.

Copyright Considerations

Charts, graphs, diagrams, drawings, cartoons, and pictures that are not individually copyrighted can be copied in multiples at the rate of one per book or periodical.

Sources of Information

The catalogs of art museums, art galleries, or reproduction distributors provide ordering information, and many serve as visual reference works. One example is the National Gallery of Art's *Color Reproductions Catalog*, which describes postcards, plaques, and reprints from the gallery's collection. Prints are reviewed in *Booklist, Elementary School Library Collection*, and *School Library Journal*.

Interactive Videos *See* Videos

Kits

A kit contains a variety of formats in one package. The materials may be pre-selected to present information in a fixed sequence for use by one person; they may be designed for user self-evaluation. Other kits and packages are less structured, such as a collection of related materials that can be used singly or in any combination by an individual or a group.

Advantages

1. Various formats relating to a specific subject are combined in one package.

2. Programmed kits are designed to bring all users to the same level of development.

3. Kits that include sound recordings of accompanying text materials can help the learner who has difficulty reading.

Disadvantages

1. One kit may include material designed for several grade levels.

2. Some kits may include materials that duplicate items in the collection.

3. Kits may be very expensive.

4. Lost non-replaceable parts may render a kit unusable.

Selection Criteria

1. Does the kit create a unified whole? Is there a relationship among its parts?

2. Is special equipment needed to use the materials in the collection?

3. Does each item in the kit meet the criteria for that format?

4. Is the kit difficult to use?

5. Are the directions clear? Is adult guidance needed?

6. Does the kit fulfill a unique purpose that other materials in the collection do not meet?

7. Is there room to store the kit?

Implications for Collection Development

Select kits on the basis of their potential use and appeal. Students and teachers may prefer to create kits using materials from the collection.

Sources of Information

Kits are reviewed in *Booklist* and *Elementary School Library Collection.*

Laser Discs *See* Videos

Magazines *See* Periodicals

Maps and Globes

Materials included are flat maps, wall maps, and globes. When a map is published in a book, evaluate it in light of the criteria listed under "Books."

Advantages

1. Maps can provide a wide range of information: place locations and spellings; significant surface features; distances between places; and scientific, social, cultural, political, historical, literary, and economic data.

2. Several people can simultaneously study wall maps.

3. Unlabeled outline maps or globes encourage children to learn the names, shapes, and locations of political and topographical features.

4. Maps are readily available at a wide range of prices.

Disadvantages

1. If a group of students is to examine the same detail in a map, multiple copies or a transparency may be needed.

2. Cartographic details, especially those on geographic, scientific, or political topics, quickly become outdated.

Selection Criteria

1. Is the map aesthetically pleasing? Does the color code help the user interpret the information?

2. Is the depth of detail suitable for the intended audience?

3. Is the map legible? Are symbols representational and clearly designed? Are printed markings of a size and type suitable to a particular map?

4. Is the item durable? Has plasticized or cloth-backed paper been used?

5. Is the surface non-glare?

6. Do the details obscure essential information?

7. Is a laminated surface that allows erasable writing for instruction available on large wall maps?

Implications for Collection Development

The collection should include maps of various sizes to meet the different needs of individuals and groups. Simple neighborhood, community, and state maps should be available to students, as should more complex geographic, political, and literary maps. Maps should be easily accessible; be sure to reinforce or otherwise protect those that students use frequently.

Copyright Considerations

For general guidelines, see the comments under Graphic Materials.

Sources of Information

Catalogs of map and globe publishers are the easiest to use and least expensive sources of information about the availability of this medium. Federal and state agencies, chambers of commerce, and travel agencies are common sources of highway and historical maps. Reviews are scarce.

Microforms

Microforms include microfilm (reel), microcards, and microfiche (a sheet of microfilm).

Advantages

1. A microform copy of a title is less expensive than the paper version.

2. Microforms can be converted to hard copy with proper equipment.

3. Primary source materials can be protected and stored.

4. Storing magazines and newspapers requires less space with these formats.

Disadvantages

1. The cost of equipment needed to use a small collection of microforms outweighs the low cost of the microforms.

2. Finding a specific section of a document often takes longer than it would if one were using the paper format.

3. These formats have less user appeal than identical content in other formats.

Selection Criteria

1. Does the collection contain the equipment needed to view the specific type of microform you are considering?

2. Does the material meet the criteria for its equivalent print format?

3. Is the equipment easy to use?

4. The media specialist should base the choice of negative or positive reproduction on the equipment available and the users' preferences.

Implications for Collection Development

Newspapers and magazines may be easier to store in microforms, but hard-back books may be easier to use than microform copies. Some media specialists find that subscribing to the microfilm edition of a newspaper such as the *New York Times* is more economical and efficient than subscribing to the paper edition. If a collection includes professional materials and the proper equipment is available, microform documents, such as those from the ERIC Clearinghouse on Information and Technology, can be obtained and stored at a lower cost. Be sure to consider equipment that can project both microcards and microfiche if both formats are in the collection.

Copyright Considerations

If the original work is copyrighted, users can make copies following the rules that apply to the format of the original work.

Sources of Information

For available titles see *Guide to Microforms in Print: Author/Title.*

Mock-ups *See* Models

Models

Models, dioramas, and mock-ups are representations of real things. A model is a three-dimensional representation of an object and may be smaller or larger than the real object. Cut-away models show the inside of an object. Dioramas provide an impression of depth, with three-dimensional foreground against a flat background. Mock-ups stress important elements of the object.

Advantages

1. These formats offer a sense of depth, thickness, height, and width.

2. They can reduce or enlarge objects to an observable size.

3. They can simplify complex objects.

4. The model and mock-up can be disassembled and reassembled to show relationships among parts.

Disadvantages

1. The size of models may limit their use with a group.

2. Some models are difficult to reassemble.

3. Loose parts are easy to misplace or lose.

4. Specially designed shelving and storage units may be needed.

Selection Criteria

1. Are size relationships of the part to the whole accurately portrayed?

2. Are parts clearly labeled?

3. Are color and composition used to stress important features?

4. Will the construction withstand handling?

Implications for Collection Development

The size of many of these materials creates storage and distribution problems. Packaging models for circulation may also be difficult. Materials produced by staff and students may lack the durability needed for permanent inclusion in the collection.

Sources of Information

Bibliographic and review information is not readily available. Suppliers of scientific equipment, such as Ward's Natural Science Establishment or Denoyer-Geppert Scientific Company list their products in catalogs.

Multimedia Kits *See* Kits

Newspapers

Two types of newspapers commonly found in media center collections are the generally circulated types, such as the *New York Times,* and those for instructional purposes, such as *Weekly Reader.*

Advantages

1. Newspapers are a familiar format as a source of information to students.

2. Local ethnic and special audience papers will appeal to members of those groups.

3. Some newspapers, such as *USA Today,* pictorially display data, making them accessible to those comfortable with figures and graphs.

Disadvantages

1. Storage can be a problem.

2. There may be periods of two to three months for the microform version of major papers to be commercially produced and one to three years for microfilming of local papers.

3. Newspapers in the CD-ROM format will provide content more consistently than the same newspaper in an online format.

Selection Criteria

1. Is the content of interest to students and teachers?

2. Are subjects treated clearly in a well-organized manner?

3. Are the illustrations pertinent and adequately reproduced?

4. Do any users need large-print editions?

5. Do the strengths of the newspaper fulfill a need within the school? For example, the *LA Times* has had extensive coverage of issues of interest to the Latino community.

6. Is the paper directed to a local, regional, national, or an international audience?

7. Who controls the editorial page? Are staff members named and articles signed?

8. Does the newspaper feature visual materials with attention-getting pictorial information and clear graphics? Is this an important feature for your users?

9. Does the newspaper offer a snapshot view of the content, or does it offer in-depth coverage? Which is needed?

10. In which formats (print, CD-ROM, or online) are the newspapers you need available?

11. Is the content the same in all formats? For example, are news items included but not syndicated columns?

12. How frequently is the information updated?

13. In the case of electronic newspapers, how easily can one retrieve back issues?

14. Does one need to use certain software to download articles?

Implications for Collection Development

Local, state, national, and international newspapers should be represented in the collection through subscriptions or through access on the Web. If classes subscribe to instructional newspapers, the media specialist may find it useful to have a copy of the teacher's edition in the media center.

Copyright Considerations

A teacher can copy a chart, graph, diagram, cartoon, picture, or an article from a newspaper for instructional use. Word limits for multiple copies for classroom use are 250 words for poetry and 2,500 words for articles. A copyright warning notice should appear on each copy. Creation of anthologies, compilations, and collective works are prohibited.

Sources of Information

Check http://www.umi.com to see which newspapers are available on CD-ROM. Check with your local public library to learn which papers and or microfilmed papers are available there. If your local university library has a newspaper librarian, contact that person. Unfortunately many libraries do not have such a position.

Online Databases

Online databases provide electronic access to information through the use of a computer with a modem connected to a telephone line. Four types of databases are the following:

1. Full text: includes all the information available for a certain record. Examples are encyclopedias, novels, magazine articles, or entire newspapers.

2. Bibliographic: provides citations and may include abstracts. An example is a magazine index.

3. Directory: provides a list of information. An example is a faculty and staff directory.

4. Numeric: contains numbers. Examples are population and census figures.

Advantages

1. Provide rapid access to large quantities of information.

2. Information is current.

3. Users can locate all the information in a one-step process.

4. Users can modify searches during the process.

5. Immediate feedback lets users know whether information is available and whether their search strategy was too narrow or too broad.

6. The information provides complete citations.

7. Bibliographies are easy to generate.

8. Users can save search strategies. This can help a user who is interrupted during a search.

Disadvantages

1. Not all the subjects in the curriculum may be included.

2. Users need training in search strategies.

3. Users need training in evaluating and selecting information.

4. Users need training in interpreting the bibliographic information.

5. Teachers and media specialists may be unable to quickly determine whether students are downloading information without analyzing it, evaluating it, or synthesizing information from several sources.

6. Teachers may need assistance in designing assignments that call for evaluation of information, rather than merely locating a predetermined number of sources on a topic.

7. Materials cited may not be available locally, and interlibrary loan requests may increase.

8. Information generated before 1970 might not be included, limiting historical searches.

9. Full text information might not include graphics from the original work.

10. Monographs are not covered as adequately as periodical articles and newspapers.

11. Downtime and malfunctions frustrate users.

Selection Criteria

1. Are the intellectual level and reading level appropriate for the intended users?

2. Will students use the disciplines covered in the database?

3. How is the database indexed? Can students conduct searches using title, author, or keywords?

4. Can students search the database using words not considered subject descriptors (that is, free-text searching)?

5. Can the searchers use Boolean logic, connecting search terms with *and, or,* and *not*?

6. Are cross-references provided?

7. How frequently is the database updated? Is this appropriate for the curriculum needs?

8. How accurate is the information?

9. What years does the database cover?

10. What services does the vendor offer? These can include offline printing, training, and help with problems.

11. How clear is the documentation? Does it include sample screens and other aids?

12. Is there a print version? Is the online search time less than that required for searching the print version?

13. Is the screen easy to read? Do directions or icons distract the user?

14. Are orientation materials, such as practice files, available in order to avoid the online costs for practice sessions?

15. What are the sources of the information on the database?

16. What criteria or standards were used in creating the database?

17. Can the users access the database from home after school hours? Is the vendor willing to negotiate this service?

Implications for Collection Development

Basic questions arise when making a decision on whether to subscribe to and use an online service. Costs may include an annual fee, a per-search fee, a per-hour fee, updates fees, and fees for other services. The users will need sufficient equipment: Should you lease or purchase it? Licensing agreements identify constraints and limits on use. When you sign such agreements, you agree to the conditions the vendor imposes. Agreements with vendors can affect use. The number of interlibrary loan requests may increase as searchers identify resources not available in the media center. Periodical collections and funds for document delivery may need to be expanded to support requests for cited articles. Future funding concerns may necessitate the formation of resource-sharing plans to accommodate the increase in requests for resources the media center does not own. Will administrators provide a separate budget for expenses?

Copyright Considerations

License agreements usually define what the publisher considers to be fair use of the product. Limitations may include the amount of information that users can download or the number of users who may access the service at the same time.

Sources of Information

In-depth reviews are found in *Online: The Magazine of Online Information Systems,* which features articles about databases and user search aids.

Pamphlets

Pamphlets are multiple-page, printed materials that are frequently housed in the vertical file rather than shelved as books. Local, state, and national governments as well as associations or businesses publish them. Pamphlets and other vertical file materials can provide a wealth of current and special treatment of timely subjects. Government documents frequently provide concise and up-to-date information about a topic, although the vocabulary may be beyond the elementary school pupil's comprehension.

Advantages

1. Pamphlets are inexpensive or free. Media specialists can readily obtain duplicate copies for topics of high interest.

2. Often information found in pamphlets is more current than that in other print media, except magazines and newspapers.

3. Pamphlets can provide a variety of viewpoints on a subject.

4. Pamphlets often discuss subjects unavailable elsewhere in the collection. Their treatment is usually brief, focusing on a specific subject.

Disadvantages

1. Because of their size and format, pamphlets are easily misfiled.

2. The flimsy construction of pamphlets limits repeated use.

3. Free pamphlets issued by organizations or corporations may take a specific position on issues or contain a great deal of advertising.

Selection Criteria

1. Because groups or businesses sponsor many pamphlets, media specialists must consider the extent of advertising. Does it dominate the presentation and distract from or distort the information?

2. Regardless of whether the item contains advertising, is the message presented without bias and propaganda? Specific instructional units may call for pamphlets that present various viewpoints. Does the viewpoint interfere with objectivity?

3. Is the information provided elsewhere in the collection?

Implications for Collection Development

Pamphlets are an inexpensive way to provide balanced information on controversial issues. Materials should be readily accessible, and media specialists should review them periodically for timeliness. Because many pamphlets are undated, media specialists find it helpful to date them as they file them. This simplifies the re-evaluation process. As new version of pamphlets arrive, the old ones should be removed.

Copyright Considerations

Some pamphlets have copyright limitations. Others, particularly those that government agencies produce, frequently have no copyright limitations. The user needs to examine each pamphlet for the copyright information.

Sources of Information

Publications from the United States Government are identified in *Guide to Popular U.S. Government Publications* and *Tapping the Government Grapevine: The User-Friendly Guide to U.S. Government Information Sources.* The U.S. Government Printing Office's *Monthly Catalog* is available at http://www.access.gpo.gov/.

Other listings appear in *The Consumer Information Catalog, Government Reference Books: A Biennial Guide to U.S. Government Publications, Monthly Catalog of United States Government Publications, U.S. Government Books,* and *Vertical File Index: A Subject and Title Index to Selected Pamphlet Materials.*

Periodicals

Three types of periodicals commonly found in media center collections are general types, such as *Time* and *Ranger Rick's Nature Magazine;* those for instruction, such as *Literary Cavalcade;* and professionally oriented titles, such as *Reading Teacher.*

Advantages

1. Periodicals offer short stories, participatory activities for young users, and extensive illustrations.

2. Some periodicals solicit contributions of writing or illustrations from students.

3. Many periodicals suggest activities that adults can use with students.

Disadvantages

1. Circulation controls are difficult to establish. Periodicals lend themselves to theft and mutilation.

2. Many magazines on popular topics disappear from collections when students take them or teachers borrow them for a "great" bulletin board pattern.

3. When a large number of children are involved, reader participation activities (such as fill in the blanks, connect the dots, or puzzles) need to be copied or laminated so they can be used more than once. Copying is subject to copyright restrictions.

4. Storage space that provides easy access to several volumes of a journal may be difficult or expensive to provide.

5. If foldouts and cutouts, such as calendars or photographs of sports figures or animals, are removed from periodicals, portions of the text may be eliminated.

6. The number of advertisements in journals may detract from their usefulness.

Selection Criteria

1. Is the content of interest to students and teachers?

2. Are subjects treated clearly in a well-organized manner?

3. Are the illustrations pertinent and adequately reproduced?

4. Is the format appropriate for the purpose of the magazine and the intended audience?

5. Do any users need large-print items?

6. Is the journal indexed? Commonly used indexes include *Children's Magazine Guide: Subject Index to Children's Magazines, Abridged Reader's Guide to Periodical Literature, Readers' Guide to Periodical Literature,* and online indexes, such as CARL's *UnCover,* and CD-ROM indexes, such as EBSCO's *Magazine Articles Summaries* (*MAS*).

7. Does the electronic version have the same coverage as the print version?

8. How easy is it to access back issues?

9. How is the electronic version updated?

10. Does the electronic version provide links to other electronic sources?

11. How easy is it to download articles?

Implications for Collection Development

The length of time one keeps periodicals will depend on patterns of use and availability of storage facilities. A common practice is to acquire microform editions for items needed after five years and to either clip the others for the vertical file or discard them. Anticipated use and whether by individuals or large groups plus cost will be key factors in deciding whether to obtain periodicals in print, online, or CD-ROM formats.

Copyright Considerations

A teacher can copy a chart, graph, diagram, cartoon, picture, or article from a periodical or newspaper for instructional use. Word limits for multiple copies for classroom use are 250 words for poetry and 2,500 words for articles. A copyright warning notice should appear on each copy. Creation of anthologies, compilations, and collective works are prohibited.

Sources of Information

Books in Print Plus includes children's titles from Bowker publications (*Ulrich's International Periodicals Directory, Words on Cassette,* and *Bowker's Complete Video Directory*), periodicals, and bibliographies.

Posters *See* Graphics

Realia

Realia include real objects, such as artifacts, stamps, postcards, plants, and animals, which may be preserved or imbedded in plastic. They bring the real world into the hands of inquisitive users.

Advantages

1. Students can handle and closely examine real objects.

2. One can inexpensively acquire some objects, such as stamps and postcards, from a wide range of sources, including the students themselves.

3. Breeders and the staff of local zoos and museums may be willing to lend or handle live specimens.

4. The handling and care of live specimens has many benefits for students and can provide an area of lively interest in the media center, especially in elementary schools.

5. Fragrant specimens, such as plants and cocoa beans, provide means for young people to learn through the sense of smell.

Disadvantages

1. Students can easily drop and break glass containers.

2. Some items may be too fragile or too small for more than one person to use at a time. Other items, such as an abandoned bird's nest, are hard to keep clean or even retain the original shape.

3. Live specimens need proper care: They may require aquariums, terrariums, or cages, and special growing conditions may need to be simulated.

4. Live specimens are most successful in media centers where adults share the students' appreciation of plants, fish, reptiles, and animals. Are you prepared to find the snake that slipped out of someone's hand or to track down the hamster scurrying in and out of the shelving units?

5. Live specimens need care when school is not in session. Sometimes one can arrange for students to take specimens home over vacations.

Selection Criteria

1. Is there a display area where several students can observe specimens at the same time?

2. Are you or is someone else willing and available to take care of the live specimens?

3. Are the specimens safe to handle?

Implications for Collection Development

Avoid duplicating specimens found in other departments of the school, such as the science laboratory.

Sources of Information

Journals such as *Science and Children,* have articles about the use of specimens and sometimes review these materials. Scientific supply houses, such as Ward's Natural Science Establishment, Denoyer-Geppert, and Hubbard Scientific Company, sell specimens and storage units. Local museums, zoos, and botanical gardens may lend materials to schools and provide speakers or visual programs about the materials.

Records, Phonograph *See* Audiorecordings

Sculpture

Sculpture and sculpture reproductions facilitate tactile learning and the development of aesthetic values.

Advantages

1. Sculpture reproductions are fairly inexpensive.

2. The use of sculpture is not limited to art study but may also be appropriate in social science, mathematics, language arts, science, and other subject areas.

3. Displaying the pieces about the media center can enhance the room's atmosphere and solve a storage problem.

Disadvantages

1. An item may be too small for a group to use.

2. Storage may pose a problem.

3. The size and weight of some pieces may make circulation awkward.

Selection Criteria

1. Is the item made of durable material that will withstand the touching that sculpture invites and which is necessary to fully appreciate the work?

2. Are reproductions true to the originals?

Implications for Collection Development

The range of subjects should reflect the various areas of the curriculum as well as the students' interests.

Sources of Information

Many museums, such as the Metropolitan Museum of Art and some commercial firms make reproductions of sculptures. You will probably find examples on display at state and national conferences. Request museum catalogs.

Slides

Two types of slides are (1) two-by-two-inch slides used with projectors with trays, carousels, or cartridges, on slide sorters, or in individual viewers and (2) microslides of biological specimens used with a microprojector.

Advantages

1. Color visuals are economical to produce.

2. Their size permits compact packaging and storage with ease of distribution and circulation.

3. Instructors can adapt sequencing and can edit according to their needs.

4. Sound can be ordered or added with the proper equipment.

5. Microslides permit an entire class to view microscopic materials, rather than requiring each student to have a microscope.

6. Slides can be projected for an indefinite time to accommodate discussion.

Disadvantages

1. Single slides are difficult to access rapidly.

2. Although slides are inexpensive to process or duplicate, this takes time and depends on the quality and speed of local laboratory services. Fast service is often available but at a substantially higher cost. Copyright restrictions apply.

Selection Criteria

1. Are art slides faithful to the original?

2. Are mountings durable?

3. Is there continuity to the set of slides?

4. Are content and length of presentation appropriate for the intended purpose and audience?

Implications for Collection Development

Effective group use of slides may require projectors with remote-control features and lenses of appropriate focal length. Ensure that slide storage and display units are compatible with the collection's equipment. Student- and teacher-produced slides should meet the same criteria as purchased items.

Copyright Considerations

Copying slide sets in their entirety, altering a program, or transferring a program to another format requires written permission. Copying a few slides is permitted when fair-use criteria are met.

Sources of Information

Examples of groups that produce slides are the American Museum of Natural History, Metropolitan Museum of Art, National Audubon Society, National Gallery of Art, and National Geographic Society.

Software *See* Computer Software

Specimens *See* Realia

Study Prints *See* Graphics

Tables *See* Graphics

Tape Recordings *See* Audiorecordings

Textbooks and Related Materials

Instructional systems encompass a broad range of materials designed to meet stated instructional objectives. Materials include textbooks (basic and supplementary), workbooks, and multimedia packages (kits). Commercial companies, school districts, and educational agencies have developed these materials. Textbooks may be used as chief sources of information or as supplementary information sources.

Advantages

1. Instruction is in a fixed sequence but is usually flexible enough for the instructor to reorganize.

2. The table of contents and index facilitate rapid access to information.

3. Each student may have a copy.

4. The teacher's editions offer suggestions for related materials and activities.

5. Textbooks are field tested, and one may request and evaluate the results of those tests.

6. Users can move at their own pace.

Disadvantages

1. Adoption of textbooks often implies they will be used over a number of years.

2. Textbooks can limit a teacher's creativity.

3. Textbooks may encourage rote learning rather than stimulate exploration.

4. The content to be covered can be determined by the limitations of the text.

5. A textbook's bibliographies may cite out-of-print materials or fail to reflect appropriate resources in the collection.

Selection Criteria

Teachers in consultation with media specialists usually select the textbooks or other instructional systems. In some situations, the media specialist may not participate, but the criteria presented here provide basic information necessary to consider in making selection decisions. A media specialist may want to buy a single copy of a particular text for its informational content, even though it is not used in a classroom. School policy may allow the school bookstore to place a copy in the center.

1. Is the content accurate and objective?

2. Does the content represent a broad spectrum of viewpoints on a given topic?

3. Are the visual materials keyed to the text?

4. Are bibliographies up to date? Do they include a wide range of formats?

5. Is the treatment appropriate for the intended purpose and audience?

6. Is the arrangement chronological or systematic?

7. Is the presentation free of racial or sexual stereotyping?

8. Is the type clear, and are the pages uncrowded?

Implications for Collection Development

In some schools, media specialists are responsible for the organization, storage, distribution, and inventory of textbooks. Regardless of whether you have this responsibility, you need to be aware of the content, the materials recommended in the bibliographies, and the potential use of textbooks as information sources. Individual titles may be useful as information works or anthologies of short stories or poetry and for the professional collection.

Copyright Considerations

Users may not copy workbooks, exercises, test booklets, and other consumable works.

Sources of Information

Textbooks and related teaching materials, such as charts and workbooks, are listed in *El-Hi Textbooks and Serials in Print*. Reviews can be found in the journals of professional teacher associations, such as *Reading Teacher*.

Toys

As with games, toys, such as blocks, puzzles, and manipulative materials, allow students the opportunity to develop coordination and to learn through touch, manipulation, and sight.

Advantages

1. Play is a way of exploring natural laws and relationships.

2. Toys can help develop perceptual motor skills.

3. Dolls or stuffed animals can help develop effective skills.

4. Individuals or groups can use toys.

5. Toys are inexpensive and can be made locally.

Disadvantages

1. Directions and parts may be lost.

2. The various shapes of toys can create storage problems.

3. Safety requirements must be observed.

4. Some toys can be used by a limited number of people.

Selection Criteria

1. Can the child play with the toy independently, or is adult guidance needed?

2. Has the user's developmental stage been considered in the selection of the toy?

3. Does color help guide the use of the toy, or is it mere decoration?

4. Is the toy constructed of solid materials?

5. Will the toy withstand use by young children?

6. Can it be used without all of its parts? Can one buy replacement parts or make them in-house?

7. Is the material nonflammable?

8. Can one wash or clean the toy?

9. Are the parts of the toy safe for children to use without injuring themselves?

Implications for Collection Development

Selection should be based on knowledge of the children's developmental needs. You may need to provide duplicate items so that more than one student can use the same toy or so that the toy can be used in the media center and also circulated.

Sources of Information

The Consumer Products Safety Commission lists toys considered unsafe for children.

Transparencies

Transparencies are single sheets of acetate or plastic that bear visual or written information that may be used in multiple sets as overlays. They can be shown to large groups by using an overhead projector. Some books and references materials use transparencies as overlays on illustrations to demonstrate relationships or sequences.

Advantages

1. The instructor or presenter can face the audience in a lighted room, thus facilitating interpersonal exchange and note taking.

2. The user can quickly edit, sequence, and review the presentation.

3. The presenters can write on the transparency while it is being projected or can use a pencil-sized or laser pointer.

4. Local production is relatively inexpensive and can be accomplished with minimum skill.

5. Overlays can be used to add information to a base visual.

6. The equipment is simple to operate and involves little maintenance, except bulb replacement.

Disadvantages

1. Storage and circulation of transparencies may be more complex than with slides.

2. Multi-color transparencies may be more expensive than 35mm slides.

3. A special tilted screen may be needed to avoid a distorted visual image.

4. Unless equipment is properly positioned, it may obstruct the view of the screen.

5. There is a lack of standardization in size and packaging of transparencies.

6. Complex overlays may create problems during presentations.

7. Action is hard to simulate without special equipment.

8. Presentations may be boring to students who prefer more interactive formats.

Selection Criteria

1. Does the subject lend itself to transparency rather than poster, mounted picture, slide, or some other medium?

2. Is the lettering clear?

3. Is the information uncluttered?

4. Is the mounting secure?

5. Is the set logically sequenced and organized?

6. Is the transparency clearly labeled?

7. Are overlays easily manipulated?

Implications for Collection Development

In schools where teachers use the lecture method, more overhead projectors are needed than in schools that utilize individualized instruction. In schools where many teachers and students use overhead projectors during the same time period, each classroom should have its own overhead projector. Production of transparencies by students or teachers requires materials, equipment, and work areas.

Sources of Information

Reviews of transparencies are scarce.

Videos

Video materials include information recorded on videodiscs and videocassettes. A laser beam reads videodiscs, which are the size of a 33rpm record. Videodisc readers can randomly search any segment and instantaneously access it. Videodisc programs provide three types of interactivity: (1) videodisc players used with or without a computer connection, (2) videodisc players used with a computer program within the videodisc, and (3) videodisc players connected to a computer controlled by software. Videodisc programs include movies; documentaries; interactive tutorials; instructional games; multimedia libraries of interrelated information from video clips, still frames, sound, maps, text, and graphics; visual databases; and simulations.

Videocassettes are videotapes that have been enclosed in a plastic case. They are available in ¾-inch format (U-matic) and ½-inch format (Beta). Video recordings of teleconferences and educational television programs may be added to the collection.

Advantages

1. Many of the visual effects used in filmmaking to enhance presentations can also aid in the production of video.

2. As in films, the content and sequence of the program is locked in, but if the program is recorded, it can be stopped or replayed.

3. Systems can be created to allow simultaneous viewing in more than one location in the school.

4. Videocassettes are easy to store, maintain, and use without damage.

5. The format is familiar to users.

6. Videodiscs provide fast and precise access to frames and segments.

7. Videodiscs can hold a still frame with no damage.

8. Videodiscs have two audio tracks, so that stereo sound or two separate tracks can be heard.

9. Videodiscs, unlike videotapes and videocassettes, cannot be erased.

10. Individuals or small groups of two to five people can use interactive videos.

11. Showing videos over closed-circuit televisions can make a presentation accessible to a large number of viewers.

Disadvantages

1. Small monitors limit the size of the audience, unless one can provide multiple monitors or video projector systems.

2. Compatible equipment is necessary.

3. On videodiscs, motion sequences are limited to 30 minutes—less than a video-tape's capacity.

4. Videodiscs can be intentionally damaged.

5. Interactive videodiscs may be expensive.

Selection Criteria

1. Does the telecast make use of the full range of television production techniques, or is it a filmed lecture?

2. Is the original case protective? Is it oversized, or does it contain another cassette or additional material, and will this cause shelving and circulation difficulties?

3. Does the interactive video provide multiple interactive paths?

Implications for Collection Development

This format has become popular because of its ease of use and range of selections. When selecting video materials for the collection, media specialists face the question of whether to buy, lease, or rent. Like other formats, video media should be previewed. When evaluating materials that originally appeared as films or filmstrips, consider the appropriateness of the format. Is the video merely a copy of the filmstrip? Videos produced by students, teachers, and staff—if they meet the selection criteria—should be retained in the collection.

Choose receiving and playback equipment for ease of use and durability.

Copyright Considerations

Copying or altering an entire video requires written permission. Off-air recordings may be retained for no more than 45 calendar days; then they must be erased. They may be shown to a class twice within 10 teaching days, and the copy should include the copyright notice. If ongoing use of the video is sought, then one needs to obtain a license.

Sources of Information

Study guides to forthcoming broadcasts are available from a number of sources, including the transmitting stations. General information is found in *TV Guide* and local television listings. State and regional public broadcasting stations frequently have announcements or newsletters for school audiences. *C-Span Newsletter* includes programming schedules and articles of interest to teachers. Check with your local station about the availability of newsletters and other guidelines.

Reviews are covered in *The Video Librarian.* Ratings are provided in *The Video Rating Guide for Libraries.*

The Video Source Book, which describes more than 125,000 programs available on videocassettes or videodiscs, provides information on the availability of video formats. *Bowker's Complete Video Directory* also includes this type of information. *Books in Print Plus* includes children's titles from Bowker publications (*Ulrich's International Periodicals Directory, Words on Cassette,* and *Bowker's Complete Video Directory*), periodicals, and bibliographies.

Videocassettes can also be obtained through federal offices, such as the National Audiovisual Center, National Gallery of Art, and Smithsonian Institution. Non-profit agencies that sell or rent videos include the Agency for Instructional Technology (AIT), which coordinates cooperative instructional television projects in the United States and Canada; Children's Television Workshop, which produces and distributes programming and television related materials, including the well-known *Sesame Street*; and Public Broadcasting Service (PBS).

Websites

Website refers to a collection of pages of documents accessible on the World Wide Web (WWW or the Web). This environment on the global computer network allows access to documents that can include text, data, sound, and video. The user can move from one location to another within the Website or use *links* to move to related Websites.

Access is by the Website's address or by the uniform resource locator (URL). The URL identifies the name of the host computer; the server; the name of the directory; the domain; the directory or server; and the Web page, or the actual filename. The domain is identified by three letters describing the sponsoring organization: .com for commercial site, .edu for educational, .k12 for a school, .org for a non-profit organization, .gov for a government agency, and .net for an Internet Service Provider, among others. The tilde symbol (~) designates a personal Web page. The user can move from one location to another within the Website or use links to move to related Websites. These letters and symbols give a clue as to the author (and authority) of the information.

Advantages

1. The Web provides access to information on a global basis.

2. The process is quick, cheap, and efficient.

3. The links connect related sources of information.

4. In following links, the user can move from information stored on one computer or database to another without being aware of the differences.

5. The information may be presented through text, sound, graphics, animation, video, and downloadable software.

6. Users can interact with the Website at their own pace.

Disadvantages

1. Searching for information takes place without the guidance of a directory, an index, or a classification scheme.

2. The content of the Website including the identified links may not be updated on a regular basis.

3. Website information may not be updated regularly.

4. Users may find more advertising than content.

5. Content may not be age appropriate.

6. Users can download a file, alter it, and (illegally) claim it is their own work.

Selection Criteria

1. Is the following information provided: name of sponsoring organization or individual, their qualifications, the full mailing address, the e-mail address, the date the page was created, the date the information was updated, and copyright information?

2. Is the purpose clearly stated?

3. Does the Website fulfill its purpose?

4. How accessible is the Website?

5. Are the links updated so that one does not get a "404 error," a sign that the link may no longer exist?

6. Does the design add to the appeal for the intended audience?

7. Is there a link back to the home page on each page?

8. Is a table of contents or outline provided for longer documents?

9. Has the site been reviewed? If so, what did the reviewer say?

10. Are the icons helpful in locating information?

11. If the Website offers a fee-based service, is it a justified and reasonable price?

Implications for Collection Development

Selection of Websites such as those of other materials should be the media specialist's responsibility, rather than having users rely on search tools. The media center's Website can be one way that users learn of links to selected sites related to their needs and interests. The media center's own Website should be updated on a regular basis. Examples could include news sources such as the BBC news site (news.bbc.co.uk/) for international news and ABC News.com (abcnews.go.com) and CNN.com (cnn.com/) for news about the United States.

Copyright Considerations

All Web pages are copyrighted. The design of the page, the HTML code, the graphics, and the collections of links are copyrightable. A notice will inform users about whether they may copy the materials. The basic procedure is, if you do not find a notice that you can reproduce the material, you must obtain permission to make more than one copy for personal use. For more information about copyrights and Websites, see the listings at the end of this chapter.

Sources of Information

Neal-Schuman Authoritative Guide to Evaluating Information on the Internet by Alison Cooke identifies additional criteria for evaluating organizational WWW sites, personal home pages, and subject-based WWW sites. *U.S. Government on the Web: Getting the Information You Need* by Peter Hernon, John A. Shuler, and Robert E. Dugan provides a comprehensive discussion of availability and use of federal government Websites. One chapter is devoted to Websites designed for children.

The "Professional Resources" listings at the end of this chapter provide a sampling of Websites devoted to the evaluation of Websites. The sites are sponsored by school districts, colleges, and universities and are updated on a regular basis. As you look at these sites and learn about others, you will find some that are directed to helping students, teachers, and parents in the evaluation process.

CONCLUSIONS

When selecting materials, consider who will use the materials, what formats they prefer, how they will use the materials, and whether appropriate equipment is available. Few collections will include every format described. Some materials may be outside the scope of a school's collection policy; others may not be suitable for a particular group of users.

Advances in technology will bring new formats to the market. As new materials and formats appear, consider their relevance to the collection. Does a new format meet needs not met by earlier formats? Will it offer enough subject coverage to justify purchasing the necessary equipment? Does the new format add a dimension to content unavailable in other media? If not, it may not be a good investment. Further developments will bring new materials to the media center if they are truly advantageous and if one selects and implements them with the user in mind.

REFERENCES

Cooke, Alison. 1999. *Neal–Schuman Authoritative Guide to Evaluating Information on the Internet*. New York: Neal–Schuman.

Crawford, Walt. 2000. Nine Models, One Name: Untangling the E-book Muddle. *American Libraries* 31, no. 8 (September): 56–59.

Hernon, Peter, John A. Shuler, and Robert E. Dugan. 1999. *U.S. Government on the Web: Getting the Information You Need.* Englewood, CO: Libraries Unlimited.

Mambretti, Catherine. 1998. *CD-ROM Technology: A Manual for Librarians and Educators.* Jefferson, NC: McFarland.

Van Orden, Phyllis. 2000. *Selecting Books for the Elementary School Library Media Center: A Complete Guide.* New York: Neal–Schuman.

ADDITIONAL READINGS

Mambretti, Catherine. 1998. *CD-ROM Technology: A Manual for Librarians and Educators.* Jefferson, NC: McFarland.
    Discusses criteria, installation, copyright issues, licensing, maintenance, and troubleshooting.

ELECTRONIC RESOURCES

Alexander, Jan, and Marsha Ann Tate. 2000. *Evaluating Web Resources.* Chester, PA: Wolfgram Memorial Library, Widener University. [http://www2.widener.edu/Wolfgram-Memorial-Library/webeval.htm]. (Accessed December 2, 2000).
    Includes checklists for evaluating advocacy, business/marketing, news, information, and personal Web pages. A frequently cited resource.

Association of Library Service to Children, Children and Technology Committee. 2000. *Great Sites: Selection Criteria.* Chicago: American Library Association. [http://www.ala.org/parentspage/greatsites/criteria.html]. (Accessed December 2, 2000).
    Helps parents evaluate authorship/sponsorship, purpose, design, stability, and content. Identifies "great sites."

Beck, Susan E. 2000. The Good, the Bad, and the Ugly, or, Why It's a Good Idea to Evaluate Web Sources. [http://lib.nmsu.edu/instruction/eval.html]. (Accessed December 2, 2000).
    Uses examples to evaluate the sources, identifies criteria, offers suggestions for teaching, and includes a bibliography.

California Instructional Technology Clearinghouse. 2000. Guidelines for the Evaluation of Instructional Technology Resources for California Schools. [http://clearinghouse.k12.ca.us]. (Accessed December 2, 2000).
    Covers distant-learning resources, online learning experiences, presentation tools, reference tools, productivity tools, California curriculum content, and multicultural aspects. Also offers reviews.

Grassian, Esther. 2000 *Thinking Critically about World Wide Web Resources*. UCLA College Library Instruction Series. Los Angles: UCLA Libraries. [http://www.library.ucla.edu /libraries/college/instruct/web/critical.htm]. (Accessed December 2, 2000).
Guides the evaluation of Websites.

Groton Public Schools, Media Technology Services. 2000. *Copyright Implementation Manual.* [http://www.groton.k12.ct.us/mts/egtoc.htm]. (Accessed December 2, 2000).
Includes updates such as Digital Millennium Copyright Act and the Sonny Bono Copyright Term Extension Act. Provides guidelines for specific applications and links to copyright resources on the Internet.

Hudak, Tina. 1999. *WWW Evaluation Guide*. Takoma Park, MD: Takoma Park Maryland Library. [http://cityoftakomapark.org/library/eval.html]. (Accessed December 2, 2000).
Helps evaluators assess the identifying factors for the site, analyze content and sources, and evaluate visuals.

Laurence, Helen. 1999. *FAU Libraries Internet Research: How to Evaluate Internet Resources.* Florida Atlantic University Libraries. [http://www.fau.edu/library/evaluate.htm]. (Accessed December 2, 2000).
Guides the evaluation of Websites.

O'Mahoney, Benedict. 2000. The Copyright Website. [http://www.benedict.com]. (Accessed December 2, 2000).
Covers current events and copyright issues and provides links.

PBS TeacherSource. 2000. Copyright. [http://www.pbs.org/teachersource/copyright/copyright .shtm]. (Accessed December 2, 2000).
A reference guide for educators who want to videotape programs from PBS. Covers copyright law, fair use, extended taping rights, educational multimedia, frequently asked questions (FAQs), and a sample template for a videotape label.

Shawhan, Joanne Parness. 1999. *Evaluating a Web Site*. Cobleskill-Richmondville High School, Cobleskill, NY. [http://www.cres.k12.ny.us/lib/hs/evaluating_web_sites.htm]. (Accessed December 2, 2000).
Calls for high-school students to evaluate content, analyze the URL (address), check background of author or sponsor, assess currency of information, and evaluate potential usefulness for their project. Provides an evaluation form.

Taylor, Jim. 2000. DVD Frequently Asked Questions (and Answers). [http://www .dvddemystified.com/dvdfaq.html]. (Accessed December 2, 2000).
November 29, 2000, version of the official Internet DVD DAQ for the rec.video.dvd Usenet news groups. Covers in a comprehensive manner basic facts about the relationship of DVD to other products. Identifies over 900 links to related information.

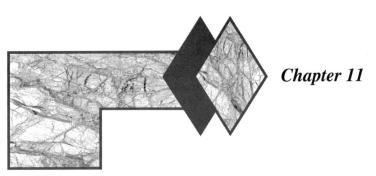

Chapter 11

Educational
Perspectives

A major purpose of the collection is to support school programs. The American Association of School Librarians and the Association for Educational Communications and Technology (1998) state this as one of the principles of information access and delivery. Their statement reads as follows:

> The collections of the library media program are developed and
> evaluated collaboratively to support the school's curriculum and to
> meet the diverse learning needs of students (83).

The wide range of instructional programs and practices in a school creates diverse demands upon its media collection. To be well versed about instructional programs, a media specialist must understand the school's approaches to education, be knowledgeable about the curriculum plans, and be aware of the purposes and demands of the teaching models used. Each model depends on a teaching support system of human and material resources. The underlying principles of a particular teaching model provide the basis for selecting resources with appropriate content and formats.

Any two schools may have identical curricula, but the teaching models may vary. Some questions to explore are the following:

♦ Does the school have a unified approach to the educational process?

♦ In what ways are the teaching methods similar?

♦ Do some teachers prefer one method rather than another?

♦ Are specific methods recommended in the curriculum plans, or do teachers have the freedom to choose their own methods?

189

As you work with teachers and other staff members, acquaint yourself with their attitudes, programs, and needs. This insight will help you plan the most appropriate services and media collection. This chapter focuses on the educational program. Chapter 12 focuses on the needs of individuals, specific groups, and services to them.

THE SCHOOL'S PURPOSE

A look at a high-school mission statement can illustrate the complexity of demands for educational support. Some high schools serve a single, overriding purpose. Sometimes this purpose is expressed in the name of the institution, with adjectives such as *vocational-technical, preparatory,* or *alternative.* For some schools the purpose is narrowly defined. The role of the media program may be narrow in scope.

More often a high school serves more than one purpose. A multi-purpose or comprehensive high school exerts varied demands on the media center collection and presents added challenges to the media specialist. In some comprehensive high schools, the purposes may not be clearly defined, which may lead to problems for budget allocations.

The media specialist will want to consult with administrators, teachers, curriculum coordinators, and students to learn about the school's purposes and programs. Is the school a comprehensive high school with both academic and practical courses and departments? Is it a vocational-technical school emphasizing specific job-related courses? Is it a performing arts or technical school offering special programs for talented students? Is there a non-traditional or an alternative program? The school board's or principal's annual report to the community can offer additional insight into the purposes of the school and its place in the district's overall education plan.

A school's purpose has implications for the collection. Each of the schools just described requires different sources in its collection. Some general materials, such as ready reference works, may be in all of these collections. In the case of a relatively expensive multi-volume work, such as Grove's *Dictionary of Music,* should all schools own a copy, or is there a way for them to share? Will all schools need a specific item? *University Press Books for Public and Secondary Libraries* will be of more interest to students in a preparatory school than to those in a vocational-technical school.

APPROACHES TO EDUCATION

In most schools philosophies have shifted from a focus on basic education (reading, writing, and arithmetic) to an emphasis on critical thinking and problem solving. Both philosophical positions can exist within one school. Whereas the principal and some teachers may emphasize critical thinking, other teachers may emphasize the basic skills.

The faculty members of Kennedy High School agree that basic education is an important goal, but they differ on how to achieve that goal. Several teachers prefer curriculum plans that detail teaching strategies and prescribe learning activities. Others prefer group investigation built on students' problem-solving abilities. The school's statement of goals may not reflect each teacher's individual approach to education. Knowing how teachers view education can help the media specialist work with them. This section describes three perspectives of education: academic, personal, and social (see Table 11.1). All three may exist in one school. Although each perspective emphasizes a specific approach to instruction, each one can draw on the others.

Table 11.1.
Perspectives of Education

Mission	Role of Student	Role of Teacher	Role of Support System
Academic			
Teach academic skills and techniques	Master information	Act as instructional manager	Provide materials developed by disciplines
	Master methods of inquiry		Provide wide range of materials and equipment
	Develop intellectual skills		
Personal			
Develop personal capacity of individuals	Develop interests and abilities	Help students help themselves	Provide space for small-group activities
			Provide materials of interest to students
Social			
Improve students' relations with peers and society	Participate in group problem-solving activities	Assign and guide group activities	Provide materials on social issues
			Provide access to community resources

Depending on its basic approach to education, a high school may teach the same general subject, for example, economics, in a number of ways. Classes that emphasize academic disciplines may stress economic theory to develop students' analytical skills. If personal development is the emphasis, economics may focus on the application of economic principles to one's personal life. Classes emphasizing the social approach may have students address the impact of the economy on the community. This simple example shows that, although primary emphasis can vary, the content and skills may be similar. Knowing the characteristics and implications of the three perspectives helps the media specialist anticipate demands on the collection.

Academic

The academic approach emphasizes academic skills and an intellectual view of the world. Scholars' ideas and techniques provide the focus for teaching. Students

♦ develop proficiency with technical and symbolic systems, for example, the technical language of biology

♦ master knowledge of a selected discipline, for example, geography

♦ master major concepts from the disciplines through the study of related fields, for example, social studies, or specific disciplines, such as physics

♦ acquire a discipline's modes of inquiry, for example, the scientific method

♦ gain an understanding of broad philosophical schools or problems, for example, aesthetics or ethics

The goal of academic instruction is to improve students' abilities to master information. The design of instructional programs may be to develop problem-solving abilities or mastery of concepts or information. Although social relationships and development of the individual are important, they are achieved through emphasis on intellectual functions.

The teacher's role is that of an instructional manager, emphasizing symbolic proficiency, or that of a trainer, emphasizing the knowledge or mode of inquiry of a discipline. Teachers may approach instruction through the inductive, deductive, or guided-discovery methods. Using the inductive method, teachers lead students through the processes of inquiry. Students collect and analyze data and learn to form concepts. In the deductive method, teachers present materials as a framework for students to master subject matter. In the guided-discovery method, the teacher leads the student progressively through a series of tasks representing intellectual processes.

Social scientists have developed research tools, such as interview guides and statistical models, that acquaint students with these models of analysis. The community serves as a source of data. Students use the tools to collect oral history or to study local government or ecology. Other learning activities take place in laboratory centers equipped with appropriate tools.

In a school that emphasizes the academic approach, the media center should have suitable, appropriately equipped spaces and laboratory areas for small groups to work. The collections should cover the disciplines, information about how scholars carry out scientific or academic inquiry, and the tools they use. One should find in the collection the usual information sources and formats, as well as materials and equipment students can use in their investigations. For example, circulating tape recorders would facilitate the collection of oral histories. Scientific and mathematics equipment may also be needed.

Personal

This approach recognizes each human being's unique character and seeks to develop every person's potential. The program emphasizes the individual. The instructional programs are designed to help students achieve self-understanding and formulate or recognize their goals. As a person's motivation for learning develops, the underlying premise is that the student will be encouraged to seek knowledge and gain mastery of academic content and skills.

Students develop one or more of the following objectives: feelings of adequacy and openness, productive thinking capacity, personal meaning, problem-solving abilities, aesthetic appreciation, or motivation to achieve.

The teacher's role is to help students teach themselves. The premise is that students are confident to direct themselves. The teacher brings new ideas and interpersonal situations to students, but the students generate their own education with the help of the counselor, teacher, and their fellow students.

The students engage in independent inquiry and creative problem solving, respond to aesthetically stimulating experiences, or react to programs designed to motive self-improvement or knowledge and skills.

The support system requires quiet places where the teacher or counselor can have private conferences with the student. In addition, space is needed for small-group activities.

The media center needs a wide range of subjects presented at different levels and formats so students can teach themselves. Students may interact with artists, musicians, writers, or scientists who teach on a part-time basis. Students may choose short courses on subjects of interest, enroll in specialized courses through distance learning, use laboratory materials, or create materials in a studio or shop. Lists of community and human resources must be available. The media specialist must know each student, be involved in each student's development, and bring resources and students together.

Social

The social approach to education emphasizes improving the students' relationships with people, society, and culture. Students learn to work cooperatively to identify and solve problems, whether academic or social. This approach has the following objectives:

◆ Develop students' cooperative problem-solving capacity (democratic-scientific approach, political and social activism).

♦ Develop students' economic independence.

♦ Introduce students to their culture and transmit the cultural heritage.

♦ Improve students' social behavior, increasing affiliation and decreasing alienation.

♦ Develop students' awareness of themselves as international citizens.

Both interpersonal (group) skills and academic inquiry skills can be emphasized to achieve these objectives. Personal development is also important. Although emphasizing social relations, the program also promotes development of the mind and the self while imparting knowledge of academic subjects. The teacher's role is that of a group leader who tries to facilitate the students' relationships with groups, society, and culture.

In a school focusing on social behavior, materials that provide opportunities for students to interact with others are certainly needed. Games and interactive videos provide such opportunities.

THE CURRICULUM

A school achieves its purpose through its educational program—the curriculum. The curriculum may be in response to mandated standards that the school district, the state, or professional organizations issue. The standards may call for specific content, establish sequencing of experiences, prescribe the teaching methods, and define the learner. Examples of content area standards linked to information literacy standards for student learning are identified in Chapter 2 of *Information Power: Building Partnerships for Learning* (American Association of School Librarians and Association for Educational Communications and Technology 1998).

The typical curriculum plan includes a statement of goals and objectives, the content teachers must cover, the organization (or sequencing) of that content, teaching strategies designed to meet the objectives or organizational requirements, and a program for evaluation. Curriculum plans may emphasize one or more of these elements. Each element of the curriculum plan has implications for the media program and its collection.

Examine the curriculum plans for your school. This may be a time-consuming task, for curriculum plans vary in scope, and there may be plans for all subject areas. Some plans are comprehensive, covering all educational programs. Others cover specific subjects or specific learning situations.

Curriculum plans may be general or give very specific directives to teachers. The general approach outlines the broad tasks of the school and identifies the teacher's responsibility. More specific curricula prescribe when, how, to whom, with what, and under what conditions the teacher is to function. More specific curricula may offer more direct practical information for the media specialist than the general curriculum. However, both plans will be helpful guides to the types of materials the media specialist will want to include in the collection.

An analysis of the curriculum plan can indicate what content or subject matter is required or recommended, when and to what depth it will be covered, and how it will be presented. If several classes will be studying the same unit simultaneously, they may need duplicate copies of specific materials. Otherwise, the media specialist can work with teachers to decide whether certain units can be taught at different times of the year. The curriculum plan may indicate why a unit is recommended for a specific time and whether altering its sequence would be detrimental to the learning process.

TEACHING MODELS

As you join teachers in collaborative efforts, you will observe the different teaching models they use. As your understanding of their approach to teaching increases, so will your effectiveness in working with them. You as a teacher probably use more than one approach.

The following sections are designed as a review or to introduce the rationale behind a sampling of models. Bruce Joyce and Marsha Weil have studied teaching models for a number of years:

> Models of teaching are really models of *learning*. As we help students acquire information, ideas, skills, values, ways of thinking, and means of expressing themselves, we are also teaching them how to learn.

> How teaching is conducted has a large impact on students' abilities to educate themselves. Successful teachers are not simply charismatic and persuasive presenters. *Rather, they engage their students in robust cognitive and social tasks and teach the students how to use them productively* (Joyce and Weil 1996, 7).

Joyce and Weil characterize four families of teaching models: social, information processing, personal, and behavioral. Each has a unique orientation to the ways people learn. Although each family emphasizes a specific approach to instruction, each draws on the others.

The social family stresses the individual's relationships to other individuals and to society. Examples include cooperative group learning, role playing, and jurisprudential inquiry. Priorities include developing the individual's ability to relate to others, to engage in democratic processes, and to work productively in society.

The information processing family is best suited to the academic mission of the school. The teaching models include concept attainment, inductive thinking, inquiry training, and mnemonics. These models develop the student's ability to acquire and organize data, sense problems, solve problems, and generate concepts. This orientation is characterized by teaching ideas and techniques from the parent disciplines.

Teachers emphasizing the personal perspective use models oriented to the individual and the development of the self. Examples within this family include non-directive teaching and enhancing self-concept. The premise is that individuals who have a productive relationship with their environment and consider themselves capable will have richer interpersonal relations and more effective information processing capabilities.

The behavioral family of models is based on social learning theory (behavior modification, behavior theory, and cybernetics). Examples within this family include contingency management, mastery learning or direct instruction, and self-training. A common characteristic is the breakdown of learning tasks into small, sequenced behaviors. Facts, concepts, skills, reduction of anxiety, and relaxation can be taught using this model.

The discussion that follows does not attempt to cover all teaching models but instead highlights examples. Each model makes different demands on the collection. No example of a model from the personal family of teaching models will be used as their support system relies more heavily on people than on materials.

Support Systems

For media specialists an important concept Joyce and Weil use is that of the support system necessary implement each model. As they examined models they identified what human, material, and technological resources were necessary for the teaching/learning process to occur. A model such as role-playing requires only a minimal level of support beyond the initial problem situation. Other models may be dependent upon prescribed materials or data. The models of group investigation, advance organizers, and simulation described in this chapter illustrate other levels of support. Media specialists can play an important role in the future success of a model by alerting administrators to the implications of the necessary support system.

Table 11.2.
Characteristics of Teaching Models

Teaching Model	Role of Student	Role of Teacher	Role of Support System
Group investigation	Solves problems	Academic counselor, consultant, friendly	Provide wide range of resources Provide access to expert opinion and to information outside the school
Advance organizers	Integrates old and new information	Lecturer, explainer, presenter	Provide data-rich, well-organized materials
Simulation model	Learns simple or complex tasks	Demonstrate, provide feedback, or proctor	Provide materials that can break down content into small tasks and provide immediate feedback

Group Investigation

This approach recognizes the student as a social being, one who cares about social order and classroom culture. The teacher builds on the students' energy to create the social order. To achieve this goal, the classroom's social system is democratic. The teacher suggests a problem to stimulate inquiry. Students identify and formulate the problem, then seek solutions through hands-on activities. Students learn by examining their experience to formulate new interpretations of principles and concepts.

The process follows six phases:

1. Encounter puzzling situations (planned or unplanned).

2. Explore reactions to the situation.

3. Formulate study task and organize for student.

4. Independent and group work.

5. Analyze progress and process.

6. Recycle activity (Joyce and Weil 1996, 84).

The teacher functions as academic counselor, consultant, and friendly critic, guiding the group experience at three levels: problem solving, task management, and group management. The teacher provides minimal structure. The atmosphere is one of reason and negotiation.

A world history class might consider the evidence for a textbook statement about the development of nationalism in Western Europe; a government class might examine the generalization that society depends on an accepted system of law. As students explore such statements, they need information from media center resources, expert opinions, and sources outside of the school.

According to Joyce and Weil the support system

> should be extensive and responsive to the needs of the students. The school needs to be equipped with a first class library that provides information and opinion through a wide variety of media; it should also be able to provide access to outside resources as well. Children should be encouraged to investigate and to contact resource people beyond the school walls. One reason cooperative inquiry of this sort has been relatively rare is that the support systems were not adequate to maintain the level of inquiry (Joyce and Weil 1996, 85).

The media specialist faces a challenge in this situation. Constraints may arise from limitations on when or how the specialist can buy materials and from lack of access to other information sources. On the other hand, the teacher who chooses this model is usually a resourceful person willing to work with the media specialist. The media specialist involved in this type of situation may get caught up in the stimulation of the experience, responding to this teacher's needs before those of other teachers who use models that depend on resources less. This is not a case of responding to the "squeaky wheel" but rather to a genuine need for information.

Other implications for the collection may seem obvious. A wide range of current materials must be available for students. Community and human resources will receive heavy use. Materials must be readily accessible, or the inquiry will be delayed and the sense of curiosity dampened. Access to electronic sources is important to students seeking a variety of viewpoints on a subject. Materials that distinguish between fact and opinion reinforce this type of learning. The media specialist will help the students locate, retrieve, select, evaluate, and apply information.

Advance Organizers

The goal of this model, which belongs to the information-processing family, is to explain, integrate, and interrelate material to be learned with previously learned material. The social system within this model is highly structured. The teacher is a lecturer, an explainer, or a presenter who controls both the social and intellectual systems.

The experience begins with the teacher clarifying the aim of the lesson, presenting and exploring the organizer (a major concept or proposition of a discipline), and eliciting the learner's prior knowledge and experience that is relevant to the learning task and organizer. This phase requires conceptually well-organized materials that are rich in data. In the second phase, the presentation of the learning task or material, the media center staff may help the teacher by preparing materials such as visuals to help the teacher clarify the aim of the lesson and display the major concepts. In phase two, the teacher and media specialist may work together to identify and evaluate information sources that present the specific content. In the third phase, strengthening cognitive organization, materials soliciting response from students will be sought. This is perhaps the most traditional, most familiar approach for many media specialists.

Simulation

The simulation model, which belongs to the behavioral family, applies to simple and complex skills, including psychomotor skills, problem-solving strategies, and interpersonal skills. Four phases in the process are orientation (or overview of the simulation), participant training, simulation operations with feedback and evaluation, and participant debriefing. The teacher's selection of materials and direction of the simulation structure the social system within this model.

The teacher may explain the theory and demonstrate the skill or may use media, such as videos or programmed learning materials. With highly structured materials, the teacher's involvement may be limited to that of facilitator, maintaining a non-evaluative but supportive attitude. Instructional systems may be simple, teacher-made games or specifically designed simulations such as driving a car or piloting an airplane.

SPECIAL PROGRAMS

Often schools initiate special programs that will influence the media center collection and program. Usually these occur after much discussion and planning at the district level. Try to involve media specialists in these discussions. Sometimes the programs are long-term, lasting several years; in other cases a program may be in place for only a year or two. Examples of such programs are literature-based reading programs, electronic reading programs, and block scheduling.

In a literature-based reading program, trade books (the types of books found in libraries and bookstores, in contrast with instructional textbooks) are used to teach reading to students. In these programs large amounts of print materials must be made available to teachers and students. If the literature-based reading program is used across disciplines, as is usually the case, then these materials must include both fiction and nonfiction materials. Often these programs are set up around thematic units developed by individual teachers or more frequently by grade-level faculty. It is essential that the media specialist be aware of these themes and the teachers' plans to use media center materials in the thematic units. The media center collection may not be adequate to support the themes the teachers select; thus, the media specialist may need to order special materials. Sitting in on grade-level curriculum-planning sessions will enable you to know in advance what types and quantities of materials might be needed (frequently sets of particular titles are used in literature-based reading programs). Such a program will greatly affect the monetary demands on the media center budget. It is advisable that you address this topic as early as possible. A meeting with the school administrators and faculty may make it possible to shift textbook funds to the media center budget to meet the needs of the literature-based reading program.

Another program that has recently had a great impact on media center collections and programs is the use of electronic reading programs, such as "The Accelerated Reader" (produced by Advantage Learning) and "Reading Counts" (produced by Scholastic). In these programs students read specific books with designated reading levels and take computer tests on those books. Thus, there is much pressure on the media specialist to have those particular titles in the media center and to have them labeled with reading levels. This may not make it possible for the media specialist to purchase other materials that are needed by the curriculum or that would be of particular interest to students. Also, a media specialist may have a philosophical problem with labeling books that teachers say are to be read by only certain students. There is much controversy about these programs, including their effects on student reading and their impact on the collections in school media centers. It is important that you be aware of these programs and the controversy. If there is discussion about initiating such a program in your school, participate in the discussions. Share your views on the programs and the ways that they might impinge on both students and the media center collection.

A third program that often affects school media centers is the initiation of block scheduling. There are numerous models used for block scheduling, but block scheduling typically involves having classes meet on only certain days of the week but for longer periods of time than in the traditional class-period scheduling. This type of scheduling can also have an impact on the school media center. Teachers whose students have not been doing research involving the media center collection may find that, by using block scheduling, they are able to have large blocks of time that can be used beneficially in the school media center. Thus, the media specialist may need to order materials to fit those research needs.

These are just a few of the special programs that have been introduced into schools that have had significant effects on the media center collection. Whenever there is discussion at your school about initiating a new program, be prepared to share your views on the program by participating in discussions and serving on committees.

DISTRIBUTION OF LEARNING MATERIALS

Another factor influencing subject- and program-oriented materials is the location of the materials themselves. When departmental libraries or resource centers are established to support particular subject areas, the centers' relationships to the collection housed in the media center must be determined. Are the centers' materials purely instructional? Are textbooks, workbooks, and supplemental materials used with specific assignments? Or are the materials considered part of the main collection and housed conveniently near the classrooms on that subject?

Another pattern of housing occurs when materials are stored in the classroom or teaching areas where they are used most frequently. For instance, cookbooks are in the home economics department, and materials on auto repairs are in the shop. A tour of the school helps you identify the distribution pattern. If materials are not housed in the media center, who is responsible for them? What are the circulation procedures? Who is responsible for inventory, maintenance, and control? Have the materials been entered on the OPAC? Are separate funds used to buy these materials, or are they purchased with media center funds? The most important question concerns the issue of convenient access to the materials.

RANGE OF COURSE OFFERINGS

To explore the school's unique demands on its collection, examine the range of courses the school offers. One high school may offer basic courses in art, computer education, dance, drama, foreign languages, health, humanities, language arts, library media, mathematics, music, physical education, political science, safety and driver education, science, and social studies. The social studies department may offer anthropology, economics, geography, history, and multicultural studies. History courses may include African, Asian, and world history. Additional courses may be designed to meet the needs of exceptional students, including gifted students and students with disabilities. The school may offer courses in agribusiness, natural resources, business, health occupations, industrial occupations, marketing, public-service occupations, and technology.

The state department of education in each state most likely has lists of approved courses. This information may be available through the department's Website or obtained from the principal or curriculum coordinator.

If a collection is to support a wide variety of courses, it must provide some level of coverage for all the subjects. Is the subject covered at an introductory, advanced, or remedial level? Are there honors courses? Do honor students have access to a nearby college collection? Has a shift in the local population created a need for materials that present concepts in simple English or bilingual formats?

How are the subjects organized or approached? For example, is art history taught as a separate course, or is it integrated into a study of humanities? As one high school moved to the integrated approach, the existing slide collection, which focused on specific artists and schools of art, was expanded. The new slides demonstrate an art medium, represent a particular technique or school of art, show the influence of philosophical thought upon art, or illustrate the influence of technology upon the subject and medium. One can draw similar comparisons with programs in elementary or middle schools.

Extracurricular groups and programs create demands for specific subject materials. A debate society needs timely information and opinions on controversial issues. A drama club needs plays, information about and patterns for costumes, and ideas for set designs. After-school programs call for information about crafts or sports.

New programs create new demands. In one district, a centrally located high-school media center is open in the evening to serve students from all schools in the district. Media specialists from various schools take turns overseeing the media center. They find that the reference collection needs to expand to meet the needs of students from diverse programs. In other communities, students in adult-education programs use the media center. They use some of the materials that the daytime students use but also need materials that cover additional subjects.

IMPLICATIONS FOR THE COLLECTION

The media specialist must know the priorities and understand the constraints of the curriculum and teaching methods in the school if the collection is to meet the needs of the school's instructional programs. To support some of these programs, the collection must include materials that have traditionally been considered instructional or classroom materials. As curricula and teaching methods change, media specialists must re-evaluate items in the collection in terms of how effectively they contribute to the teaching and learning process.

Many teaching strategies require so-called library materials as major sources of information or instruction. Teachers and media specialists can make selection decisions based on instructional needs only through cooperative efforts. General selection tools do not include the type of analysis and evaluation of materials needed to match material and teaching strategies. However, they provide a starting point for the selection process. As teachers participate in selection decisions and use materials, record their evaluations. A sample form to use when working with teachers is provided in Figure 11.1.

UNIT RESOURCE RECORD

Subject/Unit: _____

Grade: _____ Teacher: _____

Special student needs:

Objectives:

Information skills required:

Resources required:	Call number or source:	Evaluative comments:

Figure 11.1. Teacher use and evaluation form.

Janie Schomberg, a media specialist, describes how her school's culture influences collection development. She identifies the following four factors:

State guidelines for content;

Local learning outcomes based on state goals;

The community in which the school is located and the geographical area from which the students come, whether they are one and the same or distinctly different; and

> The building culture, which includes such things as the way the building is organized and the teaching and learning styles that are part of that local school. The building in which I am the school library media specialist differs greatly from individual buildings in other districts and somewhat from the other buildings in the Urbana school district (1993, 38).

Schomberg works at Leal School, a K–5 elementary school with 457 students, serving the local and also noncontiguous neighborhoods. The population is economically and culturally diverse. Each building determines what to teach in order to accomplish the learning goals that the Urbana school district curriculum establishes. Consistent with the school's philosophy, the Leal Alternatives Program includes three environmental variations within one school, all designed to meet the needs of students. Kindergarten is a full-day, self-contained classroom instructional setting. In grades 1–4, a choice of instructional styles is offered, including a team-teaching environment for grades 1–2 or 3–4, a primarily self-contained environment of grades 1–2 or 3–4, and a single-grade classroom for grades 1–4.

> Students in grades 1–4 stay with the same teacher for two years in all environment choices. These classrooms offer an alternative-year curriculum, covering the learning outcomes and content for two grades over a two-year period. . . . Fifth grade is composed of a three-teacher team that departmentalizes instruction in major content areas. All choices and configurations strive to integrate the disciplines in a curriculum subscribing to a whole language philosophy. Throughout Leal School, there are no textbooks—all teaching and learning is resource based. This philosophy and teaching style place the focus of curriculum support on the school library media center, requiring a very different collection development process than, for instance, a school that has required textbooks throughout the district and a lock-step curriculum. . . . My collection development plan is always evolving (Schomberg 1993, 39).

CONCLUSIONS

Media specialists have a responsibility to ensure that the collection meets the school's curricular and instructional needs. To carry out this responsibility, they must know the conditions for use of materials: who will use them, and how and for what purposes. Trying to learn why materials are used is more difficult than finding out who uses them and how they are used. Curriculum plans may provide this information about conditions for use.

The challenge of meeting curricular needs is complicated by the different views of what education should accomplish. Teachers and administrators may be unable to articulate their viewpoints, but if the media specialist sorts through what is seen and heard, the various approaches to education begin to become clear.

Needs for materials change. For one subject, a teacher may use a model that relies heavily on specified materials; later that same teacher may use a different model that makes no demands on the collection whatsoever.

As you get caught up in the day-to-day administrative activities and are busy coping with technological advances, do not forget that the common goal we share as educators is to create the most effective environment for the educational experience. As you collaborate with teachers, take the opportunity to learn more about how and why they are using specific approaches and models. Your professional reading should include literature on educational principles and methods. Take advantage of conversations, observation in classrooms, in-service programs, and other opportunities to further your knowledge of teaching. The knowledge you gain will enhance your ability to work with teachers and result in more effective use of the collection.

REFERENCES

American Association of School Librarians and Association for Educational Communications and Technology. 1998. *Information Power: Building Partnerships for Learning.* Chicago: American Library Association.

Joyce, Bruce, and Marsha Weil. 1996. *Models of Teaching,* 5th ed. Boston: Allyn & Bacon.

Schomberg, Janie. 1993. Tools of the Trade: School Library Media Specialists, Reviews, and Collection Development. In *Evaluating Children's Books: A Critical Look: Aesthetic, Social, and Political Aspects of Analyzing and Using Children's Books,* ed. by Betsy Hearne and Roger Sutton, 37–46. Urbana-Champaign: University of Illinois, Graduate School of Library and Information Science.

ADDITIONAL READINGS

Bishop, Kay, and Nancy Larimer. 1999. Literacy through Collaboration. *Teacher Librarian* 27: 15–20.
    Describes success stories of collaborative literacy activities in Lincoln (Nebraska) Public School Library Power schools.

Carter, Betty. 2000. Formula Failure. *School Library Journal* (July): 34–37.
    Carter points out the problems of using formulas that measure reading levels of books and tests that assign reading levels to students in school libraries.

Develop Your Core Library Collection. 2000. *Media and Methods* 36 (January/February): 10, 12, 14.
    The article provides some practical advice on how to maintain a collection by keeping up with curricular trends and subject matter.

Everhart, Nancy. 1998. Virtual Book Reports. *American School Board Journal* 185 (January): A22–A25.
    This article describes computerized reading-management programs and research findings relating to their use.

Geiken, Nancy, Julie Larson, and Jean Donham Van Deusen. 1999. Block Scheduling: Opportunities and Challenges for Collaboration. *Teacher Librarian* 27 (October): 26–31.
    The authors discuss how block scheduling can affect several aspects of the library media program, including information literacy instruction, collection development, access to the library media center, and collaboration between the teachers and teacher librarians. The article describes two schools (one middle school and one high school) that implemented block scheduling.

Gierke, Carolyn D. 1999. What's Behind Block Scheduling? *Book Report* 18 (September/ October): 8–10.
    The author surveyed colleagues on LM_NET, asking how block scheduling changed their libraries. The article is a synthesis of the responses.

Kirschenman, Jean Wolf. 1999. Internal Point/ Counterpoint: One School Library Media Specialist's Love/Hate Relationship with Accelerated Reader. *School Library Media Activities Monthly* 16 (December): 24–25.
    The author lists the cons and pros of using the Accelerated Reader reading program.

Poock, Melanie M. 1998. The Accelerated Reader: An Analysis of the Software's Strengths and Weaknesses and How It Can Be Used to Its Best Potential. *School Library Media Activities Monthly* 14 (May): 32–35.
    An explanation of the Accelerated Reader reading program and how one elementary school in Iowa used it are the topics of this article.

Prince, Robyn M., and Daniel D. Barron. 1998. Technology and Reading. *School Library Media Activities Monthly* 14 (April): 48–50.
    The authors briefly describe some of the possible side effects of using computer-based reading programs. They use several research studies to support their points.

Raphael, Taffy, and Kathryn Hu-Pei Au, eds. 1998. *Literature-Based Instruction: Reshaping the Curriculum*. Norwood, MA: Christopher-Gordon.
    This book examines literacy instruction from the perspectives of theory, contents of the curriculum, literary selection, and assessment.

Richmond, Gail. 1999. Block Scheduling: From Principles to Practice. *Book Report* 18 (September/October): 12–14.
    The author discusses how switching to a block schedule in a high school affects the media center collection and services.

Shaw, Marie Keen. 1999. *Block Scheduling and Its Impact on the School Library Media Center*. Westport, CT: Greenwood.

This book discusses the impact of block scheduling on library media usage, collection development, curriculum, resource sharing, and distance education. Some case studies at the end of the book detail the experiences of four block-scheduled schools.

Snyder, Maureen M. 1999. *Rodeo Pup*: Integrating Developmentally Appropriate Curriculum with Technology and Literature. *School Library Media Activities Monthly* 16 (September): 13–15.

This article describes a detailed collaborative lesson plan for K–1 using the book *Rodeo Pup*.

Stripling, Barbara K., ed. 1999. *Learning and Libraries in an Information Age: Principles and Practices*. Englewood, CO: Libraries Unlimited.

This series of essays examines learning, collaborative planning and teaching, the community, and research in relation to the media center program with implications for how the collection is perceived.

ELECTRONIC RESOURCES

About.com. 2000. Canada K–12 Education. [http://canadaonline.about.com/aboutcanada/canadaonline/cs/k12education/index.htm]. (Accessed November 25, 2000).

This site provides Websites for educational resources for kindergarten to grade 12 in Canada.

———. 2000. Canadian Curriculum by Province. [http://k-6educatorsca.about.com/aboutcanada/k-6educatiorsca/cs/curricbyprovince/index.htm]. (Accessed November 25, 2000).

This site contains several links to curriculum documents for Canadian provinces.

California Department of Education. 1998. California Instructional Technology Clearinghouse. [http://clearinghouse.k12.ca.us]. (Accessed November 25, 2000).

This site is "the educator's guide to high-quality instructional technology resources that support California's curriculum frameworks and standards."

Librarians Information Online Network. 2000. Lesson Plans and Teaching Activities for School Librarians. [http://www.libertynet.org/lion/lessons.html]. (Accessed November 25, 2000).

This provides a long list of useful Websites including lessons and activities in school libraries, library and information skills documents, and related books and periodicals.

McGraw-Hill School Division. 1999. State Departments of Education/Curriculum Standards. [http://www.mhschool.com/teach/music/m5.html]. (Accessed November 25, 2000).

The site is a resource for locating curriculum information for each state in the United States. It also includes a few general and national sites.

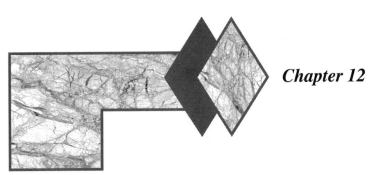

Chapter 12

Individuals and Groups

One purpose of the school media collection is to meet people's informational and recreational needs. To fulfill this purpose, media specialists must have information about those who are using the collection. This chapter focuses on materials and tools designed to help media specialists select materials that meet the typical needs of groups of people. For bibliographic and fuller descriptions of the resources cited in this chapter, see Appendix B.

When selecting materials for a collection, remember that people read, view, listen, and compute for different reasons: personal, informational, educational, cultural, and recreational. In addition to format and content, criteria for selecting materials should consider who will use the materials and how. The range of human needs is endless, varying from person to person.

STAFF MEMBERS

Staff members include people with teaching responsibilities, as well as those who work with children in other ways: administrators, guidance counselors, social workers, nurses, speech therapists, aides, secretaries, technical staff, and others. The portion of the collection designated to fulfill these people's needs is usually called the *professional collection.* Parents and other community members are sometimes allowed to use these resources.

As with the rest of the collection, a variety of formats should be available. If the collection does not contain the materials the school staff needs for their professional duties, then the media specialist needs to know where one can obtain those materials.

People who are responsible for preschoolers will find Barbara Taylor's *A Child Goes Forth: A Curriculum Guide for Preschool Children* (9th ed., Prentice Hall College Division, 1998) to be a helpful guide for selecting materials and activities for young children. *A to Zoo: Subject Access to Children's Picture Books* (R. R. Bowker, 1998) by Carolyn W. and John Lima can assist preschool and primary-level teachers in locating picture books about particular topics.

Teachers in schools using thematic units for instruction will especially appreciate *Book Links: Connection Books, Libraries, and Classrooms* (American Library Association, 1991–), which reviews old and new materials for individual units and provides suggestions for using the materials with children. *Hot Links: Literature Links for the Middle School Curriculum* (Libraries Unlimited, 1998), arranged by categories and curriculum areas, is a useful source for teachers using thematic units or literature across the curriculum.

Teachers interested in the selection and use of media will find *Instructional Media and the New Technologies* by Robert Heinich et al. (6th ed., Macmillan, 1999) helpful. Using *TV Guide* one can identify forthcoming television programs. Contact the local public television station for their programming newsletter.

The *Internet Resource Directory for K–12 Teachers and Librarians* by Elizabeth B. Miller (Libraries Unlimited, 1999) recommends Websites on particular subject areas. *Internet Books for Educators, Parents, and Children* by Jean Reese (Libraries Unlimited, 1999) assists media specialists in selecting books for the professional library and the general collection.

Teachers interested in learning about free resources (books, magazines, newsletters, posters, and other materials) can use *Vertical File Index to Selected Pamphlet Materials* (H. W. Wilson, 1955–). The *Educators Guides* series by Educators Progress Service lists free materials on a variety of subjects and in numerous formats. Teachers or guidance counselors wanting to introduce students to various careers will find *Free and Inexpensive Career Materials: A Resource Directory* (Ferguson, 1998) a useful tool. Several Websites cited in the "Electronic Resources" list at the end of this chapter identify where to obtain free materials.

LITERATURE AND GENRE MATERIALS

Survey books about children's and young-adult literature can be helpful to teachers and media specialists as they work with students in classrooms and in the media center. Two such classic works in children's literature are *Children and Books* (9th ed., Addison-Wesley, 1997) by Zena Sutherland and *Children's Literature in the Elementary School* (7th ed., McGraw-Hill, 2000) by Charlotte S. Huck et al. A smaller book focusing on literary aspects is Rebecca J. Lukens's *A Critical Handbook of Children's Literature* (6th ed., Longman, 1999). The second part of each chapter in Donna Norton's *Through the Eyes of a Child* (5th ed., Prentice Hall, 1998) includes activities on how to use each genre of children's literature in the classroom, while the first part deals with the books themselves. Carol Lynch-Brown and Carl M. Tomlinson's *Essentials of Children's Literature* (3d ed., Allyn and Bacon, 1998) interweaves the history of each genre with the selection and evaluation of such materials. Their chapter on multicultural and international literature is the most extensive coverage found in any of the titles just mentioned. John T. Gillespie and Corinne J. Naden's *Best Books for Children: Preschool Through Grade 6* (6th ed., R. R. Bowker, 1998) is another useful tool that includes annotations for 17,140 titles.

You will want to include award-winning books in your collections for teachers to use. *Newbery and Caldecott Awards: A Guide to the Medal and Honor Books* (American Library Association, 2000) provides annotations for all the winning and honor titles since the inception of the awards. Other books on award-winning titles can be found in the multicultural section of this chapter.

Teachers and media specialists will also want to use other formats to introduce children to children's literature. Two examples of titles are *Bowker's Directory of Audiocassettes* (R. R. Bowker, 1998) and *Bowker's Directory of Videocassettes* (R. R. Bowker, 1998). The information on Websites also helps teachers use children's literature with their classes. One example is "Carol Hurst's Children Literature Site" (http://www.carolhurst.com), which reviews children's books and offers ideas on how one can use the books in the curriculum.

Books for the Teen Age (New York Public Library) is an annual list of approximately 1,250 titles chosen for their appeal to teenagers. *Best Books for Young Adults* (2d ed., Young Adult Library Services Association, 2000) by Betty B. Carter, Sally Estes, and Linda Waddle provides annotations for young-adult titles organized by more than 25 themes and genres.

Some of the materials mentioned in preceding section discuss literary genres; other sources deal primarily with a specific genre. These guides are useful with reader's advisory activities.

Teachers interested in working with the popular fantasy genre will want to peruse *Fluent in Fantasy: A Guide to Reading Interests* (Libraries Unlimited, 1999). Here Diana Tixier Herald identifies numerous types of fantasy (myths and legends, sorcery, paranormal powers, fairy tales, graphic novels, etc.). She includes online resources and her personal recommendations. Herald also wrote *Genreflecting: A Guide to Reading Interests in Genre Fiction* (5th ed., Libraries Unlimited, 2000), which contains references to popular fiction (historical, western, crime, adventure, romance, science fiction, fantasy, and horror), many of which are appropriate for young-adult readers.

Another popular genre is horror. In *Hooked on Horror: A Guide to Reading Interests in Horror Fiction* (Libraries Unlimited, 1999) Anthony J. Fonseca and June M. Pulliam provide descriptions of approximately 1,000 titles. *Junior Genreflecting: A Guide to Good Reads and Series Fiction for Children* (Libraries Unlimited, 2000) by Bridget Dealy Volz, Lynda Blackburn Welborn, and Cheryl Perkins Scheer provides access to children's books of fiction in particular genres.

Reference Guide to Mystery and Detective Fiction (Libraries Unlimited, 1999) edited by James Rettig is organized thematically and is handy for locating mystery or detective titles. *Romance Fiction: A Guide to the Genre* (Libraries Unlimited, 1999) by Kristin Ramsdell is another useful reading advisory tool.

Elementary classroom teachers dealing with the genre of picture books will find over 200 books organized into categories in *Informational Picture Books for Children* (American Library Association, 2000). *Reading in Series: A Selection Guide to Books for Children* (Gale, 1999), edited by Catherine Barr, covers more than 1,000 series, which are arranged by title, and identifies genres.

Specific Subject Areas

Some of the materials you will want to provide in the media center (either in the general or the professional collection) relate to specific subjects. In the area of social studies falls *Global Voices: Using Historical Fiction to Teach Social Studies* (Addison-Wesley, 1999) by Susan B. Ouzts. Another contributor to this area is Lynda G. Adamson. Her works include the following titles:

♦ *Literature Connections to American History: Resources to Enhance and Entice K–6* (Libraries Unlimited, 1997)

♦ *Literature Connections to American History: Resources to Enhance and Entice 7–12* (Libraries Unlimited, 1997)

♦ *Literature Connections to World History: Resources to Enhance and Entice K–6* (Libraries Unlimited, 1998)

♦ *Literature Connections to World History: Resources to Enhance and Entice 7–12* (Libraries Unlimited, 1998).

Similar works in the area of science are *Science Adventures with Children's Literature: A Thematic Approach* (Libraries Unlimited, 1998) by Anthony D. Fredericks and *Science Through Children's Literature: An Integrated Approach* (2d ed., Libraries Unlimited, 2000) by Carol M. and John W. Butzow. *Exploring Science in the Library: Resources and Activities for Young People* (Libraries Unlimited, 2000) by Maria Sosa and Tracy Gath offers a bibliography of recommended science trade books and a guide for selecting the best science books for children.

Books dealing with religion and religious themes are sometimes difficult to locate. *Children's Books About Religion* (Libraries Unlimited, 1999) by Patricia Pearl Dole annotates more than 700 titles with religious themes.

Teachers and media specialists working in schools that specialize in the fine arts will have other needs. Titles such as *Halliwell's Film and Video Guide* (15th ed., HarperCollins, 1999) by Leslie Halliwell or *1-2-3-4 for the Show: A Guide to Small-Cast One Act Plays* (Scarecrow, 1999) by Lewis Heniford might be useful resources.

Journals produced by professional organizations provide worthwhile information. Many carry reviews and produce bibliographies. Titles you might consider for a professional collection are *ALAN Review* (National Council of Teachers of English), *American Music Teacher* (Music Teachers National Association), *Educational Leadership* (Association for Supervision and Curriculum Development), *English Journal* (National Council of Teachers of English), *History Teacher* (Society for History Education), *Journal of Geography* (National Council for Geographic Education), *Journal of Health Education* (American Alliance for Health, Physical Health, Recreation and Dance), *Journal of Home Economics* (American Home Economics Association), *Language Arts* (National Council of Teachers of English), *Mathematics Teacher* (National Council of Teachers of Mathematics), *Reading Teacher* (International Reading Association), *Science and Children* (American Association for the Advancement of Science), *Science Books and Films* (American Association for the

Advancement of Science), *Science Teacher* (National Science Teachers Association), and *Social Education* (National Council for the Social Studies). Appendix A lists these associations.

Professional Development

A major resource for current activities within schools are the documents in the Educational Resources Information Center (ERIC) databases. Appendix A gives further information about ERIC Clearinghouse. Manual searches can be done using *Resources in Education (RIE)* (Superintendent of Documents, 1975–) and *Current Index to Journals in Education (CIJE)* (Oryx Press, 1969–). *RIE* and *CIJE* can also be accessed through CD-ROMs and the Internet. ERIC is a particularly worthwhile resource for any faculty member taking courses for recertification or working on advanced degrees.

Another useful source for information relating to education is *Education: A Guide to Reference and Information Sources* (2d ed., Libraries Unlimited, 2000), which contains annotated bibliographies, some of which are relevant to K–12 faculty and their professional development.

REFERENCE SERVICES

Students' personal interests and classroom activities may necessitate the use of reference materials. Reference books are works, such as encyclopedias, that provide factual information and help users to locate specific information. Reference works may appear in traditional paper format, on CD-ROM, or online.

Certain titles, such as *Guinness Book of World Records,* are so popular that the collection will need a circulating copy as well as a reference copy. In schools where groups go on weeklong camping trips or nature hikes, the media center should include several copies of nature handbooks. These works can be ordered in hardback or paperback, depending on how students and teachers will use the books.

Criteria for choosing adult reference books—authority, scope, treatment of materials, arrangement, format, and special features—apply equally well to reference materials for students. Illustrations, cross-references, and pronunciation guides are important features in children's reference materials.

Basic selection tools include *Guide to Reference Materials for School Media Centers* (5th ed., Libraries Unlimited, 1998) and *Reference Sources for Small and Medium-Sized Libraries* (6th ed., American Library Association, 1999). Both recommend a wide range of titles on a variety of subjects. *Developing Reference Collections and Services in an Electronic Age: A How-to-Do-It Manual for Librarians* (Neal-Schuman, 1999) is helpful in selecting new materials and addresses the print-versus-electronic-format issue. It also provides evaluation tools and planning details for a reference collection. *The Elementary School Library Collection: A Guide to Books and Other Media* (22d ed., Brodart, 2000) includes a section recommending reference materials.

Reviews of current titles are published in *Booklist: Includes Reference Books Bulletin* and *School Library Journal.* Other review sources include *Recommended Reference Books for Small and Medium-Sized Libraries and Media Centers* (Libraries Unlimited, annual), which includes titles selected from the more comprehensive *American Reference Books Annual* (Libraries Unlimited, 2000) and *Recommended Reference Books in Paperback* (3d ed., Libraries Unlimited, 2000). *Building Electronic Library Collections: The Essential Guide to Selection Criteria and Core Subject Collections* (Neal-Schuman, 1999) by Diane Kovacs includes sources of reviews for Web-based resources.

The *Index to Poetry for Children and Young People* (H. W. Wilson, 1998) identifies more than 8,700 poems from more than 186 sources.

Many reference materials are now available as CD-ROMs or online. *CD-ROM Reference Materials for Children and Young Adults: A Critical Guide for School and Public Libraries* (Libraries Unlimited, 1999) evaluates new children's reference materials available on CD-ROMs.

MULTICULTURAL

Multicultural materials support individual needs as well as the curriculum. Multicultural materials help students learn about people whose backgrounds are different from their own. Seeing their culture represented in materials helps raise the self-esteem of members of minority groups. It is important for the school media specialist to be aware of the diversity of a school's students and to make certain that materials are available to meet those students' needs. If there is a large number of non-English-speaking students in the school population, the media center will need to have materials available in languages other than English.

The topic of multicultural materials can raise heated debate. Questions center on a variety of issues:

◆ Definition of multicultural materials: Does it include books from or about other nations? How does it define a cultural group? Should Vietnamese, Cambodian, Chinese, and Japanese materials all be labeled " Asian American" when the differences between these cultures are significant?

◆ Who is qualified to write about ethnic and cultural experiences? Should only those who are actually members of a culture write about that group? Can authors successfully write about a culture if they have gained insight into it through extensive research or experience in the culture?

◆ The quality of multicultural materials. Because you will want to select high-quality multicultural materials to include in your collection, the third issue deserves your special attention as a school media specialist. It is important to remember that the standards for any good literature also apply to multicultural and international literature. However, you need to consider some additional criteria:

• The materials should be culturally accurate. This includes the illustrations in a book as well as the text.

- Ethnic materials should contain authentic dialogue and depict realistic relationships.

- The materials should avoid racial and cultural stereotyping. Characters should be regarded as distinct individuals.

- The materials should not contain racial comments or clichés.

- Details in a story should help the reader gain a sense of the culture.

The following sources can help you provide quality multicultural materials to your collection. *The Coretta Scott King Awards Book: 1970–1999* (American Library Association, 1999) features annotations of all the winning and honor titles as well as biographies of their authors and illustrators. *Culturally Diverse Videos, Audios, and CD-ROMs for Children* (Neal-Schuman, 1999) recommends more than 1,000 multicultural titles. *Great Books for African-American Children* (Dutton/Plume, 1999) lists 250 books that celebrate the African-American culture.

Multicultural Projects Index: Things to Make and Do to Celebrate Holidays Around the World (Libraries Unlimited, 1998) is an index of multicultural projects in more than 1,700 books. *Multicultural Resources on the Internet: The United States and Canada* (Libraries Unlimited, 1999) annotates URL sites for Native American, African American, Hispanic American, Asian American, Chinese American, Japanese American, Asian Indian American, Jewish American, Americans of Middle Eastern descent, French Canadian, Cajun and Creole, and Hawaiian American cultures. *Programming with Latino Children's Materials: A How-to-Do-It Manual for Librarians* (Neal-Schuman, 1999) provides background on the Latino culture and reviews books, folktales, and recordings that can be used in programming. *Through Indian Eyes: The Native Experience in Books for Children* (American Indian Studies Center, 1998) includes critical evaluations of books by and about Native Americans.

Articles that explore current multicultural issues and reviews of new print and non-print resources can be found in *Multicultural Review: Dedicated to a Better Understanding of Ethnic, Racial and Religious Diversity* (Greenwood Publishing, 1992). This quarterly journal is designed for teachers and librarians interested in learning about new developments in the field of cultural diversity.

Two sources are particularly helpful for international materials. Carl M. Tomlinson's *Children's Books from Other Countries* (Scarecrow, 1998) contains an annotated bibliography of international titles and offers suggestions on how to share the books with children. *Bookbird* (International Board on Books for Children, 1962–) features articles of interest on international literature for children and reviews selection tools.

POOR, RELUCTANT, AND ESL READERS

Poor or reluctant readers have always challenged those who encourage reading skills and literature appreciation. The poor reader reads below capacity. This is not a reflection of that person's potential to read. A reluctant reader is one who is capable but prefers not to read. Books with high appeal and appropriate reading levels can help these students.

The phrases "high interest/low vocabulary" (hi-low) or "high interest/low reading level" (HILRL) are often used to describe these works. Criteria for evaluating such books include:

repetition of main points;

repetition of the main points in the summary;

wide margins, extra space between lines, and short chapters with space between sections;

direct and simple narrative;

use of dialogue and action;

well-organized, direct information;

illustrations to explain the text; and

simple vocabulary with sentences of varying lengths.

More Rip-Roaring Reads for Reluctant Teen Readers (Libraries Unlimited, 1999) by Betty D. Ammon and Gale W. Sherman describes both fiction and nonfiction titles for reluctant readers in middle- and high-school grades.

Selecting books for students of English as a Second Language (ESL) follows some of the same considerations. According to Laura Hibbets McCaffery, these books need to:

appeal in format,

have appropriate reading and content levels,

have appropriate illustrations,

be accurate in text and illustrations,

include access to information through an index,

define and explain terms in a glossary,

provide bibliographies for further exploration,

be representative of the culture they describe, and

effectively explain the cultures (McCaffery, 1998, xiv).

McCaffery used these criteria in selecting titles to recommend in her *Building an ESL Collection for Young Adults: A Bibliography of Recommended Fiction and Nonfiction for School and Public Libraries* (Greenwood, 1998). The bibliography identifies books and non-print materials including Websites on a range of subjects and genres.

PEOPLE WITH DISABILITIES

Although each person is unique, he or she may be part of a group sharing characteristics that require special consideration in the collection. As you consider these special characteristics, remember the message, "label cans, not people." People with special needs based on disabilities may be students, teachers, or staff members. This discussion provides basic information and identifies resources that will help media specialists, teachers, other staff members, parents, and caregivers.

Two pieces of national legislation of particular relevance for this discussion are the Education for All Handicapped Children Act of 1975 (Public Law 94-142), now called the Individuals with Disabilities Education Act (IDEA), and the Americans with Disabilities Act (ADA; Public Law 101-336). The IDEA addresses the needs of the child and calls for an individualized educational program (IEP) based on each child's needs. The media specialist should cooperate with teachers to learn about the methods they are using in the IEP in order to offer support. An older and unique work that helps media specialists, parents, and teachers understand the process of ensuring the child's rights under IDEA is *Negotiating the Special Education Maze* (3d ed., Woodbine House, 1997) by Winifred Anderson, Stephan Chitwood, and Deidre Hayden.

Information about the characteristics of disabilities and the materials recommended to meet the needs of people with disabilities can guide collection activities. The characteristics of a specific disability, however, might not apply to everyone with that disability. Furthermore many children with multiple disabilities have needs identified with more than one type of disability.

In working with these students, you have a responsibility to learn about the different characteristics and the implication for resources. School staff members can help. The teachers can describe students' behavior-management programs, abilities, and learning styles. The media specialist can learn which disabilities call for modifications or adaptations and how to implement them. Specialists at the district or state level can also provide information and advice.

Multiple Disabilities

Students with special needs use the same range of formats other students use, but in some cases alternatives or adaptations are necessary. Paperbacks are ideal for students with upper extremity weakness. Students with cognitive disabilities may find audio, video, toys, and multimedia formats useful. In *Adaptive Technologies for Learning and Work Environments* by Joseph J. Lazzaro (1993) describes available technologies and their sources. Table 12.1 lists the range of technologies Lazzaro covers. He also identifies other information sources, including organizations for people with disabilities.

Table 12.1.
Adaptive Technologies

For vision-impaired

Internal and external speech synthesis hardware
Speech synthesis software
Screen readers for graphics
Magnification systems
Software-based magnification programs
Braille systems
Optical character recognition systems

For hearing-impaired

Text telephones
Braille text telephones
Facsimile communication
Computer-assisted access
Computer-aided transcription
Computerized sign language training
Signaling systems
Captioning systems
Electronic amplification systems
Telephone amplification systems

For motor- and speech-impaired

Adaptive keyboards
Keyboard guards
Keyboard modification software
Alternative input system
Morse code systems
Word-prediction software
Voice recognition systems
Alternative communications device
Environmental control system

Based on Joseph J. Lazzaro, *Adaptive Technologies for Learning and Work Environments* (American Library Association, 1993).

Including Families of Children with Special Needs: A How-to-Do-It Manual for Librarians (Neal-Schuman, 1999) offers suggestions on how to develop special collections and resources for students with special needs. *Accessible Libraries on Campus: A Practical Guide for the Creation of Disability-Friendly Libraries* (American Libraries Association, 1999) by Tom McNulty was written for academic libraries but contains information that is helpful in accommodating patrons with disabilities in any library situation. This guide also includes a directory of resources.

Exceptional Parent: Parenting Your Child with a Disability (Psy-Ed Corp., 1971–) provides support, ideas, and resources to families of children with disabilities and the professionals who work with them. This is another suggestion for your professional collection.

Not only do media specialists need to know the people and the materials in the collection that are appropriate for children with disabilities, but they also have a responsibility to know the resources available in the community. These may include rehabilitation agencies, information agencies, and other educational or recreational programs. For example, some communities have recreation areas designed to accommodate wheelchairs or to provide information that children can learn through a variety of senses. In one recreational area, trails provide easy access to picnic areas, a fishing pier, and nature paths. Along the trails, information stations use models, large charts, printed information, and recorded messages to point out items of interest. Messages written in Braille encourage people to feel an object or to smell it. Sheltered eating areas provide spaces for wheelchairs interspersed at the picnic tables. The park is a beautiful spot everyone can enjoy. The media specialist should make information about such facilities available and possibly suggest them as destinations for field trips.

Other sources of information are national clearinghouses and organizations. The National Center on Education Media and Materials for the Handicapped (NCEMMH), located at the Ohio State University College of Education, produces evaluation guidelines and forms for instructional materials. The Council for Exceptional Children (CEC) provides information about education for both children with disabilities and gifted children. CEC hosts the ERIC Clearinghouse on Handicapped and Gifted Children, which distributes bibliographies, conference papers, curriculum guides, and other documents. The National Information Center for Children and Youth with Disabilities (NICCYD) provides free information to assist adults in helping children with disabilities become active members of their school and community.

Journals of interest to adults working with exceptional children include *Exceptional Children* (Council for Exceptional Children), *The Exceptional Parent* (Psy-Ed Corp.), and *Teaching Exceptional Children* (Council for Exceptional Children).

Visual Impairment

Children who have vision problems may require special types of materials. Some people with partial sight can use regular print materials, whereas others need large-print materials. One cannot make the assumption that large-print materials are appropriate for all children with partial sight. Low-vision aids, handheld magnifiers, or closed-circuit televisions can magnify standard print materials. Trained children can use Braille books, games, and outline maps. A blind person can read printed materials by using optical machines that allow users to feel sensation on their fingertips. For others, taped materials may be most useful.

Children with visual disabilities can participate in all media center activities. Useful pieces of equipment include rear projection screens, which permit children to get close to the screen without blocking images; tape recorders; speech compressors, which eliminate pauses between words and thus reduce the time needed to access recorded materials; talking calculators; and computers with voice-recognition capability.

People with visual and other physical disabilities can use talking books, which are tapes or records of books, textbooks, and magazines (available in English and other languages, including Spanish). Talking books are a free service of the National Library Service for the Blind and Physically Handicapped, part of the Library of Congress. Arrangements can be made through the local public library. Titles can be found in plaintext catalogs and bibliographies obtained from the National Library Service for the Blind and Physically Handicapped, or they can be downloaded online. Information on the books can be found in the print and online versions of *Braille Book Review* (1933–) and *Talking Books Topics* (1935–) from the National Service for the Blind and Physically Handicapped. These titles are available free to the blind or people with other disabilities. In 2000 the Library of Congress introduced the *Web-Braille* service, which offers Braille readers access to more than 2,700 books on the Internet.

The Complete Directory of Large Print Books and Serials (R. R. Bowker, 2000) lists adult, juvenile, and textbook titles and indicates the type size and the physical size of each book. The American Foundation for the Blind develops, publishes, and sells useful books, pamphlets, periodicals, and videos for students and professionals. They also produce the *Journal of Visual Impairment and Blindness.*

The American Printing House for the Blind (APHB) publishes Braille books and magazines as well as large-print texts. The Instructional Materials Center for the Visually Handicapped at APHB serves as the National Reference Center for the Visually Handicapped and evaluates and disseminates instructional materials related to the education of people with visual impairment.

Deafness or Hearing Impairment

Children with hearing impairments have difficulty hearing spoken language and, as a result, often have difficulty understanding written and spoken language and abstract concepts. Visual formats are useful for these children. The visuals should be large and present a single, distinct concept or idea. Illustrations and print should be immediately recognizable. Language patterns and sentence structures need to be simple. Repetition and reinforcement are helpful.

Captioned films, filmstrips, and videotapes are useful for children with hearing impairment. Information about the captioned film program can be obtained from the Captioned Media Program, whose services are available through the U.S. Department of Education. Their catalog, *Captioned Media Program* (National Association of the Deaf), which lists captioned media that can be borrowed by deaf and hard-of-hearing people, can be accessed online. Check with your local educational television station for information about captioned programming and the equipment necessary to receive it.

Children who have learned sign language will want signed books, filmstrips, and videotapes. Sources of professional materials and books in sign language are available from the Alexander Graham Bell Association for the Deaf, Gallaudet College Bookstore, and the National Association of the Deaf. The *ASHA Leader* (American Speech-Language-Hearing Association, 1996–) provides further information about people with hearing impairment. Media specialists who take a course in sign language will be able to increase rapport with these students.

CONCLUSIONS

One of the responsibilities of the school media specialist is to provide materials and services to meet the needs of people. These people may be faculty, staff, or students, and they all deserve to be treated as individuals. Media specialists are involved with students during important years of development yet seldom realize how a brief contact can affect children and their families.

One of the authors of this text recalls a first grader who came into the media center one day asking for information about logic and philosophy. He seemed to know what he wanted. With fingers crossed, the media specialist took him to the shelves. The media specialist knew there were three titles about logic and wondered whether the first grader would be able to understand them. He did. Years later, as a woman was talking to the author about media specialists' attitudes toward children, she mentioned that her young son had proudly brought home a nonfiction book. His teacher had wanted him to read a picture book rather than a book about logic. As the author listened, she wondered whether this boy could have been the child she remembered. As it turned out, she had helped the boy in his early quest to study logic. He became a champion chess player in his early teens. Every day there are children or adults whom media specialists influence, but rarely do we get the opportunity to learn the results of our efforts.

REFERENCES

Lazzaro, Joseph J. 1993. *Adaptive Technologies for Learning and Work Environments*. Chicago: American Library Association.

ADDITIONAL READINGS

Brown, Jean E., and Elaine C. Stephens. 1998. *United in Diversity: Using Multicultural Young Adult Literature in the Classroom*. Urbana, IL: National Council of Teachers of English.

   Consists of five sections including essays by famous young-adult authors on multicultural issues, reports of how teachers integrate multicultural literature in their curriculum, and issues related to the selection of multicultural books. Contains an annotated bibliography of multicultural books and resources for teachers.

Chu, Clara. 2000. See, Hear, and Speak No Evil: A Content Approach to Evaluating Multicultural Multimedia Materials. *Reference and User Services Quarterly* 39 (Spring): 255–64.

   Lists and discusses criteria for evaluating multicultural, multimedia materials. Reviews literature on the topic.

DeLaurie, Alicia. 1998. Diversity and the Library Media Teacher. *CSLA Journal* 21 (Spring): 23–24.

Discusses diversity of the content of specific multicultural books.

Feinberg, Sandra, Barbara Jordan, Kathleen Deerr, and Michelle Langa. 1999. *Including Families of Children with Special Needs: A How-to-Do-It Manual for Librarians.* New York: Neal-Schuman.

Offers suggestions for selecting materials, including toys and resources for parents in the public library setting, but content is appropriate for school media centers.

Ganss, Dawn S. 1999. Focusing on Special Needs. *The School Librarian's Workshop* 19 (June): 13–14.

Annotates several Websites that can help educators gather information on inclusion (mainstreaming special needs students into the classroom). Identifies resources for these students and for the curriculum.

Gorman, Audrey J. 1999. Start Making Sense: Libraries Don't Have to Be Confusing Places for Kids with Reading Disabilities. *School Library Journal* 45 (July): 22–25.

Provides an approach to use when working with children with learning disabilities.

Lemke, Susan Dove. 1999. The Faces in the Picture Books. *The Horn Book Magazine* 75 (March/April): 141–47.

Describes a study on diversity in picture books.

Mestre, Lori S. 2000. Improving Computer-Use Success for Students of Diverse Backgrounds. *Knowledge Quest* 28 (May/June): 20–28.

Points out that minority students' needs and learning styles differ from those of the mainstream population. Provides suggestions for working with diverse students in a computerized environment.

Morton, Kay, and Mary Forer. 1999. The Big Easy. *School Library Journal* 45 (February): 47.

Explains how, as authors, they developed an "easy to finish" collection for reluctant readers in a middle school. Suggests ways to sell the titles to students.

Shea, Pamela A. 2000. With Access for All. *School Library Journal* 46 (January): 35.

Recommends affordable products that can make the resources in a media center more accessible to students with special needs.

Wilson, Patricia. 2000. Professional Collections in Library Media Centers. *Teacher Librarian* 27 (June): 16–20.

Discusses professional collections and recommends titles.

Woody, Donna. 2000. African American Biographies: A Collection Development Challenge. *Journal of Youth Services in Libraries* 13 (Winter): 5–9.

Describes the process the author followed to try to obtain African American biographies for a Black history month project. Suggests ways to alleviate some of the problems of such a challenge.

ELECTRONIC RESOURCES

EASI. 2000. Equal Access to Software and Information. [http://www.rit.edu/~easi]. (Accessed November 25, 2000).

    Part of the Teaching, Learning, and Technology Group, an affiliate of the American Association for Higher Education. Provides links to information and publications dealing with disabilities.

Education Development Center. 2000. Speaking to Write: Realizing the Potential of Speech Recognition for Secondary Students with Disabilities. [http://www.edc.org/spk2wrt]. (Accessed November 25, 2000).

    Deals with speech recognition software and its uses in secondary school settings. Discusses and links to other Websites with information pertaining to speech recognition technology.

Florida Division of Blind Services. Florida Department of Labor and Employment Security. 2000. Florida Bureau of Braille and Talking Book Library Services. [http://www.state.fl.us/dbs/lswel.htm]. (Accessed November 25, 2000).

    Identifies services of the largest library of its kind with a collection of more than 2 million books in Braille and recorded formats available to lend to people with print disabilities.

Gallaudet University Library. 2000. Gallaudet University Library Home Page. [http://library.gallaudet.edu].(Accessed November 25, 2000).

    Provides deaf-related resources.

Laurent Clerc National Deaf Education Center. 2000. Software to Go. [http://clerccenter2.gallaudet.edu/stg/index.html]. (Accessed November 25, 2000).

    A clearinghouse for sharing software evaluation with people and agencies dealing with the educational needs of deaf and hard-of-hearing people.

Library of Congress. 2000. National Library Service for the Blind and Physically Handicapped. [http://www.loc.gov/nls]. (Accessed November 25, 2000).

    Offers steps to follow to receive talking books or Braille services.

Mele, Joe. 1996. Multicultural Book Review Homepage. [http://www.isomedia.com/homes/jmele/homepage.html] (Accessed November 25, 2000).

    Reviews of multicultural books can be submitted to this site. Designed to create a qualitative list of multicultural literature.

———. 1996. Multicultural Web Sites. [http://www.isomedia.com/homes/jmele/mcultlink.html] (Accessed November 25, 2000).

    Describes a long list of multicultural Websites. Is divided into "Educational Links" and "Multicultural Links."

RFBD. 1999. Recording for the Blind and Dyslexic. [http://www.rfbd.org]. (Accessed November 25, 2000).

    The official site of RFBD, which provides taped textbooks, references, and professional materials for people with print disabilities. Provides access to other Websites (some listed by state) that offer similar services.

University of Alberta Libraries. 1999. Special Education. [http://www.library.ualberta.ca/library_html/libraries/coutts/special.html]. (Accessed November 25, 2000).

    Provides numerous links to sites dealing with a variety of areas of special education.

Part III

Administrative Concerns

Have you ever seen a battered book in a media center? If you had a chance to glance at its title, you probably recognized it as a popular work that was rarely on the shelves. The media specialist has probably been trying for some time to rescue it to have it mended or replaced. Some books go from one student to the next with hardly a pause at the circulation desk.

Have you seen the edges of study prints crumbling from too many pinholes, games with missing pieces, or cassettes with loose tapes? Are the shelves of the media center overflowing in one section and empty in another? These situations crop up in every collection. It is a challenge to ensure that they do not happen regularly.

The media specialist is the administrator of the collection. If the word *administrator* conjures images of pushing papers and filling out forms in triplicate, then you have overlooked important administrative roles. An administrator must be a planner, organizer, policy maker, public-relations expert, business-person, and evaluator. Through these roles, the media specialist shapes a collection and accesses resources that are responsive to the changing demands of the students, curriculum, and teachers. Making selection decisions, receiving new materials, and helping students use global resources through the Internet may be the more glamorous, exciting aspects of work with the collection. Administrative decisions, however, can ensure that students and teachers obtain the resources they need.

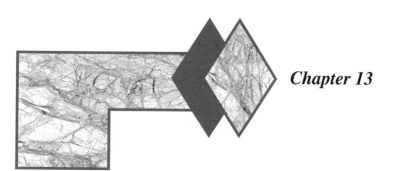

Chapter 13

Acquiring Materials

Acquisition is the process of obtaining materials. This involves confirming that materials are available, verifying order information, identifying and selecting sources of materials, arranging for order transmission and fulfillment, allocating funds, keeping records, and producing reports on expenditures of funds. Obtaining electronic products, reviewing license agreements, and negotiating for leases are additional steps in the procedure.

Speed, accuracy, and thrift are common goals of the acquisition process. Try to avoid the duplication of effort. The media center incurs costs when duplicate requests are received and unavailable materials are requested.

The media center may acquire materials through purchase, lease, and solicitation of free materials, gifts, or exchanges. Schools participating in resource-sharing programs may borrow and lend specific materials that coordinated collection development plans identify or are available through interlibrary loan.

This chapter focuses on the components of the acquisition process that are most likely to involve the building-level person directly (see Figure 13.1). It also reviews the relationship of acquisition procedures to acquisition policy, identifies the distribution systems, describes procedures for acquiring materials, and discusses the relationship between media professionals and publishers/producers. The district-level processing center may handle the acquisition procedures and serve as a clearinghouse for resource-sharing transactions. Chapter 14 discusses other ways to acquire and access materials thorough resource sharing, coordinated collection development, and electronic means.

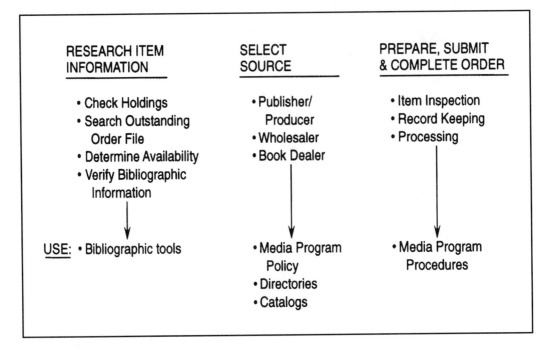

Figure 13.1. Components of the acquisition process.

Bibliographic information for acquisition tools, including those this chapter cites, appear in Appendix B. Many of these tools are available in print as well as electronic format. The list at the end of this chapter identifies works that provide information in greater depth than the scope of this discussion.

POLICIES AND PROCEDURES

Policies establish the procedures to follow and the rationale for such procedures. Procedures specify who will be responsible and spell out how they will follow the process. An acquisition policy may state that materials shall be purchased from the least expensive and most efficient source, for example, a jobber. The policy may go on to state that one may buy locally an item that one needs immediately. A policy could also state that video formats are preferable to buying or renting films.

Acquisition policies are likely to be uniform throughout the school district. The school district may also dictate the acquisition procedures. For example, the district's purchasing agent may specify the order forms that one will use. Other school districts may have agreements to use a jobber's online catalog. Procedures for accounting and record keeping are frequently established at the district level. Ask the director of the district media program for a copy of the policies and procedures. This information should be available in a handbook for all media specialists within the system.

DISTRIBUTION SYSTEMS

Choosing the best source for ordering materials is an important decision in the acquisition process. Chief distributors of materials include wholesalers, distributors, jobbers, publishers, producers, subscription agencies, dealers, remainders, vendors, and local sources such as bookstores. Other sources include retail outlets (new bookstores, used bookstores, music shops, video stores, map shops, sheet music stores, museums for slides and art reproduction, teacher supply stores for educational models and games), publishers, and producers.

Wholesalers, distributors, and jobbers are intermediaries between publishers or producers and the buyer, the media specialist. The term *jobber* is used interchangeably with the word *wholesaler*. Wholesalers buy materials from publishers and producers and sell them to bookstores and libraries. For example, one can buy books and videocassettes directly from the publisher or producer; yet the same items are often available at a lower price from a jobber or distributor. The word *distributor* may refer to a wholesaler but more frequently means a vendor of magazines, paperbacks, or audiovisual materials. Distributors may serve a region of the country or the whole country. Jobbers and distributors may provide newsletters, product hotlines, and Websites. Remainders handle materials at a discount price for items that are usually unavailable from other sources. A book remainder handles titles the original publisher is no longer keeping in stock.

If the media center has a standing order with a publisher, it will not be necessary to initiate orders for titles that the publisher delivers under the conditions of the standing order. For example, the American Library Association has categories of standing orders for materials relating to children and school libraries. Your jobber or vendor may be automatically shipping materials within specific subject, format, or award winners. Check these types of agreements to identify titles you will be receiving under the plan. Pending titles could be ones you do not want to duplicate.

Exchange programs involve two or more media centers that exchange materials, such as curriculum guides or courses of study for information skills. Other exchange programs are based on unwanted materials that are being sent to a central unit or posted so other media centers in the district can obtain those materials.

Jobbers

Libraries can expect wholesalers to have a large inventory of titles, to fill orders promptly and accurately at a reasonable cost, and to report on items not in stock. If you do not obtain satisfactory information about whether a book is out of print, out of stock indefinitely, or temporarily out of stock, contact the publisher or producer. Your concern can alert them to the need to have this item available.

Advantages/Disadvantages

Advantages to ordering materials through jobbers include the following:

You avoid the cost and paperwork of ordering through many publishers or producers.

There is only one source to contact for follow-up on orders.

Libraries receive better discounts from jobbers than from publishers or producers.

You obtain indirect access to publishers who refuse to deal directly with libraries or give poor service to small orders.

Many wholesalers provide full processing, cataloging services, circulation materials, and plastic jackets for materials.

Pre-selection plans—approval plans in which the library examines new titles at the usual discount rate with full return privileges—are frequently available.

Some jobbers offer online ordering services.

Disadvantages of using jobbers include the following:

It usually takes one month for jobbers to fill most orders, whereas publishers can deliver in one to two weeks.

The availability of older titles depends on the wholesaler's inventory.

No wholesaler can supply every available title. Some titles, such as materials that professional organizations produce, can be purchased only through direct order.

Policies on the return of defective or damaged copies may say that credit or replacement is not granted until the wholesaler has received the returns.

Selecting Jobbers

Personnel at the district level may be responsible for selecting the wholesaler or other source. If that is not the situation, contact other media specialists in the area to learn which sources they use and whether they find the service satisfactory.

Questions to consider when selecting a jobber are the following:

◆ Does the jobber offer a volume discount?

◆ Does the jobber provide a range of customer services, with clear billing and invoicing procedures and forms?

◆ Does the jobber have a toll-free telephone number?

◆ Does the jobber handle backorders and returns promptly and accurately?

◆ Is there a service representative?

◆ Does the service representative have a toll-free number?

◆ Do they have a Website?

◆ How quickly and accurately do they fill orders ?

◆ How do they figure discounts?

◆ Is the vendor financially stable?

◆ Is the vendor's automated system compatible with the media center's?

◆ What special services does the vendor offer?

◆ How much do the special services cost?

Ask other media specialists about the jobber's quality of service and handling of problems. Additional services may include the following:

Assistance with searches and verification.

Selection programs with review.

Cataloging and shelf-ready processing.

Customized management data.

Electronic financial transactions.

Electronic access to *Books in Print*.

Records for the media center's OPAC.

Distribution systems frequently offer new services. As an example, in 2000 Follett entered into an agreement with netLibrary to provide e-books over the Internet. Now media specialists can purchase e-books by using the Follett Library Resources.

As you investigate these sources, ask about their pricing schedules. Some will have two discount plans; one, a net title price, and the other based on volume orders. Batch volume orders have lower per-item costs.

The California Instructional Video Clearinghouse and the California Computer Software Clearinghouse encourage media specialists who are purchasing CD-ROMs and software to seek out producers and businesses that support the following policies:

Provide for free preview of the CD-ROM.

Provide a workstation for a limited time if needed at the site for preview of the CD-ROM.

Provide dealer support and on-site training as appropriate.

Maintain a toll-free telephone number to provide user support.

Provide a full refund for a product that fails to operate as described in advertising or in the documentation.

Provide licensing agreements that offer multiple copies at nominal cost.

Provide a network compatible version and licensing agreements that permit placing the CD-ROM on a network server.

Provide free or inexpensive updates when a new CD-ROM or version of software is available.

Replace lost or damaged disks at nominal or net cost.

Label package and disks to identify clearly the operating platform, for example, MS-DOS or MAC.

Do not require that the CD-ROM be returned when an update is received.

Provide multiple sets of consumable support materials at a reasonable cost and/or grant permission for these materials to be reproduced at each site.

State required hardware components in simple and explicit language.

List all cables, extensions, controller cards, systems, and so forth required for program operation.

Offer text only CD-ROM for either color or monochrome monitors.

Offer a subscription price for periodical indexes that is not more than twice the cost of an annual print subscription.

Offer special pricing of a CD-ROM product when purchased in combination with the same product in print (California Instructional Video Clearinghouse and California Computer Software Clearinghouse 1991b, 13).

A similar set of guidelines for software includes the following:

Provide free preview of software and documentation.

Recognize the need to provide free loan of lab packs or multiple copies of software for use in training sessions.

For extensive multi-grade programs, develop a preview disk with at least one complete interactive segment for each grade level; include sample documentation for each level.

Provide a refund for any product that fails to operate as described in documentation.

Provide a backup disk or a procedure for making one.

Replace damaged disks at nominal or no cost.

Provide free or inexpensive updates as new versions become available.

Provide licensing agreements that permit users to make multiple copies of software or provide multiple copies at a reduced cost.

Provide an explicit statement of the publisher's policy regarding permission to load a single copy of the program on multiple computers for use at the same time.

Provide a network compatible version of software with a licensing agreement that permits placing the software on a hard disk for access by multiple computers.

Provide adequate teacher support materials and training.

Accommodate a minimum of 40 students in any record-keeping component included with the program, and protect the records from unauthorized access.

Provide clear and adequate documentation for program operation.

Provide multiple sets of consumable materials at reasonable cost or permission to reproduce masters included with the program.

Make an explicit statement granting permission for students to take the software home, if this is the publisher's policy, and include a sample letter to parents that explains the copyright policy involved.

Provide a method for soliciting recommendations for the improvement of a software package and offer incentives for suggestions that are incorporated into subsequent versions (California Instructional Video Clearinghouse and California Computer Software Clearinghouse 1991a, 11).

ACQUISITION ACTIVITIES

The first stage of acquisition activities includes verifying the accuracy of bibliographic and ordering information, checking for the item in the present holdings record and in the file of outstanding orders, and checking the item's availability. The second stage is selecting the best source for the material. The third stage is preparing and submitting the order. The fourth is checking the received item against the original order and the invoice and checking the condition of the material. For example, are pages missing, or are all the elements present in a kit?

Preorder Work

As you receive requests for materials, the record-keeping process begins. Pre-order work involves verification and searching. To make wise selections, the media specialist must know what materials are available in which formats and what will be forthcoming. This involves being familiar with both bibliographic tools and sources of information about materials.

Search Procedures

The first step in the search process is to learn whether the item is already part of the collection or on order. A number of online public access computers (OPAC) can display the ordered/received status for items, making this step easier.

The requested item may be a new edition of a book recently acquired or a cassette that is part of a kit already in the collection. If the item is in the collection, one needs to check with the requester to determine whether the existing item is sufficient. If the collection does not have the item, then one determines whether the item is on order or is being processed. The "in-process file" displays whether the item is on order, has been received, or is being cataloged or processed. This record may be stored manually or electronically. Some media centers file a copy of the order slip in the card catalog under title entry; others record the information in the online catalog or the vendor's purchase order. When a work is received, the center adds a note that it is being processed. This procedure simplifies the checking process.

Verification Procedure

The verification procedure consists of two steps. The first is to establish the existence of a particular item. The second is to identify the correct author or main entry, title, publisher/producer, and other necessary ordering data. Common categories on the record are the author, title, publisher, data publication, edition, International Standard Book Number (ISBN) or International Standard Serial Number (ISSN) (unique numbers for specific titles or journals), Standard Address Number (SAN) of publisher, price, and number of copies requested. Other categories may include the requester's name, series, vendor, funding source, and the approval signature. The bibliographic data can be downloaded from some online bibliographic databases.

Sources of Information

To learn whether an item is available, one can start with a special type of bibliography called a *trade bibliography*. These tools provide ordering information for materials that are currently in print or otherwise available. Bibliographic tools that indicate availability may also state whether the item is available through purchase, rent, or loan, and the purchase or rental price

one must order the item directly from a publisher or producer or whether it is available through a jobber, distributor, or vender

there are postage or delivery charges, the person(s) responsible for pickup and return deliveries, the length of the loan, the notice required to ensure delivery on a needed date, and appropriate alternative arrangements

The information included for each item may vary from one tool to another. For print formats, the bibliographic entry usually includes the author, title, editor, publisher, date of publication, series title and number, available bindings, price, and ISBN or ISSN. For audiovisual items, the bibliographic entry usually includes the title; available formats; production and release dates; producer or distributor; physical characteristics (for example, color or black and white, captioned or sound, phono-disc or cassette, length or running time, and special equipment needed); number of pieces included (for example, four study prints and one teacher's guide); languages; price; and special conditions of availability.

Many bibliographies can be used in this process. Table 13.1 identifies a few examples that illustrate the range. To find the price of a particular book title, look under the title or authors in *Books in Print* (BIP) or on *Books in Print Plus* (R. R. Bowker), the CD-ROM version. BIP is also available online and can be searched at public and academic libraries. The *Directory of Video, Multimedia, and Audio-Visual Products* (Daniels, 1996–) contains information about equipment. Use the latest edition of these tools for the most current information on price and availability.

If you do not have access to these tools, other options are available to you. One place to find out whether titles are correct and whether a work is in print is through a commercial online bookstore. You can use these same sources to learn whether a work is forthcoming. A word of caution: Sometimes these sources do not have information about the latest edition of a work. An advantage in using these online sources is their inclusion of one or more reviews.

Electronic publishing is having an impact on publishing and bibliographic sources. The quarterly issues of *Schwann's Opus* (classical music) and *Spectrum* (pop) catalogs are being replaced with annual issues. This information will be updated on their Website (http://www.schwann.com). The Website, which was initially available only to libraries, went public with subscriptions in October 2000. The print version provides basic information about the recordings; the database provides additional information such as all the performers and their instruments. The print version will continue to have interviews and other features not found in the database. This is only one of many examples where media specialists must determine the depth of information they need and whether their collections need the print or electronic versions, or both.

Table 13.1.
Bibliographic Tools for Selected Formats

Format	Sample Tools
Books	*Books in Print* and related works
	El-Hi Textbooks and Serials in Print
Software	*Microcomputer Software Guide Online*
	Software Encyclopedia
Equipment	*Directory of Video, Multimedia, & Audio-Visual Products*
Videos	*Bowker's Complete Video Directory*
	The Video Source Book
Recordings	*Schwann Spectrum*
	Words on Cassette

Note: Appendix B provides full citations for these and other tools.

In 2000 increasing attention is being given to e-publishing. Nora Rawlinson's editorial in *Publishers Weekly* on March 6, 2000, announced a new department—"E-publishing"—reflecting the increasing number of companies publishing original e-book titles and related items.

The funds you need to buy bibliographic tools will strain even the strongest budget. Even though the cost may seem prohibitive for the CD-ROM formats, schools that can share them will find that option less expensive than purchasing print versions for each media center. In many districts, expensive bibliographies are available at the district media center. Other local sources include college and university libraries.

Websites maintained by publishers, producers, and jobbers provide information about available and forthcoming items. They may also provide information about the creators of the materials. Seeing a book jacket on a vendor program can give one a clue about its appeal to the students at your school.

Other information available at these sites includes information traditionally found in publishers' and producers' catalogs. Creating a bookmark for these companies will be helpful in learning what is available. If you decide to maintain a collection of print catalogs, remember the hidden costs in such an effort. These include clerical time for filing and maintaining the collection, storage units, and inventory-control efforts. Although bibliographic tools provide quicker access to information than catalogs do, the latter have some advantages. They are up to date and provide full ordering information and other useful information, such as suggested grade level, a possible reading level, and suggested curriculum applications.

Catalogs provide price and availability information, but they should not be used for reviews. Remember that catalogs exist to sell materials, not to offer evaluative reviews. When catalogs do quote reviews, full citations to the reviews are usually not given, so the media specialist needs to consider the limitations of incomplete reviews, words taken out of context, and the absence of more critical comments that reviews offer.

Lists of publications and products can be found in catalogs from government agencies, manufacturers, professional associations, museums, and county extension services. These listings may include free and inexpensive materials that promote or advertise products and services of the sponsoring producer.

Publications about the community may be found through announcements in local newspapers or through local civic and social organizations. The local chamber of commerce may have pamphlets about the community, businesses, industries, recreation facilities, history, forthcoming events, and geography. The local historical society may have pamphlets or slides about historic buildings or events.

Ordering

Ordering a specific title directly from a vendor or producer is called a *firm order*. *Standing order* is the term used to describe an order placed with vendors or producers for annuals and biennials that appear on an irregular basis. In these cases the vendor automatically sends the invoice with the material. Because it saves order time, this plan is advantageous if you want all the items. However, the situation is unpredictable in terms of the number that will be received and their cost. This approach requires monitoring to ensure that funds are available to pay for those items while at the same time having sufficient funds for other materials.

An *approval plan* is a form of standing order. In this situation the vendor sends the item with the invoice, and the media specialist accepts or rejects the material. The obvious advantage is the opportunity to reject the item. The disadvantage is that if one neglects to return an item, the collection can end up with a very low-use or a no-use item.

A *blanket order* is a combination of a firm order and an approval plan. The media center makes a commitment to buy all of something, such as all the Newbery Medal books or all the Caldecott Medal books. The invoice is automatically shipped with the item.

Computer-generated orders store data electronically in the library's file as well as the vendor's. For an example of how one librarian combines searching and ordering procedures using electronic resources, see Janet Foster's "Collection Development, from Text to Technology," listed in "Additional Readings" at the end of this chapter.

Common information that vendors need to ensure correct materials are the shipping address, author, title, publisher, date of publication, price, editor, number of copies, order number, instructions regarding shipping, invoicing, and method of payment. Vendors may also want the ISBN or ISSN numbers.

Receiving

Unpacking shipments calls for care. Special training may be necessary for clerical personnel and student assistants. If main office personnel, such as an account clerk, are involved in the process, establish a working rapport with them and be sure they know the exact procedure. The first item to locate is the packing slip or invoice (itemized list). This may be attached to the outside of the package or buried underneath the materials. If one does not find the packing slip, one should keep all the items in that shipment separate from those in other shipments.

As each item is received, check it against the packing slip or invoice for title match. In the case of videos, this step must take place before you remove the shrink wrap because many jobbers and distributors will not accept returns of unwrapped materials. Check the item for damage or missing parts. Know the jobber's and distributor's policy on returns and whether they will give credit for damage that occurred in shipping.

Common problems are wrong editions, items added to or deleted from the list, wrong number of copies, and damaged or incomplete items. Table 13.2 displays abbreviations and phrases that jobbers commonly use. After all items have been checked, place the property mark on them. Then record the bar code into the database. Finally, approve the invoice for payment.

Table 13.2.
Jobber Responses

OP	Out-of-print
OS	Out-of-stock
OSI	Out-of-stock indefinitely
TOS	Temporarily out-of-stock
NYP	Not yet published
NYR	Not yet received from publisher

Processing

The final stage in the acquisition process is preparing the materials for use. This involves cataloging and classifying each item, entering it on the holdings record, identifying the media center as owner, adding security strips and circulation bar codes, adding needed labels, and providing protective cases or other packaging for circulation of the materials. You will need to place copyright warnings and protection labels on the materials. Finally, you must decide how to market and display the new materials.

Record Keeping

Acquisition activities involve large amounts of detail work. You can handle the tracing of orders either manually or electronically. Manual systems often consist of keeping binders or files for purchase orders (POs) by categories such as "outstanding," "completed," or "to be paid." Other categories could be by number or budget account number.

Computers can simplify accessing information and generating records. Consideration files (the record of desired items) can be organized with a database management program, enabling one to print, in priority order, a list of items to be ordered from a single vendor. As materials are ordered and received, you can update these records. Some systems allow you to transfer the information to a different file, such as outstanding orders or new arrivals. Some systems also allow the administrator to create categories, such as a subject area, a specific format, back orders, or specified jobbers. You can use word-processing programs to create a template to print specific information on preprinted continuous forms, including purchase orders. You can also use a spreadsheet program to keep track of budget reports and projections or for organizing batch orders. Schools use databases to combine orders from several schools and to decide which schools should buy expensive materials.

If your school district is not using computer programs for management activities, consider the following questions: What jobs can best be handled through the use of computer programs? What equipment resources are available? What are the implications for staffing? What is the capability of existing software programs? Does your automated program permit online ordering, electronic invoicing, and credit-card payments?

Relationships

Media specialists share a bond with the people who are responsible for promoting the use of materials. That bond can be strengthened by two-way communication. Marketing departments have services and products to share, such as posters; media specialists can share how students respond to materials and suggest needed materials, which results in future purchases.

Communications with publishers and producers need not be limited to complaints. If students become excited about a particular work, share that information with the publisher or producer. To obtain information about authors, illustrators, filmmakers, extra book jackets, or other promotional materials, contact the people responsible for library services or library promotion at the issuing agency. For addresses of the publishers and the names of their personnel, see *Literary Market Place* (R. R. Bowker, 1973–). For similar information you can contact personnel in the audiovisual field by using *AV Market Place: The Complete Business Directory of Audio, Audio Visual, Computer Systems, Film, Programming with Industry Yellow Pages* (R. R. Bowker, 1980–).

Members of the Educational Paperback Association (paperback wholesalers) offer similar services including book examination in their warehouses, annual or biennial open houses with special sales, book fairs, reading programs, and promotional materials.

CONCLUSIONS

Acquisition activities consume time and energy. Searching for accurate information may require travel to gain access to needed tools. Detailed record keeping and correspondence demand patience. Many routines cannot be slighted or handled in haste. A media specialist's organizational abilities, mathematical skills, and business sense frequently come into play. Errors or misjudgments can be costly. Using computer-management systems can simplify procedures while controlling the information in a timely manner. Although delays or inaccurate fulfillment of orders can try one's patience, it can all be worthwhile when a student or teacher declares that the materials they have found are precisely what they wanted.

REFERENCES

California Instructional Video Clearinghouse and California Computer Software Clearinghouse. 1991a. *1991 Guidelines for CD-ROM in California Schools.* Long Beach, CA: California Instructional Video Clearinghouse and California Computer Software Clearinghouse.

———. 1991b. *1991 Guidelines for Computer Software in California Schools.* Long Beach, CA: California Instructional Video Clearinghouse and California Computer Software Clearinghouse.

Rawlinson, Nora. 2000. Developing Digital Strategies. *Publishers Weekly* 247, no. 10 (March 6): 8.

ADDITIONAL READINGS

Evans, G. Edward. 2000. *Developing Library and Information Center Collections.* 4th ed. Englewood, CO: Libraries Unlimited.
    Provides a more extensive exploration of acquisitions activities, jobbers, wholesalers, and other sources of materials.

Flood, Susan, ed. 1998. *Guide to Managing Approval Plans.* Acquisition Guidelines No. 11. Association for Library Collections and Technical Services, Acquisitions Section Publications Committee. Chicago: American Library Association.
    Provides a practical guide to the development, management, and evaluation of approval plans including the selection and evaluation of a vendor.

Foster, Janet. 2000. Collection Development, from Text to Technology. *Computers in Libraries* 20, 6 (June): 34–39.
    Describes how the Danbury (Connecticut) public libraries use electronic resources including reviews from standard reviewing publications, plus Websites of publishers and vendors in the ordering process.

Gorman, Michael. 1998. *Technical Services: Today and Tomorrow,* 2d ed. Englewood, CO: Libraries Unlimited.

    Addresses issues and trends.

Prestebak, Jane, and Konnie Wightman.2000. Losing Our Drawers. *School Library Journal* 46, no. 10 (October): 67–73.

    Explains how Z39.50 allows users of one catalog to search and retrieve information from another. Reports on a survey of media specialists' assessments of their automation systems.

Wadham, Tim. 1999. *Programming with Latino Children's Materials.* A How-to-Do-It Manual for Librarians, number 89. New York: Neal-Schuman.

    Identifies sources of Latino materials including Websites, listservs, organizations, Spanish-language book and media vendors and distributors, and Spanish-language book publishers/imprints.

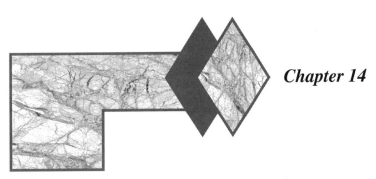

Chapter 14

Fiscal and
Access Issues

Media specialists face the reality that a single collection can neither own all available resources nor meet all of its users' demands. In meeting this challenge media specialists must address several issues. Among these is the question of ownership versus access. Should one use funds to purchase an item or to obtain a license to use that item?

Other questions deal with developing technologies. Should one add new formats such as e-books to the collection? Should e-books be circulated? If so, should the equipment to use the e-book also circulate?

Another series of questions involves accessing electronic sources of information. As media specialists make these decisions, the questions become where and how they will find the funds to support their decisions.

FISCAL MATTERS

Given this complex situation, how do media specialists allocate funds for acquiring or accessing information? Allocation can be based on curriculum areas, subject, format, users, distribution of student population (number and ability levels of students by grade level), collecting intensity rankings, and collection mapping. Other approaches include historical (how allocations were handled in the past), anticipated loss/replacement, and age of the collection. The allocation will also reflect the media center's stance on the amount of electronic access versus ownership (the more traditional position).

241

Escalating costs are another factor media specialists face. The average cost of books continues to increase. At the same time the cost of sound recordings and CDs is decreasing. One can consult the April issue of *Publishers Weekly* or the latest edition of the *Bowker Annual Library and Book Trade Almanac* (R. R. Bowker, 1955–) for an annual update on this information. Another informative source is Marilyn L. Miller and Marilyn L. Shontz's biannual report in *School Library Journal* on their national survey of media centers' collection sizes, financial resources, and expenditures.

Developing technologies bring new costs. For instance, Renee Olson, editor-in-chief of *School Library Journal,* forecasts that, with the distribution of electronic books, prices may jump. She bases her prediction on a price model from netLibrary, an e-book distributor. In addition to the price of the book in paper copy there is

> a one-time fee of 50 percent of the book's price to manage the electronic file and supply you with circulation reports. That means your book on space exploration—at an average cost of $21.26 for nonfiction—will now cost $31.89, after adding netLibrary's maintenance fee of $10.63 (Olson 2000a, 99).

This service also has limitations. One cannot print an entire work. Someone who is trying to print the entire work will see a copyright infringement notice displayed. At the end of the third such warning, the reader is cut off from using the book. In addition, only one person can view the work at one time. If multiple copies are needed, they must all be licensed.

Licensing

With the advent of accessing digital information rather than obtaining outright ownership, media specialists are learning to negotiate licensing agreements. These define appropriate use and specify a given time period. Both the media center as buyer (licensee) and vendor (licensor) are bound by the negotiated terms.

Common issues in licensing electronic resources are the following:

Resolving the issue of ownership and access. When you obtain a license, the vendor is granting the media center "permission to distribute and make available specific content for an agreed-upon duration and time."

Defining how the content may or may not be used (fair use).

Determining whether the content is to be accessed within the library or remotely.

Defining who is authorized to use the resource. In schools the user is often the faculty, staff, and students.

On a practical level Pearlmutter advises that

> [I]f your library media center has, say, only one or two workstations, it's in your best interests to negotiate a contract based on the number of users who can be online at any one time, rather than on your school's total population (Pearlmutter 1999, 28).

Other practical advice includes the following:

◆ Select the clauses in license agreements with which you agree.

◆ Create a licensing template of those terms.

◆ Develop a checklist of terms and conditions that are appropriate for your situation.

◆ Be sure the license follows the copyright laws.

◆ Avoid licenses that hold the media center liable for each and every infringement by authorized users.

◆ Avoid non-cancellation clauses.

◆ Avoid non-disclosure clauses.

◆ Time limitations should be clearly defined.

◆ Avoid licenses that permit subcontracting to an agent.

For further suggestions see the "Additional Readings" and "Electronic Resources" at the end of this chapter.

Alternative Funding

Working within the guidelines of district policies and procedures, media specialists constantly search for ways to increase resources. Their budgets may vary from year to year. Fundraising activities and grant searches are two ways to increase funding support.

Fundraising

Local efforts include sponsoring book fairs, soliciting contributions from parent groups, and obtaining support from business partners. Lisa Politzer describes how the Friends of the Torrey Pines High School Library have held two schoolwide fundraisers (a dinner dance, a rummage sale) and a gift wrapping service at a local bookstore. They found book sales weren't worth the effort, but readings by local authors have been popular. Direct mailing was their most successful fundraiser (Politzer 1999).

Grants

Media specialists may gain outside funding through grant proposals with monies coming from local, regional, or national sources. Other outside funding comes from serving as a beta-test site for the development of technology or forming partnerships with the private sector. A number of state-level networking projects require grant proposals as part of the application process.

Monies received through grants may be used for a variety of purposes. These include upgrading of technology, purchase of computer software, adding e-mail communication and online services, support for resource sharing, Web subscriptions, and facilities improvement.

Typical elements in a proposal are the following:

Cover sheet: brief identification of project, goals, and beneficiaries of the project.

Abstract: brief summary of project.

Table of contents.

Introduction: description of applicant, purpose, programs, constituents, credibility of organization and its accomplishments, credibility or proposed program.

Needs statement: need, support, data, and experiences.

Goals and objectives: intent and anticipated outcomes of the proposed project.

Project design: plan of action, activities and methods planned to achieve the project objectives.

Budget: costs and expenditures for personnel (includes wages, salaries, and fringe benefits) and non-personnel (includes equipment and supplies).

Evaluation design: plans for determining whether goals are met, assessing process and product, and identifying who will monitor and evaluate.

Dissemination: identification of what will be reported to whom and how that information will be distributed.

Plans for the future: outline of how the project will be supported after outside funding runs out.

Appendix (you should refer to these items in the narrative): Examples of items to include are the mission statement, bibliography, vita of personnel, and letters of commitment and endorsement.

The Foundation Center is a national non-profit organization devoted to fostering public understanding of the foundation field. They collect, organize, analyze, and disseminate information about foundations. At their Website (http://www.fdncenter.org) one can note the extensive number of publications and information sources they produce. Their guides are useful in identifying funding agencies interested in different aspects of education and in identifying recipients of their funds. As one example of the information they provide, see "The Foundation Center's User-Friendly Guide" (http://fdncenter.org/onlib/ufg).The Foundation Center's five main libraries are in New York; Washington, D.C.; San Francisco; Cleveland; and Atlanta.

Grantsmanship for Small Libraries and School Library Media Centers, by Frank W. Hoffman, describes the process, offers practical advice, answers the most frequently asked questions, and identifies other sources of information. The "Additional Readings" and "Electronic Resources" listings at the end of this chapter identify additional sources.

ELECTRONIC ACCESS ISSUES

A current issue is how to connect people to electronic resources. Media specialists use a variety of approaches including Websites, interactive Web-based online catalogs, and virtual libraries. The decision to make these provisions may be made at the state level. Some of the resource-sharing projects described later in this chapter will illustrate that approach. In other cases school districts are opting to have online catalogs within the district or at selected schools. A decreasing number of schools are retaining traditional card catalogs. Where users have access to electronic sources, such services usually include access to remote CD-ROMs, online databases, and online catalogs.

Like other resources, electronic ones are uneven in quality and suitability. Advertisements may dominate or be thinly disguised in virtual field trips. The purposes and goals of the sponsors may not be evident. To aid in identifying stimulating and curriculum-oriented sites, Gail Cooper and Garry Cooper provide an annotated listing in *More Virtual Field Trips* (Libraries Unlimited, 1999).

The Internet

Through telecommunication networks, students and teachers gain access to global information. Commonly used components of these systems are electronic mail, electronic bulletin boards, and electronic databases.

Media specialists use telecommunications in collection development, selection, ordering (from jobbers), and cataloging. Such services can save money and time.

Resources available through the Internet include commercial online databases. Some databases are available only at certain hours of the day or on weekends, when there is less demand for them by the original group for whom they were developed. Other resources are catalogs of hundreds of the world's libraries, free educational software, music recordings, videos, and documents. Statewide telecommunications networks are being used for state reporting of educational information, financial management systems, instructional management tools, and teacher certification.

Numerous sites have tutorials on the general use of the Internet, while other tutorials are for specific sites. The electronic resources at the end of this chapter identify a sampling of these sites.

As schools expand their use of these electronic resources, media specialists will need to decide who can access what and when. The AUPs (Acceptance Use Policies) described in Chapter 6 provide guidelines for use.

Certainly the largest, and often the cheapest, electronic network is the Internet. Much of what is available on the Internet is free. Resources on the Internet play a role in the collection as they

replace out-of-date pamphlet files,

provide materials outside the scope of the collection,

access up-to-the-minute information on current events,

provide information such as the latest values of foreign currencies,

provide materials that will not appear in print such as some government information available only in electronic format via government Websites,

allow interaction with a Website and the ability to search within a database,

offer global dialogues about specific issues, and

allow participation in discussion groups such as Kidnet, which carries information about global or national electronic projects for students and teachers.

Media Center Websites

One way media specialists help users access the Internet is through the center's Website. The purpose of the media center Website should directly reflect the media center's and the school's mission. The collection development policy should provide such a statement. Typical language "is to support the school's instructional program." That commitment would lead to providing access to Internet resources and databases related to curriculum areas or to teacher's needs. Thus the content provided at the Website should reflect the school's mission.

The media specialist selects, organizes, and disseminates information within the context of the Web environment. Selection involves identifying and evaluating relevant sites and full-text electronic resources to which links are created. Organization involves the classifying of resources with related links and creating subject bibliographies. Another important feature is creating access to the OPAC, or the Web-based searchable online catalog. Like other resources within the collection, media specialists need to re-evaluate these links and this information periodically.

Mark Stover offers "Seven Principles of Web Design" to guide the process.

1. Do preliminary planning and strategizing as to its mission, audience, and standards you'll use.

2. Consider consistency, esthetics, and appropriate use of color in the layout.

3. Provide visual cues to convey a sense of context as well as a table of contents and/or site map.

4. Create links back to the home page and other appropriate Websites.

5. Use graphics, sound, or video when appropriate in terms of size and informativeness.

6. Provide accurate content.

7. Ensure that content is reliable and authoritative (Based on Stover 1999, 208–9).

What criteria can one apply in selecting information? General criteria that apply regardless of format (see Chapter 9) can be used at this point. In addition, the criteria for evaluating Websites (see Chapter 10) also apply.

How does one identify what is available? As with information in other forms, media specialists can consult content specialists such as teachers, look at print and media sources including periodicals about computers and the Web, and use search engines.

Online Catalogs

One way media specialists help patrons access information is through the provision of electronic catalogs that have a graphical user interface (GUI). You can use these catalogs to

schedule use of audiovisual equipment;

generate and track purchase orders;

manage the record keeping of classroom reading sets;

allow patrons to search CD-ROMs, electronic databases, and the Web itself; and

provide entry points for non-media Websites within the school, such as teachers' home pages with sample projects or homework help.

A search begins in the user's classroom, an office, or at home as they move from the media center's home page to resources in the online catalog, in the online databases, and at recommended Websites. To create this interconnectivity, a media center's network needs to be connected to the Internet and have an online catalog with the communications protocol that allows the user to talk to the Web. This interconnectivity within the media center can permit every workstation an entry point to every electronic resource through the use of menuing software or links on the home page. Users can access other catalogs, such as those of a library or a vendor. Many vendors offer the Z39.50 feature, which is an international communications standard for broadcast capability that allows one to search several catalogs simultaneously. This process is similar to using a search engine on the Internet.

When purchasing a new online catalog system, Chesbro recommends that you consider the following:

1. Does the system use MARC records? Make sure that you can both import and export in either USMARC or MicroLIF MARC format.[1] Importing allows you to load MARC records into your system, and exporting permits you to take your data with you when moving to a new system in the future.

2. Is the system compatible with the network in your school or district? If it can't communicate with other systems on campus, you may have a hard time getting technical support or providing access from classrooms.

3. Does the system offer both a PC interface (Windows or Mac) and a Web interface? You might not be ready right now to put your catalog up on the Web, but the system you choose today should be able to grow with you.

4. What support services does the vendor offer? Because of staffing levels, school libraries are more likely than their public counterparts to need add-on services, like cataloging records, identifying Web resources, and providing technical support.

5. How easy is the system to learn and navigate? You will be spending a lot of time with it, and it should be easy to move, for example, from circulation to editing a student's record.

6. What nearby libraries use this system? Ask each vendor to give you the names and phone numbers of two or three schools similar to yours so that you can talk to a user of the system (Chesbro 1999, 35).

The technology to handle such networks is rapidly changing, so do not forget to consult current literature and electronic sources as you plan for your media center's future.

Virtual Library

Another way users can access electronic resources is for the media center to serve as a virtual library. The term *virtual library* can be described at several levels. At one level the user can access catalogs of media centers and libraries other than at one's own institution, with the possibility of being able to place an interlibrary loan request directly. At a more complex level, the user can access other types of databases and retrieve electronic publications.

A virtual library

provides a local collection that meets the information needs of the users;

has an online catalog that identifies the holdings of that collection;

provides access to abstracting and indexing services in machine-readable form;

provides access to other electronic subscriptions of the media center, such as databases;

has telecommunication links to other libraries' online catalogs and electronic sources;

provides access to standard Web search engines;

has telecommunications links to other sources of information, resources, and services;

links to other librarians' mediated lists; and

can send and receive information and data electronically.

How does this affect your analysis of the collection and available resources? Stielow observes that

> The Web realigns a portion of traditional collection analysis:
>
> 1. Instead of evaluating potential selections against extant holdings and applying various evaluative criteria within a limited budget, one faces an undifferentiated grab bag floating in cyberspace.
>
> 2. The presence of Internet terminals opens the entire Web as a resource, but a virtual library requires specialized professional selection from that vast resource.
>
> 3. Selection is not limited by costs, but arises from an almost overwhelming array of choices. The temptation for overreaching becomes a real danger along with the uncertainties of relying on a still unformed and transitory medium.
>
> 4. In such an environment, it is easy to reach beyond your immediate constituency and mission. Institutions may be lured into attempting to provide resources for the world.

5. Searching for sites to select can lead you through a dizzying maze of loops and links, which can easily make a reviewer unsure of what has or has not been seen (Stielow 1999, 98).

A comprehensive discussion of the Internet and virtual libraries is beyond the scope of this book. Sources cited in "Additional Readings" and "Electronic Resources" at the end of this chapter provide more in-depth coverage. Other sources explain how to locate resources through the Internet.

Resource Sharing

How are these developments affecting media centers? The basic concept of sharing bibliographic information and collections is not new. The advent of telecommunications and other technologies has increased the opportunities to share resources.

Although location of information is an important aspect, delivery of the desired items is of greater concern. Changes in technological delivery systems make it possible to address the needs of individual learners more effectively regardless of geographic location. These multi-type library organizations (that is, academic, public, school, and special libraries) establish formal cooperative organizations of independent and autonomous libraries or groups of libraries to work together for mutual benefit. Networks are not limited to regions—they can be found within a school system or at the community, county, state, national, and international levels.

The traditional library network was a cooperative in which participating members shared resources on formal and informal bases. These early consortia shared union lists of serials, provided loans through their interlibrary lending (ILL) network, or jointly owned a film collection.

The current use of the term *networking* acknowledges the development of online infrastructures through which some type of telecommunications connection links members to resources. The participants include multi-state, multi-type libraries.

Successful networks are characterized by a financial and organizational commitment from the members, who agree to perform specific tasks and adhere to specific guidelines. In return, the member library has immediate access through computer and communications technology to databases that originate in the public or private sector.

Commonly held beliefs about networks are the following:

Opportunity to access information is the right of each individual.

Networks do not replace individual collections; rather, they enhance existing ones and expand their range of services.

Participating libraries are responsible for meeting the daily needs of their users and for contributing to the network.

Networking is not free. Costs include equipment, materials, computer time, postage, telephone, copying expenses, and staff time.

Effective communication among participants is essential.

Commitment to participation is made at the school-district level.

Local, district, and regional levels of service must be clearly defined.

School-level personnel need to be notified early in the process and kept informed about plans.

Decisions must be made as to which services—for example, bibliographic retrieval, cataloging, or interlibrary loan—the network will provide.

Delivery systems for bibliographic data and information retrieval must be spelled out.

Remuneration to or from systems must be mutually agreed upon.

Legislative issues and governance must be agreed upon.

One way to judge a cooperative multi-type library organization is by the services it offers. Figure 14.1 lists some typical services.

Jane Pearlmutter observes that one of the advantages of joining a consortium is the depth of the discounts. She uses as an example the Wisconsin approach, where

> libraries, schools, colleges, and other Internet service providers have access to BadgerLink, a full text database of 4,000 magazines and journals, 29 national and regional newspapers, 13 state newspapers, 1,000 health pamphlets, and several other databases. Contracts with the vendors of the magazines' indexes EBSCOHost and UMI's ProQuest Direct allow the state to offer this wide range of resources to all of these information agencies. The Wisconsin Department of Public Instruction has estimated that the cost of providing these resources to schools and libraries on an individual (rather than a group) basis would be $50 million. How much does the consortium pay? $2.1 million! That's more than a 95-percent savings. At last count, 17 states were providing similar services (Pearlmutter 1999, 28–29).

Some of the trade-offs to consider are the state's ability to finance the renewing of the contract and the possibility that the vendor may not handle products that media specialists may want.

Lee Ireland describes recent changes:

> As libraries automated their collections, electronic union catalogues, such as those provided by Auto-Graphics, became a reality and replaced the paper union catalogues. Using this technology, which was origi- nally CD-ROM based and is now Internet based, libraries are able to automate their resource sharing efforts. These electronic union cata- logues allow libraries to share resources quickly and effectively.

For example, in the past five years, Auto-Graphics' electronic resource sharing products have enabled over 6900 libraries to share resources via the Internet and, once the item is found, to use the Internet for ILL (1999, 63).

Library Network Services

Access or referral to nonlibraries
Building and space planning
Consulting
Continuing education
Contracting for services
Contractual program administration
Cooperative acquisitions
Cooperative collection development
Cooperative programming
Database management
Delivery or courier system
Electronic bulletin board
Electronic mail
Grant writing
Graphics
Group purchasing
Handbook development
Hiring assistance
Information clearinghouse
Interlibrary loan
Loan of materials or equipment
    (temporary or permanent)
Materials examination center
Materials review
Meeting or conference planning
Newsletter

Policy development
Printing
Production facilities
Professional awareness
Professional collection
Program evaluation
Public information
Publications
Reciprocal access
Reciprocal borrowing
Reference center
Research and development
Retrospective conversion
Rotating collections
Serials cancellations
Shared licensing
Shared personnel
Shared system
    CD-ROM, microform,
    or online catalog/
    circulation
Software development
Technical services
Telefacsimile (fax)
    communications
Union list

Figure 14.1. Sample services of multi-type library organizations. Based on Association of Specialized and Cooperative Library Agencies, *Standards for Cooperative Multitype Library Organizations* **(Chicago: American Library Association, 1990), 17; and Sally Drew and Kay Ihlenfeldt, comp.,** *School Library Media Centers in Cooperative Automation Projects* **(Chicago: American Library Association, 1991), 112–13.**

Patrons using a standard Web browser in their home, office, or school workstation can access the electronic collection and make arrangements for interlibrary loans.

An example of this is the Texas Library Connection (TLC), where nearly 3,000 media centers are online with a virtual library. The Texas Education Agency handles their comprehensive, statewide, online school reference library. Begun in September 2000, the database includes a customized newspaper archive, periodical and Spanish-language databases, and a Texas almanac. In addition, through the Texas Library Connection (TLC), schools have access to over 2 million unique records, representing the holdings of approximately 3,000 schools. Individual titles represent books, videotapes, audiotapes, computer software, and other audiovisual formats. The database can be accessed from one's home, classroom, or workstation in the media centers. When doing selection and collection development activities, media specialists access the database to learn what other libraries are buying or have in their collections. The media specialists also have access to the Texas State Electronic Library, a public library consortium, and TexShare, an academic library consortium.

Renee Olson (2000b) describes Ohio's INFOhio, the online network for Ohio's public and private school libraries, which provides the following:

A unified automated system for 900 schools.

A one-million-item union catalog of full MARC records of the holdings in all the libraries.

Medianet, which allows booking of audiovisual materials on the Web.

Training for librarians and teachers.

Access to online resources such as *Encyclopaedia Britannica,* ProQuest Direct to 144 periodicals, and SIRS Discoverer.

Opportunity for schools to purchase automation services such as online catalogs and circulation systems.

Of the 900 schools, the majority (678) have their catalogs on the Web. The annual cost per student is $1 to $3, depending on the school's technical support site's fees for hardware and telecommunications. As is the case in other states, Ohio legislators have allocated more funding for public and academic library networks than to the school network. Backers of INFOhio assert that more state funding would encourage more schools to join the network.

CONCLUSIONS

The concept that each media center collection must own the resources its users need is being weighed against the opportunities that technology allows for accessing electronic resources. At the same time, media specialists are exploring alternate ways to financially support the collection. Resource sharing, particularly at the state level, with databases and electronic resources is on the increase.

A growing challenge is how to disseminate and distribute information. Media specialists are meeting this challenge by developing Websites, expanding online interactive catalogs, and creating virtual libraries. Today's media specialist is still responsible for selecting, organizing, and disseminating information, but those resources are no longer limited to those physically located in the media center.

NOTE

1. USMARC and CANMARC became MARC21.

REFERENCES

Chesbro, Melinda. 1999. The Catalog Takes to the Highway. *School Library Journal* 45, no. 5 (May): 33–35.

Hoffman, Frank W. 1999. *Grantsmanship for Small Libraries and School Library Media Centers.* Englewood, CO: Libraries Unlimited.

Ireland, Lee. 1999. The Web and Resource Sharing. *The Electronic Library: The International Journal for the Applications of Technology in Information Environments* 17, no. 2 (April): 63–65.

Kozinn, Allan. 2000. Schwann Is Revamping Its Recording Catalogs. *The New York Times,* Monday, September 11, section b, page 3.

Mattos, Jodie, and Joseph Yue. 2000. Saving Monday by Using Online Bookstores. *Computers in Libraries* 20, no. 5 (May): 42–47.

Olson, Renee. 2000a.Coming Soon to a School Near You. *School Library Journal* 46, no. 2 (February): 50–54.

———. 2000b. Replacing the Man on the Moon. *School Library Journal* 46, no. 3 (March): 99.

Pearlmutter, Jane. 1999. Which Online Resources Are Right for Your Collection? *School Library Journal* 45, no. 6 (June): 27–29.

Politzer, Lisa. 1999. You've Got a Friend. *School Library Journal* 45, no. 4 (April): 30–31.

Stielow, Frederick. 1999. *Creating a Virtual Library.* How-to-Do-It Manuals for Librarians, Number 91. New York: Neal-Schuman.

Stover, Mark. 1999. *Leading the Wired Organization: The Information Professional's Guide to Managing Technological Change.* New York: Neal–Schuman.

ADDITIONAL READINGS

The Bowker Annual Library and Book Trade Almanac. New York: R. R. Bowker, 1955– .
Provides references for research studies; statistics, such as average prices of books; news about legislation, associations, and grant-making agencies; distinguished books; and directory information.

Christensen, Deborah. 1999. Golden Retrievers. *School Library Journal* 45, no. 11 (November): 38–41.
Describes the use of metadata (data in a card catalog) to describe and locate information on the Internet. Discusses how the Gateway to Educational Materials Project (GEM), a special project of the ERIC Clearinghouse on Information and Technology, is using metatags to provide access to resources on the Internet.

Cohen, Laura B. 1999. The Web as a Research Tool: Teaching Strategies for Instructors. *Choice* Vol. 36 Supplement.
Describes basic principles, definitions, standards, and when and how to do different types of searches, and compares search engines.

Computers in Libraries: Complete Coverage of Library Information Technology. Ten times a year. Information Today.
Covers news items and general technical articles. Provides practical information on topics such as e-books, licensing, virtual libraries, fundraising, and Web designing.

Cooke, Alison. 1999. *Neal-Schuman Authoritative Guide to Evaluating Information on the Internet.* New York: Neal-Schuman.
Offers coverage of search facilities, Internet information sources, and specific types of sources. Identifies questions to consider in evaluating these information sources. Enhanced by illustrations, an annotated bibliography, and a glossary.

Cooper, Gail, and Garry Cooper. 1999. *More Virtual Field Trips.* Englewood, CO: Libraries Unlimited.
Provides annotations about informative Websites related to curriculum areas including physical education, health and safety, rural issues, and architectural field trips.

Grey, Duncan. 1999. *The Internet in School.* London: Cassell.
Takes the position of monitoring, not restricting, use of the Internet. Offers practical advice in a non-technical format about dealing with the Internet in a school serving 1,850 students ages 11–18.

Hoffman, Frank W., ed. 1999. *Grantsmanship for Small Libraries and School Library Media Centers.* Englewood, CO: Libraries Unlimited.
Offers sample language and identifies many resources as it describes the process of applying for grants.

Mambretti, Catherine. 1999. *Internet Technology for Schools.* Jefferson, NC: McFarland.
 Moves from a general overview of the issues faced in planning for and developing technology in the schools to "good Internet practices" and providing technical guidelines. Has a useful glossary.

Miller, Marilyn L., and Marilyn L. Shontz. Expenditures for Resources in School Library Media Centers, published every other year in *School Library Journal.*
 Reports on a national survey of *School Library Journal* subscribers.

Morville, Peter; Louis B. Rosenfeld, and Joseph Janes. 1999. Rev. by GraceAnne A. DeCandido. *The Internet Searcher's Handbook: Locating Information, People, and Software.* New York: Neal-Schuman.
 Guide with a practical and accessible style.

ELECTRONIC RESOURCES

The Foundation Center. 2000. The Foundation Center's User-Friendly Guide to Funding Research and Resources. [http://fdncenter.org/onlib/ufg]. (Accessed November 11, 2000).
 Describes foundations, finding a funding agency, and developing the proposal; identifies sources of information; and provides a glossary. Also from the Center, see "the Foundation Center: Your Gateway to Philanthropy on the World Wide Web" at http://www.fdncenter.org/ (Accessed November 11, 2000); Online Library at http://fdncenter.org/onlib/index.html (Accessed November 11, 2000); and "The Grantmaker Info" at http://fdncenter.org/grantmaker/index.html (Accessed November 11, 2000).

Indiana Library Resource Sharing Manual. 2d ed. 1997. [http://www.statelib.lib.in.us/www/LDO/reshman.html]. (Accessed November 11, 2000).
 Provides an example of a state's policies and procedures for interlibrary loans, reference referrals, and reciprocal borrowing.

Massachusetts Library Association/Massachusetts School Library Media Association Joint Statement on Collection Development in Schools and Public Libraries. 1999. [http://www.mlin.lib.ma.us/mblc/public_advisory/school_public/ps_jscolldev.shtml]. (Accessed November 11, 2000).
 Identifies the collection responsibilities for the public library and for the school library media center.

Open eBook Forum. 2000. [OeB]: Open eBook Forum. [http://www.openebook.org]. (Accessed November 11, 2000).
 Composed of publishers and distributors of e-books, and other interested parties. Works toward standardization of the publication structure of e-books.

Templeton, Brad. Ten Big Myths about Copyright Explained. [http://www.templetons.com/brad/copymyths.html]. (Accessed November 11, 2000).
 Focuses on copyrights in relation to Internet use.

Licensing

Brennan, Patricia, Karen Hersey, and Georgia Harper. 1997. Licensing Electronic Resources: Strategic and Practical Considerations for Signing Electronic Information Delivery Agreements. [http://www.arl.org/scomm/licensing/licbooklet.html]. (Accessed November 11, 2000).
> Addresses the needs of academic libraries and offers guidelines for licensing and copyright issues applicable to school media centers.

Librarians Information Online Network (LION). 2000. [http://www.libertynet.org/lion/lion.html]. (Accessed November 11, 2000).
> Links to automation articles and all the system vendors.

Licensing Digital Resources: How to Avoid the Legal Pitfalls? European Copyright User Platform, Netherlands. 1998. [http://www.eblida.org/ecup/docs]. (Accessed November 11, 2000).
> Discusses legal aspects.

Soete, George J. 1999. Managing the Licensing of Electronic Products. Washington, D.C.: Association of Research Libraries, Office of Leadership and Management Services. [http://www.arl.org/olms/infosvcs.html]. (Accessed November 11, 2000).
> Covers managerial aspects of licensing.

Yale University Library, Council on Library and Information Resources. 2000. Liblicense: Licensing Digital Information a Resource for Librarians. [http://www.library.yale.edu/~llicense] (Accessed November 11, 2000).
> Provides information, a draft model license, and a glossary of words and phrases commonly used in licensing agreements.

Internet

American Association of School Librarians. 1999. ICONnect. [http://www.ala.org/ICONN]. (Accessed November 26, 2000).
> Has online tutorials for students, families, and media specialists.

Auer, Nicole J. 2000. Bibliography on Evaluating Internet Resources." [http://www.lib.vt.edu/research/libinst/evalbiblio.html]. (Accessed November 11, 2000).
> Includes Internet resources, print resources, example Websites, useful listservs, and useful books.

Barker, Joe. 2000. Finding Information on the Internet. [http://www.lib.berkeley.edu/TeachingLib/Guides/Internet/FindInfo.html]. (Accessed November 11, 2000).
> Regularly revised versions from the Teaching Library Internet Workshops at the University of California, Berkeley. Covers the basics, such as a glossary of Internet and Netscape jargon, as well as exercises in finding, searching, and evaluating, and searching. Provides a link to creating your first Web-based tutorial.

Milbury, Peter. 2000. Peter Milbury's Network of School Library Web Pages. [http://www
.school-libraries.net]. (Accessed November 11, 2000).

Provides links to school library Web pages where you will find examples of
how various schools provide links to Internet sources for their users. The site is listed
in *School Library Journal Online's "Best Sites for Librarians."*

Milton S. Eisenhower Library, John Hopkins University. 2000. Evaluating Information
Found on the Internet. [http://milton.mse.jhu.edu:8001/research/education/net.html].
(Accessed November 11, 2000).

Links to "How to Search the Web" and other sites, including "Information
Retrieval and the Internet."

Rippel, Chris. n.d. Computer Training Tutorials. [http://www.ckls.org/~crippel/computerlab
/tutorials]. (Accessed November 11, 2000).

Offers advice on cleaning your mouse and other hardware, using software,
connecting to the Internet, and using the World Wide Web.

Tillman, Hope N. 2000. Evaluating Quality on the Net. [http://www.hopetillman.com
/findqual.html]. (Accessed November 11, 2000).

Covers criteria for evaluation and recommends specific evaluation tools on
the net (e.g., search engines, directory partners, guides and directories, specialized
guides, and fee-based traditional library resources).

Wisconsin Department of Public Instruction, Division for Libraries, Technology, and Community
Learning. n.d. BadgerLink: Wisconsin's Connection to the World of Information.
[http://www.dpi.state.wi.us/dpi/dltcl/badgerlink]. (Accessed November 11, 2000).

Provides access to information using existing telecommunications networks and
Internet connections. ProQuest and EdscoHost are two of the sources of information.

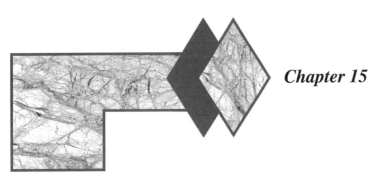

Chapter 15

Maintaining the Collection

An effective collection maintenance program serves two purposes. First, materials and equipment should be readily available for use. Second, policies and procedures for preventive maintenance help ensure economical and efficient management of the collection. Maintenance activities include keeping accurate records of what is in the collection (an inventory); inspecting materials; and repairing, replacing, or removing items.

Policies, procedures, and evaluation processes of the maintenance program are the focus of this chapter. The "Additional Readings" and "Electronic Resources" listings at the end of this chapter identify works with more specific information about the conservation and presentation of items in the collection. For bibliographic information and descriptions of the resources cited in this chapter, see Appendix B.

MAINTENANCE POLICIES

Maintenance policies frequently exist at the district, rather than at the building level. Policies related to equipment maintenance address the following issues:

when and why equipment will be traded in or discarded. The policy may guide replacement decisions by setting limitations on repair costs.

the type of repairs and maintenance that will be handled at the building level, at the district level, and through repair contracts. Simple maintenance, such as replacing light bulbs or cleaning video heads, may be done at the building level as a matter of policy, while external contractors handle major repairs and overhauls.

the records to be kept on equipment usage, repair, and maintenance. For example, one can determine the cost effectiveness of a given piece of equipment by analyzing the data collected on maintenance records.

the quantity and type of usable pieces of equipment to be provided. To meet this level of access, the policy provides a replacement schedule. For example, one might replace video units every 7 to 10 years.

The overall policy should specify that the media specialist is responsible for discarding materials and equipment. The school district should establish depreciation tables to guide the media specialist. Such tables help justify the discarding of materials and equipment. In preparing the budget, developmental items (those increasing the size of the collection) can be distinguished from replacement items (those maintaining the current level of service). The media specialist can base the replacement of materials and equipment on the rates at which the items become unusable because of wear or dated content. Although the experience of the media center staff and the condition of the existing collection are the first guides to establishing renewal rates, Table 15.1 provides some general guidelines.

Another factor to consider is loss. A loss rate greater than 2 percent suggests that a replacement or loss factor must be a budget item. In Appendix B, *Information Power: Guidelines for School Library Media Program* (American Association of School Librarians 1988) offers two budget formulas for materials and equipment.[1] For example, to replace lost, damaged, and out-of-date books, one formula multiplies by 5 percent the number of books in the collection times the average price of a book. The example uses the following illustration: For a collection with 6,000 volumes, 5 percent of the volumes (300 books) should be replaced. If the average cost of a book is $15.00, then 300 times $15.00 means $4,500 is needed to cover the replacement costs.

Policies relating to the maintenance of materials appear as a section of the collection program policy on evaluation of the collection (see Chapter 6). That section of the policy describes criteria by which materials should be evaluated for replacement, repair, or removal from the collection. Provision for replacing specific kinds of materials, such as encyclopedias and CD-ROM materials, should be included.

The maintenance policy should identify criteria for evaluating and weeding the collection, including characteristics of materials to be permanently discarded. The policy must address concerns frequently voiced when the removal of items from a collection is proposed.

◆ What will occur when someone needs the materials that have been removed?

◆ How can we provide a replacement policy to ensure that a decrease in number of items held will not lead to a budget cut?

◆ If additional personnel are needed to re-evaluate the collection, how will the media center fund those costs?

◆ How will the media center handle the transferring or disposal of materials and equipment?

Table 15.1.
Sample Replacement Rates

Type of Item	Average Years of Practical Usefulness
Materials	
Books	
hardback, K-8	6-8
hardback, 9-12	8-10
paperback	2
Software	6
Film formats	10
Recordings, audio and video	10
Transparencies	12-15
Equipment	
Computer terminals	8
Headphones	4-6
Library furniture	20-30
Microcomputers	8
Projectors	
filmstrip	10
opaque	12
overhead	8-10
16-mm	10
slide	10
sound filmstrip	8
sound slide	8
Players	
audio cassette	5
record	8
tape	8
video cassette	8
Television monitor or receiver	10
Video cameras	8

From *South Dakota Planning Guide for Building Library Media Programs,* 2d ed. (Pierre, SD: South Dakota State Library and Archives, 1985), 42; Washington Library Media Association, Certification and Standards Committee, and superintendent of Public Instruction, *Information Power for Washington: Guidelines for School Library Media Programs* (Olympia, WA: State Superintendent of Public Instruction, 1991), 22; and Charles W. Vlcek and Raymond. V. Wiman, *Managing Media Services: Theory and Practice* (Englewood, CO: Libraries Unlimited, 1989), 118.

The policy can also identify materials that are not to be discarded. Examples include local and state history, unless collected by another agency; major publications of the school, unless another department is responsible for the school's archives; and items incorrectly classified or poorly promoted, which might circulate under changed circumstances.

The policy should also specify when re-evaluation and inventory are to take place. The policy may recommend continuous, intermittent, or periodical weeding. The continuous plan, which takes place on a daily basis, may be difficult to handle without disrupting established routine. The intermittent plan calls for designating specific times for re-evaluating and inventorying specific areas or types of media. The periodic plan makes use of days when the media center is not scheduled for use. Careful planning can avoid disrupting services to students and teachers.

ESTABLISHING PROCEDURES

Working within parameters of the district policies, the media specialist is responsible for establishing collection maintenance procedures for systematic inspection of all materials and equipment. While technicians and aides can repair and clean materials and equipment, the media specialist identifies maintenance problems, diagnoses causes, establishes corrective measures, and monitors the quality of the work completed by media center staff or an outside contractor.

Routine internal maintenance procedures include the following:

Books and printed materials: replacing protective jackets, repairing torn pages, mounting pictures.

Audio materials: splicing tapes, wiping CDs.

Equipment: cleaning areas of heavy use, such as playback heads and lenses.

Monitors and screens: using anti-static wipes.

Other maintenance procedures relate to the identification and listing of holdings. Procedures should state how the media center would accomplish record-keeping activities and systematic inspection of materials. For materials, the *holdings record* serves this purpose, noting where the center should store an item and how many copies it owns. Often a similar list does not exist for equipment. If the district has an inventory control and maintenance form for equipment, establish a procedure for keeping these records up to date. If one does not exist, initiate a record. Devise a system for listing the purchase date for the equipment; its location; and dates for maintenance, cleaning, and repair.

Emergency Planning and Security

Be sure to plan for damage from fire, flood, a leaky roof, tornadoes, earthquakes, or vandalism. Does the school district have a disaster plan or a cooperative agreement with the public library? If not, develop a disaster plan to answer the "what if" questions one faces in such situations. The plan can begin with attention to local conditions. Where are the fire extinguishers and smoke alarms? The plan should list their locations, how frequently and when to check them, and the training scheduled for staff members. The local fire department will provide training. Emergency telephone numbers and people who can give advice on what to do with fire- or water-damaged materials should be readily available. Plan to store emergency supplies in the media center or be certain to know their location in the school. For instance, emergency supplies for water damage include paper towels, plastic drop cloths, and rolls of freezer wrap.

Develop procedures and information about what, where, and how to keep records. Some relevant questions are as follows: Which member of the school's staff has a copy of the insurance policy? What evidence will the school need to make a claim on the insurance policy? Is there a copy of the holdings record? How often should the copy be updated? Will the school keep pictures and negatives or a videotape of furniture and equipment?

Keep the original pictures and negatives in separate locations, in the hope that damage will occur in only one location. Maintain one record (a photograph, negative, or videotape) and a copy of the holding record in a fireproof safe in the school's administrative offices or in the media center. At least one school administrator should know the location and nature of the records.

Security procedures should provide access to equipment while preventing loss. As a security precaution, permanently affix the school identification number assigned by the National Center for Educational Statistics (NCES) in Washington, D.C., to all equipment. Your state department of education or office of public instruction can provide the number. The first two digits of this number identify the state; the next five digits identify the school. With this number, you can easily verify your ownership of recovered stolen equipment.

Preventive Maintenance

With diminishing funds for media centers, developing protective practices is an important step in the collection program. General practices should include keeping the media center clean; storing materials properly—vertically, loosely, and adequately supported; dusting materials regularly; controlling temperature and humidity; securing heavy equipment to a cart; purchasing books that will be heavily used in library binding or pre-binding; and using CD-ROM formats for heavily used reference works.

Preventive measures for equipment include the following:

1. Keep warranties, manuals, and repair records in an accessible file.

2. Test each machine by operating it yourself.

3. Train media staff and students in the proper operation and care of equipment.

4. Offer faculty in-service sessions on proper use of the equipment.

5. During the yearly inventory, check equipment, including electrical cords, for problems.

6. Regularly schedule maintenance checks with vendors of computers and video equipment.

7. Cover machines not in use.

8. Keep a log of use, rotating the machines.

9. Keep equipment in a climate controlled area.

10. Fasten televisions and VCRs to designated carts.

11. Do not allow students to move television equipment.

12. Clean the heads of VCRs and audiocassette players.

13. Create a maintenance area or a workspace with basic tools for minor repairs.

14. Attach "trouble-shooting" telephone numbers to equipment (Streiff 1992, 152–53).

To carry out these procedures, Jane E. Streiff (1992, 153) recommends having the following items:

a toolbox containing cotton swabs on six-inch sticks;

anti-static wipes;

a drawer or box containing screwdrivers of assorted sizes, needle-nose pliers, wrenches, scissors, and a utility knife;

head-cleaning tapes for VCRs and audiocassette players; and

a computer disk for cleaning computer drives.

Streiff recommends affixing a sign bearing instructions for users to each piece of equipment (see Figure 15.1).

For the User of This Equipment

1. If machine does not function properly, check the instructions and the power source.

2. Have a problem? Call the media specialist before forcing parts or jamming the machine.

3. Rewind tapes after use.

4. Remove software materials from the machine after use.

5. Allow bulbs to cool before turning off the machine fan.

6. Secure reels, electrical cords, other movable components.

7. Replace covers on machines.

8. Inform the media specialist of any problems you have had with this machine.

9. Do not allow students to move televisions.

Figure 15.1. Suggested instructions to be posted on media center equipment. From Jane E. Streiff, *The School Librarians' Book of Lists* **(West Nyack, NY: Center for Applied Research in Education, 1992), 153–54.**

INVENTORY AND REEVALUATION OF ITEMS

The evaluation of the collection as a whole is discussed in Chapter 17. The current discussion focuses on inventory and on re-evaluating individual items to decide which you should repair, replace, or remove from the collection.

The importance of establishing and holding to a designated time for inventory cannot be overemphasized. Maintenance easily can be put off, resulting in neglect. Continuous weeding, once established in the daily routine, may be the most manageable, effective, and least disruptive plan. The school library media specialist, who knows the demands upon the collection, must take the initiative to start the task.

Inventory is the process of verifying holding records. During the process the media specialist assesses the physical condition of the each item. In this context, inventory is more than the mere matching of bar codes with records to obtain a count of the holdings. Inventory, as described here, is the process of examining each item physically and also checking the records for accuracy. A videotape may be in the wrong container, or a teacher's guide for a set of study prints may be missing. A detailed examination of materials can uncover problems overlooked during the routine checking of items at the circulation desk.

Some schools close collections for inventory, thus freeing the staff from other duties so they can review the collection in depth. However, closing the collection during the school year is in direct conflict with efforts to work collaboratively with the school. Some school districts recognize this conflict and hire media personnel for a period when schools are not in session. In one school district a team is appointed to inventory and weed various collections throughout the summer months. This practice can prevent the emotional strain that removing items entails. The disadvantage is losing the insight of the person who knows the needs of the school.

Other districts rotate sections of the collection for inventory, including re-evaluation, over a three-year period. Inventory can take place when items are in circulation. Through notations on the holdings and circulation records, media specialists can determine whether unexamined materials are on the shelves or still circulating. The size of the staff, the size of the collection, available time, and user demands influence the decision whether to evaluate the entire collection at once or one section at a time.

Benefits of Discarding Items

These activities involved with discarding items take time but are beneficial because they

♦ create space;

♦ create an atmosphere of order, neatness, and care;

♦ reflect changes in students' interests and the school's program;

♦ ensure having accurate materials and avoid the cost of maintaining unwanted items;

♦ create a more attractive collection by the removal of dull and drab materials;

♦ retain a reputation for being a source of reliable information;

♦ save time in locating items; and

♦ avoid giving the impression of a larger, better collection.

The case study that follows this section illustrates the time involved and the attitudes one encounters when weeding a collection. You may face similar situations; people will test your conviction about the value of removing materials. Avoiding this responsibility may be more comfortable than facing it. Use your knowledge of the benefits and your skills with people to prepare them, and then set a professional example of thoughtful collection management to ensure better service to the users.

Why People Don't Weed

People give many reasons and excuses for avoiding weeding. Typical attitudes are these:

Books are sacred objects; only vandals destroy books.

Someone may need this in the future.

I don't have enough time to examine every item in the collection.

There will be a scene if teacher X wants this.

We don't have time to remove the bibliographic and holding records for all these items. (What about the users' time and attitudes on finding useless materials?)

Our policy doesn't justify the removal of materials bought with public funds.

I cannot decide when a fiction title is out of date.

Kits are expensive to replace, and this one has at least half of the original items.

These study prints are no longer available. (Even when the corners are torn and the explanatory text is missing.)

Someone may want to compare these editions.

A class could probably use this 10-year-old set of encyclopedias. (Although we have the electronic version on our LAN.)

I remember when Abdul made that model. (Abdul now holds a master's degree in engineering.)

This software package has gone through several revisions, adding features we could learn to use, but many of us know how to use this version.

I hate to admit I bought this shelf sitter.

As you consider those statements, prepare to hear yourself thinking them as you make decisions. Remember that you are responsible for the collection. You can involve others in the process, but you lead the way by knowing the criteria for removing items. You may experience fatigue and doubt if you tackle a large-scale re-evaluation project. To reassure yourself, refer to the policies as you apply the criteria for deciding whether to discard an item.

Criteria for Weeding

As criteria guide decisions to add items to the collection, they also guide decisions to discard an item. The media specialist uses both objective and subjective criteria. Discarding an item because of its age is a form of objective weeding. Subjective criteria involve judging the appropriateness of content.

Table 15.2.
Age and Circulation Guidelines

Class	Subject of Format	Age	Last Circulated (Years)	Comments
000	General	5	NA	
030	Encyclopedia	5-10	NA	New edition every 5 years
100	Philosophy/ Psychology	10	3-5	
200	Religion	5-10	3-5	
290	Mythology	10-15	3-5	
300	Social science	10-15	5	Retain balance on controversial subjects
310	Almanacs and Yearbooks	2-5	NA	Have latest
398	Folklore	10-15	5	Keep standard works
400	Language	10	3-5	
	Dictionaries	NA	NA	Keep basics
500	General	5	3	Closely examine anything over 5 years old, except botany and natural history
600	General	5	3	Most materials outdated after 5 years
620	Applied science	5-10	3-5	Retain car manuals
640	Home economics	5	3	Weed old patterns, keep cookbooks
700	General	NA	NA	Keep all basic, especially art history. Keep catalogs up-to-date
745	Crafts	NA	5	Keep well-illustrated items
770	Photography	5	3	Avoid dated techniques, equipment
800	Literature	NA	NA	Keep basic, especially criticism; discard minor, unassigned writers; check indexes
900	General	15	5	Evaluate demand, accuracy
920	Biography	NA	3-5	Keep until demand wanes, unless outstanding in content or style and still used
940	History	15	5	Keep outstanding broad histories
	Local history			Keep all books, local newspapers, local authors; consider oral history
F	Fiction/Easy	NA	2-5	Keep high demand; evaluate literary merit; classics should be replaced as new, more attractive editions become available
VF	Vertical file			Current information not found in other sources
	Government documents	5-10		
Ref	Reference			
	Indexes	3-5		As new annual or cumulations appear, discard old copies
	Atlases	5		
	Newspapers	1 week		For nonindexed
		2 years		For indexed
		Microform		If use requires
	Maps and globes			Check for accuracy
	Vocational files	2-5	2	Date items as added to collection to assist weeding
	College catalogs	2	NA	
	Periodicals	5	NA	Discard nonindexed
		5-8		Indexed
		10		Bound
Prof	Professional materials	8-10		
AV	Audiovisual and software			Weed worn or out-of-date items
	Films	8-12		
	Filmstrips	8-10		
	Transparencies	12-15		
	Records	8-12		
	Audiotapes	12-15		
	Videotapes	3-5		
	Software	6		

You can make selection decisions about removing or adding materials in the same way. Find out what criteria were used for selecting the materials; these can then apply to removing them. In addition, criteria related to the condition of materials can serve as a basis for deciding when you should remove them. These criteria should be recorded as were the criteria for selection. Criteria for removal of materials can include the following:

- ◆ Appearance and condition: unattractive covers or packaging, small print, dull or faded illustrations, missing pages or parts, garbled sound tracks, warped sound recordings, dirty beyond the state where they can be cleaned, dingy.

- ◆ Poor content: out of date (see Table 15.2), mediocre writing or presentation, inaccurate or false information, materials not listed in standard works or indexes.

- ◆ Inappropriate for the specific collection: neither circulated nor used for reference during the past five years, unneeded duplicates, interest or reading level inappropriate for students, works in languages students do not read, or materials no longer needed in the curriculum (see Table 15.2).

- ◆ Age of materials (note any exceptions to these criteria): materials 10 years old and not listed in standard selection tools; out-of-date materials (for example, photographs or videos that show automobiles or fashions from 10 years ago) (see Table 15.2).

If you find materials published before 1900 that you think might be rare, ask an appraiser about their value. Be prepared to pay a fee for this service. Appraisers are listed in the yellow pages or business sections of telephone directories. If the item is indeed valuable, you might sell it or donate it to a special collection. If you decide to sell the item, you can contact a dealer. In the case of old books the dealer needs to know the bibliographic information, including edition, printing, whether it has an autograph, whether the author or illustrator is of local or state interest, and the condition of the work.

Exceptions

The policy identifies materials that are not to be discarded. Examples include

classics, unless more attractive formats are available;

local and state history, unless another agency maintains a collection;

major publications of the school, unless another department is responsible for the school's archives;

items incorrectly classified or poorly promoted, which might circulate under changed circumstances; and

items identified in currently used indexes, such as quotation books or poetry anthologies.

Case Study

An example at Roosevelt High School illustrates the problem. Since its beginning in 1947, this school's collection has been a model for other schools. The previous media specialists and the principals prided themselves on the size of the collection in comparison with those at other schools.

In 1999, when Brittany, the new media specialist, arrived, the scene was chaotic. Stuffed shelves, dusty boxes, and jammed closets held more than 30,000 items. In one corner piles of 8mm cartridges were found, but no projectors. One could see books with drab bindings. A typical example was a 1968 home economics book still used by students doing assignments on average family income and expenses. Boxes were overflowing with old filmstrips. Two closets held a complete run of *Life* magazine. Bibliographic records did not match holdings.

Fortunately, the district hired the media center staff to do a badly needed inventory the week after school closed. Brittany began by removing the 8mm films, obsolete film-strips, old filmloops, and warped recordings. Then she removed 10 sets of encyclopedias that were 20 years old. By removing these materials, she was able to create a workspace and an area for temporary shelving of other materials.

The first step in the inventory process was to arrange the collection according to the shelf list. The overflow books were piled on the floor in front of the appropriate stacks. Missing items were noted. Second, the media center staff checked the equipment against the inventory listing. Found items were noted with the date.

Next it was time to decide which section of the collection they should re-evaluate first. Many nonfiction titles, purchased with Roosevelt funds, had not circulated for more than 10 years. Brittany asked two staff members to look at the publication dates of the nonfiction titles. They pulled old items using criteria related to age of information, last circulation date, and possible use in the curriculum. Meanwhile, Brittany and another staff member began examining the fiction section.

Both teams found books with small print, unattractive bindings, and missing pages. There were many unneeded duplicate copies, which made for easy withdrawal decisions. Of the 38 copies of John Bunyan's *Pilgrim's Progress,* Brittany kept two illustrated copies. Later she would inquire whether anyone still needed that title. Each team identified items to mend, rebind, give to another media center, discard, or re-catalog. They considered the following questions in deciding whether to repair an item:

♦ Is the repair cost effective?

♦ Is the title worth the time, supplies, and effort required to restore it?

♦ Is the title a unique item in the collection?

♦ Is it out of print or readily available?

♦ Is the title a duplicate copy?

♦ How useful is it?

As the teams examined the materials, they used photocopied slips on which they could check whether to mend, rebind, replace, trade, sell, recycle, or discard the item.

Basic supplies were set out in the work area, including these items:

Opaquing liquid (different shades) for pencil and ink marks

Soft rubber erasers

Fine-grade sandpaper for dirt and ink marks

Rubber cement

Scissors

Ink eradicator for ink and marking pen

Cleaning fluid for grease, dirt, and markings on the spine

Soft rags

Rice paper for holes and tears (based on Streiff, *School Librarians' Book of Lists*, 149, 150)

The removal of unattractive and obsolete materials made a positive impression. Supporters admired the improved atmosphere created by less crowded shelves and the removal of worn and unattractive materials. Teachers learned when their favorite titles would be repaired or replaced. Dealing with the assistant principal, who was upset over the decrease in the number count, provided an opportunity for Brittany to remind him about the value of usefulness over quantity. Her public-relations skills were useful in explaining the disposal of the materials to parent volunteers who were upset about the removal of materials bought with taxpayers' funds.

Involving Others

As in other aspects of the collection management, the media specialist should involve teachers and others in the decisions about what items to remove. If they have not participated in setting the goals and objectives for the collection or in framing the maintenance policy, you may need to remind them about these documents.

Teachers and their students can provide subject area expertise. For example, high-school science students can help spot inaccurate information in science materials. Teachers can be encouraged to bring to your attention materials that are no longer useful.

There are different techniques for involving users in the decision-making process about which items to remove. One technique is to display materials with tags on them on which the faculty can check off "retain," "discard," or "don't know" and then initial the item. Another technique is to use the *book slip* method. In that approach you put a colored label on duplicate or low-use titles. The call number, the date, and a notice of the intent to remove the item from the collection should be clearly visible. Users are asked to remove the slip and turn it in at the circulation desk if they think the item should be kept. Six months or a year later, the staff checks for materials with slips and removes those materials. As in all cases when the media staff remove items from the collection, they should also remove their records.

Disposal of Discarded Materials

Discarded materials can be disposed of by trading, selling, recycling, or destroying. Check your school district's policy about withdrawing and discarding materials. Practices vary. Some schools recycle paper items, others burn discarded materials, sell them, or give them away to other agencies. In some large school districts, exchange centers provide temporary storage for materials the schools no longer need. A listing of the materials may be circulated to all schools, thus providing individuals with an opportunity to identify materials they could use. In other systems such materials are stored for a given period of time, during which media specialists can browse through the materials and select those that are useful to their school.

The general public is quite sensitive to the physical destruction of materials that public funds have paid for. When large-scale discarding is occurring, the school community and the general public need information about the reasons for it. Putting materials into a dumpster can create bad press. Even taking materials to another community's dumpsite can lead to bad press or retrieval of the material by a well-meaning citizen. Whenever the media center staff plan to discard materials, they should remove all identifying marks of ownership and clearly mark the items as discarded!

CONCLUSIONS

Broken equipment, speakers that distort sound, puzzles with missing pieces, and books with missing pages are common in school collections. A user who finds such items may lose interest in looking further. Collection maintenance is easy to delay. There is always someone who needs the media specialist's attention. Materials can wait, as they did at Roosevelt High School, until the task is overwhelming. The chore of straightening out records can be boring and time consuming. The amount of disposed materials and equipment can become excessive, resulting in emotional responses and negative reactions.

Regularly maintaining materials and keeping records can help you avoid many of these problems. There always will be surprises and circumstances beyond your control. A brief story reveals how unusual maintenance problems can be. An odor pervaded the media center. It did not seem to come from the air ducts, and, at first, it filled the entire room. As the sniffing investigators toured the room, they detected the strongest smell at the beginning of the fiction section. The center staff removed books and checked and moved shelves. They found nothing on or behind them. As the books were being replaced, one of them felt damp. A bookmark was found—a juicy dill pickle.

NOTE

1.   American Association of School Librarians and Association for Educational Communications and Technology. 1988. *Information Power: Guidelines for School Library Media Programs.* Chicago: American Library Association; Washington, D.C.: Association for Educational Communications and Technology. This information is not presented in the 1998 guidelines (*Information Power: Building Partnerships for Learning.* Chicago: American Library Association).

REFERENCES

American Association of School Librarians and Association for Educational Communications and Technology. 1988. *Information Power: Guidelines for School Library Media Programs.* Chicago: American Library Association; Washington, D.C.; Association for Educational Communications and Technology.

Streiff, Jane E. 1992. *The School Librarians' Book of Lists.* West Nyack, NY: Center for Applied Research in Education.

ADDITIONAL READINGS

DePew, John N. 1991. *A Library, Media and Archival Preservation Handbook.* Santa Barbara: ABC-Clio.
    Covers care and handling of library materials; the environment; binding and in-house repair of books; care of photographic, audio, and magnetic media; disaster preparedness and recovery; preservation services; and suppliers.

Fortson, Judith. 1992. *Disaster Planning and Recovery: A How-to-Do-It Manual for Librarians and Archivists.* New York: Neal-Schuman.
    Offers a practical approach to planning for disasters and recovery.

Gwinnett County Public Library. 1998. *Weeding Guidelines.* Gwinnett County, GA. Distributed by the Public Library Association, a division of the American Library Association.
    Applicable to the school setting, although written from the public library perspective.

Lavender, Kenneth, and Scott Stockton. 1992. *Book Repair: A How-to-Do-It Manual for Librarians.* New York: Neal-Schuman.
    A practical, carefully illustrated manual.

Weihs, Jean Riddle. 1991. *The Integrated Library: Encouraging Access to Multimedia Materials.* Phoenix: Oryx Press.
    Covers care, handling, and storage of analog sound discs, magnetic tapes, film media, two-dimensional opaque materials, three-dimensional and boxed materials, computer disks, and optical discs.

ELECTRONIC RESOURCES

Florida Department of Education. 1999. SUNLINK Weed of the Month Club. [http://www.sunlink.ucf.edu/weed]. (Accessed November 11, 2000).

      Offers practical suggestions and criteria for weeding collections one subject at a time. Makes recommendations for purchases of additional current titles on the topic.

Library of Congress. 1999. Preservation: Caring for Your Collections. [http://lcweb.loc .gov/preserv]. (Accessed December 3, 2000).

      Covers books, motion-picture film, photographs, manuscripts, prints, posters, maps, audiorecordings, and the drying of water-damaged materials.

Preservation Services, Dartmouth College Library. 1996. A Simple Book Repair Manual. [http://www.dartmouth.edu/~preserve/repair/repair index.htm]. (Accessed December 3, 2000).

      A handy, informative, online repair manual.

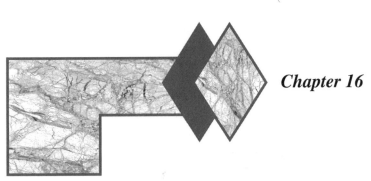

Chapter 16

Evaluating the Collection

How can a media specialist determine the worth of a collection? The concepts of collection discussed in Chapter 2 suggest several types of values to consider. You will recall that a collection (1) is a physical entity; (2) includes materials in print, visual, auditory, tactile, and electronic formats with appropriate forms of delivery; (3) serves school goals and programs; (4) meets the developmental, cultural, and learning needs of all students; (5) provides both physical and intellectual access to information resources of all types; (6) provides access to human and materials resources in the local and global community; (7) accesses information and materials from other libraries and information systems through interlibrary loan, resource sharing, and electronic resources; and (8) is only one element of the media program. Each of these concepts identifies something that the media specialist can measure or evaluate.

Evaluation is the process of (1) identifying a problem; (2) establishing methods of measure; (3) collecting, analyzing, and interpreting data; and (4) reporting the information. This process, often a continual assessment of the collection, provides a basis for decision making. One can measure how well the collection meets the defining concepts and how effectively each concept is addressed at any given time.

Three types of measures can help the media specialist evaluate a collection. Collection-centered measures include checking lists, catalogs, and bibliographies; examining the collection directly; age analysis; compiling comparative statistics; and applying collection standards. Use-centered measures include circulation studies, in-house studies, user opinion surveys, shelf-availability studies, and analysis of interlibrary loan statistics. Simulated-use studies include citation studies and document delivery tests. This chapter discusses the advantages, disadvantages, and application of each measure in the school setting.

WHY EVALUATE?

Those who fund media programs need facts on which to base decisions regarding basic funding, shifts in financial resources, expansion of programs, and cutbacks. As managers, media specialists need information on which to base decisions about the collection and for communicating the needs of the collection to administrators. The evaluation process (see Figure 16.1) reveals answers to the following questions: Is the collection responsive to changes in the school's program? Is the collection integral to curricular and instructional needs? Does the collection meet the users' needs? Does it provide access to materials from outside the school? Does it include formats that users prefer? Does it hinder or facilitate the media program? These questions identify general areas of investigation that are broad and complex. One cannot examine all these questions simultaneously; to do so would be an overwhelming task. One can more readily evaluate smaller issues—components of the larger questions.

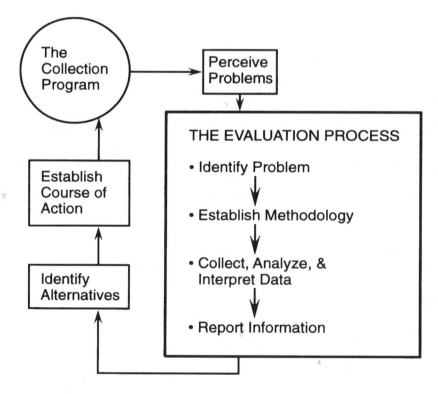

Figure 16.1. The use of the evaluation process in the collection program.

Before beginning an evaluation project, one must identify what information to collect, how to record it, how to analyze it, how to use it, and with whom to share it and why.

The Lincoln (Nebraska) school district effectively used documentation to obtain increased funding. Marjorie J. Willeke and Donna L. Peterson (1993) describe a study of the size, age, and assessment of the collections' responsiveness to curricular demands. They observe that although earlier principals, teachers, and media center staff had reported the outdated status of the collections, "[I]t was the objective data, supporting subjective opinion, that resulted in the district's allocating additional monies for collection renewal" (105).

Further evidence of the power of objective data to gain support is reported in Carol A. Doll and Pamela Petrick Barron's *Collection Analysis for the School Library Media Center: A Practical Approach* (1991). They emphasize that the length of the report is important. A single-page report serves as an example of the amount of information an administrator can read briefly. They describe a number of situations in which media specialists use such reports to obtain internal and external funding and support. Doll and Barron provide directions and sample work forms for analyzing collections in terms of (1) the average age of the collection; (2) the circulation patterns of collections; (3) comparison of the collection to standard bibliographies, textbooks, and periodical indexes; (4) an estimate of updating costs and benefits; (5) an estimate of replacement costs; and (6) the recording of unmet teacher and curriculum needs. One media specialist can accomplish each of these techniques within a realistic time frame.

EVALUATION AND MEASUREMENT

Evaluation is the process of deciding worth or value; measurement, a component of the evaluation process, is the process of identifying extent or quantity. We can count the number of items that circulate in any given period, but that information is not evaluative; counting provides quantitative data, an objective measure. The count gives us information about the number of items that circulated; there is no information about who used the materials (or whether anyone did) and under what set of circumstances, whether additional materials were used in other places, or even what materials were used within the media center. Merely counting the number of circulated science titles does not measure how adequately the collection supports the science curriculum. One must interpret additional quantitative data and perhaps consider some qualitative assessments before beginning to evaluate. The reason for the evaluation determines whether one should use quantitative or qualitative techniques, or a combination of both. Although quantitative data give an objective measure but lack the element of judgment found in qualitative data, quantitative analysis does give us an objective basis for changing a collection policy.

Measurement can lead to meaningful evaluation. Professional judgment helps us decide what to measure, whether we can measure it, and how we interpret the results. The process can provide knowledge about alternatives, possible consequences, the effectiveness of operations, and insight into the managerial aspects of the collection program. Evaluation produces information that can be judged by four criteria: validity, reliability, timeliness, and credibility. If the information is essential to a decision, it has validity. If we can reproduce the information when repeating the same techniques, the evaluation has reliability. If the information reaches the decision-makers when they need it, it has timeliness. If decision-makers trust the information, it has credibility. One should consider these criteria when planning how and when to evaluate.

BARRIERS TO EVALUATION

As with weeding, media specialists can fall into the trap of finding reasons for putting off or avoiding evaluation. Sharon L. Baker and F. Wilfrid Lancaster (1991) identify five barriers to evaluation. First, some people believe library services are intangible and library goals are impossible to measure objectively. However, media specialists who use the planning process recognize evaluation as a crucial component in the process. The cyclical planning process builds on the uniqueness of each media center. Assessment occurs in the context of each collection's philosophy, mission statement, constraints, users, and environment. Long-range goals guide the direction of the organization. The process also involves short-term, measurable objectives to guide day-to-day activities. Strategies help us to meet the objectives and identify measures for evaluating them. (Figure 3.2 illustrates how evaluation is an integral part of the planning process, not an isolated event.)

A second barrier is concern about lack of staff time. Automation answers this argument. Automated circulation systems provide a means to easily obtain circulation figures and to analyze use of the collection. This information helps one see patterns in the media center. Online public access catalogs can help media specialists to analyze other aspects of the collection. These analyses can lead to evaluation, which in turn can lead to more efficient and effective operations, thus saving staff time.

Third, media specialists may lack experience with or knowledge about collecting and analyzing empirical data. There are several ways to overcome this problem. For example, other members of the school's faculty can be asked to help with these operations. Courses and workshops on research methods provide opportunities to gain confidence in these activities. At the end of this chapter are resources that include guides for evaluation activities.

Fourth, people who are unfamiliar with evaluation may fear the results. The results should be objective data that identify program strengths and weaknesses. The data can help one to make collection decisions. An informed manager can use documented weaknesses to gain additional support of funds.

A fifth barrier is uncertainty about what to do with the results. Those responsible for the collection, including its funders, must be ready to use the results to make the necessary changes. The results of evaluation need to be shared and used, not filed away.

TECHNIQUES FOR MEASURING COLLECTIONS

There are many ways to measure the value of a collection. The following sections describe the most commonly used techniques for measuring collection value. As you read about them, think about their appropriateness for your purposes. How will the results help you present the media center program to others? What type of data will you collect? What effort must you make to collect the data? How many people will you need? What will the costs be? How much time will it take? What will the instrument measure? What will it not measure? Once you have obtained the information, how should you organize it? With whom can you share the information? How can you use the information to communicate with others? Analyzing evaluation techniques with these questions in mind can help you select the most appropriate technique.

COLLECTION-CENTERED MEASURES

To determine the size, scope, or depth of a collection, one can use collection-centered techniques. These are often used to compare the collection with an external standard. They include checking lists, catalogs, and bibliographies; examining the collection directly; age analysis; compiling comparative statistics; and applying collection standards.

Checking Lists, Catalogs, and Bibliographies

In this procedure, the shelf list, catalog, or other holdings record is compared with a bibliography, list, or catalog of titles recommended for a certain purpose or type of collection. During the procedure, record the number of titles the center owns and does not own. From this data you can obtain the percentage of recommended titles that the collection contains.

Lists that you can use in the technique include standard catalogs; specialized bibliographies; basic subject lists; current lists; reference works; periodicals; lists designed to meet a specific objective; citations in textbooks or curriculum guides; or catalogs from jobbers, publishers, and producers. Examples of current lists include the Association for Library Service to Children's *Notable Children's Books, Notable Children's Videos, Notable Computer Software*, and *Notable Children's Recordings*; or the Young Adult Library Services Association's *Best Books for YAs, Selected Videos for Young Adults*, and *Outstanding Books for the College Bound* series. Current lists of this nature identify highly recommended titles, but you must determine whether the collection needs those titles.

The purpose of an evaluation indicates which list is appropriate. If the purpose is to measure the general coverage of titles appropriate for the audience served, standard catalogs, such as the H. W. Wilson series titles *Children's Catalog, Middle and Junior High School Library Catalog,* and *Senior High School Library Catalog* or Brodart's *Elementary School Library Collection,* would be useful. If comparison reveals that the collection has many of the recommended titles, then, presumably, the collection is successful. The more closely the purpose of the tool matches the purpose of the collection, the more beneficial the comparison will be. The collection development policy can provide a basis for judging the appropriateness of a specific list.

Advantages

1. A wide range of lists is available.

2. Many lists are selective and include informative annotations.

3. Lists of this nature are frequently updated and revised.

4. Lists can be compiled to meet the needs of a collection.

5. Searching lists is a comparatively easy way to evaluate a collection.

6. Most compilations have been prepared by competent professional media specialists or subject specialists.

Disadvantages

1. The only available lists may be those used as purchasing guides.

2. Some items may be out of print.

3. The cost of the list may outweigh the benefit of its use.

4. No single list can cover every subject or need.

5. Bibliographies cover materials for all ages and may have limited usefulness for evaluating a collection established to serve a specific age group.

6. This approach does not give credit to titles in the collection that could be equal to or better than those the list recommends.

Application

This approach is especially helpful for identifying titles on a specific subject or checking certain sections of the collection. At Roosevelt High School, several teachers were so successful in motivating students to read short stories that the short-story section of the stacks was often empty. Brittany, the media specialist, compared the holdings with selection tools and indexes to short stories. In addition to identifying titles not in the collection, she recorded two items of information. First, on the index pages that list the works included, she recorded the call numbers of titles in the collection. This information helped students locate anthologies containing specific works. Second, on the holding record for each short-story collection, Brittany recorded the name of the tool that indexed that particular work. This information was useful later when she was weeding the short-story collections. At that time, if a particular work was in good condition and indexed, she kept the item for the collection.

In schools where teachers use textbooks or curriculum guides that include bibliographies of recommended materials, the media specialist can measure the collection against those titles. Teachers appreciate having a list of available titles with their call numbers. Creating such a list for teachers can also alert you to gaps in the collection and simultaneously provide teachers with an opportunity to suggest alternate materials. A limitation of this approach is that titles listed in textbooks and curriculum guides may be out of print. Newer materials may provide the same content, however.

Examining the Collection Directly

A physical examination of the materials can reveal the size, scope, and depth of a collection. An assessment of the timeliness of materials and their physical condition can help identify which items need to be mended, repaired, bound, replaced, removed, or discarded.

The examiner can be a member of the media center staff or an outsider. The latter is usually someone knowledgeable about materials on a specific subject. Fermi Middle School had a science consultant who was knowledgeable about science materials for middle-school students examine the collection and recommend additional materials.

The media center staff can examine the collection on two levels. The more cursory approach is to examine only the shelves. Are some shelves consistently empty? Is that a sign of popularity or improper distribution? Are teachers giving assignments that call for those materials? Does the collection development policy provide for adequate coverage in this area? Do some shelves have materials that are seldom used? Have students turned to electronic forms for this information? This cursory approach takes little time and can indicate a section of the collection that calls for more careful study.

A more in-depth approach is a systematic review of the collection. One examines the materials while considering the collection development policy. If users' needs have changed, a policy change is imperative. For subjects that have low priority in a collection, infrequently used materials are probably unnecessary. Knowledge of the collection policy and the extent to which materials are added, withdrawn, or replaced can help the media specialist to establish goals for the review program.

Selection criteria such as those presented in Chapter 9 can guide these decisions. Ideally, such a review is an ongoing process. It is easy to check the physical condition of books and periodicals when users return them. More time is required to check damage to software. Chapter 15 describes other aspects of this process.

David V. Loertscher and May Lein Ho developed *Computerized Collection Development for School Library Media Centers* (1986) as a way to map a collection. This computerized system allows one to analyze a collection in terms of curricular areas and numbers of students enrolled in courses. The resulting collection map provides a graphic presentation of the analysis of the collection. The process involves four phases of activity. In phase 1 the media specialist identifies the collection's areas of strength, diversity of formats, publication dates, and duplicate titles. Phase 2 includes an analysis of the map in terms of meeting curriculum demands, identifying areas of the collection that need emphasis, re-mapping for proposed changes, and creating budget allocations to reflect the proposed changes. In phase 3, an automated acquisition system is designed to match the map. This is used to maintain the consideration file, create purchase orders, record received items, and track the budget. As these data are collected, the map is revised. Phase 4 provides ways to evaluate and monitor the collection's progress. For example, an assessment form provides teachers a way to evaluate how effectively the collection meets the needs of a specific unit. Media specialists using this technique reported cases in which they were surprised at finding unexpected weaknesses in the collection. They also obtained objective data to support concerns about inadequacies in the collection.

Advantages

1. A cursory examination can be accomplished quickly.

2. Media specialists considering resource sharing can readily identify a collection's weaknesses and strengths.

3. Reviewing a collection on a systematic and ongoing basis ensures that both the collection policy and the collection are responsive to school goals and user needs.

4. Establishing criteria for decisions about relegating, repairing, binding, replacing, and discarding materials facilitates and standardizes those processes.

Disadvantages

1. One must check on the holdings record any materials that are being circulated during the examination study.

2. The process, unless computerized or focused on one aspect of the collection, is time consuming and requires trained personnel.

3. If one does not consider the collection development policy and the rate of growth, individual items, rather than the collection as a whole, will be evaluated.

4. Resources available through cooperative efforts are not considered. If a media center is participating in a resource-sharing program where another collection is responsible for collecting on a specific subject, those materials will not appear in the examination.

5. People who are knowledgeable about the school program, as well as a subject area, may be difficult to locate and expensive to hire.

Application

At Roosevelt High School, when Brittany found materials that had not circulated in three years and that standard catalogs did not recommend, she placed the materials in the appropriate departmental areas. Department chairpersons provided assistance in deciding which items to remove. When Brittany found several titles relating to a specific course, she sought the aid of the teacher and used the occasion to suggest newer materials that would suit the same purpose as the items being considered for withdrawal. As teachers became more aware of the collection, their support increased.

The Los Angeles Unified School District used the technique of collection mapping to analyze collections in terms of materials in languages other than English (O'Brien n.d.). The October enrollment figures help to identify the native languages of the student population. This information is translated into the percentages of the students that read each specific language. O'Brien observes:

> Another factor to consider is the percentage of Spanish readers at the given grade levels. In many schools, the majority of students in grades K–3 read in Spanish. However, the percentage drops off sharply in grades 4–6. Even if 90 percent of the children in grades K–3 are reading in Spanish, the collection should reflect a balance of English and Spanish books. It is important to provide high quality English books at both the primary and the upper grade levels. Easier English books are useful for teaching ESL and for giving older students who are transitioning into English reading books that they can easily read. As students become more proficient English readers, they need models of excellent English language use (O'Brien n.d., 3).

For each language, the collection analysis work form used in Los Angeles includes the following categories: Dewey area; recommended percentage of the collection, total recommended number of books (goal); the number of items in that language owned by the library; the number of items in that language that the collection should have; and the number of items in that language the collection needs. Media center staff complete the portion of the form that reports the actual count. The district office staff calculates the columns for items the collection should have and needs. Table 16.1 is an example for an elementary school with 802 students. The example is for Spanish; similar analyses are done for Korean, Chinese, Vietnamese, Armenian, Farsi, Khmer, and Filipino titles. You can display this information and the analysis of holdings by decade of publication as graphs to visually present the information. The results guide the media specialist in removing out-of-date materials and selecting materials to meet the needs of non-English readers.

Table 16.1.
Analysis of Spanish-Language Titles

Dewey Area	Recommended Percent	Recommended Number of Books (Goal)	Spanish Holdings: Actual	Spanish Holdings: Should Have	Spanish Holdings: Needed
398.2	6%	481	92	121	29
500	10%	802	19	201	182
900	6%	481	7	121	114

Based on Bonnie O'Brien, *Collection Mapping* (Los Angeles: Institutional Media, Library Services, Office of Los Angeles Unified School District, n.d.).

Age Analysis

One method of examining the collection is to estimate the age of the information in the materials. Carol Doll (1997) explains that this can be done by selecting a random sample of materials and then computing the average copyright date.

Advantages

1. Others can easily understand the result.

2. It is possible to match the result with anecdotal information, such as noting that the average age of the materials in the collection is 25 years and then recalling what was happening in the world at that time.

Disadvantages

1. It is difficult for one number to represent an entire set of materials. Sometimes it is better to use one number for fiction and another number for non-fiction.

2. One must consider how old is too old for a children's collection. There are presently no standard guidelines that determine the appropriate age for children's collections.

Application

When trying to obtain funds to update an outdated collection, either by adding print materials or buying accessibility to online materials, a school media specialist could obtain the average copyright date of the print materials in the media center and present that date to the principal or site-based advisory committee. Using anecdotal information to emphasize the age of the collection ("In our library no one has yet walked on the moon."), the listeners can easily realize the importance of having current materials available in the media center.

Compiling Comparative Statistics

Although the limitations of quantitative methods were discussed earlier in this chapter, there are reasons for collecting these types of data. For example, comparing data collected at various times of the year reveals patterns of use. State and federal agencies, professional associations, and accrediting agencies typically request circulation statistics.

Several writers have expressed concern about the lack of comparative national statistics that could document the contributions of media centers or the status of their collections. This information would be useful for policy makers. Kathleen Garland (1993) found that a majority of state agencies collect three types of statistics from media centers: expenditures, holdings, and personnel. Comparing statistics among states is impossible because no single statistic is collected uniformly by all states, nor are terms or time periods standard. Garland found that elementary- and middle-school media specialists collect circulation statistics for a variety of reasons, including reports to principals, superintendents, and boards of education. Viewing the importance of statistics as documentation of the contributions media programs make to education, Garland (ibid.) points out the need to share this information with policymakers at the state and national levels:

> Unfortunately, statistics describing the condition of library media centers and assessing their performance are rarely published. Library media specialists must make policymakers aware of the contributions of library media programs to the schools they support, and they must have supporting data (107).

Lillian N. Gerhardt (1991) addresses the consequences of not providing this information at the local level:

> If your position is not a quantifiable part of the full plan for improving local education, then school librarians can remain a fringe benefit to be added, divided, or subtracted according to the whims and worries of the local taxpayers (4).

Marilyn Miller and Marilyn Shontz (1993) call for data to document the deterioration of collections. Statewide data, regional accrediting association data, and data collected on a national basis by the National Center for Education Statistics could provide information needed by the states, the U.S. Department of Education, and Congress:

> There seems to be one avenue left to us, and that is for state associations to become militant on the issue of sinking school library media centers. We are talking about rural children, inner-city children, the children of migrant workers, and the parents of tomorrow. Local control, local autonomy, local decision making means local exposure of conditions that are crippling and will continue to cripple the learning possibilities for our children. Local leadership has to be developed, organized, motivated, and led by state associations. These may be our last hope (36).

There are several types of statistics to use with local, state, and national policymakers. Statistics can be collected about the following aspects of the collection:

size: total number of volumes or titles, number of titles in various formats, subjects, or classification

growth rate: volumes added within a given period of time; number of volumes by format, subject, or classification; cataloging statistics; or volumes compared to circulation

expenditures for materials: by format, classification, or genre; percentage of total budget; or amount per user or category of user

collection overlap: how many individual titles are held in common among two or more collections. This information is helpful in assigning areas of collection responsibility for resource sharing.

Advantages

1. If records have been kept, statistics are easy to compile.

2. If the application is clearly defined, it is easy to understand and compare the statistics.

3.   The method relates directly to the users in the case of requests filled or not filled.

Disadvantages

1.   There is a lack of standard definitions of the content or quantity of a unit.

2.   It is difficult to count non-print items and sets of materials.

3.   Significance may be difficult to interpret.

4.   Possible inaccuracy or inconsistency in data collection and recording exists.

5.   Statistics are usually inapplicable to a media center's goals and objectives.

Application

The gathering of statistics is commonly used to compare one collection with another, examine subject balance within a collection, and decide whether to share resources or to allo-cate monies. Media specialists lack a universally accepted set of definitions. When using data for comparative purposes, the participating agencies need to agree on the definition of each statistical component and use identical measurement methods. Learn what your district or state considers a statistical component and which data-collecting methods it uses.

If the collections in your district or state are being compared, data must be gathered in the same way. Check for the district's or state's guidelines. Are you to use a volume or title count? If you are to count each volume of an encyclopedia set or each record in an album, the total size of the collection may be distorted. Some districts with centralized processing may count an item as it appears in its main entry. For example, because each school may have a separate main entry, a school that owns a kit containing two filmstrips, five books, and a teacher's guide might record one kit; another school with only one of the filmstrips and one of the books might record two items—a book and a filmstrip. An encyclopedia set cataloged as one item would count as one title. A multi-volume set in which each volume is separately cataloged would be recorded as the number of individual titles.

Automated catalog systems use bar codes, generally with each volume having an individual bar code. If an item in a kit can be checked out separately, each item would have a separate bar code. However, if the intent is for the kit to be checked out with all items included, then one bar code is used for the kit. It is relatively easy to determine the number of volumes in a collection when the items are separately bar coded.

The use of online databases to access titles that are not physically in the media cen-ter can also complicate the counting of volumes and titles. Although the materials may not be physically in the media center, they are accessible, and the media center budget is being used to purchase their accessibility.

When information is to be used for allocating funds, there is an advantage to having uniform data about the quantity of materials accessible to each student. One could argue that several students can use the encyclopedia set; however, circulating materials, such as kits, are usually checked out to one person at a time. Data that include both a title and a volume count reveal more about the accessibility of materials than does a volume count alone. This dual procedure accounts for duplicate titles that can serve more people for a specific item but records the limit of the total resources available.

Statistics about unfilled requests can help determine what materials to add to a collection. It is a good idea to record requests by students and teachers for information or specific items not in the collection. You can then use these records when making selection decisions.

Applying Standards

In this procedure, the collection is compared to quantitative and qualitative recommendations that various standards, guidelines, or similar publications list. The issuing body may be professional associations, such as the American Association of School Librarians (AASL) and the Association for Educational Communications and Technology (AECT), who jointly published *Information Power: Guidelines for School Library Media Programs* (1988). The guidelines, which focus on qualitative standards and a planning approach based on the needs of individual media centers, note that

> Quantitative descriptions are limited in value because the quantitative characteristics of programs vary in relation to needs and program activities. They are, by no means, the sole criteria by which individual programs should be evaluated (AASL and AECT 1988, 115).

The guidelines provide qualitative and quantitative descriptions of state-of-the-art schools, which provide a basis for comparison of performance standards. Media specialists can compare their schools with others at the same level of service and with similar student populations.

Although the more recent school library media standards, such as *Information Power: Building Partnerships for Learning* (American Association of School Librarians and the American Association of School Association for Educational Communications and Technology 1998), do not include quantitative descriptions of school media collections, they do address the importance of the collections in their principles, which AASL and AECT approved. Principle 5 under "Information Access and Delivery" emphasizes collaborative evaluation:

> The collections of the library media program are developed and evaluated collaboratively to support the school's curriculum and to meet the diverse learning needs of students (90).

The principles also relate to the document's information literacy standards, which note that

> Through collaborative collection development and evaluation, the program's collections promote active, authentic learning by providing a variety of formats and activities linking information literacy with curricular objectives (90).

Accreditation agencies, for example, the Southern Association of Colleges and Schools, are another source of standards. Typically such standards include basic criteria for evaluation of materials, level of financial support, size and condition of the collection, and access to materials. Accreditation agency standards are based on resources or inputs, such as the amount of money spent per student. Regional accrediting bodies are listed at the end of the chapter.

Advantages

1. The guidelines generally are relevant to the media center and the school's goals and objectives.

2. Educators usually accept standards and guidelines and consider them authoritative.

3. They can be used in persuasive ways to solicit support.

Disadvantages

1. The recommendations may be stated so generally that a high degree of professional knowledge and judgment may be needed to interpret the statements.

2. Knowledgeable people may disagree about the application and interpretation of the statements.

3. Minimum standards may be perceived as sufficient.

Application

Judge the appropriateness of standards and guidelines for your purpose by considering the following questions: Who (people, associations, or agencies) created the document? What was their purpose? Who approved, accepted, or endorsed the standards, and how did they do so? Are the recommendations rigid, or do the guidelines suggest alternative approaches? Do the guidelines represent the long-range goals of your program, or has your program developed beyond the scope of the recommendations? Are the philosophy and rationale of the guidelines acceptable? On what basis would you recommend these guidelines to others? These questions imply some of the uses of standards.

Standards and guidelines allow media specialists to compare the collection to accepted measures or goals so that they can identify weaknesses in the collection. However, standards represent only an opinion of the collection level needed to support a program; accreditation agencies use them in this way.

Be familiar with state and national guidelines. You can use these documents with administrators, teachers, and others to interpret the concept of the media program, articulate needs, and formulate goals and objectives. Some media specialists obtain copies of such documents for their administrators, highlighting sections applicable to the media program.

USE-CENTERED MEASURES

Use-centered measures can be used to determine whether, how often, and by whom materials are used. Circulation studies, in-house studies, user opinion surveys, shelf-availability studies, and analysis of interlibrary loan studies focus on the users and the use of materials.

Circulation Studies

Analysis of circulation data can help you examine the collection as a whole, or any part of it, in terms of publication data, subject, or user group. You can use this information to identify (1) low-usage materials, which may be ready to be removed from the collection; (2) high-usage materials, which may be titles to duplicate; (3) patterns of use in selected subject areas or by format; and (4) materials that specific user groups favor.

Advantages

1. Data are easily arranged into categories for analysis.

2. Flexibility in duration of study and sample size is possible.

3. Units of information are easily compiled.

4. Information is objective.

5. Data can be readily available with automated circulation systems.

6. Types of user can be correlated with the types of material they use.

Disadvantages

1. In-house use is excluded, thus underrepresenting actual use.

2. It reflects only materials found by users and does not record whether the user did not locate a desired item or whether the collection did not have that item.

3. Bias may be present because of inaccessibility of heavily used materials.

4. The method is not suitable for non-circulating collections, such as periodicals.

Application

Kathleen Garland (1992) compares the results of sampling circulation activity over short periods of time with activity over the period of one school year. The results of her study of an elementary school showed a high correlation between a typical week's activities and that of the whole year. One can use the evidence from such studies to show how well the collection supports the curriculum. Increased circulation of reading for pleasure may result from whole-language or electronic reading motivation programs. By documenting this increase, a media specialist could justify an increased budget allocation for fiction. New media specialists can use this technique to identify which courses and teachers make extensive use of which sections of the collection. By identifying weak areas of the collection, teachers and media specialists can work together to identify materials to fill those gaps. Garland (ibid.) offers practical advice for elementary-school media specialists who want to try this technique.

Acknowledging the limitations of circulation analysis, Linda H. Bertland (1991) used an automated circulation system to analyze use of materials. She notes that the analysis can indicate which materials will probably not circulate again, show how people use a collection, and help one evaluate past acquisitions decisions. In turn, these results can provide justification for future expenditures or other management decisions. She describes locating fiction paperbacks in several locations in the media center. Regardless of location, even when intershelved with hardback copies of the same titles, her students prefer paperbacks. This information helped her make a collection development decision. Paperback fiction books became a selection priority.

In-House Use Studies

In-house studies can focus on either the use of non-circulating materials or on the users of materials within the media center. During these studies, users are asked not to shelve materials. This allows the media center staff to record use of the materials as they reshelve them. Other examples include keeping logs of computerized database use.

Advantages

1. Types of users can be correlated with the types of material they use.

2. A circulation study combined with the in-house use study about the same part of the collection provides more in-depth information about the use of that section.

3. The method is appropriate for non-circulating materials.

4. It can help one determine which journals to keep and for how long, which databases meet students' needs, areas in which students need help in developing search strategies, and gaps in the collection.

Disadvantages

1. Users' cooperation is needed.

2. If conducted during a high- or low-use period, results may be biased.

3. Circulating items will not be included, and this may create bias.

4. The method does not reflect a student's failure to locate and find desired information.

Applications

As an example, this analysis can help media specialists study the amount of use of the reference collection. During the period of the study, students are asked not to shelve the reference materials they use but to leave them on the tables. At designated time periods, a staff member collects, counts, and reshelves the reference materials.

Another example is recording which materials are utilized by particular classes while in the media center. This could involve counting the various formats or types of materials by classification number. When compared with the characteristics of the learners or the teaching methods used, this information may help one anticipate future needs.

Yet another example is the analysis of automated logs or logs students keep as they conduct searches online or on CD-ROMs. Media specialists can analyze the logs in terms of (1) the database used, (2) the search terms used, (3) the number of items retrieved, (4) the number of retrieved items meeting the user's need, (5) types of formats retrieved, and (6) whether the user found the material in the collection or borrowed it through an interlibrary loan or other resource-sharing plan.

Output Measures for School Library Media Programs, by Frances Bryant Bradburn (1999), is a practical guide to quantifying and measuring outputs of service. The output measures include (1) media center use, such as curriculum support request rate; (2) resource availability: curriculum support fill rate, information fill rate, and online resources success rate; and (3) access measures such as media specialist availability measures. The manual provides three case studies including one about collection development before a new course is added to the curriculum.

User Opinion Surveys

A survey of users and user groups requires soliciting verbal or written responses through interviews, questionnaires, or a combination of methods. User opinions can be gathered informally, leading the media specialist to think that users' needs have been identified. Examples of informal surveys include asking students as they check out materials whether they found what they wanted and recording their answers.

A formal survey is more systematic and thorough. The formal approach involves a series of steps: identifying the objectives, selecting and designing the data collection technique, developing and testing the instrument, selecting the sample (the subgroup of the population), collecting and analyzing the data, data, and interpreting the results.

Whether using a written questionnaire or conducting interviews, one can use carefully worded questions to identify the strengths and weaknesses of the collection as perceived by the users. The questions should be directed to specific goals, which may or may not be of significance to the user. Formulating questions that solicit the type of information you need can be time consuming. Interviews, which take longer to administer, can provide more in-depth information. However, the length of time involved may mean that fewer individuals participate in the process. The results of either type of survey can provide the basis for making changes in the collection development policy.

Advantages

1. The survey can be developed to relate directly to the needs of users and to the goals and objectives of the collection.

2. The information collected may reflect current interests.

3. A survey can be used for most types of users.

Disadvantages

1. The method requires aggressive seeking of opinions.

2. Those polled may be passive about participating or lack a point of comparison.

3. Users' interests may be narrower than the collection development policy.

4. Designing written questionnaires for young children may be difficult.

Application

Users' needs can be assessed formally and informally. At one level a student may ask for a specific title that a cousin recommended, while another may ask for the latest recording by a favorite singer. These requests reveal students' interests. A busy media specialist may forget to write down the request or be unable to obtain sufficient information on which to initiate an order. Individual requests may not reflect priorities that the collection development policy established. Through a more formal approach, one can obtain a consensus and direct the inquiry in accordance with the goals of the school. Resources listed at the end of this chapter include a number of works that provide further information about designing surveys. Examples of questionnaires can be found in guides used for preparing self-studies when seeking accreditation.

Shelf-Availability Studies

To determine whether users are finding specific works they seek, users can be interviewed or handed a brief questionnaire that asks them to identify titles they could not find. These data can help identify titles the center does not own, titles for which the center needs duplicate copies, items that have been improperly shelved, and insufficient directions for locating materials. One may also learn that the user had an incomplete or inaccurate citation, copied the call number incorrectly, or did not know where to locate the materials. This information about the collection and the user identifies areas that call for corrective action and changes.

Advantages

1. The method identifies failures that users face in trying to find materials.

2. Data on possible changes in library policies and procedures are provided.

3. The method can be used repeatedly to measure changes in library performance.

Disadvantages

1. User cooperation is required.

2. Staff time in planning and collecting data is involved.

3. The needs of nonusers are not identified.

4. Users may not remember the titles.

Application

Using a simple questionnaire, a media specialist could have students indicate what they were looking for and whether they found it. The results can indicate areas of the collection that need strengthening or areas where circulation is high and duplicate copies may be needed. Staff members may need to follow up on the survey by determining whether students had the wrong call number or whether materials were shelved incorrectly.

Interlibrary Loan Statistics Analysis

Interlibrary loan requests represent materials people did not find in the collection and sought to obtain from other sources. Analyzing these requests can identify subject or format weaknesses in the collection, identify specific titles needed, and monitor resource-sharing agreements. You should compare analyses of subject areas with similar analyses of acquisition and circulation data to identify areas of heavy use or lack of materials. The results must be evaluated in terms of the collection development policy and existing resource-sharing agreements involving interlibrary loan.

Advantages

1. The data are often readily available. For example, statistics on requests for periodical titles are usually kept to avoid copyright infringement.

2. The items are needed by at least one person.

3. Requests may indicate weaknesses in the collection.

Disadvantages

1. The significance of the data may be difficult to interpret because it represents the request of only one person.

2. Needs of users who personally go to other collections and skip making interlibrary loan requests are not identified.

Application

Records of interlibrary loan requests can be analyzed to identify titles that users request. The results can be analyzed in terms of frequently sought subjects for which the collection needs additional materials. Analysis of requests for articles can reveal heavily used periodicals that the collection may need. Suzanne, the high-school media specialist, uses this type of evaluation to identify which magazines are used most frequently. Then she determines whether the magazines in the collection cover the same subjects and whether they have the same appeal as the borrowed items. This information indicates which titles to add and which should not be renewed.

When Bruce, an elementary-school media specialist, receives materials that teachers have requested through interlibrary loan, he asks them to fill out a brief questionnaire. He enters the bibliographic information describing the item and asks, "Was the item useful?" and "Will you need it again?" If teachers indicate they will need the material in the future, Bruce adds the item to the "to be purchased" list.

SIMULATED-USE STUDIES

Information about the use of the collection can be gathered without directly involving the user. These simulated situations include citation studies and document delivery tests.

Citation Studies

This method can be used if the users of the collection use other libraries. If students write term papers or do independent projects, media specialists can check the bibliographies of student papers or projects to identify titles cited that are not holdings of the school collection.

Advantages

1. Lists are easily obtained from the students' project bibliographies.

2. The method relates directly to the user.

3. The procedure is easy to apply.

4. This method identifies works not in the collection.

Disadvantages

1. The value is limited if students use only the collection being evaluated.

2. Citations are limited to the subject of the paper, a small portion of the total collection.

3. The method is limited by the number of students who write papers.

Application

One example of how this technique can be used is from Fermi Middle School's program for students gifted in science. These students' projects were judged outstanding at the district science fair. One of their assignments was to write term papers on a recent advance in science. They were encouraged to use resources at other libraries, including the nearby university and industrial libraries. When the students completed their projects, the media specialist checked their citations to see which titles were not in the school's collection. Titles that several students cited were considered for addition to the school's collection.

Document Delivery Tests

This technique is similar to the shelf-availability study, but library staff—rather than users—do the searching. It also carries the citation study a step further. It helps determine whether the collection includes a specific title, whether one can locate the item, and how long it takes to do so. The purpose of document delivery tests is to assess the capability of a library to provide users with the items they need at the time they need them. A typical approach is to compile a list of citations that reflects users' needs and determine the time it takes to locate each item.

Advantages

1. Objective measurements of the capability of the collection to satisfy user needs are provided.

2. Data can be compared between libraries if identical citation lists are used.

Disadvantages

1. A representative list may be difficult to create.

2. Because library staff perform the searches, the test understates the problems users encounter.

3. To be meaningful, tests need to be repeated or compared with studies conducted in other libraries.

Application

Logs can be kept of interlibrary loan requests to record the requested item, the date of the request, the date the item was available to the requestor, and the response time (days between request and availability). The same type of information can be recorded about the response time for a teacher requesting a title for purchase. Further information can be gleaned by asking whether the requestor still needs the item.

When Lisa, an English teacher, complained that the students at Bubbling Brook High School could not find the materials they needed for their term papers, Suzanne, the media specialist, took action. She checked the reading list against the holdings and compared this information with the titles that were in circulation during the assignment. Later she repeated the comparison and realized that she needed to either add more titles or establish a reserve system.

COMBINATION OF MEASURES STUDIES

Between 1990 and 1991 the Birmingham, Alabama, schools surveyed the status of their collections through a study of the availability of materials, the age of the collections, and the number of unfulfilled requests due to lack of materials, combined with an assessment of circulation statistics. They found that 66 percent of the books in the collection were 10 years old or older. In a two-week period in January, they documented 4,000 unfilled requests due to a lack of materials or a lack of current ones. Using these figures and the average costs of books, they projected a three-year budget to buy the needed materials. Geraldine Watts Bell (1992) reports the study. Her article includes copies of the directions and work forms used, which demonstrate that the planners adhered to the dictum that for comparative statistics data, all participants must follow the same procedures and use the same formulas. Graphs of the findings show how visuals can impart information to administrators.

CONCLUSIONS

Techniques for measuring and evaluating collections are not limited to those this chapter describes. The "Additional Readings" and "Electronic Resources" at the end of this chapter can serve as a starting point for learning more about the techniques described here and about other methods of evaluation.

The techniques this chapter describes include qualitative and quantitative measures. Often two or more methods are used together to obtain more meaningful results. The evaluation process provides an opportunity to work with students, teachers, and administrators to ensure that the collection meets their needs. Their involvement can lead to understanding why certain decisions are made.

REFERENCES

American Association of School Librarians and Association for Educational Communications and Technology. 1988. *Information Power: Guidelines for School Library Media Programs.* Chicago: American Library Association; Washington, D.C.: Association for Educational Communications and Technology.

———. 1998. *Information Power: Building Partnerships for Learning.* Chicago: American Library Association.

Baker, Sharon L., and F. Wilfrid Lancaster. 1991. *The Measurement and Evaluation of Library Services,* 2d ed. Arlington, VA: Information Resources Press.

Bell, Geraldine Watts. 1992. Systemwide Collection Assessment Survey. In *School Library Media Annual 1992,* vol. 10, ed. Jane Bandy Smith and J. Gordon Coleman, Jr., 135–47. Englewood, CO: Libraries Unlimited.

Bertland, Linda H. 1991. Circulation Analysis As a Tool for Collection Development. *School Library Media Quarterly* 19 (Winter): 90–97.

Bradburn, Frances Bryant. 1999. *Output Measures for School Library Media Programs.* New York: Neal-Schuman.

Doll, Carol A. 1997. Quality and Elementary School Library Media Collections. *School Library Media Quarterly* 25 (Winter): 95–102.

Doll, Carol A., and Pamela Petrick Barron. 1991. *Collection Analysis for the School Library Media Center: A Practical Approach.* Chicago: American Library Association.

Garland, Kathleen. 1992. Circulation Sampling as a Technique for Library Media Program Management. *School Library Journal* 21, no. 2 (Winter): 73–78.

———. 1993. An Analysis of School Library Media Center Statistics Collected by State Agencies and Individual Library Media Specialists. *School Library Media Quarterly* 21 (Winter): 108.

Gerhardt, Lillian N. 1991. News in Contrast. *School Library Journal* 37 (June): 4.

Loertscher, David V., and May Lein Ho. 1986. *Computerized Collection Development for School Library Media Centers.* Fayetteville, AR: Hi Willow Research and Publishing.

Miller, Marilyn L., and Marilyn Shontz. 1993. Expenditures for Resources in School Library Media Centers, FY 1991–1992. *School Library Journal* 39 (October): 26–36.

O'Brien, Bonnie. n.d. *Collection Mapping.* Los Angles: Los Angeles Unified School District, Office of Instructional Media, Library Services.

Willeke, Marjorie J., and Donna L. Peterson. 1993. Improving the Library Media Program: A School District's Successful Experience with Change. *School Library Media Quarterly* 21 (Winter): 101–5.

ADDITIONAL READINGS

Everhart, Nancy. 1998. *Evaluating the School Library Media Center.* Englewood, CO: Libraries Unlimited.
> Provides useful forms for evaluating collections and developing surveys.

Kachel, Debra E. 1997. *Collection Assessment and Management for School Libraries.* Westport, CT: Greenwood.
> Deals with the assessment of school library media collections. Includes charts, timetables, and sample policies, most coming from documents used in the Ephrata Area School District in Ephrata, Pennsylvania.

Loertscher, David V. 1999. *Building a School Library Collection Plan*: *A Beginning Hand-book with Internet Assist*. San Jose, CA: Hi Willow Research and Publishing.
> Deals with evaluating school library media collections and mapping collections. Provides directions to some Internet sites.

———. 2000. The Information Infrastructure. In *Taxonomies of the School Library Media Program*, 2d ed., 210–17. San Jose, CA: Hi Willow Research and Publishing.
> Presents an explanation and illustrations of collection mapping.

ELECTRONIC RESOURCES

Glass, Colby. 2000. Collection Development Evaluation Plan. [http://www.accd.edu/pac/lrc/evaluatn/eval-cd.htm]. (Accessed November 11, 2000).
> Lists purposes of collection evaluation and raises questions one should ask regarding evaluation. Includes examples for evaluation of a collection.

Massachusetts School Library Association. 1996. Standards for School Library Media Centers in the Commonwealth of Massachusetts. [http://www.doe.mass.edu/doedocs/LMstandards/lmstandards.html]. (Accessed November 11, 2000).
> Provides some quantitative evaluation measurements for a school library collection.

Middle States Association
> See also Commission on Elementary Schools (CES/MSA). See also Commission on Secondary Schools.

Missouri Department of Elementary and Secondary Education. 2000. School Library Media Standards. [http://www.dese.state.mo.us/divinstr/curriculum/library/index.html]. (Accessed November 11, 2000).
> Includes information on collection analysis, evaluation, and development.

New England Association of Schools and Colleges (NEASC)

Northwestern Association of Schools and Colleges (NASC)

Regional Accreditation Agencies
> Note: See Appendix A for their addresses.

Southern Association of College and Schools (SACS)

Texas Department of Education. 2000. School Library Standards: Resources. [http://www.tea.state.tx.us/technology/libraries/resources.html]. (Accessed November 11, 2000).
> Provides quantitative measurements of evaluating collections at three levels (exemplary, recognized, and acceptable).

Western Association of Schools and Colleges (WASC)

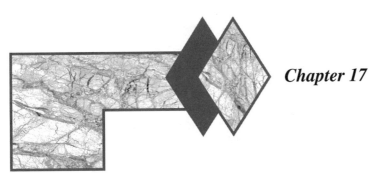

Chapter 17

Creating, Shifting, and Closing Collections

When student populations shift or there is a change in grade levels served by the school, media specialists respond by creating an initial collection, combining collections, or closing a collection. And the media center may even be moved to a different location within the same school campus. Each situation presents different demands upon media specialists' knowledge and skill. A media specialist's human-relations skills may be tested in the tensions of these stimulating experiences. Emotions can run high when a school is closed or a favorite group or grade level is lost.

CREATING COLLECTIONS

The opening of a new school calls for the creation of an initial collection. When a new building is being planned, various patterns of preparation for the initial collection can occur. The optimal time to begin planning is when the building contract is awarded. In the ideal situation, the media specialist and faculty are hired to plan during the year preceding the opening of the building. This procedure has definite advantages. The media specialist can benefit from participating with the faculty members as they identify philosophies and goals, create the curriculum, and develop plans. The media specialist's major responsibility during the year is to ensure that the desired types of learning environments will be ready on opening day. The media specialist must place orders early enough to allow for delivery, processing, and time to make any necessary substitutions. Admittedly, school districts rarely have the financial resources or educational foresight to provide a whole year of planning.

Regardless of whether the entire faculty is engaged in planning during the year prior to opening the school, the collection needs to be ready on opening day. If the school's staff has not been appointed, the responsibility often rests with district-level staff. Those planning the new facility need to be aware of the long-range goals and objectives of the district's educational program and the equipment and materials needed for an initial collection. Planners should design flexibility into the plans to accommodate changes that may occur in teaching styles, subjects taught, and the needs of unknown users.

Districts follow various patterns for handling orders for a new building. Some districts use one-third of the initial collection budget to buy materials to have on opening day. One-third is reserved for recommendations by the principal and professional staff. The remaining third is reserved for orders generated by the media specialist, who works with teachers and students to make selections. Other districts spend the entire first-year's budget prior to the opening of the school. The district must also consider the cost of licensing electronic resources for the collection when making a budget.

School districts with recent student population growth patterns often have lists of recommendations for the initial collection or have automated holdings records of such collections. In some cases, such districts are willing to share or sell their lists. This type of list is designed to cover the broad scope needed by teachers and students in widely varying school communities and is frequently revised annually.

Major book jobbers also offer prepackaged opening-day collections. Even though this package, or any list developed by other school districts, may not address your school's unique needs, there are some advantages to the packages: Current costs are known, out-of-print titles are excluded, time and effort is saved by not having to consider unavailable items, the media specialist can add additional materials, and the printout of online orders saves time. Such a list has the following disadvantages: Direct-order and standing-order items will not be covered, items requiring licensing will not be included, and the unique needs of the school may not be met.

General guidelines about the number of items that should be in an initial collection may also be available from the state's school library media consultant or state association. These guidelines may outline the formats, as well as stages of development, from the initial collection to one considered to be excellent.

By using selection-aid tools, one can identify specific titles for a collection. Useful sources include *Children's Catalog* (H. W. Wilson), *Elementary School Library Collection* (Brodart), *Middle School Library Collection* (H. W. Wilson), and *Senior High Library Collection* (H. W. Wilson). The broad scope and coverage of these tools help the media specialist identify titles to match the wide range of information needs that will be experienced during the opening days of the collection.

SHIFTING AND MOVING COLLECTIONS

Sometimes it becomes necessary to shift or move entire collections. This might occur because of redesigning, remodeling, or simply outgrowing space for the present collection. Moving or shifting a collection is no easy task. Planning is essential in order to avoid many of the frustrations that can result from such a move. The following suggestions can help you successfully complete the task with a minimum number of problems:

1. Weed the collection before making a move or shift. There is no reason to move books that are not being used.

2. Read the shelves to ensure that all the books are in order.

3. Measure the floor, wall, and shelf space that will be available for the collection.

4. Make a paper model (to scale) of the media center to which you are moving. Be sure to draw in windows, furniture, and cabinets. Also indicate the electrical outlets.

5. Measure and log the amount of space needed for each section of books (as they presently line the shelves). Write in the sections on your paper model, making certain you leave adequate space for each section.

6. Choose sturdy boxes that are not too large for packing the books. Books are heavy, and you may need to move some of them yourself.

7. Pack boxes in reverse order beginning with the last book on each shelf. When you unpack, the books will be in shelf order.

8. In large letters, label the boxes on the side, identifying which books are in each box. For instance, the easy picture books might be labeled: E AAR-ADA.

9. Place all the boxes near the bookcases where they will be shelved to avoid overlooking a box.

10. Do not fill all the shelves. Leave at least one-quarter of each shelf to allow for expansion.

11. If space allows, do not use the bottom shelves. It is difficult to read the labels on the spines on the bottom shelves. Also, this will again leave room for expansion in individual sections.

12. Do not forget to plan for your online collection as well. Plan the location of computers so they are accessible to electrical outlets and away from the heavy traffic areas. Be sure adequate work surfaces are available next to each computer.

CLOSING COLLECTIONS

When schools are closed, consolidated, or have attendance districts reorganized, the full impact may not be felt until the formal announcement is made. Someone should be responsible for determining the procedures for removing materials. Media specialists must be involved in the planning to avoid confusion and inefficiency.

Consolidation and reorganization of attendance districts can be "hot" issues calling for special handling by the media specialist. A sense of standards, diplomacy, and tact, along with sensitivity to the politics of the situation, will help. Perhaps the loss can be turned into a gain for other schools in the district. Planning is the key factor in retaining items the collection needs while preparing for the transfer of other items. Send information about the available items, with plans for their transfer, to the receiving school. Assess each of the newly formed collections in terms of their weaknesses and strengths in meeting the new demands.

When schools close, answers to the following questions can guide the planning process: What will the disposition of the materials, equipment, and furniture be? What legal guidelines are there for the disposition of materials and equipment? Are there local constraints? What are the closing deadlines? Will extra help be available?

Once the target date is known, create a timeline with specific goals. Post this information to alert the users and staff. Notify students and teachers when the media center plans to curtail services.

Teachers who are moving to other schools can help by indicating the titles they want available. Reallocate these items first so they can be processed into the collections.

Chapter 15 describes important criteria for weeding materials. Does the policy on gift materials provide for transferring the materials to another school? Are there additional materials that other regulations or agreements cover? Check such policies before deciding on how to dispose of items.

You can distribute a list of the remaining materials throughout the system so that other media specialists can request specific titles. Unclaimed items must be stored, distributed, or discarded. Distribution possibilities include storing materials at an exchange center, where they can be examined, or donating the materials to other agencies serving children, such as hospitals or day-care centers. You could advertise the materials for sale to beginning collections. Policies within the district will govern how you can disperse materials; they may grant approval for sale to individuals for fundraising.

CONCLUSIONS

A logically developed plan using a logical organization approach can help the transitions of starting or closing a collection. Equally important is a sense of tact and good humor on the part of the media specialist.

ADDITIONAL READINGS

Habich, Elizabeth Chamberlain. 1998. *Moving Library Collections: A Management Handbook*. Westport, CT: Greenwood.

  Provides comprehensive information about moving collections, regardless of the size of the collection or type of library.

Smallwood, Carol. 1998. A Do-It-Yourself, Low-Cost Move to a New Library. In *School Library Media Management,* 4th ed. Compiled by the editors of *The Book Report, Library Talk* and *Technology Connection,* 159–61. Worthington, OH: Linworth Publishing.

Describes moving into a new high-school library. Offers tips on moving books and other materials.

ELECTRONIC RESOURCES

American Library Association. 1998. "Moving Libraries." [http://www.ala.org/library /fact14.html]. (Accessed November 10, 2000).

Lists moving companies that specialize in moving libraries. Provides a bibliography of sources dealing with moving libraries.

Stevens, Shirien. 1997. Planning Shifts of Library Collections. [http://libweb.uoregon.edu /acs_svc/shift/shiftplan.html]. (Accessed November 10, 2000).

Identifies basic steps for shifting library collections and provides additional links.

Postscript

There may be days when you feel you are operating in a vacuum, isolated from anyone who shares your enthusiasm for what a media program can be. This is not unusual, particularly for the media specialist who works alone at the building level. Remember that through electronic mail, listservs at the state and national levels, telephone calls, or a letter you can contact someone who shares your concerns. You can contact media specialists you meet at professional meetings, staff members of professional associations, and former professors. Like the media program, you are part of a larger circle of people who share common interests.

Information and dialogue are available, if you initiate the contact. You will find others who welcome you.

ELECTRONIC RESOURCES

Bertland, Linda. 2000. "School Libraries on the Web." [http://www.sldirectory.com/index .html]. (Accessed December 2, 2000).

A directory of school libraries around the world also has links to library/media services at the district, state, and national level.

Milbury, Peter. "Welcome to LM_NET On the World Wide Web!" [http://ericir.syr.edu /lm_net]. (Accessed December 2, 2000).

Hosted by AskERIC and the ERIC Clearinghouse on Information & Technology. This site provides information and links to various LM_NET services and to other sites of interest to school library media specialists.

Appendix A
Agencies, Associations, and Suppliers

Agency for Instructional Technology (AIT)
    Box A, 1800 North Stonelake Drive
    Bloomington, IN 47402-0120
    812-339-2203
    800-457-4509
    Fax 812-333-4218
    E-mail info@ait.net
    http://www.ait.net

Alexander Graham Bell Association for the Deaf
    3417 Volta Place NW
    Washington, D.C. 20007-2778
    202-337-5220 Voice and TTY
    Fax 202-337-8314
    http://www.agbell.org
    Publishes *Volta Review* (ISSN 0042-8639, seven issues per year); includes reviews of books for parents and teachers of deaf children. Also publishes books and audiovisual materials.

American Alliance for Health, Physical Education, Recreation, and Dance
    1900 Association Drive
    Reston, VA 20191-1599
    800-213-7193
    800-321-0789
    703-476-3400
    Fax 703-476-9527
    E-mail info@aahperd.org
    http://www.healthfinder.gov/text/orgs/HR1396.htm
    Journals include *Health Education* (ISSN 0097-0050, bimonthly) and *Journal of Physical Education, Recreation, and Dance* (ISSN 0730-3084, monthly August–May); each has information about professional resources and occasionally includes reviews or features on materials for students.

American Association for the Advancement of Science (AAAS)
1200 New York Avenue NW
Washington, D.C. 20005
202-326-6400
Fax 202-789-0455
E-mail webmaster@aaas.org
http://www.aaas.org
Publishes *Science Books and Films* (ISSN 0098-324X, five issues per year) (sometimes listed as *AAAS Science Books and Films*). Includes reviews of books, films, and filmstrips on mathematics and the sciences (social, physical, and life).

American Association of School Administrators (AASA)
1801 North Moore Street
Arlington, VA 22209-9988
703-528-0700
Fax 703-841-1543
http://www.aasa.org
Publishes *School Administrator* (ISSN 0036-6439), 11 issues per year, pamphlets, filmstrips, and books; sponsors conferences, conventions, and other information services.

American Association of School Librarians (AASL)
50 E. Huron Street
Chicago, IL 60611
800-545-2386
800-545-2433 (for Illinois residents)
312-280-4386
Fax 312-664-7495
E-mail AASL@ala.org
http://www.ala.org/aasl
Publishes *Knowledge Quest* five times a year, bibliographies, and other materials. *School Library Media Research* publishes refereed original research studies and is accessible at http://www.ala.org/aasl/SLMR. "Learning through the Library" Web pages can be accessed directly at http://www.ala.org/aasl/learning (includes information about teaching-learning practices, summaries of research studies, and Websites dealing with instructional improvement).

American Association of University Women (AAUW)
1111 16th Street NW
Washington, D.C. 20036
800-326-AAUW
Fax 202-872-1425
TDD 202-785-7777
E-mail info@aauw.org
http://www.aauw.org
Promotes education and equity for all women and girls.

American Civil Liberties Union (ACLU)
125 Broad Street, 18th Floor
New York, NY 10004-2400
212-549-2500
http://www.aclu.org
Has affiliates in all 50 states. Publishes materials on intellectual freedom and students' rights.

American Council on Consumer Interests
240 Stanley Hall
University of Missouri-Columbia
Columbia, MO 65211
573-882-3817
Fax 573-884-6571
http://consumerinterests.org
Publishes *Journal of Consumer Affairs* (ISSN 0022-0087, two issues per year); contains reviews of books and articles on consumer matters.

American Federation of Teachers
555 New Jersey Avenue NW
Washington, D.C. 20001
202-879-4400
E-mail online@aft.org
http://www.aft.org
Publications include the periodicals *American Teacher* (ISSN 0003-1380, monthly) and *American Educator* (ISSN 0148-432X, monthly), newsletters, pamphlets, books, films, and videotapes.

American Foundation for the Blind
11 Penn Plaza, Suite 300
New York, NY 10001
212-502-7600
800-AFB-LINE
Fax 212-502-7777
TDD 212-502-7662
E-mail afbinfo@afb.org
http://www.afb.org
Publishes *Journal of Visual Impairment and Blindness* (ISSN 0145-482X, monthly September–June); includes reviews of books, films, and so on. The foundation's publications include books, films, pamphlets, and bibliographies.

American Library Association (ALA)

50 E. Huron Street
Chicago, IL 60611
800-545-2433
312-944-6780
Fax 312-440-9374
TDD 312-944-7298
http://www.ala.org
Publishing Services (ALA Books and Production Services)
312-280-5416
800-545-2433, ext. 5416

Publications, such as books or journals (e.g., *Booklist*), can be purchased through the order department. See separate entries for the American Association of School Librarians (AASL), Association for Library Service to Children (ALSC), Office of Intellectual Freedom (OIF), and Young Adult Library Services Association (YALSA).

Washington Office

202-547-4440, Fax 202-547-7363
Publishes the *ALA Washington Newsletter* (ISSN 001-1746, at least 12 issues per year); communicates legislative activities and issues.

American Museum of Natural History

Central Park West at 79th Street
New York, NY 10024
212-769-5100
http://www.amnh.org

American Printing House for the Blind (APHB)

1839 Frankfort Avenue
Box 6085
Louisville, KY 40206-0085
800-223-1839
502-895-2405
Fax 502-899-2274
E-mail info@aph.org
http://www.aph.org

Publishes Braille books, magazines, and Talking Book records; manufactures educational aids for the blind. The Instructional Materials Center for the Visually Handicapped at APHB evaluates and disseminates instructional materials and serves as the National Reference Center for the Visually Handicapped.

American Speech-Language-Hearing Association
>10801 Rockville Pike
>Rockville, MD 20852-3294
>888-321-ASHA
>Fax 1-877-541-5035
>TTY 301-571-0457
>http://www.asha.org

Produces audiocassettes and videotapes; publishes *ASHA: A Journal of the American Speech-Language-Hearing Association* (ISSN 0001-2475), which reviews games, kits, and learning materials designed for use with children who have hearing or speaking impairments.

Association for Childhood Education International (ACEI)
>17904 Georgia Avenue, Suite 215
>Olney, MD 20832
>800-423-3563
>301-570-2111
>Fax 301-570-2212
>E-mail aceihq@aol.com
>http://www.udel.edu/bateman/acei

Publishes *Childhood Education: Infancy through Early Adolescence* (ISSN 0009-4056) six times a year (fall, winter, spring, summer, Annual Theme Issue, and Annual International focus issue). Includes departments of "Books for Children" and "Professional Books."

Association for Educational Communications and Technology (AECT)
>1800 N. Stonelake Drive, Suite 2
>Bloomington, IN 47401
>812-335-7675
>877-677-AECT
>Fax 812-335-7678
>http://www.aect.org
>E-mail aect@aect.org

Publishes *TechTrends* (ISSN 8756-3894, six issues per year), books, pamphlets, and audiovisual materials of interest to media specialists. Provides information about copyright questions.

Association for Library Service to Children (ALSC)
>50 E. Huron Street
>Chicago, IL 60611
>800-545-2433, ext. 2163
>312-280-2163
>http://www.ala.org/alsc

Publishes *Journal of Youth Services in Libraries* (ISSN 0040-9286) with YALSA. This division's *Caldecott Calendar* can be ordered directly from ALSC.

Association for Supervision and Curriculum Development (ASCD)
　　1703 North Beauregard Street
　　Alexandria, VA 22311-1714
　　800-933-ASCD
　　703-578-9600
　　Fax 703-575-5400
　　http://www.ascd.org
　　Publishes *Educational Leadership* (ISSN 0013-1784, monthly), which contains reviews
of professional books. ASCD publishes books, pamphlets, videotapes, and audiocassettes.

Association of American Publishers
　　71 Fifth Avenue
　　New York, NY 10003-3004
　　212-255-0200
　　Fax 212-255-7007
　　http://www.publishers.org/home/index.htm
　　Frequently publishes or co-sponsors activities related to freedom to read and collection matters.

Canadian Library Association
　　200 Elgin Street, Suite 602
　　Ottawa, ON K2P 1L5
　　Canada
　　800-267-6566
　　613-232-9265
　　Fax 613-563-9895
　　http://www.cla.ca
　　Publishes the annotated critical bibliography *CM: Canadian Materials for Schools
and Libraries* (ISSN 0363-9479, six issues per year).

Captioned Films for the Deaf Distribution Center
　　5034 Wisconsin Avenue NW
　　Washington, D.C. 20016
　　202-363-1308
　　This branch of the U.S. Department of Education, Bureau of Education for the Handicapped provides educational and full-length entertainment subtitled films to deaf persons
free of charge.

Children's Book Council, Inc.
　　568 Broadway, Suite 404
　　New York, NY 10012
　　212-966-1900
　　http://www.cbcbooks.org
　　Publishes *CBC Features* and other informational packets about children's books.
Provides an examination center and information about new titles for children.

Children's Television Workshop
1 Lincoln Plaza, Floor 2
New York, NY 10023
212-595-3456
http://www.ctw.org

Commission on Elementary Schools (CES)
Middle States Association of Colleges and Schools
GSB Building, 1 Belmont Avenue, Suite 618
Bala Cynwyd, PA 19004
610-617-110
Fax 610-617-1106
http://www.ces-msa.org
Accredits in Delaware, the District of Columbia, Maryland, New Jersey, New York,
Pennsylvania, Puerto Rico, and the U.S. Virgin Islands.

Commission on Secondary Schools (CSS)
Middle States Association of College and Schools
3624 Market Street
Philadelphia, PA 19104-2680
215-662-5603
Fax 215-662-0957
http://www.css-msa.org/pub/html
Accredits in Delaware, the District of Columbia, Maryland, New Jersey, New York,
Pennsylvania, Puerto Rico, and the U.S. Virgin Islands.

Consumer Education Resource Network (CERN)
1500 Wilson Boulevard, Suite 800
Rosslyn, VA 22209
800-336-0223
A resource and service network in the consumer-education field.

Consumer Products Safety Commission
4330 East-West Highway
Bethesda, MD 20814-4408
800-638-2772
301-504-0580
TTY 800-638-8270
http://www.cpsc.gov

Council for Exceptional Children (CEC)
> 1920 Association Drive
> Reston, VA 22091-1589
> 888-CEC-SPED
> 703-620-3660
> Fax 703-264-9494
> TTY 703-264-9446
> http://www.cec.sped.org

Publishes *Teaching Exceptional Children* (ISSN 0040-0599, quarterly), which includes articles on instructional methods and materials. Other publications include newsletters, books, and media. CEC is the ERIC Clearinghouse on Handicapped and Gifted Children and publishes *Exceptional Child Education Resources* (ECER) (ISSN 0160-4309, quarterly), a print presentation of all citations in the ECER database.

C-SPAN
> 400 N. Capitol Street NW, Suite 650
> Washington, D.C. 20001
> 800-523-7586
> http://www.c-span.org

Publishes *C-SPAN Newsletter,* which includes programming schedules and articles of interest to teachers.

Denoyer-Geppert Scientific Company
> 5225-T N. Ravenswood Avenue
> Chicago, IL 60640
> 800-621-1014
> 312-561-9200
> Fax 312-561-4160

Provides models, charts, and realia.

Educational Paperback Association
> Box 1399
> East Hampton, NY 11937
> 212-879-6850
> http://www.edupaperback.org

Trade organization of paperback distributors who specialize in working with schools and libraries in the United States and Canada. They offer services including book fairs and examination opportunities.

Educational Resources Information Center (ERIC)
> Office of Educational Research and Improvement (OERI)
> U.S. Department of Education
> 555 New Jersey Avenue NW
> Washington, D.C. 20208-5720
> 202-219-2290
> Fax 202-219-1817
> E-mail accesseric@accesseric.org
> http://www.accesseric.org:81

The ERIC program staff manages the ERIC system, which consists of clearinghouses, adjunct clearinghouses, and support components. Basic ERIC reference tools are *Resource in Education* (RIC), a monthly journal of abstracts of current education-related documents, published by the Superintendent of Documents, Washington, D.C. 20402; *Current Index to Journals in Education* (CIJE), a monthly journal of abstracts of education-related articles, published by the Oryx Press, 4041 North Center Avenue, Phoenix, AZ 85012, 800-279-ORYX; *Thesaurus of ERIC Descriptors,* a master list of subject headings used in indexing and searching, available from Oryx Press.

ERIC Clearinghouses
Each publishes research summaries, bibliographies, information analysis papers, and other products. They offer free reference and referral services of their subject area. Clearinghouses not listed here include Higher Education (HE) and Community Colleges (CC).

Adult, Career, and Vocational Education
> Ohio State University
> Center on Education and Training for Employment
> 1900 Kenny Road
> Columbus, OH 43210-1090
> 614-292-7069
> 800-848-4815 ext. 2-7069
> Fax 614-292-1260
> TTY/TDD 614-688-8734
> E-mail ericacve@postbox.acs.ohio-state.edu
> http://www.ericacve.org

Counseling and Personnel Services
> ERIC/CASS
> University of North Carolina at Greensboro
> School of Education
> 201 Ferguson Building UNCG
> Greensboro, NC 27402-6171
> 800 414-9769
> Fax 336-334-4116
> E-mail ericcass@uncg.edu
> http://ericcass.uncg.edu

Disabilities and Gifted Education
Council for Exceptional Children (CEC)
1920 Association Drive
Reston, VA 20191-1589
888-CEC-SPED
703-620-3660
TTY 703-264-9446
Fax 703-264-9494
E-mail ericec@cec.sped.org
http://www.cec.sped.org/index.html

Educational Management
1787 Agate Street
5207 University of Oregon
Eugene, OR 97403-5207
800-438-8841
541-346-5043
Fax 541-346-2334
E-mail eric@eric.uoregon.edu
http://eric.uoregon.edu

Elementary and Early Childhood Education
University of Illinois at Urbana-Champaign
Children's Research Center
51 Gerty Drive
Champaign, IL 61820-7469
800-583-4135
217-333-1386
Fax 217-333-3767
E-mail ericeece@uiuc.edu
http://ericeece.org

Information and Technology
Syracuse University
621 Skytop Road, Suite 160
Syracuse, NY 13244-5290
800-464-9107
Fax 315-443-5448
E-mail eric@ericir.syr.edu
http://ericir.syr.edu/ithome

Language and Linguistics
ERIC Clearinghouse on Languages and Linguistics
4646 40th Street NW
Washington, D.C. 20016-1859
Attention: Acquisitions Coordinator
E-mail eric@cal.org
http://www.cal.org/ericll

Reading, English, and Communication Skills
Indiana University
Smith Research Center, Suite 140
Bloomington, IN 47408-2698
800-759-4723
812-855-5847
Fax 812-855-4220
http://www.indiana.edu/~eric.rec

Rural Education and Small Schools
Appalachia Education Laboratory
Box 1348
Charleston, WV 25325-1348
800-624-9120
304-347-0400
Fax 304-347-0487
E-mail aelinfo@ael.org
http://www.ael.org/eric

Science, Mathematics, and Environmental Education
Ohio State University
1929 Kenny Road
Columbus, OH 43210-1080
800-276-0462
614-292-6717
Fax 614-292-0263
E-mail ericse@osu.edu
http:// www.ericse.org

Social Studies Social Science Education
Indiana University
Social Studies Development Center
2805 East 10th Street, Suite 120
Bloomington, IN 47408-2698
800-266-3815
812-855-3838
Fax 812-855-0455

E-mail ericso@ucs.indiana.edu
http://www.indiana.edu/~ssdc/eric_chess.htm

ERIC Clearinghouse on Teaching and Teacher Education

American Association of Colleges for Teacher Education
1307 New York Avenue NW, Suite 300
Washington, D.C. 20005-4701
800-822-9229
202-293-2450
Fax 202-457-8095
E-mail query@aacte.edu
http://www.ericsp.org

Urban Education

Teachers College Box 40
Columbia University
Institute for Urban and Minority Education
New York, NY 10027-9998
800-601-4868
E-mail ef29@columbia.edu
http://eric-Web.tc.columbia.edu/

ERIC Adjunct Clearinghouses

New clearinghouses with narrower scopes are called *adjunct clearinghouses.*
The broader-based clearinghouse with which the adjunct is affiliated handles the cataloging, indexing, and abstracting of the documents. Like the clearinghouses, the adjuncts
provide free reference and referral services, as well as research summaries, bibliographies,
information analysis papers, and other products.

Adjunct ERIC Clearinghouse for Consumer Education

National Institute for Consumer Education
Eastern Michigan University
559 Gary M. Owen Building
300 W. Michigan Avenue
Ypsilanti, MI -48197
734-487-2292
Fax 734-487-7153
E-mail NICE@online.emich.edu
http://www.nice.emich.edu

Adjunct ERIC Clearinghouse for ESL Literacy Education

National Clearinghouse for ESL Literacy Education (NCLE)
4646 40th Street NW
Washington, D.C. 20016-1859
202-362-0700, ext. 200
Fax 202-363-7204
E-mail ncle@cal.org
http://www.cal.org/ncle

National Clearinghouse for U.S.–Japan Studies

Indiana University
Social Studies Development Center
2805 East 10th Street, Suite 120
Bloomington, IN 47408-2698
800-266-3815
812-855-3838
Fax 812-855-0455
E-mail japan@indiana.edu
http://www.indiana.edu/~japan

Adjunct ERIC Clearinghouse on Chapter 1

Chapter 1 Teaching Assistance Center PRC Inc.
2601 Fortune Circle East
One Park Fletcher Building, Suite 300-A
Indianapolis, IN 46241-2237
800-456-2380
317-244-8160
Fax 317-244-7386
http://www.trc.com/ees

Adjunct ERIC Clearinghouse on Clinical Schools

American Association of Colleges for Teacher Education
1307 New York Avenue NW, Suite 300
Washington, D.C. 20005-4701
800-822-9229
202-293-2450
Fax 202-457-8095
http://www.aacte.org/menu2.

American Association of Colleges for Teacher Education

1307 New York Avenue N.W., Suite 300
Washington, D.C. 20005-4701
202-293-2450
Fax 202-457-8095
http://www.aacte.org

ERIC Support Components

Production, publication, and dissemination of ERIC documents and services are handled by:

ACCESS ERIC

2277 Research Boulevard, 6L
Rockville, MD 20850
800-LET-ERIC (538-3742)
301-519-5157
Fax 301-519-6760
E-mail accesseric@accesseric.org
http://www.accesseric.org

ACCESS ERIC's publications include *A Pocket Guide to ERIC, All About ERIC, The ERIC Review, ERIC User's Interchange, The Catalog of ERIC Clearinghouse Publications,* and the following reference directories: *ERIC Information Service Providers, Education-Related Information Centers,* and *ERIC Calendar of Education-Related Conferences.*

ERIC Document Reproduction Service (EDRS)

DynEDRS, Inc.
7420 Fullerton Road, Suite 110
Springfield, VA 22153-2852
800-443-ERIC (3742)
703-440-1400
Fax 703-440-1408
E-mail service@edrs
http://www.edrs.com

EDRS produces and sells microfiche and paper copies of documents announced in *Resources in Education* (RIE). EDRS products can be ordered online through BRS, DIALOG, OCLC, or by Fax.

ERIC Processing and Reference Facility

Computer Sciences Corporation
4483-A Forbes Boulevard
Lanham, MD 20706
800-799-ERIC (3742)
301-552-4200
Fax 301-552-4700
E-mail ericfac@inet.ed.gov
http://ericfac.piccard.csc.com

This facility serves as the central editorial and computer-processing agency and prepares *Resources in Education* (RIE). To order *Resources in Education,* contact:

U.S. Government Printing Office
Superintendent of Documents
Box 371854
Pittsburgh, PA 15250-7954
202-512-1800
Fax 202-512-2250
http://www.access.gpo.gov

ORYX Press (ORYX)

Box 33889
Phoenix, AZ 85067-3889
800-279-ORYX (6799)
602-265-2651
Fax 800-279-4663 or 602-265-6250
E-mail info@oryxpress.com
http://www.oryxpress.com
Publishes *Current Index to Journals in Education* (CIJE), the *Thesaurus of ERIC Descriptors,* and other ERIC publications.

Freedom to Read Foundation

50 E. Huron Street
Chicago, IL 60611
800-545-2433, ext. 4226
312-280-4226
Fax 312-440-9374
http://www.ftrf.org
Promotes and defends the First Amendment right of free expression. Provides legal counsel and other support to libraries and librarians.

Gallaudet University

800 Florida Avenue NE
Washington, D.C. 20002-3695
TTY/V 202-651-5050
http://www.gallaudet.edu
Write to Gallaudet University Bookstore for a catalog of their materials for deaf people.

Handicapped Learner Materials-Special Materials Project (HLM-SMP)

624 East Walnut Street, 2nd Floor
Indianapolis, IN 46204
317-636-1902
A small fee covers usage of captioned films and other materials for children or teachers.

Hubbard Scientific
  401 W. Hickory Street
  Box 2121
  Fort Collins, CO 80522
  800-446-8767
  970-484-7445
  Fax 970-484-1198
  http://www.hubbardscott.com

Institute for First Amendment Studies
  357 North Plain Road
  Great Barrington, MA 01230
  413-274-0012
  http://www.ifas.org
  Research organization dedicated to protecting First Amendment freedoms.

International Communications Industries Association, Inc.
  11242 Waples Mill Road, Suite 200
  Fairfax, VA 22030
  800-659-7469
  703-273-7200
  Fax 703-278-8082
  http://www.icia.org
  Provides information about the copyright law. As the trade association for the communications-technologies industries, it has publications, products, and services relating to the use of this technology.

International Reading Association
  800 Barksdale Road
  Box 8139
  Newark, DE 19714-8139
  800-336-Read, ext. 266
  302-731-1600
  Fax 302-731-1057
  http://www.reading.org
  Publishes *Reading Teacher* (ISSN 0034-0561, nine issues per year) on reading instruction at the elementary-school level and *Journal of Reading* (ISSN 0022-4103, eight issues per year) on teaching reading at the high-school through adult level. Both journals include reviews and articles of interest. Also publishes books, bibliographies, and audio recordings. Sponsors "Teacher's Choices" ("the best books to use with kids").

Library of Congress
> 101 Independence Avenue SE
> Washington, D.C. 20540
> 202-707-5000
> E-mail lcweb@loc.gov
> http://www.loc.gov
> Publications include *Talking Books Topics* (large-print edition, ISSN 0039-9183) and *Braille Book Review* (large-print edition, ISSN 0006-873X), bimonthly magazines that announce books and magazines available in these formats. The agency also provides information about equipment, bibliographies, and information about blindness and other physical handicaps.

MENC: The National Association for Music Education
> 1806 Robert Fulton Drive
> Reston, VA 20191
> 800-336-3768
> 703-860-4000
> Fax 703-860-1531
> http://www.menc.org
> Publications include *Music Educators Journal* (ISSN 0027-4321, nine issues per year); includes reviews.

Metropolitan Museum of Art
> 1000 Fifth Avenue at 82nd Street
> New York, NY 10028-0198
> 212-535-7710
> TTY 212-570-3828
> http://www.metmuseum

Middle States Association of Colleges and Schools
> 3624 Market Street
> Philadelphia, PA 19104-2680
> 215-662-5600
> Fax 215-622-5950
> http://www.css-msa.org

Middle States Association, Commission on Elementary Schools
> See Commission on Elementary Schools (CES/MSA).

Middle States Association, Commission on Secondary Schools
> See Commission on Secondary Schools (CSS/MSA).

National Association of Elementary Principals

1615 Duke Street
Alexandria, VA 22314
800-38-NAESP [800-386-2377]
703-684-3345
http://www.naesp.org
Publishes *Principal* (ISSN 0271-6062, five issues per year), books, pamphlets, and films.

National Association of Independent Schools

1620 L Street NW
Washington, D.C. 20036-5605
202-973-9700
Fax 202-973-9790
http://www.nais.org
Publishes *Independent School* (ISSN 0145-9635, quarterly), books, reports, and curricular materials.

National Association of Partners in Education (NAPE)

901 North Pitt Street, Suite 320
Alexandria, VA 22314
703-836-4880
Fax 703-836-6941
http://www.napehq.org
Publishes *The Partners in Education* (nine issues per year).

National Association of Secondary Schools Principals (NAASP)

1904 Association Drive
Reston, VA 20191-1537
800-253-7746
703-860-0200
Fax 703-476-5432
http://www.nassp.org
Publications include *NASSP Bulletin* (ISSN 0192-6365, nine issues per year), *Curriculum Report* (ISSN 0547-4205, bimonthly), and *The Practitioner* (ISSN 0192-6160, quarterly) (sometimes listed as *The NASSP Practitioner*).

National Association of the Deaf (NAD)

814 Thayer Avenue
Silver Spring, MD 20910-4500
Fax 301-587-1791
E-mail NADinfo@nadorg
http://www.nad.org
Publications include children's books and materials for parents and teachers; some are in sign language, and some are about sign language.

National Audiovisual Center
http://www.ntis.gov/nac

National Audubon Society
700 Broadway
New York, NY 10003
212-979-3000
Fax 212-979-3188
http://www.audubon.org

National Catholic Educational Association
1077 30th Street NW, Suite 100
Washington, D.C. 20007-3852
202-337-6232
Fax 202-333-6706
http://www.catholic.org/ncea/index.html
Publications include journals, books, pamphlets, and audiocassettes. The association offers workshops, seminars, and consulting services.

National Center for Audio Tapes (NCAT)
c/o Academic Media Services
Campus Box 379
University of Colorado
Boulder, CO 80309
303-492-7341
Associated cooperatively with Association for Educational Communications and Technology (AECT); reproduces audiotapes on direct order from educational institutions.

National Center for Educational Statistics (NCES)
1990 K Street NW
Washington, D.C. 20006
202-502-7300
http://nces.ed.gov/index.html
Includes "Highlights of the School Library Media Centers Survey" covering 1993-1994, which was published in August 1998 at http://bces.ed.gov/surveys/libraries/highlights.html.

National Center for Health Education (NCHE)
72 Spring Street, Suite 208
New York, NY 10012
212-334-9470
Fax 212-334-9845
E-mail nche@nche.org
http://www.nche.org/nchehome.html
Provides information to schools interested in developing or redesigning their health curriculum. Will direct people to programs and contacts within the Center's School Health Education Project (SHEP).

National Clearinghouse for Bilingual Education
George Washington University
Center for the Study of Language and Education
2121 K Street NW, Suite 260
Washington, D.C. 20037
202-467-0867
800-321-6223
Fax 800-531-9347
E-mail askncbe@ncbe.gwu.edu
http://www.ncbe.gwu.edu
Offers information about organizations involved in bilingual education, publishes information analysis products, offers a computerized information database with limited online search services, and provides field representatives.

National Coalition Against Censorship
275 Seventh Avenue
New York, NY 10001
212-807-6222
Fax 212-807-6245
E-mail ncac@ncac.org
http://www.ncac.org
Publishes *Censorship News* (ISSN 0749-6001, quarterly). Provides technical help to individuals and groups on how to fight censorship. NCAC's Clearinghouse on Book-Banning Litigation helps lawyers and educators keep current on library and school issues.

National Conference for Community and Justice
475 Park Ave South, 19th floor
New York, NY 10016-6901
http://www.nccj.org

National Council for Geographic Education
16A Leonard Hall
Indiana University of Pennsylvania
Indiana, PA 15705-1087
724-357-6290
Fax 412-357-7708
E-mail NCGE-ORG@grove.iup.edu
http://www.ncge.org
Publishes *Journal of Geography* (ISSN 0022-134, seven issues per year), reviews textbooks and other books of interest to teachers.

National Council for the Social Studies (NCSS)
>3501 Newark Street NW
>Washington, D.C. 20016
>202-966-7840
>Fax 202-966-2061
>E-mail info@ncss.org
>http://www.ncss.org

Publishes *Social Education* (seven issues a year), dealing with middle and high schools; *Social Studies and the Young Child,* dealing with elementary schools. Both journals include the annual "Notable Children's Trade Books in the Field of Social Studies."

National Council of Teachers of English (NCTE)
>1111 W. Kenyon Road
>Urbana, IL 61801-1096
>800-369-4283
>217-328-3870
>Fax 217-328-9645
>E-mail public-info@ncte.org
>http://www.ncte.org

Publications include *Language Arts* (elementary) (ISSN 0360-9170) and *English Journal* (middle school and junior and senior high school) (ISSN 0013-8274), each is eight issues per year; plus a wide range of materials: professional topics, literary maps, cassettes, and booklists. NCTE has a Committee on Censorship and offers resources, aid, and support. Assembly on Literature for Adolescents of NCTE (ALAN) publishes three times a year, *The ALAN Review,* which emphasizes new books, research, and methods of teaching. The Children's Literature Assembly (CLA) publishes twice a year, *The Journal of Children's Literature,* with discussions of issues and trends. The Junior High/Middle School Assembly's (JH/MSA) publication provides a network for those working with this age group.

Within the NCTE structure, two assemblies publish items of interest. These are the *ALAN Review* (ISSN 0882-2840, three issues per year; reviews hardbacks and paperbacks), by the Assembly on Literature for Adolescents; and *The Bulletin of the Children's Literature Assembly,* which provides in-depth discussion on specific topics in this subject area.

National Council of Teachers of Mathematics
>1906 Association Drive
>Reston, VA 20191-9988
>800-235-7566
>703-620-9840
>Fax 703-476-2970
>E-mail nctm@nctm.org
>http://www.nctm.org

Publishes *Arithmetic Teacher* (elementary) (ISSN 0004-136X) and *Mathematics Teacher* (junior high school through teacher education) (ISSN 0025-5769); each is nine issues per year; both include reviews and articles of interest.

National Education Association
1201 16th Street NW
Washington, D.C. 20036
202-833-4000
http://www.nea.org
Publishes *Today's Education: General Edition* (ISSN 0272-3573, monthly during the school year), plus books, pamphlets, curricular resource materials, and audiovisual materials.

National Gallery of Art
6th Street and Constitution Avenue NW
Washington, D.C. 20565
202-737-4215
http://www.nga.gov

National Geographic Society
Education Services Division
1145 17th Street NW
Washington, D.C. 20036-4688
800-647-5463
TDD 800-548-9797
http://www.nationalgeographic.com

National Library Service for the Blind and Physically Handicapped
Library of Congress
Washington, D.C. 20542
202-707-5100
Fax 202-707-0712
TDD 202-707-0744
E-mail nls@loc.gov
http://www.loc.gov/nls

National PTA, National Council of Parents and Teachers
National PTA Headquarters
330 N. Wabash Avenue, Suite 2100
Chicago, IL 60611
800-307-4782
312-670-6782
Fax 312-670-6783
E-mail info@pta.org
http://www.pta.org/index.htm

National Public Radio Educational Cassette Programs
> National Public Radio
> 635 Massachusetts Avenue NW
> Washington, D.C. 20001
> 202-414-2000
> http://www.npr.org

National School Boards Association
> 1680 Duke Street
> Alexandria, VA 22314
> 703-838-6722
> Fax 703-683-7590
> E-mail info@nsba.org
> http://www.nsba.org

National Science Teachers Association
> 1840 Wilson Boulevard
> Arlington, VA 22201-3000
> 703-243-7100
> http://www.nsta.org
> Publishes *Science and Children* (elementary) (ISSN 0420-8767, eight times a year)
and *Science Teacher* (ISSN 0036-8555, nine issues per year); both include reviews of materials
for teachers and students.

National Study of School Evaluation
> 1699 East Woodfield Road, Suite 406
> Schaumburg, IL 60173-4958
> 800-THE-NSSE (800-843-6773)
> 847-995-9080
> Fax 847-995-9088
> http://www.nsse.org
> Publishes evaluation instruments.

National Technical Information Service
> Technology Administration
> U.S. Department of Commerce
> Springfield, VA 22161
> 703-605-6000
> Fax 703-605-6900
> http://hplustest.harvard.edu:81/alpha/ovid_ntis.html

New England Association of Schools and Colleges

209 Burlington Road
Bedford, MA 01730
617-271-0022 ext. 307
Fax 617-271-0950
E-mail vferrandino@neasc.org
http://www.neasc.org

Northwest Association of Schools and Colleges

1910 University Drive
Boise, ID 83725-1060
208-427-5727
Fax 208-427-5729
http://www2.idbsu.edu/nasc
Accredits schools in Alaska, Idaho, Montana, Nevada, Oregon, Pennsylvania, Utah, Virginia, and Washington. Standard IV covers the Library Media Program.

Office for Intellectual Freedom

800-545-2433, ext. 4223
312-280-4223
http://www.ala.org/alaorg/oif
Publishes interpretations of the *Library Bill of Rights* and other materials dealing with intellectual freedom and challenges.

PBS Video (Public Broadcasting Service)

1320 Braddock Place
Alexandria, VA 22314
703-739-5000
http://www.pbs.org

People for the American Way

2000 M Street NW, Suite 400
Washington, D.C. 20036
800-326-7329
202-467-4999
Fax 202-293-2672
E-mail pfaw@pfaw.org
http://www.pfaw.org
Concerned with issues such as the freedom to learn, free expression, religious library, equal rights, building a democracy, and monitoring the religious right; provides news, articles, and links to related topics.

Recordings for the Blind, Inc.
20 Roszel Road
Princeton, NJ 08540
800-221-4792
800-221-4793
609-452-0606
Fax 609-987-8116

Smithsonian Institution
Smithsonian Information
SI Building, Room 153
Washington, D.C. 20560-0010
202-357-2700
TTY 202-357-1729
E-mail info@info.si.edu
http://www.si.edu

Southern Association of Colleges and Schools (SACS)
1866 Southern Lane
Decatur, GA 30033
404-679-4500
http://www.sacs.org/pub/sacs.htm
Commission on Elementary Schools
Commission of Secondary schools
Publishes *Guide to Evaluation and Accreditation of Schools.*

Speech Communication Association
5105 Backlick Road, Bldg. E
Annandale, VA 22003
703-750-0533
Fax 703-914-9417
http://www.cios.org/www/sca1.htm

Communication Institute for Online Scholarship (Speech Communication Association)
Box 57
Rotterdam Junction, NY 12150
518-887-2443
Fax 518-887-5186
Comserve@cios.org
Publishes *Communication Education* (ISSN 0363-4523, quarterly); includes reviews
of books and non-book materials useful to teachers of speech. The association publishes
books, pamphlets, and audiocassettes.

United States Board on Books for Young People (USBBY)
> Box 1017
> Honesdale, PA 18431-1017
> http://www.usbby.org
> 302-731-1600
> Fax 302-731-1057

Encourages interest in international children's literature through the *United States Board on Books for Young People* newsletter and meetings.

U.S. Copyright Office
> Public Information Office
> 101 Independence Avenue SE
> Washington, D.C. 20559-6000
> 202-707-3000
> E-mail copyinfo@loc.gov
> http://lcWeb.loc.gov/copyright

Information specialists are available from 8:30 am to 5:00 pm Eastern time, Monday through Friday. Recorded information is available 24 hours a day. The hotline number for copyright forms is 202-707-9100.

U.S. Government Printing Office
> http://www.gpo.gov

Ward's Natural Science Establishment, Inc.
> 5100-T N. Henrietta Road
> Box 92912
> Rochester, NY 14692-9012
> 716-359-2502
> Fax 716-334-6174
> http://scrtec.org/track/tracks/foo879.html

Western Association of Schools and Colleges (WASC)
> 533 Airport Boulevard, Suite 200
> Burlingame, CA 94010
> 650-696-1060
> Fax 650-696-1867
> E-mail wasc@ed.co.sanmateo.ca.us
> http://www.wascWeb.org

Covers educational institutions in California, Hawaii, Guam, and other areas of the Pacific. Publications: directory, annual.

WLN

> Box 3888
> Lacey, WA 98509-3888
> 1-800-DIALWLN

Can provide additional information about WLN Collecting Analysis and Assessment Services. Publications include *Using the Conspectus Method: A Collection Assessment Handbook* by Mary Bushing, Burns Davis, and Nancy Powell (1997).

Young Adult Library Services Association (YALSA)

> 50 E. Huron Street
> Chicago, IL 6-611
> 800-545-2433, ext. 439
> 312-280-4391
> Fax 312-664-7459
> E-mail YALSA@ala.org
> http://www.ala.org/yalsa/index.html

Publishes *Journal of Youth Services in Libraries* (ISSN 0040-9286) with the Association for Library Service to Children. The division's publications and bibliographies can be ordered directly from YALSA.

Appendix B
Resources

This list identifies books, journals, and electronic sources useful in dealing with collection matters. The topics include bibliographies, sample policy statements, intellectual freedom manuals, copyright recommendations, guidelines for preservation of materials, and selection tools. The chapter number at the end of the entry indicates the chapter(s) of this book in which the title is specifically mentioned or the chapter(s) that discusses activities for which the reference would be helpful. Use the index to find page numbers. For additional sources see listings at the end of chapters. Addresses are provided for journals; see Appendix A for associations' addresses.

A to Zoo: Subject Access to Children's Picture Books. 5th ed. Carolyn W. Lima and John A. Lima. New York: R. R. Bowker, 1998. ISBN 0-8352-3916-0. Chapter 12.

  Identifies more than 18,000 titles (fiction and nonfiction) for preschoolers through second-graders. Author, title, and illustrator indexes provide access.

Abridged Readers' Guide to Periodical Literature. See *Readers' Guide to Periodical Literature*.

Accessible Libraries on Campus: A Practical Guide for the Creation of Disability-Friendly Libraries. Tom McNulty, ed. Chicago: Association of College and Research Libraries, 1999. ISBN 0-83898-035-X. Chapter 12.

  Focuses on academic libraries but is equally appropriate for other institutions. Covers creating a Web page accessible to the blind and visually impaired. Has a directory of resources.

ALAN Review. Athens, GA: Assembly on Literature for Adolescents, National Council of Teachers of English, 1979– . ISSN 0882-2840. Chaps. 8, 10, and 12.

  Three times per year. Available on microfiche. Reviews new hardback and paperback titles for adolescents. Subscription: ALAN/NCTE, 1111 Kenyon Road, Urbana, IL 61801. (http://scholar.lib.vt.edu/ejournals/ALAN)

American Book Publishing Record. New Providence, NJ: R. R. Bowker, 1960– . ISSN 0002-7707. Chapter 10.

  Monthly. Related Work: *American Book Publishing Record Cumulative*, 1984– (published annually). Compiles titles cataloged by the Library of Congress. Dewey classification arrangement. Provides full cataloging data, LC and DDC numbers, subject headings, and price. Author index.

American Music Teacher. Cincinnati, OH: Music Teachers' National Association, 1951– . ISSN 003-0112. Chapter 12.

   Bi-monthly. Covers earliest music history to the latest developments in music technology. Features articles on teaching methods and techniques. Reviews teaching materials, music publications, videocassettes, music software, and other new technology. (http://www.mtna.org/amt/amt.htm)

American Reference Books Annual. Englewood, CO: Libraries Unlimited, 1970– . ISSN 0065-0112. Chapter 12.

   Reviews reference books published in the United States and Canada. Author/ title and subject index.

Appraisal: Science Books for Young People. Boston: Children's Science Books Review Committee, 1967– . ISSN 0003-7052. Chaps. 8 and 10.

   Quarterly. Reviews of trade books and series by librarians and science specialists. Annual cumulation. Subscription: Appraisal, 605 Commonwealth Avenue, Boston, MA 02215.

ASHA Leader. Rockville, MD: American Speech-Language-Hearing Association, 1996– . ISSN 1085-9586. Chapter 12.

   Twice monthly. Formerly *ASHA.* Reports on emerging issues and news of the profession. Subscription: *The ASHA Leader,* 10801 Rockville Pike, Rockville, MD 20852. (http://www.asha.org/publications/leader.htm)

AV Market Place: The Complete Business Directory of Audio, Audio Visual, Computer Systems, Film, Programming with Industry Yellow Pages. New York: R. R. Bowker, 1989– . ISSN 0067-0553. Chapter 13.

   Annual. Lists addresses and services of producers, distributors, production services, manufacturers, and equipment dealers.

Authoritative Guide to Evaluating Information on the Internet. Alison Cooke. New York: Neal-Schuman, 1999. ISBN 1-55570-356-9. Chapter 14.

   Covers search facilities, Internet information sources, and specific types of sources. Provides questions to guide evaluation of these information sources.

Best Books for Children: Preschool Through Grade 6. 6th ed. John T. Gillespie and Corinne J. Naden. New York: R. R. Bowker, 1998. ISBN 0-83524-099-1. Chapter 12.

   Includes brief annotations for 17,140 titles that had two or three recommendations in leading journals. Provides bibliographic and order information and citations to reviews. Indexes for author, title, illustrator, and subject.

Best Books for Young Adults. 2d ed. Betty B. Carter, Sally Estes, and Linda Waddle. Chicago: Young Adult Library Services Association, 2000. ISBN 0-83893-501-X. Chapter 12.

   Provides annotations for books published between 1966 and 1999. Organized by more than 25 themes. Lists formatted so they can be reproduced for handouts.

Book Links: Connecting Books, Libraries, and Classrooms. Chicago: American Library Association, 1991– . ISSN 1055-4742. Chapter 12.

> Six times per year. Discusses old and new titles. Includes "Book Strategies," "Classroom Connections," "Visual Links," "The Inside Story," and "Poetry" columns. Subscription: American Library Association, 50 E. Huron Street, Chicago, IL 60611. (http://www.ala.org/BookLinks/)

The Book Report: The Journal for Junior and Senior High School Libraries. Worthington, OH: Linworth, 1982– . ISSN 0524-0581. Chapter 10.

> Bimonthly during the school year. Reviews books, films, filmstrips, videocassettes, and software for junior and senior high school use. Subscription: Linworth Publishing, 5701 North High Street, Suite 1, Worthington, OH 43214. (http://www.linworth.com/bookreport)

Book Review Digest. New York: H. W. Wilson, 1905– . ISSN 0006-7326. Chaps. 8 and 10.

> Monthly. Quarterly and annual cumulations. Available on CD-ROM and online. (http://www.silverplatter.com/catalog/wbrd.htm)

Book Review Index. Detroit, MI: Gale Research, 1965– . ISSN 0524-0581. Chaps. 8 and 10.

> Annual cumulation or subscription basis of six bimonthly issues. Indexes more than 500 publications for reviews of books, periodicals, and books on tape. Related Gale titles: *Children's Book Review Index* and *Young Adult Book Review Index*.

Bookbird: A Journal of International Children's Literature. North York, ON, Canada: International Institute for Children's Literature Research and International Board on Books for Young People, 1962– . ISSN 0006-7377. Chaps. 10 and 12.

> Quarterly. Available on microform. Covers books of international interest and reviews of selection tools. Subscription: Evelyn Holmberg, University of Toronto Press, 5201 Dufferin Street, North York, ON M3H 5T8, Canada.

Booklist: Includes Reference Books Bulletin. Chicago: American Library Association, 1905– . ISSN 0006-7385. Chaps. 8, 10, and 12.

> Semimonthly. Available in microform. Reviews current books, videos, and software on regular basis. Reviews foreign language materials and materials on special topics in irregular columns. Provides monthly author/title index and semiannual cumulative indexes. Includes *Reference Books Bulletin* with reviews of encyclopedias, dictionaries, atlases, and other books using a continuous revision policy. Subscription: ALA, 50 E. Huron Street, Chicago, IL 60611. (http://www.ala.org/booklist.html)

Books for the Teen Age. New York Public Library, Committee on Books for Young Adults, 1929– . ISBN 0-87104-744-6. Chapter 12.

> Annual. Describes titles chosen on the basis of their appeal to teenagers. Title index. Order: Office of Branch Libraries, New York Public Library, 455 Fifth Avenue, New York, NY 10016. (http:www.nypl.org/branch/teen/1999)

Books in Print. New York: R. R. Bowker, 1948– . ISSN 0068-0214. Chaps. 10 and 13.
> Annual. Related works include *Subject Guide to Books in Print, Books in Print Supplement, Forthcoming Books in Print with Book Reviews Plus,* and *Publishers Trade List Annual.* Various titles available in print, CD-ROM, microfiche, online, and data tapes formats. Related entry: *Children's Books in Print.* (http://www.bowker.com)

Books in Print Supplement. See *Books in Print.*

The Bowker Annual Library and Book Trade Almanac. New York: R. R. Bowker, 1955– . ISSN 0068-0540. Chapter 14.
> Available in print and CD-ROM (Library Reference Plus). Includes research and statistics, such as average prices of books; news about legislation, associations, and grant-making agencies; lists of distinguished books; and directory information.

Bowker's Complete Video Directory 1999. New York: R. R. Bowker, 1999. ISSN 1051-290X. Chapter 10.
> Annual. Identifies videos for entertainment and/or education. Available as part of *Variety's Video Directory Plus* on CD-ROM.

Bowker's Directory of Audiocassettes for Children, 1999. R. R. Bowker, 1999. ISSN 0000-1740. Chaps. 10 and 12.
> Provides information about subject, author, reader, grade level, review citations, length, and price for 10,000 audiocassettes. Indexes by subject, title, author, reader/performer, and producer/distributor.

Bowker's Directory of Videocassettes for Children K–12, 2000. R. R. Bowker, 2000. ISBN 0-83524-323-0. Chaps. 10 and 12.
> Provides subject, age recommendation, description, review notation, release data, and ordering and/or rental information for more than 23,000 titles.

Braille Book Review. Washington, DC: National Library Service for the Blind and Physically Handicapped, 1933– . ISSN 0006-873X. Chapter 12.
> Bimonthly. Describes books for children and adults. Provides title, order code, author, number of volumes, and date of original print edition. Indexed monthly and annually. Address: National Library Service for the Blind and Physically Handicapped, 1291 NW Taylor Street, Washington, DC 20542. (http://www.loc.gov/nls/bbr.html)

Building a School Library Collection Plan: A Beginning Handbook with Internet Assist. David V. Loertscher and Blanche Woolls with Janice Felker. San Jose, CA: Hi Willow Research and Publishing, 1999. ISBN 0-93150-70-7. Chapter 16.
> Discusses evaluating and mapping collections. Distributor: LMC Source, P.O. Box 720400, San Jose, CA 95172-0400.

Building an ESL Collection for Young Adults: A Bibliography of Recommended Fiction and Nonfiction for School and Public Libraries. Laura Hibbets McCaffery. Westport, CT: Greenwood, 1998. ISBN 0-31329-937-4. Chapter 12.
> Describes titles in a wide range of subjects. Identifies reading level, interest level, and other characteristics important for this audience. Author and title indexes.

Building Electronic Library Collections: The Essential Guide to Selection Criteria and Core Subject Collections. Diane Kovacs. New York: Neal-Schuman, 1999. ISBN 1-555-70362-3. Chapter 12.

      Covers collecting, evaluating, and Web-based information. Recommends specific sites with major subject areas. Includes a section in one chapter on resources to support K–12 education.

Bulletin of the Center for Children's Books. Champaign, IL: University of Illinois Press, 1945– . ISSN 0008-9036. Chaps. 8 and 10.

      Monthly. Uses codes to indicate level of recommendation. Author/title index in each volume. Subscription: University of Illinois Press, BCCB, 54-E. Gregory Dr., Champaign, IL 61820. (http://edfu.lis.uiuc.edu/puboff/bccb)

Canadian Books in Print: Author and Title Index. Toronto: University of Toronto Press, 1975– . ISSN 0702-0201. Chapter 8.

      Annual. Supplemented quarterly *by Canadian Books in Print: Update on Fiche*, 1979– . Includes English- and French-language titles published by predominantly English-language Canadian publishers.

Captioned Media Program. Silver Spring, MD: National Association of the Deaf. Chapter 12.

      Former *Captioned Films/Videos Program.* Offers loans of films, videos, and other teaching materials through this service of the U.S. Department of Education. (http://www.cfv.org)

CD-ROM Reference Materials for Children and Young Adults: A Critical Guide for School and Public Libraries. Stephen Del Vecchio. Englewood, CO: Libraries Unlimited, 1999. ISBN 1-56308-711-1.

      Evaluates new children's reference available on CD-ROM. Considers usability, design, and extra features.

CD-ROM Technology: A Manual for Librarians and Educators. Catherine Mambretti. Jefferson, NC: McFarland, 1998. ISBN 0-78640-501-5. Chapter 10.

      Discusses criteria, installation, copyright issues, licensing, maintenance, and troubleshooting.

A Child Goes Forth: A Curriculum Guide for Preschool Children. 9th ed. Barbara J. Taylor. New York: Prentice-Hall College Division, 1998. ISBN 0-1391-6354-9. Chapter 12.

      Describes criteria for selecting materials for young children.

Children and Books. 9th ed. Zena Sutherland. Reading, MA: Addison-Wesley, 1997. ISBN 0-67399-733-2. Chapter 12.

      Discusses children's literature including sources of information for teachers and media specialists.

Children's Book Review Index. Detroit: Gale Research, 1976– . ISSN 0001-0335. Chapter 10.

      Provides review citations for books recommended for children through age 10. Illustrator and title indexes.

Children's Books from Other Countries. Carl M. Tomlinson, ed. Lanham, MD: Scarecrow Press, 1998. ISBN 0-81083-4X7-2. Chapter 12.

Provides annotations for 724 titles from 29 countries. Offers suggestions for using them in the curriculum. Includes listings for the Hans Christian Andersen and Mildred Batchelder awards.

Children's Books in Print. New York: R. R. Bowker, 1969– . ISSN 0069-3480. Chapter 10.

Annual. Related work: *Subject Guide to Children's Books in Print.* Provides bibliographic and ordering information. *Subject Guide to Children's Books in Print* uses Sears subject headings, supplemented by LC headings. Excludes textbooks.

Children's Catalog. 17th ed. Anne Price and Juliette Yaakov, eds. Standard Catalog Series. New York: H. W. Wilson, 1996. ISBN 0-8242-0983-5. Chaps. 8, 10, 16, and 17.

Four annual supplements. Preschool through grade 6. Abridged Dewey Decimal Classification. Provides bibliographic and order information, recommended grade level, subject headings, and descriptive/critical annotations. Index lists authors, subjects, titles, and analytical references to composite works.

Children's Literature in the Elementary School. 7th ed. Charlotte S. Huck et al. New York: McGraw-Hill, 2000. ISBN 0-07232-228-4. Chapter 12.

Guides teachers and media specialists in the selection and use of literature with children.

Children's Magazine Guide. New York: R. R. Bowker, 1948– . Nine issues per year with an annual cumulation. ISSN 0743-9873. Chapter 10.

Indexes 52 children's magazines. Provides name of article, author, magazine, issue date, and number of pages.

Choice. Middletown, CT: Association of College and Research Libraries, 1963– . ISSN 0009-4978. Chapter 8.

Monthly (except bimonthly July/August). Available on microfilm. Related works: *Choice Reviews on Cards.* Reviews periodicals, books, non-print media (films, audiotapes, videos, slides, microforms, software, CD-ROMs, Websites, and filmstrips.) Annual cumulated index published separately. Subscription: Choice, 100 Riverview Center, Middletown, CT 06457.

CM: Canadian Review of Materials. Winnipeg, MB Canada: The Manitoba Library Association, 1971– . ISSN 1201-9364. Chapter 8.

Biweekly. Electronic reviewing journal. Reviews books, videotapes, audiotapes, and CD-ROMs. Includes news, feature articles, interviews, and Web reviews. No charge for reading Website or receiving their e-mail version, but they ask regular readers to contribute $42 to help defray expenses. Subscription: CM Subscriptions, 606-100 Arthur Street, Winnipeg MB R3B 1H3 Canada. (http://www.umanitoba.ca/cm /index.html)

Collection Assessment and Management for School Libraries: Preparing for Cooperative Collection Development. Debra E. Kachel. Westport, CT: Greenwood, 1997. ISBN 0-31329-853-8. Chaps. 6 and 16.

Contains the Ephrata Area School District (Pennsylvania) "Written Collection Policy Documents" including copyright, selection, acceptable use, and curriculum mapping.

The Complete Directory of Large Print Books and Serials 2000. New Providence, NJ: R. R. Bowker, 2000. ISBN 0-83524-312-5. Chapter 12.

Lists adult, juvenile, and textbook titles available in large print. Includes the type size and physical size of each book listed.

Computers in Libraries: Complete Coverage of Library Information Technology. Westport, CT: Meckler, 1989– . ISSN 1041-7915. Chapter 14.

Ten times per year. Carries news items and general technical articles designed to provide practical information. Recent topics include e-books, licensing, virtual libraries, fundraising, and Web designing. Subscription: Information Today, Inc., 143 Old Marlton Pike, Medford, NJ 08055-8750. Telephone: 609-654-4266.

The Consumer Information Catalog. Washington, DC: Consumer Information Center, General Services Administration, 1977– . Chapter 10.

Quarterly. Free. Subscription: Consumer Information Center-R, P.O. Box 100, Pueblo, CO 81002. (http://www.pueblo.gsa.gov)

Consumer Reports. Mt. Vernon, NY: Consumers Union, 1942– . ISSN 0010-7174. Chapter 10.

Monthly (December issue is annual buying guide issue). Provides evaluative comparisons of equipment including emerging technologies. Available in microform. Subscription address: Consumer Reports, P.O. Box 2480, Boulder, CO 80322. (http://www.consumerreports.org)

The Copyright Primer for Librarians and Educators. 2d ed. Janis J. Bruwelheide. Chicago: American Library Association, 1998. ISBN 0-83890-642-7. Chapter 6.

Offers practical guidance on issues and questions about copyright. Includes "Web Do's and Don'ts" and a reprint of "Fair Use in the Electronic Age: Serving the Public Interest: A Working Documents from the Library Community," which was approved in principle by the ALA Council on February 8, 1995.

Coretta Scott King Awards Books, 1970–1999. Henrietta Smith, ed. Chicago: American Library Association, 1999. ISBN 0-83893-496-X. Chapter 12.

Provides annotation and biographical information about works by African American authors and illustrators for the designated award or honor books. Includes example of each winning illustration.

Creating a Virtual Library: A How-to-Do-It Manual. no. 91. Frederick Stielow, ed. New York: Neal-Schuman, 1999. ISBN 1-55570-346-1. Chapter 14.

Provides practical guidance through designing, managing, developing policies, and selecting virtual resources.

Critical Handbook of Children's Literature. 6th ed. Rebecca J. Lukens. New York: Longman, 1999. ISBN 0-321-00361-6. Chapter 12.

    Discusses the literary elements of children's literature.

Culturally Diverse Videos, Audios, and CD-ROMS for Children and Young Adults. Irene Wood, ed. New York: Neal-Schuman, 1999. ISBN 1-55570-377-1. Chapter 12.

    Recommends more than 1,000 titles including African American, Asian, Latino, Native American, Arab, Jewish, Cajun and various European American. Provides bibliographic information, list price, and suggested audience.

Dealing with Selection and Censorship: A Handbook for Wisconsin Schools and Libraries. no. 0046. Carolyn Winters Folke. Madison, WI: Wisconsin Department of Public Instruction, 1999. Chapter 7.

    Offers practical advice. Available for $21.00 from Publication Sales, Wisconsin Department of Public Instruction, Drawer 179, Milwaukee, WI 53293-1079, 1-800-243-8782. Also available at http://www.dpi.state.wi.us/pubsales

Developing Library and Information Center Collections. 4th ed. G. Edward Evans. Englewood, CO: Libraries Unlimited, 2000. ISBN 1-56308-832-0. Chapter 13.

    Provides a comprehensive overview with focus on the issues and processes of collection development.

Developing Reference Collections and Services in an Electronic Age: A How-to-Do-It Manual for Librarians. Kay Cassell. New York: Neal-Schuman, 1999. ISBN 1-55570-363-1. Chapter 12.

    Discusses selection criteria, advantages and disadvantages of print versus electronic sources, space requirements, and other considerations. Provides model policies.

Directory of Video, Multimedia, and Audio-Visual Products. Fairfax, VA: International Communications Industries Association; Overland Park, KS: Daniels Publishing Group, 1996– . ISSN 1086-9565. Chapter 9.

    Also available with text with CD-ROM. Provides photographs and specifications for video, projection systems, accessories, audio visual, audio, and furniture products. Includes glossary and ISIA Membership Directory. Indexes by product, company, and directory section.

Education: A Guide to Reference and Information Sources. 2d ed. Nancy P. O'Brien, ed. Reference Sources in Social Sciences Series. Englewood, CO: Libraries Unlimited, 2000. ISBN 1-56308-626-3. Chapter 12.

    Annotations describe sources in educational technology, multilingual/multicultural education, curriculum, instruction, content areas, educational research, and others. Author, title, and subject index.

Educational Leadership: Journal of Department of Supervision and Curriculum Development. Washington, DC: NEA, 1943– . ISSN 0013-1784. Chapter 12.

    Monthly. Online version has selected full-length articles and several abstracts of articles. Reviews professional books. Subscription address: ASCD, 1250 North Pitt Street, Alexandria, VA 22314-1453. (http://www.ascd.org/pubs/el/elintro.html)

Educational Media and Technology Yearbook. Englewood, CO: Libraries Unlimited, 1973– . ISSN 8755-2094. Chapter 14.

    Published annually. Published in corporation with and cosponsored by the Association for Educational Communications and Technology. Lists pertinent organizations.

Educators Guides (annuals). Available from Educators Progress Service, 214 Center Street, Randolph, WI 53956. Chapter 12.

    Titles include:

> *Educators Grade Guide to Free Teaching Aids*
>
> *Educators Guide to Free Films, Filmstrips and Slides*
>
> *Educators Guide to Free Guidance Materials*
>
> *Educators Guide to Free Health, Physical Education, and Recreation Materials*
>
> *Educators Guide to Free Home Economics Materials*
>
> *Educators Guide to Free Science Materials*
>
> *Educators Guide to Free Social Studies Materials*
>
> *Educators Guide to Free Materials*
>
> *Elementary Teachers' Guide to Free Curriculum Materials*
>
> *Guide to Free Computer Materials*
>
> *Educators Guide to Free Videotapes*

El-Hi Textbooks and Serials in Print, including Related Teaching Materials K–12 Annual. New York: R. R. Bowker, 1985– . ISSN 0000-0825. Chapter 10.

    Indexes textbooks by subject, author, title, series, and publisher. Indexes serials by subject, title, and publishers.

The Elementary School Library Collection: A Guide to Books and Other Media, Phases 1-2-3, 2000. 22d ed. Lauren K. Lee, ed. Williamsport, PA: Brodart, 2000. ISBN: 0-8727-2114-0. Chaps. 4, 7, 10, 11, 16, and 17.

    Includes useful appendixes and indexing by title, author, and subject. CD-ROM version available. Recommends children's books, periodicals, audiovisual materials, professional materials, and computer software.

English Journal. Urbana, IL: National Council of Teachers of English, 1912– . ISSN 0013-8274. Chapter 12.

    Monthly (September-April). Available in microform. Reviews young adult literature, films, videos, software, and professional publications. Subscription: NCTE Subscription Service, 1111 W. Kenyon Road, Urbana, IL 61801-1086. (http://www.cc.ysu.edu/tej)

Essentials of Children's Literature. 3d ed. Carol Lynch-Brown and Carl M. Tomlinson. Boston: Allyn & Bacon, 1998. ISBN 0-20528-136-2. Chapter 12.
>Surveys children's literature, featuring genres, authors within the genre, and recommended titles. Includes a chapter on multicultural and international literature.

"Evaluating Web Resources." Jan Alexander and Marsha Ann Tate. Chester, PA: Wolfgram Memorial Library, Widener University. Date Mounted: August 1996. Updated September 11, 1999. Copyright 1996–1999. http://www2.widener.edu/Wolfgram -Memorial-Library/webeval.htm. Chapter 10.
>Is frequently cited as a worthwhile Website. Provides checklists for evaluating advocacy, business/marketing, news, informational, and personal Web pages.

Evaluating the School Library Media Center: Analysis Techniques and Research Practices. Nancy Everhart. Englewood, CO: Libraries Unlimited, 1998. ISBN 1-56308-085-0. Chapter 16.
>Discusses qualitative and quantitative research techniques. Guides conducting research, collecting statistics, and evaluating the media center program.

Exceptional Children. Reston, VA: Council for Exceptional Children, 1934– . ISSN 0014-4029. Chapter 12.
>Four times a year. Research-based articles. Reviews professional books.

Exceptional Parent: Parenting Your Child with a Disability. Boston: Psy-Ed, 1971– . ISSN 0046-9157. Chapter 12.
>Twelve issues per year. Provides information and support for families with children with disabilities and the professionals who work with them. Subscription: Dept. Exceptional Parent, Box 2078, Marion, OH, 43306-2178.

Exploring Science in the Library: Resources and Activities for Young People. Maria Sosa and Tracy Gath. Chicago: American Library Association, 2000. ISBN 0-83890-768-7. Chapter 12.
>Co-published with American Association for the Advancement of Science (AAAS). Includes supplemental activities for science instruction in the library, Web references, a guide to selecting books, information about fundraising, and an annotated bibliography of science trade books.

Fiction Catalog. 13th ed. Bronx, NY: H. W. Wilson, 1996. ISBN 0-82420-894-3. Chapter 10.
>Four annual supplements. Recommends 5,450 books in the main volume (1996). Provides access by subject and genre.

Fluent in Fantasy: A Guide to Reading Interests. Diana Tixier Herald. Englewood, CO: Libraries Unlimited, 1999. ISBN 1-56308-655-7. Chapter 12.
>Provides an overview of the genre. Recommends titles and online resources.

For Younger Readers: Braille and Talking Books. Washington, DC: National Library Service for the Blind and Physically Handicapped, The Library of Congress, 1967– . ISSN 0093-2825. Chapter 12.

Biennial. Annotates braille, disc, and cassette books announced in *Braille Book Review* and *Talking Books Topics*. Available in braille, sound recording, and large type. Free.

Free and Inexpensive Career Materials: A Resource Directory. Elizabeth H. Oakes, ed. Chicago: Ferguson, 1998. ISBN 0-89434-221-5. Chapter 12.

Lists more than 800 sources of career information materials. Provides fax numbers, Websites, and e-mail addresses for many of the organizations.

Genreflecting: A Guide to Reading Interest in Genre Fiction. Diana Tixier Herald. Englewood, CO: Libraries Unlimited, 2000. ISBN 1-56308-638-7. Chapter 12.

Describes eight fiction genres (romance, westerns, fantasy, crime, science fiction) including subgenres. Identifies more than 6,000 titles.

Global Voices: Using Historical Fiction to Teach Social Studies. Susan B. Ouzts. Reading, MA: Addison-Wesley, 1998. ISBN 0-67336-395-3. Chapter 12.

Provides lessons incorporating contemporary literature from many cultures for use in language arts and social studies classes in middle schools.

Grantsmanship for Small Libraries and School Library Media Centers. Sylvia D. Hall-Ellis et al. Frank W. Hoffman, ed. Englewood, CO: Libraries Unlimited, 1999. ISBN 1-56308-484-8. Chapter 14.

Describes the writing of planning, project design, project narrative, project personnel, budget development, and project evaluation for grant writing. Includes appendixes with an annotated bibliography, frequently asked questions, and a glossary.

Great Books for African-American Children. Pamela Toussaint. New York: Dutton/Plume, 1999. ISBN 0-45228-044-3. Chapter 12.

Reviews 250 titles and provides ordering information.

"Great Sites: Selection Criteria." Children and Technology Committee of the Association of Library Service to Children. Chicago, IL: American Library Association, Stephanie Stokes design, October 15, 1998. http://www.ala.org/parentspage/greatsites/criteria.html (Accessed November 10, 1999). Chapter 10.

Helps parents evaluate authorship/sponsorship, purpose, design, stability, and content. Recommends sites for children.

Guide to Managing Approval Plans. Susan Flood, ed. Acquisition Guidelines no. 11. Association for Library Collections and Technical Services, Acquisitions Section Publications Committee. Chicago: American Library Association, 1998. ISBN 0-8393-481-1. Chapter 13.

Provides a practical guide to approval plans. Covers description of types of plans, vendor selection, an agreement, developing a profile, and monitoring the plan.

Guide to Microforms in Print: Author/Title. Munich, Germany: K. G. Saur, 1975– . ISSN 0164-0747. Chapter 10.

Annual. Lists microforms by author and title.

Guide to Popular U.S. Government Publications. 5th ed. Frank W. Hoffmann and Richard J. Wood. Englewood, CO: Libraries Unlimited, 1998. ISBN 1-56308-607-7. Chapter 10.
　　　　Covers 2,500 publications. Provide bibliographic information, illustrative material, stock number, price, SuDocs classification number, and annotation.

Guide to Reference Materials for School Library Media Centers. 5th ed. Barbara Ripp Safford. Englewood, CO: Libraries Unlimited, 1998. ISBN 1-56308-545-3. Chapter 12.
　　　　Covers more than 2,000 titles including electronic resources with age and reading levels, presentation styles, strengths and weaknesses, comparison with other works, and citations to reviews.

"Guidelines for the Evaluation of Instructional Technology Resources for California Schools." Stanislaus County (California) Office of Education, 1999. http://clearinghouse.k12.ca.us (Accessed December 3, 2000). Chapter 10.
　　　　Identifies evaluation rubrics in terms of California curriculum content, instructional design, program design, assessment, and instructional support materials. Appendixes cover other aspects of selection. Appendix D Legal Compliance "Standards for Evaluation of Instructional Materials Respect to Social Content," 1986 Edition, California State Department of Education, Abbreviated Edition (Education Codes 60040-60044).

Halliwell's Film and Video Guide, 1999. 15th ed. John Walker, ed. New York: HarperCollins, 1999. ISBN 0-06273-692-2. Chapter 12.
　　　　Includes more than 23,000 reviews. Provides country of origin, rating, format, year releases, alternate title, brief description, quotes from reviews, and awards. Arranged alphabetically by title. Lists Academy Award winners, four-star reviews by title and by year, three-star reviews by title and by year.

The History Teacher. Long Beach, CA: Society for History Education, 1967– . ISSN 0018-2745. Chapter 12.
　　　　Quarterly. Available on microfilm. Reviews books, textbooks, supplementary readers, and professional books. Subscription: Society for History Education, Department of History, California State University, 1250 Bellflower Boulevard, Long Beach, CA 90840.

Hooked on Horror: A Guide to Reading Interests in Horror Fiction. Anthony J. Fonseca and June Michele Pulliam. Genreflecting Advisory Series. Englewood, CO: Libraries Unlimited, 1999. ISBN 1-56308-671-9. Chapter 12.
　　　　Describes approximately 1,000 contemporary and classic titles for English literature classes and horror fans. Focuses on widely available titles.

The Horn Book Magazine. Boston: Horn Book, 1924– . ISSN 0018-5078. Chaps. 8 and 10.
　　　　Six issues per year. Available in microform. Related work: *The Horn Book Guide to Children's and Young Adult Books*, 1990– , ISSN 1044-405X. Reviews hardback and paperback books. Includes books in Spanish. Subscription: Circulation Department, Park Square Building, 31 James Avenue, Boston, MA 02116. (http://www.hbook.com/mag.shtml)

Hot Links: Literature Links for the Middle School Curriculum. Cora M. Wright. Englewood, CO: Libraries Unlimited, 1998. ISBN 1-56308-587-9. Chapter 12.

>Recommends titles arranged by curriculum areas. Indicates high interest/low reading level titles.

Including Families of Children with Special Needs: A How-to-Do-It Manual for Librarians. Sandra Feinberg, Kathleen Deerr, Barbara Jordan, and Michele Langa. New York: Neal-Schuman, 1999. ISBN 1-55570-339-9. Chapter 12.

>Offers suggestions for selecting materials, including toys and resources for parents.

Index to Poetry for Children and Young People, 1993–1997. Bronx, NY: H. W. Wilson, 1998. ISBN 0-82420-939-7. Chapter 12.

>Covers approximately 8,700 poems from more than 186 sources. Indexes by title, author, first line, and subject.

Information Power: Building Partnerships for Learning. American Association of School Librarians and Association for Educational Communications and Technology. Chicago: American Library Association, 1998. ISBN 0-83893-470-6. Chaps. 1, 2, 5, 6, 7, 13, and 16.

>Guides for school library media centers.

Informational Picture Books for Children. Patricia J. Cianciolo. Chicago: American Library Association, 2000. ISBN 0-83890-774-1. Chapter 12.

>Annotates 250 titles (published between 1994 and 1999) of interest to preschoolers through middle-school students

Instructional Media and the New Technologies of Instruction. 6th ed. Robert Heinich et al. Upper Saddle River, NJ: Prentice-Hall, 1999. ISBN 0-13859-159-8. Chaps. 9, 10, and 12.

>Discusses selection and use of media. Includes software package for teachers to use in creating, maintaining, printing, and evaluating lesson plans and the materials used in them.

Intellectual Freedom Manual. 5th ed. ALA Office of Intellectual Freedom. Chicago: American Library Association, 1996. ISBN 0-83890-677-X. Chapter 6.

>Includes policies and their interpretations. Offers guidelines for developing policies and practices.

Internet Books for Educators, Parents, and Children. Jean Reese. Englewood, CO: Libraries Unlimited, 1999. ISBN 1-56308-697-2. Chapter 12.

>Recommends approximately 100 titles. Index for author and title.

The Internet in School. Duncan Grey. New York: Continuum International, 1999. ISBN 0-30470-531-4. Chapter 14.

>Takes the position of monitoring, not restricting, use of the Internet. Offers practical advice in a non-technical format about dealing with the Internet in a school serving 1,850 students ages 11–18.

Internet Policy Handbook for Libraries. Mark Smith. New York: Neal-Schuman, 1999. ISBN 1-55570-345-3. Chapter 6.

>Includes examples from school library media center policies, describes the process of developing, and discusses the issues involved.

Internet Resource Directory for K–12 Teachers and Librarians, 1999/2000 Edition. Elizabeth B. Miller. Englewood, CO: Libraries Unlimited. Annual, 1999. ISBN 1-56308-812-6. Chapter 12.

>Describes selected resources on a wide range of subjects including resources to help teachers and media specialists, lesson plans, AUP, copyright, Intellectual Freedom, and selections. Posts changes and updates monthly at http://www.lu.com /Internet_Resource_Directory.

Internet Technology for Schools. Catherine Mambretti. Jefferson, NC: McFarland, 1999. ISBN 0-78640-727-1. Chapter 14.

>Moves from a general overview of the issues faced in planning for and developing technology in the schools to "good Internet practices" and on to providing technical guidelines. Glossary.

Journal of Geography. Macomb, IL: National Council for Geographic Education, 1902– . ISSN 0022-1341. Chapter 12.

>Bimonthly. Reviews textbooks and professional materials; has a column on free and inexpensive materials. Subscription: National Council for Geographic Education, Western Illinois University, Macomb, IL 61455.

Journal of Health Education. Reston, VA: American Alliance for Health, Physical Education, Recreation and Dance, 1991– . ISSN 1055-6699. Chapter 12.

>Bimonthly. Available in microform. Subscription: American Alliance for Health, Physical Education, Recreation and Dance, 1900 Association Drive, Reston, VA 22091.

Journal of Home Economics. Washington, DC: American Home Economics Association, 1909– . ISSN 0022-1570. Chapter 12.

>Quarterly. Available in microform. Reviews trade and professional books. Subscription: American Home Economics Association, 2010 Massachusetts Avenue NW, Washington, DC 20036.

Journal of Visual Impairment and Blindness. New York: American Foundation for the Blind, 1977– . ISSN 0145-482X. Chapter 12.

>Monthly (except July and August). Available in regular print or in Braille. Available in microform, on audiocassette, and online. Subscriptions: Subscription Services, The Sheridan Press, 450 Fame Avenue, Hanover, PA 17331, or telephone 1-888-522-0220 (United States), or 1-717-632-3535 (international), or http:www .afb.org/jrib.html.

Junior Genreflecting: A Guide to Good Reads and Series Fiction for Children. Bridget
Dealy Volz, Lynda Blackburn Welborn, and Cheryl Perkins Scheer. Genreflecting
Advisory Series. Englewood, CO: Libraries Unlimited, 2000. ISBN 1-56308-556-9.
Chapter 12.
   Describes titles for children in grades 3–8. Arranges titles by specific
themes and subtopics.

Kirkus Reviews. New York: Kirkus Service, 1933– . ISSN 0042-6598. Chapter 10.
   Semimonthly. Available in microform. Reviews trade books. Entries provide bibliographic/order information, paging, month and day of release, type of
book, and grade level. Subscription: Kirkus Service, 200 Park Avenue South, New
York, NY 10003.

Kliatt: Reviews of Selected Books, Educational Software and Audiobooks. Wellesley, MA:
Kliatt, 1978– . ISSN 1065-8602. Chaps. 8, 10, and 12.
   Eight issues per year. Available in microform. Reviews software, paper-
backs, and audiobooks for ages 12–19. Subscription: Kliatt, 33 Bay State Road,
Wellesley, MA 02481, Telephone 781-237-7577, Fax 781-237-7577.

Language Arts. Urbana, IL: National Council of Teachers of English, 1975– . ISSN 0360-9170.
Chapter 12.
   Monthly (September through May). Available in microform. Reviews chil-
dren's books and professional materials. Subscription: National Council of
Teachers of English, 1111 Kenyon Road, Urbana, IL 61801.

Learning and Libraries in an Information Age: Principles and Practice. Barbara K. Stripling,
ed. Englewood, CO: Libraries Unlimited, 1999. ISBN 1-56308-666-2. Chapter 11.
   Discusses the role of the media center in meeting informational and instructional needs and in establishing collaborative efforts with teachers.

Libraries, the First Amendment, and Cyberspace: What You Need to Know. Robert S. Peck.
Chicago: American Library Association, 2000. ISBN 0-8389-0773-3. Chapter 4.
   Answers questions relating to censorship and access. Appendixes include
important First Amendment documents.

Library Journal. New York: Cahners/R. R. Bowker, 1876– . ISSN 0363-0277. Chaps. 8 and 10.
   Semimonthly (monthly January, July, August, and December). Available
in microform. Reviews books, magazines, videos, CD-ROM, software, and
audiobooks. Monthly author index to reviews. Includes annual buyer's guide to
hardware and equipment. Subscription: Box 1977, Marion, OH 43305-1977. (Library
Journal Digital http://www.ljdigital.com)

Library Talk: The Magazine for Elementary School Librarians. Carolyn Hamilton, ed.
Worthington, OH: Linworth, 1988– . ISSN 1043-237X. Chapter 10.
   Five issues per year. Reviews trade books, including Spanish and professional
books, multicultural materials, reference materials, videos, CD-ROMs, and software. Identifies free and inexpensive materials. Includes the formerly separately

published *Technology Connection.* Subscription: 480 E. Wilson Bridge Road, Suite L, Worthington, OH 43085. (http:www.linworth.com/libraryTalk)

Literary Market Place : The Directory of the American Book Publishing Industry with Industry Yellow Pages (two-volume set). New York: R. R. Bowker, 1973– . ISSN 0161-2905. Chapter 13.

> Annual. Available in print, CD-ROM (Library Reference Plus), or online. (http://lmp.bookwire.com)

Literature Connections to American History, K–6: Resources to Enhance and Entice. Lynda G. Adamson. Englewood, CO: Libraries Unlimited, 1998. ISBN 1-56308-502-X. Chapter 12.

> Describes historical fiction novels, biographies, history trade books, CD-ROMs, and videotapes covering from "North America before 1600" through "since 1975."

Literature Connections to World History, Grades K–6: Resources to Enhance and Entice. Lynda G. Adamson. Englewood, CO: Libraries Unlimited, 1998. ISBN 1-56308-504-6. Chapter 12.

> Covers from prehistoric times to recent ones. Index of author, titles, and subjects.

Literature Connections to World History, 7–12: Resources to Enhance and Entice. Lynda G. Adamson. Englewood, CO: Libraries Unlimited, 1998. ISBN 1-5630-8505-5. Chapter 12.

> Describes materials (trade books, CD-ROMs, and videos). Indexes by author/illustrator, title, and subject.

Massachusetts Library Association/Massachusetts School Library Media Association Joint Statement on Collection Development in Schools and Public Libraries. 1995. Available at http://www.mlin.lib.ma.us/mblc/public_advisory/school_public/ps_jcolldev .shtml (Last modified December 20, 1999). (Accessed January 29, 2000). Chapter 14.

> Identifies the collection responsibilities for the public library and for the school library media center.

Mathematics Teacher. Reston, VA: National Council of Teachers of Mathematics, 1954– . ISSN 0004-136X. Chapter 12.

> Monthly (except June-September). Available in microform. The column "Reviewing and Viewing" covers teaching materials, including games, videotapes, workbooks, software, and books for teachers. Subscription: NCTM, 1906 Association Drive, Reston, VA 22091. (http://www.nctm.org/mt/mt.htm)

Media Review Digest. Ann Arbor, MI: Pierian Press, 1970– . ISSN 0363-7778. Chapter 8.

> Lists reviews of educational and feature films, videocassettes, videodiscs, filmstrips, educational spoken records, tapes, compact discs, slides, transparencies, kits, maps, globes, charts, and games. (http://www.pierianpress.com/mrd-list.htm)

Middle and Junior High School Library Catalog. 8th ed. Bronx, NY: H. W. Wilson, 2000. ISBN 0-82420-880-3. Chaps. 8, 16, and 17.

> Four annual supplements. Recommends more than 4,200 fiction and non-fiction books in the main volume (2000). Arranged by Abridged Dewey Decimal Classification. Indexes: author, title, subject, and analytics.

Monthly Catalog of United States Government Publications. Washington, DC: Government Printing Office, 1895– . GP 3.8. Chapter 10.

> Available on CD-ROM GP 3.8/7: Identifies publications by major branches, departments, and bureaus of the U.S. government. Provides depository and order information.

More Rip-Roaring Reads for Reluctant Teen Readers. Betty D. Ammon and Gale W. Sherman. Englewood, CO: Libraries Unlimited, 1999. ISBN 1-56308-571-2. Chapter 12.

> Describes 40 titles (fiction and nonfiction) in terms of ways to motivate reluctant readers in middle and high school. Listings include genre, themes, and reading and interest levels.

More Virtual Field Trips. Gail Cooper and Carry Cooper. Englewood, CO: Libraries Unlimited, 1999. ISBN 1-56308-770-0. Chapter 14.

> Covers additional sites to those identified in *Virtual Field Trips* (Libraries Unlimited, 1997). Pays more attention to physical education, health and safety, rural, and architectural field trips than the earlier edition does.

Moving Library Collections: A Management Handbook. Elizabeth Chamberlain Habich. Westport, CT: Greenwood, 1998. ISBN 0-31329-330-9. Chapter 17.

> Offers suggestions for moves handled by staff or professional movers. Includes pest-management advice.

Multicultural Projects Index: Things to Make and Do to Celebrate Festivals, Cultures, and Holidays around the World. 2d ed. Mary Anne Pilger. Englewood, CO: Libraries Unlimited, 1998. ISBN 1-56308-524-0. Chapter 12.

> Identifies multicultural projects in more than 1,700 books.

Multicultural Resources on the Internet: The United States and Canada. Vicki L. Gregory, Marilyn H. Karrenbrock Stauffer, and Thomas W. Keene Jr. Englewood, CO: Libraries Unlimited, 1999. ISBN 1-56308-676-X. Chapter 12.

> Identifies sources for Native, African, Hispanic, Asian, Chinese, Japanese, Asian Indian, Jewish, Middle Eastern-North African, Hawaiian, and Cajun-Creole Americans.

Multicultural Review: Dedicated to a Better Understanding of Ethnic, Racial and Religious Diversity. Westport, CT: Greenwood, 1992– . ISSN 1058-9236. Chaps. 8 and 12.

> Quarterly. Includes articles, often bibliographic essays, and reviews of materials for juvenile and adult audiences. Subscriptions: Greenwood Publishing Group, Inc., 88 Post Road W., Box 5007, Westport, CT 06881-5007. (http://www.mcreview.com/mcorder.htm)

Neal-Schuman Authoritative Guide to Evaluating Information on the Internet. Alison Cooke. New York: Neal-Schuman, 1999. ISBN 1-55570-356-9. Chaps. 10 and 14.
>Discusses criteria for a range of types of sources including Websites, electronic journals, newsgroups, databases, current awareness services, and FAQs.

Negotiating the Special Education Maze: A Guide for Parents and Teachers. 3d ed. Winifred Anderson, Stephen Chitwood, and Deidre Hayden. Rockville, MD: Woodbine House, 1997. ISBN 0-93314-972-7. Chapter 12.
>Provides basic information on the special education process, particularly as it applies to schools and parents.

Newbery and Caldecott Awards: A Guide to the Medal and Honor Books. Chicago: American Library Association, 2000. ISBN 0-83893-495-1. Chapter 12.
>Annual. Provides background information about the titles and their creators.

Newsletter on Intellectual Freedom. Chicago: Intellectual Freedom Committee of the American Library Association, 1952– . ISSN 0028-9485. Chapter 7.
>Bimonthly. Available on microform. Reports events relating to intellectual freedom and censorship. Subscription American Library Association Committee on Intellectual Freedom, 50 E. Huron St., Chicago, IL 60611.

1-2-3-4 for the Show: A Guide to Small-Cast One-Act Plays. Lewis W. Heniford. Lanham, MD: Scarecrow, 1999. ISBN 0-81083-600-9. Chapter 12.
>Provides bibliographic information and genre. Describes how to obtain scripts through publishers or library collections.

Online: The Magazine of Online Information Systems. Wilton, CT: Online, 1970– . ISSN 0146-5422. Chapter 10.
>Six times per year. Provides articles about online applications and in-depth evaluative reviews. Subscription: Online, Inc., 462 Danbury Road, Wilton CT 06897. (http://onlineinc.com/onlinemag)

Output Measures for School Library Media Programs. Frances Bryant Bradburn. New York: Neal-Schuman, 1999. ISBN 1-55570-326-7. Chapter 16.
>Describes various measures and their use.

Preservation: Caring for Your Collections. 1999. Library of Congress. http://www.lcWeb.loc .gov/preserv (Accessed December 3, 2000). Chapter 15.
>Covers books, motion-picture film, photographs, manuscripts, prints, posters, maps, audiorecordings, and the drying of water-damaged materials.

Programming with Latino Children's Materials: A How-to-Do-It Manual for Librarians. Tim Wadham. New York: Neal-Schuman, 1999. ISBN 1-55570-352-6. Chapter 13.
>Provides background information, annotated bibliographies, and suggestions for selection policies and identifies acquisition sources.

Publishers, Distributors, and Wholesalers of the United States. New Providence, NJ: R. R. Bowker, 1979– . ISSN 0000-0671. Chapter 13.

Annual. Lists more than 50,000 publishers, wholesalers, distributors, software firms, and museum and association imprints. Access by name, imprint, subsidiaries, divisions, state, firms with toll-free numbers, ISBN prefix, and publisher's field of activity.

Publishers Weekly. R. R. Bowker, 1872– . ISSN 0000-0019. Chaps. 10 and 13.

Weekly. Reviews books and audiovisual materials. Discusses trends in the book industry. (http://www.publishersweekly.com/)

Quill and Quire. Toronto: Key Publishers, 1935– . ISSN 0033-6491. Chapter 8.

Monthly. Available in microform. Special supplement: *Forthcoming Books = Livres á Paraitre.* Reviews books and has advertisements for tapes and records. Subscription: Customer Service, 35 Riviera Drive, Unit 17, Markham, Ontario L3R 8N4 Canada.

Readers' Guide to Periodical Literature. H. W. Wilson, 1901– . ISSN 0034-0464. Chapter 10.

Monthly. Available in print, CD-ROM, and online. Indexes journals including books reviews. Related source: *Abridged Readers' Guide to Periodical Literature.*

Reading in Series: A Selection Guide to Books for Children. Catherine Barr, ed. New Providence, NJ: R. R. Bowker, 1999. ISBN 0-835243-011-8. Chapter 12.

Covers more than 1,000 series. Provides author, current publisher, genre, grade level, brief description, list of all titles in the series, and reference to similar series. Includes a series for ESL readers.

The Reading Teacher. Newark, DE: International Reading Association, 1950– . ISSN 0034-0561. Chaps. 10 and 12.

Eight issues per year. Available on microform. Includes teaching tips, insights into theory, research findings, and reviews of children's literature. Subscription: International Reading Association, Box 8137, Newark, DE 19714. (http://www.reading.org/publications/journals/RT/rt.htm)

Recommended Reference Books for Small and Medium-Sized Libraries. Bohdan W. Wynar, ed. Englewood, CO: Libraries Unlimited, 1982– . ISSN 0277-5948. Chapter 12.

Annual. Selected from *American Reference Books Annual.* Lengthy reviews coded to identify titles of interest to school library media centers.

Recommended Reference Books in Paperback. 3d ed. Jovian P. Lang and Jack O'Gorman. Englewood, CO: Libraries Unlimited, 2000. ISBN 1-56308-583-6. Chapter 12.

Annotates appropriately 1,000 titles covering a wide range of subjects.

Reference Guide to Mystery and Detective Fiction. Richard Bleiler. Reference Sources in the Humanities Series. James Rettig, ed. Englewood, CO: Libraries Unlimited, 1999. ISBN 1-56308-380-9. Chapter 12.

Provides a comprehensive guide to mystery and detective titles.

Reference Sources for Small and Medium-Sized Libraries. 6th ed. Scott E. Kennedy, ed. Chicago: American Library Association, 1999. ISBN 0-83893-568-4. Chapter 12.

    Describes reference sources recommended by the Reference Sources for Small and Medium-sized Libraries Editorial Committee, Collection Development and Evaluation Section, Reference and User Services Association of the American Library Association.

Resources in Education. U.S. Department of Education, Office of Educational Research and Improvement, National Library of Education, Educational Resources Information Center, 1975– . ISSN 0098-0897. Chapter 12.

    Monthly. Also available from ERIC as part of a computer file, online sources, and CD-ROMs. Provides summaries of the documents and abstracts available from the ERIC Document Reproduction Service (EDRS). Distributor: U.S. Government Printing Office, Washington, DC 20402.

The Reviewing Librarian. Toronto: Ontario School Library Association, 1974– . ISSN 0318-0948. Chapter 8.

    Quarterly. Reviews books, audiovisual materials, government publications, and magazines. Subscription: Ontario Library Association, 73 Richmond Street West, Toronto, Ontario M5H 1Z4 Canada.

Romance Fiction: A Guide to the Genre. Kristin Ramsdell. Genreflecting Advisory Series. Englewood, CO: Libraries Unlimited, 1999. ISBN 1-56308-335-3. Chapter 12.

    Provides background information. Identifies selected titles for young adults.

School Libraries in Canada. Ottawa, Ontario: Canadian School Library Association, 1980– . ISSN 0227-3780. Chapter 8.

    Quarterly. Available on microform. Reviews books, films, videos, and CDs for grades K–12. Subscription: SLIC Subscriptions, Canadian Library Association, 328 Frank Street, Ottawa, Ontario K2P OXB Canada.

School Library Journal: The Magazine of Children's, Young Adult, and School Libraries. New York: R. R. Bowker, 1954– . ISSN 0000-0035. http://www.slj.com/. Chaps. 4, 8, and 10.

    Twelve issues per year. Available on microform. Reviews books (preschool through adult titles for young people, Spanish language, references), videos, recordings, CD-ROMs, and software. Includes checklists of pamphlets, posters, and free materials. Includes monthly index, annual author/title book review index, and audiovisual index. Subscription: Box 1978, Marion, OH 43305-1978.

Schwann Opus. Santa Fe, NM: Stereophile, 1949– . ISSN 1066-2138. Chaps. 10 and 13.

    Lists available classical music titles. Subscription: Schwann Publications, 1280 Santa Anita Court, Woodland, CA 95776.

Schwann Spectrum. Santa Fe, NM: Stereophile, 1992– . ISSN 1065-9161. Chaps. 10 and 13.

    Lists available pop recordings. Subscription: Schwann Publications, 1280 Santa Anita Court, Woodland, CA 95776.

Science and Children. Washington, DC: National Science Teachers Association, 1963– . ISSN 0036-8148. Chaps. 10 and 12.

      Eight times per year (September through May). Available on microform. Reviews software, curriculum materials, and children's books. Subscription: National Science Teachers Association, 1742 Connecticut Avenue, Washington, DC 20009-1171.

Science Books and Films. Washington, DC: American Association for the Advancement of Science, 1965– . ISSN 0098-342X. Chapter 12.

      Nine issues per year. Available on microform. Reviews books, films, filmstrips, videos, and software and lists what is on the Public Broadcasting System. Covers preschool through professional materials. Subscription: American Association for the Advancement of Science, 1333 H Street NW, Washington, DC 20005.

The Science Teacher. National Science Teachers Association, 1934– . ISSN 0036-8555. Chapter 12.

      Monthly (September-May). Available in microform. Reviews software, books for students, and professional books. Subscription: National Science Teachers Association, 1840 Wilson Boulevard, Arlington, VA 22201.

Science Through Children's Literature: An Integrated Approach. 2d ed. Carol M. Butzow and John W. Butzow. Englewood, CO: Teachers Ideas Press, 2000. ISBN 1-56308-651-4. Chapter 12.

      Features more than 30 books with science in the story line.

Selecting Books for the Elementary School Library Media Center: A Complete Guide. Phyllis Van Orden. New York: Neal-Schuman, 2000. ISBN 1-55570-368-2. Chapter 10.

      Describes the selection process and identifies criteria for picture books, fiction, folk literature, poetry, information books, reference works, and professional books. Glossary.

Senior High School Library Catalog. 15th ed. New York: H. W. Wilson, 1997. ISBN 0-82420-921-4. Chaps. 8, 10, 16, and 17.

      Four annual supplements. Abridged Dewey Decimal Classification. Provides bibliographic and order information, availability of paperback editions, Sears subject headings, and descriptive/critical annotations. Index by author, title, subject, and analytics.

"A Simple Book Repair Manual." 1996. Preservation Services, Dartmouth College Library. http://www.dartmouth.edu/~preserve/repair/repairindex.htm (Accessed December 3, 2000). Chapter 15.

      Presents a handy, informative online repair manual.

Social Education. Arlington, VA: National Council for the Social Studies, 1937– . ISSN 0037-7724. Chapter 12.

      Seven issues per year. Reviews books for children and young adults. Subscription: National Council for the Social Studies, 3501 Newark Street NW, Washington, DC 20016.

Software Encyclopedia: A Guide for Personal, Professional, and Business Users. 2 vols. New Providence, NJ: R. R. Bowker, 1985– . ISBN 0-83524-223-4. Chapter 10.
> Annual. Provides annotated listings for over 21,000 software programs. Index by title, compatible system, and application.

Software Reviews on File. New York: Facts on File, 1985– . ISSN 8755-7169. Chapter 10.
> Monthly. Reviews over 600 software programs per year. Indexes by subject and company. Provides publisher, address, price, and publisher's description. Condenses and cites reviews.

Speaking Out! Voices in Celebration of Intellectual Freedom. Ann K. Symons and Sally Gardner Reed. Chicago: American Library Association, 1999. ISBN 0-83890-763-6. Chapter 4.
> Read these brief essays for their insight, breadth of perspective, and challenges to your personal and professional position.

Subject Guide to Books in Print. See *Books in Print.*

Subject Guide to Children's Books in Print. See *Children's Books in Print.*

SUNLINK Weed of the Month Club. 1999. Florida Department of Education. http://www.sunlink.ucf.edu/weed (Accessed July 6, 1999). Chapter 15.
> Offers practical suggestions and criteria for weeding collections one subject at time. Recommends current titles on the topic being weeded.

Talking Book Topics. Washington, DC: Library of Congress, National Library Service for the Blind and Physically Handicapped, 1975– . ISSN 0039-9183. Chapter 12.
> Bimonthly. Annotates magazines and books available through the cooperating libraries. (http://www.loc.gov/nls/tbt/tbt.html)

Tapping the Government Grapevine: The User-Friendly Guide to U.S. Government Information Sources. 3d ed. Judith Schiek Robinson. Phoenix, AZ: Oryx Press, 1998. ISBN 1-57356-024-3. Chapter 10.
> Provides bibliographic information, publishers' addresses, Websites, Internet addresses, and practical guidelines for locating U.S. government sources.

Teacher Librarian. Vancouver, BC: Rockland Press, 1973– . ISSN 0315-8888. Chapter 10.
> Formerly *Emergency Librarian.* Five times a year. Available on microform. Reviews professional reading, children's recordings, magazines, and paperbacks. Subscription: Rockland Press, Department 284, Box C34069, Seattle, WA 98124-1069. (http://www.teacherlibrarian.com)

The Teacher's Complete and Easy Guide to the Internet. 2d ed. Ann Heide and Linda Stilborne. New York: Teachers College, Columbia University, 1998. ISBN 0-80773-779-8. Chapter 12.
> Describes how teachers and students are using Internet resources. Discusses controversial materials and acceptance use policies.

Teaching Exceptional Children. Reston, VA: The Council for Exceptional Children, 1968– . ISSN 0040-0599. Chapter 12.

> Six times a year. Covers methods, materials, and current issues. Subscription: Council for Exceptional Children, 1920 Association Drive, Reston, VA 20191-1589, or call 1-888-CEC-READ, or visit their Web page at http://www.cec.sped.org/bk /abtec.htm.

Tech Trends. Bloomington, IN: Association for Educational Communications and Technology, 1985– . ISSN 8756-3894. Chaps. 6 and 10.

> "Copyright and You" is a regular column. Six times a year. Included in membership dues. Subscription: AECT, 1800 North Stonelake Drive, Suite 2, Bloomington, IN 47404-1517, telephone 812-335-7675, e-mail chulce@ait.net.

Technology and Copyright Law: A Guidebook for the Library, Research, and Teaching Professions. Arlene Bielefield and Lawrence Cheeseman. New York: Neal-Schuman, 1997. ISBN 1-55570-267-8. Chaps. 6 and 10.

Technology and Learning. Dayton, OH: Peter Li, Inc., 1980– . ISSN 1053-6728. Chapter 10.

> Eight issues per year. Reviews computer software and multimedia for elementary and secondary students. Provides hardware requirements, emphasis, grade level, publisher, description of software manuals and guides, rating, strengths, and weaknesses. Subscription: Peter Li, Inc., 2451 E. River Rd., Dayton, OH 45439.

Teen Legal Rights. Kathleen A. Hempelman. Westport, CT: Greenwood, 2000. ISBN 0-31330-968-X. Chapter 4.

> Covers discrimination issues, freedom of expression, school libraries, and school newspapers.

Through Indian Eyes: The Native Experience in Books for Children. 4th ed. Contemporary American Indian Issues, no. 7. Beverly Slapin and Doris Seale. Los Angeles: American Indian Studies Center, 1998. ISBN 0-93562-646-8. Chapter 12.

> Expands on earlier editions of *Books without Bias: Through Indian Eyes.* Critically evaluates and offers guidelines for selection of books on Native Americans.

Through the Eyes of a Child: An Introduction to Children's Literature. 5th ed. Donna E. Norton and Saundra E. Norton. Prentice-Hall, 1998. ISBN 0-13667-973-0. Chapter 12.

> Treats multicultural literature as a separate chapter as well as integrated throughout. Includes a database on CD-ROM of over 2,600 titles.

"TV Guide." http://www.tvguide.com. Chapter 12.

> Provides a daily listing of television programs.

U.S. Government Books. U.S. Government Printing Office, 1982– . GP 3.17/5. Chapter 10.

> Lists available books.

U.S. Government on the Web: Getting the Information You Need. Peter Hernon, John A. Shuler, and Robert E. Dugan. Englewood, CO: Libraries Unlimited, 1999. ISBN 1-56308-757-X. Chapter 10.

Describes issues, types of publications, search engines, and Websites. Includes a chapter about Websites for children. Indexes by government body, title, and author.

University Press Books Selection for Public and Secondary School Libraries. Association of American University Presses. ISSN 1055-4173. Chapter 12.

Annual. Selected by a committee from the American Association of School Libraries (AASL) and the Public Library Association (PLA). Rates books in terms of general audience, regional interest, and in-depth collections for students in grades 6–12. For publishers listed see Website for the AAUP On-Line Catalog—at http://aaup.uchicago.edu. Members of AASL and PLA automatically receive copies. Librarians can obtain a free copy of the bibliography by writing on their school's stationery to the Association of American University Presses, Inc., Marketing Department, 71 West 23rd Street, Suite 901, New York, NY 10010.

Vertical File Index: A Subject and Title Index to Selected Pamphlet Materials. New York: H. W. Wilson, 1955– . ISSN 0042-4493. Chaps. 10 and 12.

Monthly (except August). Available online. Provides order information for over 3,000 sources of free and inexpensive materials including reading lists, charts, posters, maps, and government publications. Arranged by subject with title index. Subscription: H. W. Wilson, 950 University Avenue, Bronx, NY 10452.

Video Librarian, The. Randy Pitman, 1986– . ISSN 0887-6851. Chapter 10.

Bimonthly except combined in July and August. Reviews nearly 200 videos for public, school, and university libraries. The magazine's supplement is available online at http://www.videolibrarian.com/indexx.html. E-mail: vidlib@kndaco.telebyte .com. Subscription: *Video Librarian,* 8705 Honeycomb Court NW, Seabeck, WA 98380.

Video Rating Guide for Libraries, The. Beth Blenz-Clucas, ed. Santa Barbara: ABC-Clio, 1990– . ISSN 1045-3393. Chapter 10.

Quarterly. Provides rating, bibliographic, ordering, and cataloging information. Indexes by subject, title, price, audience, and the best videos of each issue. Index is cumulated in the fourth quarterly issue.

Video Source Book, The. 22d ed. Terri Schell, ed. Farmington Hills, MI: Gale Research, 1979– . ISSN 0748-0881. Chapter 10.

Annual. Covers prerecorded video programs currently available on videocassette, videodisc, and videotape. Provides date of release, running time, major plot, theme, closed captions, or signing for people with a hearing impairment, and availability. Order from: Gale Research, Book Tower, Detroit, MI 48226.

VOYA: Voice of Youth Advocates. Virginia Beach, VA: Voice of Youth Advocates, 1978– . ISSN 0160-4201. http://www.voya.com. Chaps. 8 and 10.

Bimonthly. Available on microform. Reviews books (trade, paperbacks, reprints, professional), reference titles, films, videotapes, and recordings.

"Web Braille." Library of Congress, National Library Service for the Blind and Physically Handicapped. http://www.loc.gov/nls/nls-wb.html (Accessed December 3, 2000). Chapter 12.

> Provides information on how to access electronic Braille books.

Weeding Library Collections: Library Weeding Methods. 4th ed. Stanley J. Slote. Englewood, CO: Libraries Unlimited, 1997. ISBN 1-56308-511-9. Chapter 15.

> Discusses the policies and practices used in weeding collections.

Words on Cassette. 14th ed. New Providence, NJ: R. R. Bowker, 1999. ISBN 0-83524-095-9. Chapter 10.

> Annual. Provides reader's name, author, title, playing time, number of cassettes, purchase/rental price, order number, and publisher. Indexed by title, subject, author, producer/distributor, and reader.

"WWW Evaluation Guide." Tana Hudak. Takoma Park, MD: Takoma Park Maryland Library. http://cityoftakomapark.org/library/children/eval.html (Accessed December 3, 2000). Chapter 10.

> Evaluation guide listed under "School Resources." Helps the evaluator assess the identifying factors for the site, analyze content and sources, and evaluate visuals.

Appendix C
Statements on People's Rights

This appendix includes two statements regarding intellectual freedom. As you read these statements, consider the rationale for, and the meanings and interpretations of, the words. Do you share the beliefs these statements express? Are they ones you will recommend for adoption by your school board?

LIBRARY BILL OF RIGHTS: THE POLICY[*]

The American Library Association affirms that all libraries are forums for information and ideas, and that the following basic policies should guide their services.

1. Books and other library resources should be provided for the interest, information, and enlightenment of all people of the community the library serves. Materials should not be excluded because of the origin, background, or views of those contributing to their creation.

2. Libraries should provide materials and information presenting all points of view on current and historical issues. Materials should not be proscribed or removed because of partisan or doctrinal disapproval.

3. Libraries should cooperate with all persons and groups concerned with resisting abridgement of free expression and free access to ideas.

4. Libraries should cooperate with all persons and groups concerned with resisting abridgment of free expression and free access to ideas.

5. A person's right to use a library should not be denied or abridged because of origin, age, background, or views.

6. Libraries which make exhibit spaces and meeting rooms available to the public they serve should make such facilities available on an equitable basis, regardless of the beliefs or affiliations of individuals or groups requesting their use.

---

[*]Adopted June 18, 1948. Amended by the ALA Council on February 2, 1961; June 27, 1967; and January 23, 1980.

Reprinted with permission from *Intellectual Freedom Manual*, 5th ed., pages 3–4. Copyright 1996. Permission is granted by the American Library Association. Reprinted with permission of the American Library Association and the Office for Intellectual Freedom (50 E. Huron Street, Chicago, IL 60611) from *Intellectual Freedom Manual,* 5th ed. Copyright 1996.

ACCESS TO RESOURCES AND SERVICES IN THE SCHOOL LIBRARY MEDIA PROGRAM: AN INTERPRETATION OF THE *LIBRARY BILL OF RIGHTS*[*]

The school library media program plays a unique role in promoting intellectual freedom. It serves as a point of voluntary access to information and ideas and as a learning laboratory for students as they acquire critical thinking and problem solving skills needed in a pluralistic society. Although the educational level and program of the school necessarily shapes the resources and services of a school library media program, the principles of the *Library Bill of Rights* apply equally to all libraries, including school library media programs.

School library media professionals assume a leadership role in promoting the principles of intellectual freedom within the school by providing resources and services that create and sustain an atmosphere of free inquiry. School library media professionals work closely with teachers to integrate instructional activities in classroom units designed to equip students to locate, evaluate, and use a broad range of ideas effectively. Through resources, programming, and educational processes, students and teachers experience the free and robust debate characteristics of a democratic society.

School library media professionals cooperate with other individuals in building collections of resources appropriate to the developmental and maturity levels of students. These collections provide resources which support the curriculum and are consistent with the philosophy, goals, and objectives of the school district. Resources in school library media collections represent diverse points of view on current as well as historical issues.

While English is, by history and tradition, the customary language of the United States, the languages in use in any given community may vary. Schools serving communities in which other languages are used make efforts to accommodate the needs of students for whom English is a second language. To support these efforts, and to ensure equal access to resources and services, the school library media program provides resources which reflect the linguistic pluralism of the community.

Members of the school community involved in the collection development process employ educational criteria to select resources unfettered by their personal, political, social, or religious views. Students and educators served by the school library media program have access to resources and services free of constraints resulting from personal, partisan, or doctrinal disapproval. School library media professionals resist efforts by individuals to define what is appropriate for all students or teachers to read, view, or hear.

---

[*]Adopted July 2, 1987; amended January 10, 1990, by the ALA Council.

Reprinted with permission from *Intellectual Freedom Manual,* 5th edition, pages 36–37. Copyright 1996. Permission granted by the American Library Association. Reprinted with permission of the American Library Association and the Office for Intellectual Freedom (50 E. Huron Street, Chicago, IL 60611) from *Intellectual Freedom Manual,* 5th ed. Copyright 1996.

Major barriers between students and resources include: imposing age or grade level restrictions on the use of resources, limiting the use of interlibrary loan and access to electronic information, charging fees for information in specific formats, requiring permissions from parents or teachers, establishing restricted shelves or closed collections, and labeling. Policies, procedures, and rules related to the use of resources and services support free and open access to information.

The school board adopts policies that guarantee students access to a broad range of ideas. These include policies on collection development and procedures for the review of resources about which concerns have been raised. Such policies, developed by persons in the school community, provide for a timely and fair hearing and assure that procedures are applied equitably to all expressions of concern. School library media professionals implement district policies and procedures in the school.

Bibliography

Chapter 1

American Association of School Librarians and Association of Educational Communications and Technology. 1988. *Information Power: Guidelines for School Library Media Programs.* Chicago: American Library Association; Washington, D.C.: Association for Educational Communications and Technology.

———. 1998. *Information Power: Building Partnerships for Learning.* Chicago: American Library Association.

Camarena, Janet. 2000. "A Wealth of Information on Foundations and the Grant Seeking Process." *Computers in Libraries* 20, no. 5 (May): 26–31.

Coatney, Sharon. 1998. "Information Power: Building Partnerships for Learning." *Teacher Librarian* 26 (September–October): 9–10.

Guenther, Kim. 2000. "Making Smart Licensing Decisions." *Computers in Libraries* 20, no. 6 (June): 58–60.

Hammer, Sebastian. 2000. "Dr. Metadata, or: How I Learned to Stop Worrying and Love Z39.50." *American Libraries* 31, no. 9 (October): 54–56.

Harada, Violet, and Jean Donham. 1998. "Information Power: Student Achievement Is the Bottom Line." *Teacher Librarian* 26 (September–October): 14–17.

Mancall, Jacqueline. 1991. "(Un)changing Factors in the Searching Environment." *School Library Media Quarterly* 19 (Winter): 84–89.

Chapter 4

American Library Association. Office of Intellectual Freedom. 1996. *Intellectual Freedom Manual,* 5th ed. Chicago: American Library Association.

———. 2000a. "The Censor: Motives and Tactics." [http://www.ala.org/alaorg/oif/censormotives .html]. (Accessed December 3, 2000).

———. 2000b. "Intellectual Freedom and Censorship Q & A." [http://www.ala.org/alaorg /oif/intellectualfreedomandcensorship.html]. (Accessed December 3, 2000).

———. 2000c. "The 100 Most Frequently Challenged Books of 1990–1999." [http://www.ala .org/alaorg/oif/top100bannedbooks.html]. (Accessed December 3, 2000).

Haycock, Ken, Betty Chapin, and David Bruce. 1999. "Information Age Dilemma: Filtering the Internet for Young People." In *Bowker Annual Library and Book Trade Almanac,* 44th ed., 235–65. New Providence, NJ: R. R. Bowker.

Moshman, David. 1986. "Children's Intellectual Rights: A First Amendment Analysis." In *Children's Intellectual Rights.* David Moshman, ed., 27–38. New Directions for Child Development Series, no. 33. San Francisco: Jossey-Bass.

———. 1989. *Children, Education, and the First Amendment: A Psychological Analysis.* Lincoln, NE: University of Nebraska Press.

Chapter 6

Smith, Mark. 1999. *Internet Policy Handbook for Libraries.* New York: Neal-Schuman.

Chapter 7

American Library Association. Office for Intellectual Freedom. 1996. *Intellectual Freedom Manual,* 5th ed. Chicago: American Library Association.

Buckingham, Betty Jo, ed. 1995. *Selection of Instructional Materials: A Model Policy and Model Rules,* 4th ed. Des Moines, IA: State of Iowa. Department of Education. Also available at [http://www.iema-ia.org/IEMA116.html]. (Accessed December 3, 2000).

Dealing with Selection and Censorship: A Handbook for Wisconsin Schools and Libraries. 1999. State of Wisconsin, Department of Public Instruction, no. 0046. Madison, WI: Department of Public Instruction.

Jones, Barbara M. 1999. *Libraries, Access, and Intellectual Freedom: Developing Policies for Public and Academic Libraries.* Chicago: American Library Association.

Minnesota Coalition Against Censorship. 1991. *Selection Policies and Reevaluation Procedures: A Workbook.* Minneapolis: Minnesota Educational Media Organization.

Chapter 8

Callison, Daniel. 1990. "A Review of the Research Related to School Library Media Collections: Part I." *School Library Media Quarterly* 19 (Fall): 57–62.

Hearne, Betsy, and Roger Sutton, eds. 1993. *Evaluating Children's Books: A Critical Look: Aesthetic, Social, and Political Aspects of Analyzing and Using Children's Books.* Urbana-Champaign: University of Illinois, Graduate School of Library and Information Science.

Chapter 10

Bielefield, Arlene, and Lawrence Cheeseman. 1997. *Technology and Copyright Law: A Guidebook for the Library, Research, and Teaching Professions.* New York: Neal-Schuman.

Bruwelheide, Janis H. 1998. *The Copyright Primer for Librarians and Educators,* 2d ed. Chicago: American Library Association.

Heinich, Robert, Michael Molenda, James D. Russell, and Sharon E. Smaldino. 1999. *Instructional Media and Technologies for Learning,* 6th ed. Upper Saddle River, NJ: Prentice-Hall.

Laurence, Helen. 1999. "FAU Libraries Internet Research: How to Evaluate Internet Resources." Florida Atlantic University Libraries. Updated July 14. [http://www.fau.edu/library/evaluate.htm]. (Accessed December 3, 2000).

Liu, Y. Peter. 1999. "Non-print Trading." In *Understanding the Business of Library Acquisitions,* 2d ed. Karen A. Schmidt, ed., 224–61. Chicago: American Library Association.

Mambretti, Catherine. 1998. *CD-ROM Technology: A Manual for Librarians and Educators.* Jefferson, NC: McFarland.

Schmidt, William D., and Donald A. Rieck. 2000. *Managing Media Services: Theory and Practice.* Englewood, CO: Libraries Unlimited.

Taylor, Jim. 2000. "DVD Frequently Asked Questions (and Answers)." [http://www.dvddemystified.com/dvdfaq.html]. (Accessed December 3, 2000).

Chapter 11

Joyce, Bruce, and Marsha Weil. 1996. *Models of Teaching*, 5th ed. Boston: Allyn & Bacon.

Chapter 13

Evans, G. Edward. 2000. *Developing Library and Information Center Collections,* 4th ed. Englewood, CO: Libraries Unlimited.

Chapter 14

Hoffman, Frank W. 1999. *Grantsmanship for Small Libraries and School Library Media Centers.* Englewood, CO: Libraries Unlimited.

Mambretti, Catherine. 1999. *Internet Technology for Schools.* Jefferson, NC: McFarland.

Stover, Mark. 1999. *Leading the Wired Organization: The Information Professional's Guide to Managing Technological Change.* New York: Neal-Schuman.

Chapter 15

Slote, Stanley J. 1997. *Weeding Library Collections: Library Weeding Methods,* 4th ed. Englewood, CO: Libraries Unlimited.

Chapter 16

Baker, Sharon L., and F. Wilfrid Lancaster. 1991. *The Measurement and Evaluation of Library Services,* 2d ed. Arlington, VA: Information Resources Press.

Bradburn, Frances Bryant. 1999. *Output Measures for School Library Media Programs.* New York: Neal-Schuman.

Doll, Carol A., and Pamela Petrick Barron. 1991. *Collection Analysis for the School Library Media Center: A Practical Approach.* Chicago: American Library Association.

Index